BIG-BOX SWINDLE

BIG-BOX
SWINDLE

THE TRUE COST OF
MEGA-RETAILERS AND THE
FIGHT FOR AMERICA'S
INDEPENDENT BUSINESSES

STACY MITCHELL

Beacon Press, Boston

BEACON PRESS
25 Beacon Street
Boston, Massachusetts 02108-2892
www.beacon.org

Beacon Press books
are published under the auspices of
the Unitarian Universalist Association of Congregations.

09 08 07 06 8 7 6 5 4 3 2 1

This book is printed on acid-free paper
that meets the uncoated paper ANSI/NISO specifications
for permanence as revised in 1992.

Text design and composition by Wilsted & Taylor Publishing Services

Library of Congress Cataloging-in-Publication Data
Mitchell, Stacy.
Big-box swindle : the true cost of mega-retailers and the fight
for America's independent businesses / Stacy Mitchell.
p. cm.
Includes bibliographical references.
ISBN-13: 978-0-8070-3500-9 (hardcover : alk. paper)
ISBN-10: 0-8070-3500-9 (hardcover : alk. paper) 1. Chain stores—United States.
2. Retail trade—United States. 3. Small business—United States. I. Title.

HF5468.M58 2006
381′.120973—dc22   2006013818

For Jacob

CONTENTS

INTRODUCTION

IN THE LATE SUMMER OF 2005, Kepler's, a fifty-year-old independent bookstore in Menlo Park, California, abruptly shut down. Owner Clark Kepler explained that bookstore chains and Amazon.com had displaced so much of the store's sales that he could no longer pay the bills. But before Kepler could file for bankruptcy, the business was swept up in an outpouring of community grief. Hundreds of local residents rallied outside the shuttered store, which was soon covered in forlorn love letters from customers describing how the bookstore had been the center of community life and what a loss it was. "Can't the store be saved? You're one of the main reasons I'm in Menlo Park," read one. Another lamented, "My husband and I dated here." Many offered money: "How about a monthly donation? I can do $50/mo . . . Give us a Web site so we can all support you. Let us help. Please." Soon someone set up SaveKeplers.com and the pledges poured in. Five weeks after it had closed, Kepler's was back, saved by a group of local investors who vowed to return the business to sound financial footing, and numerous small donations from residents.

One of the more remarkable aspects of this community effort to save a bookstore is that many of the people who rallied—who so adored this business that they could not conceive of their town without it and were willing to give their time and even their money to save it—confessed in interviews with reporters covering the story that they, too, had been buying more and more books online and at Target and Borders. They loved the store for its many author events and for the joy of browsing and meeting neighbors, and for the sense of community it fostered, but that devotion did not always translate into regular patronage. The store's near closure brought into stark relief just what was at stake.

Across the country, people are coming to similar realizations about the value of locally owned, independent businesses[1]—the beloved bookstores, century-old family hardware stores, local grocers, and funky neighborhood record stores—as well as the high cost to communities and local economies of the corporate retailers that have grown to dominate so much of our landscape. The first part of this book makes a case for reversing the precipitous shift from locally owned businesses to chains, while the second part charts how a growing number of communities are doing so. Since 2000, some two hundred big-box development projects have been halted by groups of ordinary citizens, shattering the conventional wisdom that these stores are unstoppable. These groups have succeeded by educating and galvanizing their neighbors and by learning how to harness the local planning process.

Many communities are going further: Dozens of cities and towns have adopted laws that actively favor small-scale, local business development and limit the proliferation of mega-retailers. Some have enacted store size-caps, which effectively ban big-box retail. Others require that retail development proposals pass comprehensive economic- and community-impact reviews before gaining approval. Many are funneling new investment into neighborhood and downtown business districts by outlawing sprawling shopping centers on the outskirts. Much is happening at the state level too. Citizens and lawmakers in several state capitols are working to enact legislation to put an end to the sizable public subsidies and tax breaks that are frequently granted to big-box development. In 2004 Vermont became the first of what is hoped will be many states to close a common state tax loophole that allows chains, but not independent retailers, to skirt their tax obligations.

People are working not only to prevent mega-retailers from overtaking their communities, but also to strengthen and rebuild locally owned businesses. Local groups are busy restoring long-desolate downtowns and neighborhood business districts, setting up retail incubators to nurture start-up enterprises, and wrestling with ways to channel more capital into financing local business creation. Independent businesses, meanwhile, are banding together in coalitions and purchasing cooperatives that marry the advantages of scale with the benefits of local ownership. The Coalition of Independent Music Stores, for instance, has become a force in introducing new artists, and has given independent music stores newfound clout with record labels. Independent bookstore owners have pooled their resources to develop e-commerce engines that enable their customers to shop locally on the Web with the same broad database of titles found on Amazon.com. Trade associations, like the National Community Pharmacists Association, and retailer-owned cooperatives, like Ace Hardware, have started programs to train and mentor a new generation of business owners.

Independent Business Alliances have sprung up in more than three dozen communities since the late 1990s and, through creative marketing and educational campaigns, are making "locally owned" something residents are increasingly seeking and supporting. The Austin (Texas) Independent Business Alliance, which has a membership of 350 local businesses that collectively rank as the city's fifth largest employer, has undertaken a lively four-year educational effort that highlights the economic and community benefits of homegrown enterprises and urges residents to "Break the Chain Habit" and "Shop Locally Owned." The effort is having an effect on people's shopping choices, the actions of the Austin city government, and even retail developers, who are looking to include more independents in their projects. Similar campaigns are under way in cities as far flung as Bellingham, Washington, and Raleigh, North Carolina.

This explosion of activity may well herald the beginnings of a sea change in our priorities as a society. This book argues that, to a scandalous degree, big-box retailers are a product of public policy, not simply consumer choice. Driven by an erroneous conviction that chain retailers boost employment and expand the economy, elected officials have actively fostered and underwritten their proliferation. It began in the late 1950s with massive tax breaks that fueled the explosion of shopping malls, and accelerated dramatically in the 1990s as cities began funneling billions of dollars in development subsidies to big retailers. Although pressure is mounting to put an end to these giveaways, they continue, with chains like Target and Lowe's picking up multimillion-dollar subsidies to build new stores. Since the early 1990s, Wal-Mart alone has grabbed over $1 billion in local and state subsidies to fund construction of its new stores and warehouses.

The favoritism does not end there. Many states have provisions in their tax codes that enable chains, but not independent retailers, to skirt paying income taxes. This tax loophole has been so heavily utilized by the chains—they shelter billions in profits every year—that tax experts have even given it a nickname, the Geoffrey Loophole, after the Toys "R" Us mascot, Geoffrey the Giraffe. The playing field has been tilted too by the failure of state and federal officials to adequately police predatory pricing and other abuses of market power, which has allowed mega-retailers to force out smaller rivals, not by being better competitors, but simply by being bigger.

Fueled partly by these policies, a handful of global chains have grown to dominate the retail market. The top ten alone have doubled their market share since 1996 and now capture almost 30 percent of the more than $2.3 trillion Americans spend at stores each year. The largest, Wal-Mart, grew tenfold in fifteen years, and in 2005 accounted for one out of every ten dollars Americans spent on everything from groceries and toys to hardware and clothing. Target is eight times larger than it was in 1990. Home Depot and Lowe's, barely a blip on the radar screen in 1990, now have half of the hardware and building-supply market. Electronics are dominated by Best Buy; books by Borders and Barnes & Noble; videos by Blockbuster. Walgreens, Rite Aid, and CVS have exploded to more than thirteen thousand outlets. Meanwhile, tens of thousands of locally owned businesses have disappeared since the early 1990s—a die-off unprecedented in history.

This is progress—or so we have imagined. Independent businesses, we have long assumed, are necessary casualties on the road to economic advancement and prosperity. And indeed, the big chains appear to bring communities economic growth, new jobs, and tax revenue. This book argues, however, that these apparent gains are illusory, that mega-retailers impose a variety of hidden costs on society and contribute far less to our economic well-being than they take away.

Although a new big-box store rising on the edge of town might appear to be economic growth, it is not. The vast majority of these stores are built not to satisfy increased consumer demand—the acreage of retail store space has been expanding ten times faster than household incomes—but because a chain sees a predatory opportunity to displace sales at other businesses. These companies purposely flood local markets with an excess of retail space in order to dilute the available consumer dollars and capsize their smaller competitors, which, no matter how skilled, may lack the deep financial resources necessary to outlast such an assault. As local stores contract and close, communities end up losing as many or more retail jobs as they gain from the new superstore. Indeed, retail employment actually fell in counties that added Wal-Mart stores, according to a national study. Still, the myth that new big-box stores and shopping centers expand job opportunities persists, in part because the gains—the two hundred people donning orange aprons at Home Depot—are visible, while the losses are scattered across many businesses and may take months to fully materialize.

The impact on the local economy does not end there. When chains displace local businesses, dollars that once circulated locally, generating economic activity and jobs, cease to do so. Independent retailers bank at local banks, advertise in local newspapers, carry goods produced by local companies, and hire a range of professionals, from accountants to Web designers. Corporate chains require very little in the way of local goods and services. Instead, most of the money that consumers spend at a big-box store is siphoned out of the community's economy. The resulting job losses are another hidden cost of mega-retailers.

The chains are driving the contraction of manufacturing as well. Their market dominance has given them near-total control over how and where goods are produced. Most big retailers have their primary procurement offices in China, where they contract directly with low-wage factories to produce a growing share of the goods they stock. In 2005, upward of 20 percent of the goods that Wal-Mart and other big-box retailers sold were their own products. With their top customers also their biggest competitors, U.S. manufacturers are left with two options: they can either make their products in those same factories or give up shelf space and market share to other suppliers or the chains themselves. Black & Decker is one of many that have succumbed. Pressured to lower costs by Home Depot and Lowe's, Black & Decker began closing its U.S. factories in 2002, laying off thousands of workers. Producers of everything from toys to television sets have done the same thing.

The relentless drive to cut costs continues abroad, as the chains press even the lowest wage factories to lower their prices even more, often demanding that they make the same products for less than they did the year before. Workers in these factories suffer not only miserable wages and working conditions, but they have little hope for a better life. Should their wages rise, the chains can cut ties and move production to another factory or even another country in a matter of weeks. Some ten thousand factory jobs have been eliminated in the once-booming maquiladoras along Mexico's northern border since 2000, as mega-retailers and their suppliers shifted to China, where wages were considerably lower. Then, in 2005, when costs in China showed some signs of increasing, the chains began looking in India and other countries for workers who could be had for less.

Owning a small business and working in manufacturing are two long-standing occupational pillars of the American middle class. As these sectors have contracted, so has the middle class. The share of national income flowing to the middle 60 percent of families has declined since 1985. And the situation is getting worse: in all but two states, new jobs being created

pay less than those being lost. Mega-retailers are both driving this disturbing trend and, insidiously, growing because of it: as incomes shrink, the
prospect of a bargain becomes ever more irresistible. But we are shopping
ourselves out of decent jobs with good wages.

The poor have fared even worse in the big-box economy. Their share of
the nation's income is dropping even faster. Poverty is no longer confined
to the under- and unemployed; a stunning number of full-time workers do
not earn enough to meet basic needs. Many work in retail. The chains have
used their immense market power to hold down retail wages, which have
not kept pace with wage growth in the rest of the economy. Work at most
of the big boxes is grueling and demoralizing, with pay well below the
poverty line. Store managers are under such intense pressure to cut labor
costs, surreptitiously deleting hours from employees' time cards has become an appallingly widespread practice. Turnover rates hover around
50 percent at many of these chains, meaning that half of all workers quit or
are fired within a year, which keeps wage levels down. Sporadic union-
organizing drives at Home Depot, Target, and Wal-Mart stores have met
with fierce resistance, often collapsing amid allegations that managers illegally intimidated workers. When Wal-Mart employees in a small town in
Quebec became the first to form a union at one of the company's superstores, the chain retaliated by closing the store and laying off all two hundred employees.

This is not a recipe for broad prosperity. Rather, this book contends, the
economic structure that mega-retailers are propagating represents a modern variation on the old European colonial system, which was designed not
to build economically viable and self-reliant communities, but to extract
their wealth and resources. Yet many cities eagerly usher in these corporate
colonizers. Some envision a tax windfall, only to discover that these sprawling stores impose a significant burden on public infrastructure and services. Or worse, after their local economies have been bulldozed, they find
that they are utterly dependent on a few big boxes that might raise prices,
lay off employees, or threaten to move to a neighboring town if they don't
receive a tax break.

As they reorganize the economy for their own ends, mega-retailers
are remaking the American landscape. While a one-hundred-thousand-
square-foot store once required an acre of land, because it was two stories
and located downtown, today a big-box store of that size, with its moat of

parking, consumes at least a dozen acres. The aggregate effect of this is staggering. In the Cleveland metro alone, some nine thousand acres of forest, wetlands, and rich farm fields have fallen to big-box stores and shopping centers, even as the metro's population has declined. A similar land binge is under way nationwide. Between 1990 and 2005 the amount of retail space per person in the United States doubled, from nineteen to thirty-eight square feet. Because most of this development was auto-oriented in nature, for every square foot of new store space, another three to four square feet was paved for cars. What's propelling this expansion is not growth in spending; adjusted for inflation, median household incomes rose less than 10 percent over that fifteen-year period.

Rather, the culprit is a kind of development arms race in which the big chains continually invent and unroll new formats and bigger stores in an effort to undercut not only Main Streets but other shopping centers. We do not need or utilize all of this excess retail and much of the country is now strewn with the wreckage: about one in five enclosed malls has either already gone dark or is teetering on the verge of financial collapse. Hundreds of strip shopping centers are vacant. Thousands of big-box stores have been abandoned as well, usually because the company opted to build an even bigger box nearby. Wal-Mart alone has some three hundred empty stores, vacated as it built larger supercenters with full grocery departments. These blighted shells often remain vacant for years, because the chains, determined to prevent their competitors from taking the locations, continue to pay the rent. Many cities, especially those that depend heavily on sales tax revenue, are caught up in this development contest, going to great lengths to lure massive new retail power centers that will pull shoppers from neighboring towns. But the only sure bet in this retail merry-go-round is that today's winners invariably become tomorrow's losers, as their bright new shopping centers are surpassed by even bigger and newer retail venues elsewhere in the region.

As retail sprawls outward, running errands entails more driving. The 1990s saw a jump of more than 40 percent in the number of miles driven by the average household for shopping—which translates into an increase of almost 95 billion miles a year for the country as a whole. Mega-retailers are thus fueling smog, acid rain, and global warming. Retail sprawl has also emerged as a top threat to our rivers, lakes, and estuaries. The specific culprit is pavement, which does not allow rain to soak into the ground, but sends it, loaded with oils and other pollutants, rushing into nearby bodies of water. No other category of land use creates more pavement and polluted runoff than big-box stores and shopping centers.

Not only are the true costs of mega-retailers becoming ever more apparent, but there is also a growing sense of what our communities lose when locally owned businesses disappear. Local owners are both financially and personally vested in their communities and, as a result, their business decisions often reflect a broader range of concerns than simply maximizing the bottom line. Their face-to-face relationships with employees and customers and their own personal connections to the places where they do business influence how they operate and the choices they make about such things as whether, for example, to support a tax increase that would reduce profit but improve the local schools their children attend. This complex set of motivations differs from the narrow range of factors that drive stockholders and distant boards of directors, and, as shown in this book, produces valuable community benefits.

Local retailers breathe life into our downtowns and neighborhood business districts. They provide a setting for casual socializing with our neighbors—standing in line at the bakery or walking along the sidewalk—which builds a sense of camaraderie and responsibility for one another. This kind of informal interaction has a tangible impact on community health. Studies show that people who live in places where a larger share of the economy is in the hands of locally owned businesses take a more active role in civic affairs. These communities come out ahead on various measures of social well-being. They have lower rates of poverty, crime, and infant mortality, and are more resilient in times of adversity. Their citizens are far more likely to attend public meetings, volunteer, and even vote than those living in areas dominated by big corporate chains.

Independent businesses play an important and unique role in the marketplace. Their decline is a significant material loss to consumers. Local business owners often possess a level of expertise and knowledge that is unmatched by their big-box counterparts. Video store owners are frequently film aficionados. Many local toy-store owners have played with every game and toy their stores carry and, as a result, tend to hold their suppliers to high standards. Independent pharmacists provide a level of health care and personal attention that is far superior to that offered by chain drugstores and superstore pharmacies, according to a 2003 study by *Consumer Reports*.

Although the chains present themselves as consumer advocates, their true loyalty is to stockholders. Meeting consumer needs is incidental to the main enterprise, hitting growth and profit targets. One consequence of the mega-retailers' drive to cut costs is that manufacturers have had to sharply curtail investment in product research and development. Innovation in many product categories is suffering. A small but growing number of manufacturers have opted out of the big-box game, deciding that they would rather develop and make innovative products in the United States. But their success will depend on whether local retailers survive and continue to provide an alternative avenue to consumers.

Local retailers are thus crucial to ensuring that a diversity of goods is available on store shelves. Although individually they are considerably smaller than their big-box rivals, collectively, independent stores stock a much wider array of products. This is because they each make their own decisions about what to carry, while at the chains these choices are determined by a handful of buyers at corporate headquarters. This is especially important with regard to books, music, and movies. Independent retailers in these categories play a much larger role in introducing and promoting new writers and artists than their relatively modest market share would suggest. Many acclaimed authors and bands insist that no one would have heard of them had it not been for enthusiastic independent merchants putting their books and albums into customers' hands.

That chains are bigger and must therefore offer lower prices is such an ingrained notion that even critics often give them a free ride on this point. But this is not in fact always the case. Surveys in several states have found that independent pharmacies, most of which belong to buying groups, have the lowest prices on average, beating drugstore chains, supermarkets, and even Wal-Mart and Target. Independent appliance dealers had better prices than Wal-Mart and most large chains, according to a 2005 *Consumer Reports* analysis. Another survey found that the cost of an identical cartload of groceries varied widely at different Wal-Mart stores across Nebraska, apparently in relation to the level of nearby competition. As shown in this book, many chains rely on sophisticated pricing strategies to foster a perception among consumers that their prices overall are lower than they actually are, and they often enter new markets sporting steep discounts only to raise prices once rival businesses have closed. The only way to ensure vigorous competition and protect consumer welfare over the long term is to maintain a market with numerous competitors.

There is nothing preordained or inevitable about the rise of mega-retailers or about their continued dominance. We could change course. When American colonists forced their way onto three ships docked in Boston harbor in 1773 and dumped more than ninety thousand pounds of tea into the sea, their actions were as much a challenge to global corporate power as they were a rebellion against King George III. The ships were owned by the East India Company, a powerful transnational corporation. The company had recently suffered losses, in part because of an American boycott of its merchandise. In response, the British parliament passed the Tea Act, which exempted the East India Company from paying taxes on tea it sold in the colonies. The aim was to enable the company to undercut small competitors, all of which were subject to the tax, and drive them out of business.[2]

The British government and the East India Company were betting that the lure of cheap tea would overpower any sense of principle. But they misjudged. The colonists continued to support independent merchants and boycott East India tea. The Boston Tea Party, and the British retaliation that followed, ultimately led to an organized American boycott of all British goods—homegrown and locally made became the fashion of the day—and, two years later, to the Declaration of Independence. Local self-reliance and dispersed ownership, the colonists judged, were essential to political freedom and democratic self-government.

Our communities are fast becoming colonies once again, subject to a new crop of transnational corporations that exercise an extraordinary degree of power over our economy, and are remaking the American landscape for their own ends. They are in part a product of government policy, which has ignored their full cost, as well as created the context for our own, often shortsighted, shopping choices. Fortunately, there is a spreading public realization of the true cost of mega-retailers. Across the country, citizens, local business owners, and elected officials are taking steps to curb their proliferation and rebuild local enterprises. Taken together, these strategies offer a road map for a more prosperous and sustainable future.

PART ONE

ONE

CHAIN STORE WORLD

CONCERNS ABOUT THE POWER OF LARGE RETAILERS are sometimes dismissed on the grounds that such worries are nothing new. Chains have been around for more than a century, and over the years various retailers have risen to the top only to fade and be eclipsed by new competitors. Long before Wal-Mart, the case goes, there was A&P. One of the earliest chains, A&P—shorthand for the Great Atlantic & Pacific Tea Company—was founded in 1859 by George Gilman and George Hartford. They started with a simple tea store on Vesey Street in Lower Manhattan, but began opening additional outlets almost immediately. Over the years, they expanded into groceries. By 1910 the chain had more than 350 outlets. By World War I, A&P had become the largest food retailer and largest chain in the country. It would dominate grocery retailing for decades. As powerful as A&P was, however, it never came close to Wal-Mart's current size. At its height, A&P captured 2.5 percent of all retail sales. Wal-Mart today has 10 percent.

Nor had chains as a whole captured much more than 20 percent of the market by midcentury. They had undergone one big growth spurt in the 1910s and 1920s, during which the Woolworth's variety store chain grew from three hundred to nineteen hundred outlets and Kroger grocery stores multiplied from a few dozen to more than five thousand—although most of these were very small, often one-man, operations. Cars had not yet become central to American life and so the chains moved into modest storefronts within city neighborhoods and along small-town Main Streets. Other big retailers of the period included mail-order giants Sears, Roebuck & Co. and Montgomery Ward, which had developed the first mechanized distribution centers—where goods arrived from suppliers and were repackaged for shipping to customers via an elaborate conveyor-belt system

—and began setting up retail stores during the 1920s, opening more than eight hundred over the course of the decade.[1]

But despite this expansion, the vast majority of retail trade was still dispersed among hundreds of thousands of small businesses. By 1929 chains controlled 22.2 percent of the market, while Americans continued to spend nearly four of every five dollars with independent retailers. This ratio remained virtually unchanged for the next twenty-five years. By the mid-1950s, the overall market share of chain stores had inched up only slightly, to 23.7 percent. Chains suddenly stopped growing partly because of the collapse of the stock market, but also because of widespread public animosity, which ensured that, even as the economy recovered, chain store expansion did not resume. Concerns about the impact of chain retailers had first surfaced in the 1920s and then intensified into a full-blown backlash during the 1930s and 1940s. Many Americans had come to believe that the chains were driving down wages across the economy and undermining democracy by concentrating economic power in the hands of a few. As discussed in Chapter 8, chain store boycotts and campaigns in support of locally owned businesses took root in cities and towns across the country.[2]

National chains, led by A&P, countered with a massive public relations campaign. They dismissed the broad economic and civic issues raised by chain store critics, arguing that all that truly mattered, the real test, was whether chain stores benefited consumers. Proponents claimed they did, by offering lower prices. It was a viewpoint that began to gain ground in the 1950s in the context of larger shifts in American society. The politics of shopping was changing. The concerns about concentrated economic power and job quality that commonly influenced spending decisions and spawned boycotts in the preceding decades gave way to the idea, familiar to us today, that consumers have little responsibility to the pubic good other than to simply consume, the more the better, in order to guard against recession and spur economic growth.[3]

Rapid suburbanization beginning in the 1950s created fertile ground for national chain stores. Initially developers did not incorporate stores into their subdivisions. The suburbs were strictly residential and families traveled downtown or back to the old neighborhood to do their shopping. But developers and retailers soon recognized the potential, and by the late 1950s auto-oriented, suburban-shopping-center construction was in full swing. Strip shopping centers, set back from the street with parking spaces in front, along with freestanding fast-food outlets, sprung up on major roadways. Chain grocers built vast supermarkets, while the department store chains opened suburban branches that would soon eclipse their downtown flagships in sales and importance. Then came regional shopping centers, and in 1956 the first fully enclosed mall opened in a Minneapolis suburb. Chain stores thrived in these new centers, while independent businesses were largely excluded. Shopping center development was a big business, orchestrated from afar by large companies. These developers had little interest in local businesses to begin with, and were further prevented from offering them leases by their investors, mostly big insurance companies and pension funds, which explicitly barred independents and insisted on contracts with large well-known national brands (today, 90 percent of space in large malls is leased to chains).[4]

Not only were locally owned stores excluded, but the neighborhood business districts and downtowns where they had long operated were losing customers as families left for the suburbs. Cars became increasingly integral to daily life, with disastrous results for downtowns. Easy highway access and ample parking gave suburban-style shopping centers an edge with consumers. As people drove more, downtowns became congested and parking more of a challenge, making a trip into the city even less appealing. The drop in consumer traffic downtown discouraged new investment there, further contributing to a downward cycle of business failures and decline. Even the best-run independent stores struggled to stay afloat in such an environment. By 1967, independents' market share had dropped to about two-thirds of retail sales. Community life suffered as well. While downtowns had nurtured a fluid mix of community and commercial functions, the new suburban shopping centers were strictly private spaces designed to produce a profit.[5]

The market was not the only force driving these changes. Public policy played a major role. To a significant degree, the chain store expansion that began in the late 1950s was underwritten by the federal government. Taxpayers picked up the tab for massive road-construction projects—including $130 billion for the interstate highway system—giving the United States more paved mileage per capita than any other country. Newly created federal mortgage guarantees strongly favored new suburban homes and restricted lending in established neighborhoods. These policies indirectly supported the chains by fueling suburbanization at the expense of central cities and creating the automobile infrastructure that would make giant shopping centers possible.[6]

The federal government also intervened more directly in 1954, when Congress adopted changes to the tax code that suddenly made shopping centers highly lucrative tax shelters. Under tax law, buildings are assumed to deteriorate and lose some of their value every year. The government allows owners to set aside a portion of the value of their buildings tax-free each year to cover the eventual cost of replacement. Prior to 1954, the tax code assumed a commercial building would last forty years, so the owner was allowed to deduct one-fortieth of the structure's value each year from his or her income. Although families were moving to the suburbs in large numbers in the early 1950s, very few shopping centers were built during these years. They were challenging to develop, incredibly expensive, and it took many years for owners to recoup their investments. Some of those that were built went bankrupt. Retail grew in the suburbs, but at a more incremental pace and on a smaller scale that, if left alone, might have provided more opportunities for local entrepreneurs.

But in 1954 Congress accelerated and front-loaded the depreciation timetable, allowing commercial-property owners to take massive deductions in the early years. The result was that shopping centers, even highly profitable ones, were able to show major losses on paper. Kratter Corp, for example, took in nearly $10 million in revenue from real estate investments in 1960. Less expenses, this left a sizable profit of $5.2 million. But Kratter was able to take a $6.9 million depreciation deduction, transforming the profit into a $1.7 million loss for tax purposes. Not only did Kratter's investors walk away with millions of dollars in tax-free income, but they could apply this paper loss to other kinds of income, further reducing their tax liability. Shopping center construction thus became a tax shelter. It was far more lucrative than buying stocks. Not surprisingly, after 1954 money poured in to commercial real estate development. Developers put up new shopping centers, took the big deductions allowed in the first few years, and then sold the property, moving on to build other, often bigger, retail projects. In 1953 new shopping center construction totaled 6 million square feet. Three years later, that figure had increased more than 500 percent. Over the next twenty years, eighteen thousand shopping centers and malls were built in the United States.[7]

According to historian Thomas Hanchett, the effect of the tax code change becomes readily apparent by comparing the rates of shopping center construction in the United States and Canada, which did not adopt accelerated depreciation. In the mid-1950s, the two countries had about the same number of shopping centers per capita. A decade later, the United States had twice as many. There were other consequences as well. "Structures built under accelerated depreciation were intended to be disposable," noted Hanchett. "You reaped the tax break as long as the law allowed, usually seven to fifteen years, then unloaded the project. So builders got out of the habit of building for the ages." Because accelerated depreciation was available only for new construction, not renovation, downtown businesses and property owners could not take advantage of the new tax shelter. Shopping center development grew into an even bigger business, closely connected to national chains and affording little opportunity for independent retailers.[8]

BIRTH OF THE BIG BOX

It was into this world of rampant shopping center growth that Sam Walton opened the first Wal-Mart store in the small town of Rogers, Arkansas, on a warm summer day in 1962. Walton owned a modest downtown variety store in the neighboring community of Bentonville, but had bigger ambitions. He wanted to become a shopping center developer, but banks and investors were unwilling to lend him that kind of money, so he decided to open a large department store instead. Many of the characteristics that would come to define the Wal-Mart empire in later years were present in that first store. "Wal-Mart Discount City," as the sign read, occupied a cheap, single-story building half a mile west of downtown. It was designed for the automobile: situated at the intersection of two major roadways and surrounded by blacktop parking. The store itself spanned sixteen thousand square feet, dwarfing nearly every other business in town. It sold a broad assortment of merchandise, from housewares and clothing to cameras and automotive supplies. Goods were trucked in from the far corners of the country, sourced wherever they could be bought the cheapest. Popular items like shampoo and toothpaste were sold as loss leaders—stacked high at the front of the store and priced well below cost. The idea was to undercut local competitors and draw into the store customers who then stocked up on other items that were priced to produce a profit. There were three checkout stands and a staff of twenty-five. Most of the employees were women. Wal-Mart exploited a legal loophole to pay them just 50–60¢ an hour, well below the federal minimum wage of $1.15 an hour.[9]

Two years later founder Sam Walton opened a second Wal-Mart in

Springdale and a third in Harrison, just off the highway bypass. By 1969 there were eighteen Wal-Mart stores in Arkansas, Missouri, and Oklahoma. The company built its first distribution center that year: a giant warehouse, two football fields in size, where shipments arrived by truck and were unloaded, repacked, and shipped out to individual stores. The pace of Wal-Mart's expansion steadily accelerated. Rather than leapfrogging into new markets, the company favored fully saturating a region with stores before moving on to colonize new territory. By 1973 there were fifty-five stores, spanning five states. In those early years, Wal-Mart avoided major population centers, staking its claim exclusively in small towns. Here, land was cheap, workers nonunion and low-paid, and zoning nonexistent. In small towns, Wal-Mart's giant stores—they averaged forty-five thousand square feet, or about one acre, in the mid-1970s—constituted an overwhelming force, capable by virtue of their sheer scale and financial might to undercut and devour much of the local retail trade.[10]

Wal-Mart was not the only company building big-box superstores. Hundreds of similar stores were opening across the country in low-rent locations far removed from traditional commercial centers. In 1962, the same year Sam Walton launched his chain, the department store company Dayton's debuted four Target stores in the Minneapolis and Duluth suburbs, while S. S. Kresge, a foundering sixty-year-old variety store chain, opened the first Kmart in Garden City, thirty miles outside Detroit. There were many others, mostly regional in scope, including Mammoth Mart, Bradlees, and Zayre in New England; Korvettes, Caldor, and Two Guys in New York; Fred Meyer in the Northwest; Gemco and FedMart in California; and Venture and Value City in the Midwest. Most of these companies no longer exist. They expanded in the 1970s and then began to collapse and disappear in the 1980s. Some were acquired, while others went out of business, as the big three—Kmart, Wal-Mart, and Target—extended their reach. By the mid-1980s, Kmart had taken the lead with two thousand stores, Wal-Mart had mushroomed to nine hundred outlets, and Target had grown to three hundred.[11]

The success of these mass merchandisers soon inspired other variations on the big-box format. One was the "category killer"—a superstore that carries a large selection of one category of goods, such as toys or consumer electronics—so named by the retail industry because of its ability to wipe out smaller competitors and dominate an entire category. Toys "R" Us is widely considered to be the first category killer. Although the chain traces its origins to a baby furniture store founded in Washington, D.C., shortly after World War II by Charles Lazarus, the son of a bicycle retailer, the company's modern history began in 1978, when Toys "R" Us went public and started building vast toy superstores. Another early entrant was Home Depot, which got its start when Bernard Marcus and Arthur Blank, having been fired from management jobs with the Southern California hardware chain Handy Dan, bought a pair of defunct Treasure Island discount stores on the outskirts of Atlanta and reopened them as home-supply superstores in 1979. Circuit City, another early category killer, opened its first thirty-thousand-square-foot consumer electronics superstore in North Carolina in 1981.[12]

Still another variation on the big-box format that first appeared in the late 1970s was the warehouse store. These bare-bones retailing outlets typically have cement floors, simple metal shelves, and unfinished ceilings. They sell everything from office supplies to groceries, mostly in bulk quantities. The selection is broad, but not deep; a typical warehouse store carries about four thousand individual items, while a Wal-Mart supercenter might have as many as one hundred thousand. In 1976 veteran retailer Sol Price—who had founded the FedMart chain, on which Sam Walton based his early Wal-Mart stores—opened the first warehouse store, called Price Club, in an abandoned airport hangar in an industrial section of San Diego. Six years later two of the company's executives left to create their own warehouse chain, opening the first Costco in Seattle in 1983. That year, Wal-Mart, still a regional chain, took another page from Sol Price's playbook, launching Sam's Club in a vacant building on the outskirts of Oklahoma City.[13]

HYPERGROWTH

Although the growth of chain retailers since 1990 can be seen as a continuation of a longer-running trend, it is also entirely unprecedented in both scope and speed. The chains have built a staggering number of stores. They've expanded, colonized land, and consumed market share at a stunning pace. Consider that in 1996, the top ten retail chains accounted for a remarkable 15 percent of consumer spending. Less than a decade later, in 2005, the top ten captured nearly 30 percent of the more than $2.3 trillion that Americans spend in stores each year. Two or three corporations now dominate each retail sector. As the chains have gained market share, tens of thousands of independent businesses have disappeared.[14]

Target grew eightfold from 1990 to 2005; it had 1,400 stores and $53 billion in annual sales in 2005. Two category killers, Home Depot and Lowe's, account for nearly half of all hardware and building-supply sales, double the share they held in 1998. Home Depot had 1,900 stores that captured $73 billion in sales in 2004, while Lowe's, which opened its first superstore in the early 1990s, ranked as the nation's eighth largest retailer, with 1,200 outlets and $36 billion in annual revenue. Since 1990, about 5,000 independent hardware stores have closed. Three office-supply chains—Staples, Office Depot, and OfficeMax—all of which were founded in the late 1980s, have grown to 3,800 outlets and $41 billion in annual sales. Meanwhile, small and medium-size office-supply stores have shrunk to less than 5 percent of the market. Costco, which merged with Price Club in 1993, has nearly tripled in size since 1995. The company currently operates 440 warehouse stores and takes in $47 billion a year. Best Buy, which opened its first superstore in 1989, captures one of every five dollars Americans spend on consumer electronics. Another 10 percent of the market is held by Circuit City.[15]

Some of the most dramatic consolidation has occurred in the grocery industry. Food sales represent the largest segment of the U.S. retail market, accounting for about one-fifth of all store spending. Not that long ago, Americans did most of their shopping at independent grocers and small regional chains, which in turn bought their stock from a large number of independent wholesalers. Today, much of our food flows through a handful of national companies. The top five grocers—Wal-Mart, Kroger (which owns Fred Meyer and Ralph's), Albertson's (which owns Jewel-Osco and Acme), Safeway (which owns Vons and Dominick's), and Ahold (which owns Stop & Shop, Bi-Lo, and Giant)—now capture 46 percent of sales nationally, more than double the share they held in 1998. Independent grocers have dropped to just 17 percent of the market. Because many of the big chains buy directly from manufacturers and handle their own warehousing and distribution, the number of independent grocery wholesalers has also declined since 1990, from more than 350 to fewer than 100.[16]

Clothing sales are likewise increasingly dominated by just a few companies. Mass merchandisers like Target are major clothing sellers, as are specialty chains like Gap Inc., which owns The Gap, Banana Republic, and

Old Navy. Since 1997, Gap Inc. has grown from two thousand to three thousand outlets and more than doubled its revenue. Americans also rely on an ever-diminishing number of corporate retailers for their prescription medications. Chain pharmacies—led by Walgreens, CVS, and Rite Aid—account for 40 percent of prescription drug sales, while the market share of independent drugstores has dropped to 20 percent (supermarkets, mass merchandisers, and mail-order companies account for the rest). The pharmacy chains plan to expand even more rapidly in the near future. Walgreen Co. alone intends to open stores at the rate of one a day to attain its goal of seven thousand outlets by 2010.[17]

Books, movies, and music are rapidly becoming the province of a handful of global retailers. Two megachains, Barnes & Noble and Borders, which started as single outlets and only began unrolling superstores in 1990, now account for about one-fifth of all books sold in the United States and half of all sales made at bookstores. The volume of books sold online and at big-box retailers like Wal-Mart also increased sharply during the 1990s. The number of independent bookstores meanwhile fell by half between 1990 and 2002, and their market share shrank from about 30 to 10 percent. Independent video stores are dropping off the map in record numbers as well; some four thousand have closed since 2000. Blockbuster, which opened its first store in 1985, now has more than nine thousand outlets and accounts for 40 percent of all movie rentals. The second largest video chain, Hollywood Video, captures another 11 percent of the market. Music sales are also increasingly dominated by big chains like Best Buy and Wal-Mart. Since 1998, about one-third of independent music stores have closed; independents' share of album sales has dropped to just 12 percent.[18]

Chain restaurants have grown rapidly as well. Chains and franchises already control much of the fast-food and casual-dining markets, and are now taking over more of the midrange and even fine-dining markets. Shopping malls and big-box complexes across the country are ringed by the same brands: Chili's, Outback Steakhouse, Ruby Tuesday, TGI Friday's. Companies like The Cheesecake Factory and Panera Bread are expanding by more than 20 percent each year, adding still more seats to cities that are already oversaturated. Most ubiquitous of all is Starbucks. The company started the 1990s with fewer than one hundred outlets, finished the decade with two thousand, and has since quintupled in size to more than ten thousand locations. As Starbucks spreads its logo to every corner, other chains are taking a more stealth approach. Some fine-dining restaurant chains give each of their outlets its own name and decor to obscure the centralized management and give patrons the impression of independent ownership. Even ethnic segments long dominated by immigrant families are not immune. Chains like P. F. Chang's and Paul Lee's Chinese Kitchen, which is owned by Outback Steakhouse, are expanding rapidly and hoping to do for the Chinese restaurant market what Olive Garden did for Italian dining. Overall, restaurant sales are more dispersed than other sectors, but the general trend has been the same: greater concentration among the largest chains and diminishing market share for locally owned competitors. The top one hundred chains currently capture 52 percent of all restaurant spending.[19]

What about the Web? At one time, the Internet was seen as a savior of small businesses. The Web would level the playing field: at little expense, independent entrepreneurs could go online and gain access to the same worldwide market their big competitors enjoy. Meanwhile, big-box chains, saddled with vast brick-and-mortar empires, would struggle in this new dynamic. But e-commerce has not developed the way many imagined. While some independents have thrived on the Web, setting up busy electronic stores, often connected to shopping portals like eBay and Abebooks, much of online retailing is dominated by the same retailers that control a commanding share of offline sales. "Web retailing is fast becoming a microcosm of the overall retailing industry," according to Jack Love, publisher of *Internet Retailer*. The top twenty Web retailers captured 30 percent of the $70 billion Americans spent online in 2003 (which represents almost 3 percent of retail sales). Twelve of the twenty are major chains, including Office Depot, Best Buy, Target, Wal-Mart, The Gap, and Barnes & Noble. A few computer makers and catalog retailers also make the cut. Topping the list, of course, is Amazon.com, the bookstore-turned–mass merchant that had over $5 billion in sales in 2003. (Amazon got to the top in part because shareholders allowed it to lose money—more than $3 billion between its founding in 1995 and 2003, when it turned its first, modest, profit.)[20]

By far the biggest chain—one that stands in a league all its own—is Wal-Mart. To even begin to get a sense of how big Wal-Mart is and how much it has grown requires a legion of statistics. In 2005 Wal-Mart had $312 billion in revenue. It operated more than six thousand stores worldwide, including thirty-eight hundred in the United States, each of which averages three football fields in size. With 600 million square feet of floor space in the United States, Wal-Mart could fit every man, woman, and child in the country inside its stores. No company has more trucks on North American roads than it does. Wal-Mart is five times the size of the nation's second largest retailer, Home Depot. It's bigger than Target, Sears, Costco, JC Penney, Walgreens, Best Buy, The Gap, Staples, Toys "R" Us, Nordstrom, Blockbuster, and Barnes & Noble combined.

Wal-Mart is an economic heavyweight of global proportions. It ranks as the thirty-fourth largest economy in the world, bigger than the gross domestic product of most countries, including Austria, Chile, and Israel. Its purchasing power is vast. Wal-Mart bought $18 billion worth of goods from China in 2004, making it the country's fifth largest trading partner, ahead of Great Britain, Germany, and Russia. With 1.5 million employees, Wal-Mart stands as one of the world's largest private employers. Millions more work indirectly for the chain, laboring in factories to produce goods for its shelves or in ports loading shipping containers bound for its stores. To keep this global empire running, Wal-Mart has built a computer system so vast it is said to rival the Pentagon's in size.[21]

Wal-Mart captures an extraordinary share of American consumer spending in nearly every category. Since the advent of its supercenter format in 1988, the retailer grew from selling virtually no groceries to being the country's top food seller. The chain now captures one of every five dollars Americans spend on groceries, and is even more dominant in some markets, such as Dallas–Fort Worth, where Wal-Mart's 104 stores account for one-third of food sales. Wal-Mart also ranks as the number one clothing retailer. It sells more home furnishings than any other company. It is the nation's largest music seller, accounting for one in five albums sold, and the largest toy retailer, with 27 percent of that market. Wal-Mart sells 31 percent of all DVDs, 18 percent of cameras and film, and 16 percent of consumer electronics. It has nearly one-third of the market for numerous household staples, including toothpaste, diapers, and shampoo.[22]

Not only is Wal-Mart driving out independent competitors, it has even begun to devour other large chains. Kmart is foundering, while regional department store companies such as Ames and Caldor have already gone belly-up. Supermarket chains are vulnerable. Of the thirty supermarket chains that filed for bankruptcy protection between 1995 and 2005, Wal-Mart was a catalyst in twenty-six of those cases. And the losses are likely to continue. According to an analysis by the market research firm Retail Forward, for every Wal-Mart supercenter that opens in the next few years, two grocery stores will close. The casualties will include independents as well as stores operated by big national retailers like Kroger and Safeway. Sears and

Kmart merged in an effort to withstand the giant, as did Federated and May, parent companies to numerous department store chains, including Macy's, Bloomingdale's, and Lord & Taylor. Major toy chains are also in trouble. In the late 1990s, Wal-Mart made an aggressive push into the toy market, surpassing Toys "R" Us to become the nation's top toy seller. Determined to steal yet more market share, Wal-Mart, industry analysts say, then began selling toys at cost or even at a loss, making up the revenue in other departments. The tactic sent Toys "R" Us into a tailspin and thrust two other national toy chains, FAO Schwartz and KB Toys, into bankruptcy. Next in Wal-Mart's sights are the consumer-electronics chains. Since 2001, Wal-Mart has increased its market share in this category by 60 percent, surpassing Circuit City to become the second largest consumer-electronics retailer after Best Buy. On Thanksgiving Day in 2005, there were more visitors to Wal-Mart's Web site than to Amazon's—a first.[23]

There seems to be no end to the goods and services Wal-Mart plans to conquer. The company has opened health clinics in many stores and has been working to overturn government regulations that bar it from going into banking. More than fifteen hundred of its outlets are now equipped with gas stations. Doubts over the chain's capacity to expand any further in the United States have surfaced periodically in the business press for more than a decade. Wal-Mart seemed impossibility large in 1999 when *Money* magazine headlined a feature on the retail juggernaut with the query, "How Big Can It Get?" Since then it has doubled in size. Consider too that half of its supercenters are located in just eleven states in the Southeast and Midwest. There are five to ten times as many Wal-Mart stores per capita in Oklahoma and Mississippi than there are in California and New Jersey. And while Wal-Mart accounts for a stunning 10 percent of all U.S. retail sales, in Arkansas it captures close to 20 percent of the pie. Wal-Mart itself sees plenty of room for expansion. The company's executives approve an average of $1 billion in real estate spending every month. CEO Lee Scott has said, "We are finding we can put more supercenters closer together than we ever dreamed of in our life."[24]

Such aggressive building is imperative if a chain is to keep its shareholders content and its stock price buoyant. To grow at the rate shareholders have come to expect, retailers must not only boost sales at their existing stores, they must continually build new stores in order to grab new market share. Indeed, less than half of the annual revenue growth for many big chains can be attributed to increased sales at established stores. In 2004, for example, only one-third of Lowe's $4.7 billion in new revenue was derived from stores open for a year or more. The rest of the company's gains came from opening new outlets. The same was true of Wal-Mart; increased sales at established stores accounted for only one-third of its $27 billion in added revenue. Maintaining this growth rate requires relentless construction. Since 1995, Target and Wal-Mart have expanded their total floor area by an average of 8–10 percent a year. To stay on track, Wal-Mart must build more than 50 million square feet of new store space a year.[25]

Where will all of these new stores go? One place is urban neighborhoods, which many big-box retailers are now targeting as a source of growth. "In general, the inner city is undersaturated with chain retail space. It's a lot of mom and pops," contended Al Meyers of the market research firm Retail Forward. Meyers conceded that, for big-box retailers, the inner city is "last on their list," but they're running out of opportunities elsewhere. Where space allows, big-box retailers prefer to impose their standard suburban formats on city neighborhoods. Shuttered industrial sites are common targets. In Philadelphia, a trio of suburban-style big-boxes—Ikea, Lowe's, and Best Buy—recently debuted on former shipyard land not far from City Hall. In the heart of historic New Orleans, the demolition of a public-housing complex provided sufficient acreage for Wal-Mart to build a two-hundred-thousand-square-foot supercenter surrounded by an ocean of parking. But where necessary, big-box developers are finding ways to wedge massive stores into even the most densely built urban areas. Whole blocks of storefronts in Manhattan have been converted to Bed Bath & Beyond, Best Buy, Circuit City, Old Navy, Staples, and Kmart outlets. Home Depot has opened two Manhattan superstores and is planning more, while Wal-Mart and Target are looking for sites.[26]

TOMORROW, THE WORLD

Although we often refer to them as national chains, these retailers are in fact global chains. One can now visit Starbucks on Avenue de l'Opéra in Paris, shop at Borders in Singapore, or rent a video at Blockbuster in Glasgow, Scotland. Home Depot has erected its orange box just beyond the fortified walls of Quebec City, the four-hundred-year-old cradle of French culture in North America, while Wal-Mart has built a superstore at the base of the ancient pyramids of Teotihuacán in Mexico. The global spread of U.S.-based chains is not a new phenomenon. McDonald's has 32,000 outlets around the world. But what is new is the scope of the megastore appetite: the sheer scale of the stores themselves and their capacity to seize, wherever they go, a dominant share of the local trade in basic necessities, including groceries, clothing, and building supplies.

"Our priorities are that we want to dominate North America first, then South America, and then Asia, and then Europe," David Glass, then CEO of Wal-Mart, announced in the late 1990s. Today the chain operates on all four continents, with more than fifteen hundred outlets outside of the United States, and derives one-fifth of its revenue from its international division. "The United States is 37 percent of the world's economy, which leaves 63 percent for international," John Menzer, CEO of Wal-Mart International, explained. "If we do our job, international operations should someday be twice as large as the United States." Other big chains have declared similar intentions. In an interview with the Associated Press, Home Depot CEO Bob Nardelli dismissed stockholder concerns that the chain may be reaching the saturation point by noting that the company so far has captured only 10 to 12 percent of the global home-improvement market.[27]

Close at hand and sharing much in common with the United States, Canada was an early target for American megachains, which first appeared in the mid-1990s and have since grown to dominate the market. Wal-Mart arrived in Canada in 1994 and now operates 235 superstores and ranks as the country's largest retailer. Costco comes in fourth, with sixty-three warehouses and $5 billion in annual sales. Home Depot is the top retailer of hardware and building supplies. Best Buy leads in consumer electronics, while Staples is the largest seller of office products. The proliferation of these large-scale stores is transforming Canada's landscape. "We've had this view in Canada about how wonderful our downtowns are and that this separates us from the Americans," reported Dr. Ken Jones, director of the Centre for the Study of Commercial Activity at Ryerson University. But now, "downtowns in Canada are in trouble." The Toronto metro has more than seven hundred big-box and category-killer stores, twice as many as there were in the late 1990s.[28]

Megastores are also overrunning Mexico, upending local economies and changing daily life. Wal-Mart built its first Mexican outlet in 1991. Today, it's the largest retailer by a wide margin, with 633 stores and more than one hundred thousand employees. As it commonly does in foreign countries, Wal-Mart expanded in Mexico partly by acquiring existing chains. Many of these, like the Bodega Aurrerá supermarkets, are still operated under their old names, which makes Wal-Mart's takeover of the country's economy not quite as obvious. Wal-Mart has been especially aggressive in the food sector and now controls more than one-third of Mexico's grocery sales, a level of market concentration that alarms antitrust authorities, as well as local farmers and suppliers who have fewer buyers for their products. Two years ago, the Mexican Federal Competition Commission launched an investigation into whether Wal-Mart was strong-arming suppliers, ultimately ordering the company to follow a code of conduct governing its dealings with vendors. More recently, the government authorized Mexico's three competing supermarket chains to form a joint purchasing alliance. The unprecedented move may enable these larger retailers to hold on, but it does nothing to stem the fallout from Wal-Mart's expansion that is occurring in neighborhood after neighborhood as thousands of family-owned businesses, small food producers, and open-air markets disappear.[29]

As they do in the United States, big-box chains rarely give any consideration to local preferences and tend to arrive in waves, one after the other, so rapidly that citizens have little time to react. Cuernavaca, a growing city about ninety minutes south of Mexico City, provides a case in point. In 2001 Costco purchased a historic hotel and casino from the local government. Surrounded by twenty-four acres of Amanalco forest, including hundreds of century-old trees, this fine old art deco hotel, called the Casino de la Selva, was adorned throughout with murals painted in the early 1930s. It had long served as a getaway for politicians, artists, and writers, but had been shut down and confiscated by the government when its owner died in the late 1980s. Costco bought the property with the intention of leveling both the hotel and the forest and erecting one of its standard warehouse stores in their place.

When Costco's plans became public, local environmentalists, small-business owners, and preservationists formed the Civic Front for the Defense of the Casino de la Selva and called on the city to preserve the hotel and turn the land into a park. They organized rallies, the largest of which drew more than fifteen thousand people, collected petition signatures, and reached out to organizations around the world. But Cuernavaca city officials, who'd sold Costco the property for less than market value, remained adamantly in favor of the big box. They arrested dozens of the Civic Front's leaders on charges of sabotage and gave Costco the green light. In the fall of 2002, the company demolished the hotel, cut down the trees, and built two massive concrete boxes—the Costco store and a large chain supermarket.

Virtually overnight, Cuernavaca was flooded with chain store construction. First came Wal-Mart, then two cineplexes and an Office Depot. Sam's Club, Home Depot, Staples, Blockbuster, and several fast-food outlets, including KFC and McDonald's, followed. Cuernavaca, long known as the "city of eternal spring" for its lush climate, may soon become the "city of the eternal megastore." Locally owned businesses are fast disappearing, while the global chains, according to Civic Front member Flora Guerrero Goff, "impose a lifestyle which destroys our culture, environment, and local economy."[30]

Costco, like most big chains, makes little effort to adapt its standard store formula to different cultures. Mike Sinegal, head of the chain's Japan division, bluntly explained, "The bottom line is that the uniqueness of these markets is overrated." Fourteen thousand miles from Cuernavaca, Costco operates another mammoth warehouse store, this one on the outskirts of Tokyo, in the city of Machida. With its glowing red and blue sign and 146,000 square feet of bare-bones selling space, this Costco is virtually indistinguishable from the one in Cuernavaca or from any of the chain's 440 other outlets. About all that sets it apart are the two stories of parking garage stacked on top of the building, a variation made necessary by Japan's high land costs, and a slightly altered product mix that includes cases of seaweed and green tea stacked alongside the more familiar two-pound boxes of potato chips, giant cans of Dinty Moore stew, and oversize packs of beef jerky. Costco plans to build at least fifty outlets in Japan. It's not alone. Spurred by the government's decision to lift long-standing rules restricting construction of large stores, megachains are popping up across the country. Wal-Mart, which bought and is expanding a chain of stores called Seiyu, recently unveiled its first Japanese supercenter, an 85,000-square-foot, single-story outlet, situated within view of Mount Fuji in the fishing community of Numazu.[31]

The success of megastores in Japan and elsewhere around the world depends not on these global retailers' ability to understand local customs and shopping habits, but rather on their power to thoroughly remake them. Traditional practices of visiting several small neighborhood stores three or four times a week, often on foot or by bicycle, are giving way to a more suburban American approach to running errands. It's inherent in the megastores' very design. The sheer scale of these stores and their location on the outskirts of town make picking up a few things every other day impractical. What these stores are actually designed for, what they foster, is a big once-a-week shopping trip. Hauling a week's worth of groceries and other goods home on a bicycle is not an option, and so the car becomes essential to shopping. It's a self-reinforcing cycle: once the car enters the picture, the difficulty of parking downtown or along dense neighborhood streets further erodes the convenience and appeal of locally owned stores. As these businesses begin to decline and close, people have a harder time finding what they need within the neighborhood, and so begin to rely ever more on the superstores.

U.S.-based chains are not the only retailers building global empires. Four of the world's top ten retail corporations are based outside the United States: France's Carrefour, Germany's Metro, the Dutch firm Ahold, and Britain's Tesco. (To get a sense of their relative size, all four of these companies combined would still be smaller than Wal-Mart.) While some European countries have taken steps to limit megastores, others are being overrun by the same kind of retail development that has sprawled across much of North America. In Britain, massive, edge-of-town hypermarkets are draining the life from many town centers. "We are witnessing the slow death of small independent retailers," contended Andrew Simms of the London-based New Economics Foundation. "A new retail feudalism is emerging across Britain as a handful of brands take over our shopping." Four hypermarket giants—Tesco, Asda (owned by Wal-Mart), Sainsbury, and Safeway—now account for 75 percent of the country's food sales. As greengrocers, butchers, druggists, and other merchants disappear from town centers and urban neighborhoods, miniature versions of the big four, like Tesco's Express stores, along with global chains like The Gap, Blockbuster, and Starbucks, have moved into the void.[32]

In much the same way that U.S.-based chains have annexed the Canadian and Mexican markets, when the iron curtain lifted, western European chains rushed into Hungary, the Czech Republic, Slovakia, and Poland. Tesco now has 150 hypermarkets in central and eastern Europe. British journalist Joanna Blythman described one on the outskirts of the Czech town of Hradec Králové: "The Tesco hypermarket . . . sits on no man's land where town meets country . . . an anonymous terrain of roads, warehouses, car showrooms, fast-food drive-throughs and big-box retail developments. It could be France, it could be the U.S., it might be Germany, Mexico, Belgium, Malaysia, the U.K. or Chile. Just another global retail zone, stripped of any geographical or national character." In the space of a few years, Croatians shifted from primarily shopping in small stores and markets to buying most of their food from global chains. The ancient Polish city Kraków now has more megastores per capita than any other European city. Between 2002 and 2004 alone, more than three thousand of Kraków's twenty thousand small businesses folded.[33]

Now the European chains are racing against Wal-Mart and other U.S.-based retailers to conquer countries as far-flung as Brazil and Malaysia. Tesco is a major player in Taiwan, South Korea, and Thailand. Carrefour has erected hypermarkets in thirty-one nations, including Chile, Indonesia, and Turkey. For global retailers, one particularly enticing conquest is China, with its massive population, fast-growing economy, and oppressed workforce. Recent policy changes in China—required to gain entrance to the World Trade Organization—have opened the way for unlimited big-box construction and full foreign ownership of retail stores. Wal-Mart, which sources much of its inventory in China, has opened fifty-five superstores in the country, while both Carrefour and the German chain Metro have dozens more. One retail analyst predicts that by 2010, a handful of global chains will control half of China's retail sales. Should that occur, China will have bypassed any sort of entrepreneurial free market, shifting from a top-down economy directed by state-owned industries to one that is equally centralized, but controlled by multinational corporations.[34]

VENDORVILLE

A handful of corporate chains have become so powerful, they have the capacity not only to refashion local retail economies the world over but to determine what goods the global economy produces, how they're made, and by whom. At one time, the big power players in the economy were manufacturers, like US Steel and General Motors. Today the kingpins are the big chains. They are the gatekeepers. With as much as one-third of the market for certain products, they have near-absolute power to dictate terms and to force even the largest manufacturers to meet their demands. To get a sense of this dynamic, visit the head offices of any of the dominant retailers. Stop by Lowe's in Mooresville, North Carolina, or Costco in Issaquah, Washington. Orbiting around each of these corporate headquarters are the branch offices of hundreds of manufacturers and vendors, staffed by thousands of employees whose sole task is to keep their companies in the chains' good graces.

Nowhere is this balance of power more apparent than in northwest Arkansas. About eight miles from Wal-Mart's first store in Rogers, just on the other side of I-540, is the town of Bentonville, population twenty-five thousand. Sam Walton's hometown for much of his life, Bentonville remains home to Wal-Mart's corporate headquarters, which looks a lot like one of the company's superstores: a low-slung, featureless box in a sea of parking. Wanting to be within reach of the world's largest customer, more than four hundred companies have opened offices nearby, massing along the I-540 corridor from Bentonville south to Fayetteville in an area nicknamed Vendorville. Many of America's most famous brands are here: General Electric, Kraft, Levi Strauss, Clorox, Dial, Del Monte, General Mills, Disney.

One of the first to arrive in the late 1980s was Procter & Gamble, a household-goods powerhouse with a portfolio today that includes Pampers, Tide, Downy, Crest, Folgers, Duracell, Gillette, Right Guard, and Pringles. As big as it is, P&G is dwarfed by Wal-Mart and largely at its mercy. The chain accounts for 15 percent of P&G's revenue, or about $10 billion a year. If Wal-Mart dropped P&G's products, the company would have to double sales to its next nine largest accounts just to stay even—a fate the company is working hard to avoid. In an office not far from Wal-Mart headquarters, P&G has 250 employees who spend their days analyzing sales data from Wal-Mart stores, developing products according to Wal-Mart's instructions, and figuring out ways to reduce Wal-Mart's costs. "Every vendor has many people who are really Wal-Mart employees," explained one executive interviewed by *Advertising Age*.[35]

While the media have reported fairly extensively on the harsh methods corporate retailers employ to extract ever lower prices from their suppliers—Wal-Mart famously insists that its vendors reduce their prices year after year, while Target has perfected online reverse-auctions in which competing companies undercut one another's bids in real time—what has received less attention are the ways chains use their clout to shift some of their own costs onto suppliers. Much of the work done at manufacturers' Bentonville branch offices benefits Wal-Mart at no cost to the company. Retailers also commonly require vendors to adopt expensive new technologies that are of little benefit to themselves, but that reduce labor costs for the chains. Costco, Target, and Wal-Mart, for example, are beginning to demand that suppliers embed radio frequency identification (RFID) tags in their merchandise. These tiny microchips, about the size of a grain of sand, emit signals that can be picked up by specialized scanners. They make managing and tracking inventory much easier for retailers. Wal-Mart expects the tags to reduce payroll at its distribution centers by as much as 10 to 20 percent. But the average supplier—Wal-Mart has thousands—will spend an estimated $9 million implementing the technology.[36]

An even more fundamental and far-reaching cost-shift is now under way as major chains shed ownership of the goods that line their shelves. Traditionally, retailers owned products during the time from when they were delivered until they were purchased by a customer. Capital was thus perpetually tied up in inventory, and managing inventories created expenses and risks for retailers. Now, under new accounting systems being adopted by Wal-Mart and other chains, suppliers are only paid after their products are scanned at the checkout counter. Basically, the chains are becoming vast consignment stores, with manufacturers assuming the burden and expense of owning the inventory. Which party shoulders the cost of lost, stolen, or damaged merchandise is the subject of negotiations, but one doubts the suppliers come out ahead. One analyst predicts that by 2010, Wal-Mart will have wiped all inventory costs from its balance sheet.[37]

To sell to the big chains, companies must follow extensive rules established by each retailer, setting out how goods are to be packaged, labeled, and shipped. They must meet pinpoint delivery times, rolling their trucks up to the right bay at the distribution center at exactly the right moment. The rules vary from retailer to retailer and change constantly. The slightest infractions result in fines, known as chargebacks, which retailers deduct from suppliers' invoices without notice or negotiation. The practice was pioneered by Wal-Mart and spread to other chains in the 1990s. Afraid to offend their biggest customers, companies rarely discuss chargebacks publicly. One anonymous supplier reported being fined $120,000 by Kmart for delivering shipments out of sequence. Kmart eventually reduced the fine to $40,000, but only after the vendor painstakingly assembled documentation showing the fine was unjustified. According to the Credit Research Foundation, chains use chargebacks to discount suppliers' invoices by an average of 4 to 10 percent.[38]

Perhaps the most shocking penalty of all is one corporate retailers call "margin relief"—a fine that vendors must pay if their products fail to generate sufficient profits for the chain. One anonymous vendor reported being assessed $30,000 by Lowe's, because the company's merchandise was not selling as well or as fast as the chain had anticipated. "This is an everyday occurrence," an executive with a lighting and electrical supplier told *National Home Center News.* "We sell a product into a retailer that doesn't sell [in the stores], we have to take it all back and then get penalized on top of that." Essentially, doing business with the chains entails guaranteeing that your products will yield profits, regardless of the circumstances or the retailers' own miscalculations.[39]

Companies that depend on one or two chains for a large portion of their revenue, as many now do, are perpetually at risk of being crushed and losing everything. In an interview in *Fast Company,* Frank Garson II, president of The Lovable Company, a lingerie maker founded in 1926, described his firm's relationship with Wal-Mart: "They have such awesome purchasing power that they write their own ticket. If they don't like your prices, they'll go vertical and do it themselves—or they'll find someone that will meet their terms." After negotiating a contract with the Lovable, Wal-Mart decided to change the terms unilaterally, forcing the manufacturer to give up the business. Three years later, Lovable folded. "Wal-Mart chewed us up and spat us out," Garson said. Rubbermaid similarly imploded under Wal-Mart's vice-like grip. In 1994, faced with rapidly escalating prices for resin, a key ingredient in many of its products, Rubbermaid asked Wal-Mart to accept a price increase. The chain not only refused, but retaliated by clearing Rubbermaid products from its shelves, replacing them with goods made by competitors. With Wal-Mart no longer a customer, Rubbermaid instantly lost almost 20 percent of its revenue. The company, which had just been named one of America's most admired companies by *Fortune,* began to founder. Three years later Rubbermaid was gone, consumed by Newell Company.[40]

Today, Newell Rubbermaid products are back on Wal-Mart's shelves. But any notion of two equals negotiating in their own interest has given way to a form of corporate feudalism, complete with the sort of pageantry that commonly marked medieval hierarchies. Newell's Bentonville branch office houses fifty employees, only part of the company's Wal-Mart division. The office itself is designed to imitate Wal-Mart's own corporate headquarters, down to the cheap carpet, tiny cubicles, and plastic chairs. Pictures of Sam Walton and his aphorisms are tacked to the walls. On the first floor, an exact replica of a Wal-Mart store has been constructed in miniature, showing the placement of Newell Rubbermaid's products. Newell CEO Joe Galli spends at least four weeks every year touring the real thing.[41]

While doing business with the chains is dangerous and sometimes fatal for large manufacturers, small producers fare even worse. In 2003 a judge ruled that Home Depot's dealings with a small door-and-shutter manufacturer were "malicious . . . and fraudulent." The judge concluded that the chain had not only abused this particular supplier, Santa Fe Custom Shutters and Doors, but routinely mistreated other small suppliers. The owners of the company, which had folded after taking on substantial debt to build enough manufacturing capacity to fulfill a contract with Home Depot, which the chain later canceled, were awarded $12 million in damages. Consultant Howard Davidowitz, who has advised some of his clients not to do business with giant retailers, warns, "If you do, you can get destroyed in a thousand ways." But if the chains continue to absorb an ever-larger share of consumer spending, and more independent retailers disappear, small firms may have no choice but to take their chances supplying the big boxes.[42]

Market concentration often leads to more market concentration, and indeed, the excruciating pressure of dealing with the megachains has set off a wave of mergers among manufacturers, notably Procter & Gamble's acquisition of Gillette in 2005 and Whirlpool's purchase of Maytag in 2006. The point is not so much to gain leverage; that's an impossible goal given that the biggest manufacturers are not even in the same league as the chains. The top five book publishers, for instance, produce nearly half of all the books sold in the United States, but their combined revenue is still smaller than Barnes & Noble's. The world's largest and best-known consumer brands are only a fraction of the size of Wal-Mart. Manufacturers have no hope of becoming big enough to hold their own in negotiations with the chains; they're merging because a certain scale is necessary just to keep up with the demands of supplying these retailers. According to the executive of a food company that recently merged with another, suppliers in the supermarket industry need to do at least $15 billion in annual sales to function effectively. "The reason," he explained, "is that at $15 billion, you start having the scale to put a significant number of people in Bentonville."[43]

More ominous for manufacturers is the fact that the chains are not only their largest customers but, increasingly, their competitors too. Suppliers to Wal-Mart and Target risk losing the business not only to another vendor but to the chain itself. Store-brand, or private-label, products now account for 20 percent of sales at large chains. Wal-Mart-manufactured dog food, sold under the Ol' Roy label, has surpassed Purina as the world's top-selling brand. The chain's in-house juice label outsells Ocean Spray, while its toy trucks take up more shelf space than Mattel's. Wal-Mart has recently moved into more sophisticated product lines. In 2004 it unveiled its own electronics brand, iLo, producing plasma television sets and DVD recorders; Wal-Mart may eventually manufacture everything from cell phones to computers. It's not alone. Best Buy has started making DVD players, televisions, and computers under its Insignia label. Target has developed an extensive array of private-label clothing, beauty, and food products. Home Depot sells exclusive lines of tools and other products. While the chains are free to compete directly with their vendors, the reverse is not true. A few years ago, Home Depot sent a letter to its suppliers demanding that they stop selling their products on their own Web sites: "We trust you can understand that a company may be hesitant to do business with its competitors."[44]

The rapid expansion of private-label sales is due in part to a remarkable transfer of knowledge from manufacturers to retailers. Not long ago, retailers lacked the expertise and understanding of consumer preferences needed to truly compete with major brands. But that's no longer the case. The primary directive of the legions of manufacturers' employees stationed in Bentonville is to help Wal-Mart sell more goods, which they accomplish by giving the retailer access to all of their research and expertise about the market for dog food or toys or DVD players. As a result, when Wal-Mart launches its own private-label version, it knows about as much about making and selling that product as any of the leading brands. Procter & Gamble's Bentonville employees, for example, spent years teaching Wal-Mart about the laundry business. The chain repaid the favor in 2001 when it unveiled its own laundry detergent, priced well below Tide, P&G's pride and joy.[45]

Big retail chains are manufacturers' top customers and largest rivals. Soon they may become their primary source for raw materials as well. Wal-Mart has begun to leverage its vast international procurement network to negotiate deals on inputs, like denim and polar fleece, that its suppliers use to manufacture products for superstore shelves. Mattel and Hasbro are among the companies that have reportedly already begun to purchase their inputs through Wal-Mart. As Ken Eaton, head of international procurement at Wal-Mart, explained, "There's no reason we can't be buying oranges for orange juice, paper for notebooks or tomatoes for tomato juice."[46]

WALTON 5 & 10

Sam Walton had become a legendary figure in America even before his death in 1992. His story is the ultimate tale of the hometown merchant who made it to the big time. Before opening Wal-Mart Discount City, Walton owned a variety store in downtown Bentonville. Named Walton 5 & 10, the store sold clothing, household goods, sewing supplies, cookware, toys, and cosmetics. The location was ideal: a prime spot on what was, in the 1950s, a bustling town square buttressed by the county courthouse and lined with small businesses. Like many local merchants, Walton was actively involved in the community. He took a turn as president of the Rotary Club, served on the hospital board, helped launch a Little League program, sponsored the high school football team, taught Sunday school, and was elected to the city council. In 1962 Walton launched the Wal-Mart empire. Twenty-three years later he was the richest person in America. According to the legend that permeates the business press, Wal-Mart's miraculous rise was owed to Walton's feisty entrepreneurialism, seven-day workweeks, and notorious thrift. He worked in a small, unadorned office and drove a '79 Ford pickup until the day he died.[47]

There's certainly truth to the Walton legend. But much as the rags-to-riches stories of Horatio Alger once served to keep the country's poor docile and hardworking, the Walton tale is told to shore up a now dubious tenet of the American economic system: namely, that anybody with a good idea and a willingness to work hard can grow a business from scratch. It helps mollify concerns about Wal-Mart's power, because the underlying implication of the Walton legend is that at any moment another clever, gutsy entrepreneur could start up a small business and go head-to-head with Barnes & Noble or Home Depot or even Wal-Mart.

But is this really still possible? Could Sam Walton himself open an independent retail store today and make it? Downtown Bentonville tells its own story about the state of American entrepreneurialism. The town square is about as lifeless as the towering statue of a Confederate soldier overlooking the green. A small stationery store has managed to hang on, along with a diner and a "country store" for tourists. Gone is Bentonville Furniture's "four floors of fine furniture." So too the shoe store, doughnut shop, the dry cleaner. The red-lettered sign of Walton 5 & 10 remains, but the business ceased functioning decades ago. The storefront is now a museum churning out the Walton legend, replete with artifacts, including Sam Walton's pickup truck and a stuffed version of his dog, Ol' Roy.[48]

Independent businesses are few and far between in Bentonville. Much of the town's economic activity has migrated out to Sam Walton Boulevard, a sprawling commercial strip of fast-food outlets and gas stations anchored by a Wal-Mart supercenter, or to one of the many clusters of chain stores that have sprung up along the I-540 corridor east of town. Like many Americans, Bentonville residents do much of their shopping and dining at places like Scottsdale Center, a massive array of the same big chains found everywhere: Lowe's, Linens 'n Things, Old Navy, The Gap, Kohl's, Barnes & Noble, Chili's, and Applebee's.

For independent businesses, surviving in this environment is a considerable challenge. It's not simply a matter of competition. The chains have certain inherent advantages, to be sure, but local businesses do too. The problem, many contend, is that corporate chains use their financial resources and market power to gain an unfair edge over their smaller rivals. In an economic system designed to reward companies for being better, the major chains have managed to grab market share in large measure simply by being bigger. It's a rigged game. Even the most popular, innovative, and best-managed independent businesses face an uphill battle, which raises a critical question. Are corporate retailers creating an economy that is more competitive and dynamic, or one that is decidedly less so?

A favorite tactic employed by corporate retailers is to flood a market with far more retail space than local consumers can actually support. "The reading population is not growing, but there are so many more bookstores," said Ann Christopherson, co-owner of Women & Children First, a longstanding and highly regarded Chicago bookstore. Since the early 1990s, Barnes & Noble and Borders have built nearly forty superstores in the Chicago metro. Meanwhile, consumer spending on books has been stagnant. With those dollars spread ever more thinly over a much larger number of stores, many of Chicago's independent booksellers, predictably, have slipped into the red and closed. Retail profit margins are slim and, while a chain has the financial resources to ride out losses at some of its superstores indefinitely, only a small decline in revenue can make the difference for an independent. "You can be stuck just by virtue of the fact that enough of your customers are picking up at Borders a few of the things they would have bought from you," Christopherson said. Sales at her store fell during the early 1990s when the superstores first expanded in Chicago. She and co-owner Linda Bubon have managed to get revenue back up to a viable level, but the chains keep on coming. Borders has opened yet another superstore less than a mile from Women & Children First.[49]

Much the same scenario has played out nationwide. "Our best estimates are that since 1991, the retail square footage devoted to the sale of books in the United States has quadrupled and that, over the same period, total book sales (in units) have remained about the same," said Oren Teicher of the American Booksellers Association. Overbuilding has occurred in nearly every retail sector. "We're willing to cannibalize ourselves," Home Depot chief executive Bob Nardelli said recently as he briefed shareholders on the company's strategy of blanketing the country with so many outlets that their market areas overlap.[50]

This carpet-bombing tactic worries Scott Lockwood, owner of Robnett's Hardware in Corvallis, Oregon. Home Depot is building a 130,000-square-foot store in this city of fifty thousand and, if another developer's plans succeed, Lowe's will soon follow. Home Depot already has an outlet in the neighboring town of Albany and plans to open several more in the region. The market is not large enough to support all of this new capacity, Lockwood contends. He wonders if Robnett's, which was founded in 1857 and ranks as the oldest continuously operated business in Oregon, will survive. "We're not going to roll over," Lockwood vowed, but big-box saturation may prove an even more dire threat than the Great Depression. Two locally owned hardware stores in Albany have already closed.[51]

Business experts advise independent merchants like Lockwood to carve out a niche, a specialized area of the market in which the chains are not directly competing. By this logic, independent businesses no longer have a place in the mainstream of the American economy, but can survive only on the outer margins, selling extraneous products rather than everyday goods and services. But even accepting this, what's really left for independents? "They don't leave those crumbs for long," Lockwood said. He pointed out that local garden centers have focused more on advanced gardeners in an effort to differentiate themselves from Home Depot, which has a large gardening department aimed primarily at the "starter" market. But now, having seen how attractive the advanced market is, Home Depot is beginning to expand in that direction. "When they see a market is viable, they move into it," Lockwood contended. "Soon there will be no fringe left."[52]

Corporate retailers commonly offer very low prices at newly opened stores, sometimes sustaining losses at those outlets for months or even years to gain market share. Once people have gotten into the habit of shopping the big box, however, prices rise. That's happened at the Home Depot store in Albany, according to Lockwood, who has kept tabs through a network of contractors that shop both his store and Home Depot. "They all tell me the same thing," he said. Prices have risen appreciably since the Home Depot opened two years ago. Individual items may vary, but if you look across a broad range of goods, prices at Robnett's and Home Depot are now about the same. Lockwood conceded that this surprises even him. "They have the marketing ability to create this sense of lower prices," whether it's true or not, he explained.[53]

"We're so inundated with the advertising that people are convinced the big stores are the only way to go," concurred Tom Tracy, who owns Bay Copy & Data, an office-supply business in Tampa, Florida. When he launched the business in 1986, there were at least fifty local office-supply businesses in the area. Today there are a handful. Marketing, he argued, has conditioned people to think of the chains first and foremost whenever they need something. If you need office supplies, you automatically think of Staples or Office Depot. Few people consider the impact of their choices on the community. "I asked a teacher recently where she goes for supplies. She told me Staples," Tracy said. "Then I asked her where she goes for donations for school programs. She named an independent business."[54]

"One of the biggest problems facing independent music stores is loss-leader pricing," argued Don VanCleave, president of the Coalition of Independent Music Stores and former owner of Magic Platter CD in Birmingham, Alabama. The nation's two largest music sellers, Wal-Mart and Best Buy, he explained, sell CDs at a loss to get customers in the door; according to the chains' market research, once inside, these customers buy other higher-value items. Someone lured in for the latest Céline Dion album, for example, might pick up a new pair of jeans or shop for a DVD player. Independents that sell only music must find a way to compete with mass merchandisers that treat their entire music departments as loss leaders.[55]

The power that Wal-Mart in particular has over its suppliers is creating "an economic and competitive imbalance," according to Burt Flickinger, managing partner at the New York–based consulting firm Strategic Resource Group. While suppliers set up offices in Bentonville and devote hundreds of employees to keeping Wal-Mart happy and profitable, they cannot afford to provide the same support to other retailers. "Other stores are not getting their fair share," Flickinger explained. As large retailers shift more of their own costs onto manufacturers, who absorbs these added expenses? Certainly manufacturers are not charging the chains higher prices, just the opposite. Suppliers are bridging the gap to a degree, by making their business more efficient and by moving production to lower-wage countries. But some of these expenses are almost undoubtedly reflected in the prices manufacturers charge other, less powerful, customers, namely the wholesalers that supply independent businesses. "I have a price sheet for Wal-Mart and a price sheet for everyone else," one toy company executive told the *Washington Post*.[56]

"Wal-Mart is destroying the free enterprise system," Bob Allen, a forty-year veteran of retailing, asserted. In 1964 Allen and his wife, Georgene, opened a large department store two blocks east of downtown Hastings, Nebraska. Allen's did brisk business through the 1970s and 1980s. Then in 1990 Wal-Mart arrived on the outskirts of town. Soon after it opened, Bob Allen contended, the superstore started selling many of its health and beauty products at a loss. According to records kept by Allen, in 1993 Wal-Mart sold Crest toothpaste for 62¢, compared with $1.89 at Allen's, and priced a large bottle of Bayer aspirin at $1.56, while Allen's had it for $4.99. To hit the point home, the superstore posted signs under many items showing Allen's price versus Wal-Mart's. Persuaded that the superstore offered better deals, many of Allen's customers jumped ship and started shopping at Wal-Mart. Few seemed to notice as prices slowly inched up. By 2000, Bob Allen said, prices for the products he'd tracked over the years were about the same at both stores. The Hastings Wal-Mart sold the large bottle of Bayer aspirin for $5.78, while Allen's priced it at $5.49. The Crest toothpaste went for $1.87 at Wal-Mart and $2.15 at Allen's. But by then it was too late. Wal-Mart had captured the business. "It's so un-American," lamented Allen, whose store has been losing money for the last few years.[57]

As challenging as it is to survive today as an independent business, it's even more difficult to launch one. Chain store saturation has made viable locations hard to come by. The vast majority of developers and their financial backers are as inclined toward corporate retailers and as reluctant to include independent businesses as they were when the shopping center building craze began in the late 1950s. "If [investors] see Joe's Coffee on the tenant list, they discount the rent," explained Peter Rubin, president of Coral Co., a real estate development firm. "They see Red Lobster and they say, 'That makes me feel good,' even though the food sucks." Obtaining capital to launch an independent business, always difficult, is even more so. "I started in 1974 with an initial investment of five hundred dollars in a tiny space and grew with the community," said Gayle Shanks, owner of Changing Hands Bookstore in Tempe, Arizona, which now has thirteen thousand square feet of selling space and forty-five employees. "Many of the great bookstores in this country got started that way," she added, but it is harder today. Changing Hands stands as the last general independent bookstore in the Phoenix metro, which now has twenty-one Borders and Barnes & Noble outlets.[58]

Just a few miles north of Changing Hands, yet another Barnes & Noble is under construction. It's part of a massive 130-acre big-box development called Tempe Marketplace. The center includes the usual array of chains—Target, Old Navy, Best Buy, PetSmart, Office Max, and so on—and was financed in part by over $40 million in tax breaks provided by the city of Tempe. Five miles to the south of Changing Hands is another Barnes & Noble, this one part of the Chandler Fashion Center, which is also on the public dole, having been granted tax breaks worth $42 million. On the other side of the metro, in Glendale, lies the Arrowhead Towne Center Mall, built with $17 million in government subsidies and home to a B. Dalton outlet, a subsidiary of Barnes & Noble. Subsidies for retail developers are not unique to the Phoenix area; they're provided by cities and counties nationwide. Perhaps more than anything else, more than the loss-leader pricing or the special favors wrested from suppliers, it is this pervasive government support for chain retailers—through not only subsidies but, as we'll see in Chapter 7, a host of regulatory and tax advantages—that has undermined locally owned businesses.[59]

The current trends are sobering, to say the least. But trends are not destiny. There are three things worth keeping in mind. One is that tens of thousands of locally owned retail businesses still exist. Given the circumstances, this is a remarkable testament to their ingenuity—and to the potential of rebuilding a more diversified and decentralized economy. Second, the power of corporate chains, vast and unprecedented on the one hand, is also fragile and tenuous. It hinges on the choices we make every day. Wal-Mart's tremendous might, and its ultimate fortunes, rests on its ability to ring up

$790 million in sales tomorrow, and more the next day and the day after that. Lastly, the future depends on our public policy decisions. Should we continue to shower chains with subsidies and tax advantages denied to independent businesses, the current trends are likely to continue. Policy-makers have eagerly supported chain store expansion out of a sense that their growth was both inevitable and beneficial. But as we'll see, corporate chains have left us worse off—as wage earners and even as consumers —and they've imposed significant costs on the environment and our communities.

TWO

FADING PROSPERITY

FOR MIKE CASTLES, THE HARDEST PART of closing his family's seventy-two-year-old hardware store was letting down the employees. "We had great people: Jake, who'd been with us for forty years; Kent, my shop man, another forty years; Doris, the bookkeeper. She was here forty years, too," he said. "They all started with my grandfather." In 1932 Mike's grandfather opened Castles Ace Hardware in the town of Carlisle in the south-central part of Pennsylvania. It was a sizable store: twenty-eight thousand square feet with about two-thirds devoted to hardware and the other third to a large lumberyard and millwork shop, where employees would custom cut and plane boards to any size and thickness at no extra cost. In the late 1950s, Mike's uncle Lee dropped out of college and came to work at the store, eventually inheriting it in 1974. He asked Mike to take over the day-to-day management a few years ago, but continued to make any big decisions about the business. The final decision to close was his. The store had been hard hit by the opening, in rapid succession, of three massive superstores in Carlisle. Sales dropped when Wal-Mart arrived in 2002 and then again when Lowe's opened just a few blocks away in early 2004. Home Depot announced that it would build its own store and open by the fall of that year. In July, Lee Castles decided to liquidate his family's business. "It was a bitter pill for him," said Mike.[1]

Twenty people lost their jobs when the store closed. Most had made thirteen to sixteen dollars an hour with benefits, according to Mike Castles, but those who had been there the longest earned close to fifty thousand dollars a year. There were other losses as well. Local contractors, most of whom had remained fiercely loyal after the superstores opened, could no longer get certain specialty items locally. "When I run into them on the street now, they all bend my ear for fifteen or twenty minutes about how much they miss me," said Mike. All of the spending that Castles had done with other local businesses in town disappeared when the store closed. "If it was available through someone in the community, we bought it in the community," Mike recounted. Gone from the local economy were the dollars the store spent on advertising, repairs, supplies, inventory, remodeling, and various professional services. Castles had also been a longtime contributor to local charities and nonprofits. "Very few of them were turned away," said Mike, who serves on two nonprofit boards himself and contends that it is much harder to secure a donation from the chains, where decisions are made far from Carlisle. Today, Mike Castles often finds himself replaying those final months in his mind, wondering what he could have done differently to save his family's business. "It was such an emotional time," he said.[2]

Many other local stores also lost sales or closed after the superstores arrived. With a population of just eighteen thousand, plus another thirty thousand in the surrounding area, Carlisle's market proved too small to absorb all of that new retail without losses to existing businesses. Margins are thin in retail and only a modest drop in revenue can be enough to plunge a business into the red. Two other local hardware stores—Handy Hardware and Cochran & Allen—also folded. Shopping at an independent hardware store is no longer an option in Carlisle. The community's 250-year-old downtown operates on the economic margins; it's quiet, with more than a few vacancies. Driving along the highway, what now marks Carlisle's existence is the giant Wal-Mart supercenter. It is one of four in a row, spaced about every nine miles on the way to Harrisburg. These stores loom large on the landscape and local economy, but somewhere at Wal-Mart headquarters, one can imagine that they are just four little pins on a map.[3]

This is progress—or so we are told. "Progress" is a favorite word among big-box retailers and their boosters. Typical of its use was a full-page newspaper ad that Wal-Mart ran in the town of Westbrook, Maine, in the summer of 2005, as the city was considering new zoning rules that would interfere with the company's plans to build a two-hundred-thousand-square-foot supercenter. The ads opposed the rules and urged residents to "let the City Council know that you support progress." This idea of progress is powerful and pervasive. It suggests that, while we may regret the loss of our hometown grocer or the neighborhood pharmacy, these are necessary casualties on the path to economic advancement and prosperity. And indeed, the big chains seem to deliver exactly what most communities want most: economic growth, lower prices, new jobs, and tax revenue.

But the megachains contribute far less to our local economies than they take away. For all of the new jobs that the chains have created, they have destroyed many thousands more—at small businesses and American factories especially, but also, as we will see, at enterprises as diverse as family farms and local newspapers. Many of these jobs came with good paychecks, and their loss is shrinking the middle class. The poor have fared even worse, as global retailers have used their immense market power to drive down wages for those at the bottom, while simultaneously closing off avenues— like starting a small business or getting a good manufacturing job—that generations of Americans have used to pull themselves out of poverty. What poor families are saving at the big-box till is no match for what they have given up in income. Nor are the tax benefits any less of a mirage; these sprawling stores place a major burden on roads and other pubic infrastructure and many of their employees must rely on pubic assistance to get by.

Perhaps the greatest economic danger of all is that, as local businesses disappear, our communities are becoming ever more dependent on a handful of corporations that have no allegiance to the places where they do business. None of this really looks much like progress. It certainly is not an economic model designed to foster broad prosperity.

THE JOBS MIRAGE

New big-box stores and shopping centers are almost invariably sold to communities as job creators. Developers, supportive local officials, and even newspapers routinely refer to the number of new jobs a particular project will bring. The *Dayton Daily News* reported that a new Target in Sugarcreek, Ohio, "will create 150 to 200 new jobs." Wal-Mart is "expected to create 250 jobs," *Crain's Chicago Business* reported during the debate leading up to the approval of a superstore on the city's west side. In Salem, Oregon, "the big-box store the Home Depot envisions could create nearly 200 jobs," according to the *Statesman Journal*. Many local officials, under pressure to demonstrate job growth during their terms, are only too eager to go along, appearing at ribbon-cuttings for the stores and hailing them as job generators. Many communities, having suffered through recent plant closures and economic instability—trends for which the retail chains are partly to blame—are desperate to believe these claims, welcoming anything that appears to create work, no matter how low-paid.[4]

But the employment boost promised by the chains is nothing more than an illusion. It's true that big-box stores create hundreds of retail jobs. But they eliminate as many by forcing other businesses to downsize or close. When Bob Sowers closed his three grocery stores in Athens, Ohio, 135 people lost their jobs. Sowers had spent twenty-seven years building up the business from the small convenience store he had started back in college. Then Wal-Mart arrived, opening a supercenter the size of four football fields. At first Sowers thought he would survive. Sales dropped only 8 percent in the first year. "I was ecstatic. I thought, we can live with this," he said. But that 8 percent turned out to be all of his profit and then some. "When revenue drops, your expenses as a ratio of sales go way up. Then you are on a downward spiral," he said. "You find yourself not able to pay your bills and it's humiliating. I ended up filing for bankruptcy." The 135 people who lost their jobs were earning about 20 percent more than their counterparts at the new Wal-Mart, and had health insurance as well. "It's just sickening what Wal-Mart has done to this community," Sowers lamented. "I was just one of many in their path." At least a dozen other businesses have closed in Wal-Mart's wake, including a shoe store, two record stores, another grocer, and an optician.[5]

It may take a few years for the fallout from a new superstore to fully materialize, but ultimately the number of jobs created is offset by at least an equal number of job losses at other stores. The reason is fairly simple: retail development does not represent real growth. It does not generate new economic activity. Opening a Target superstore will not increase the amount of milk people drink or how many rolls of paper towels they use in a year. It will not increase their disposable income. The size of the retail spending "pie" in a local market is a function of how many people live in the area and how much income they have. Building new stores does not expand the pie; it only reapportions it.

Corporate retailers know this, of course. Although city officials often assume that chains pick locations based on data that show an area has unmet demand, in fact they more often choose sites because they believe they can steal market share from nearby businesses. "When I first started as a retail consultant, I developed all of these models to see what categories had unmet demand. But after a while, I realized that was futile," said Chris Boring, president of Boulevard Strategies. Most retail development is based on "predatory opportunity," according to Boring. "You do it bigger than the other guy and just knock him out of the market. That's where most of the action is these days."[6]

Grabbing market share from rivals is part of competition. But the chains' vast resources and their ability to oversaturate markets, sell goods below cost, and operate individual outlets at a loss indefinitely gives them an edge that can hardly be described as true competition. As Bob Sowers found, a superstore does not even need to appeal to a majority of a local competitor's customers; all it has to do is skim off enough sales to push the independent into the red and then wait it out. This phenomenon has produced some rather curious success stories in the retailing world. Take Blockbuster, which has captured more than 40 percent of the video-rental market and forced out thousands of profitable independent video stores as it expanded, often by locating next door to or across the street from competitors. Yet by 2005 the chain had not actually turned a profit. In fact, since Blockbuster went public in 1999, it has lost more than $3 billion. Independents, no matter how beloved and popular, lack this ability to succeed while losing money.[7]

As local stores contract and close, communities end up with no overall growth in retail sales or employment. It's what Dr. Kenneth Stone, an economist at Iowa State University who has studied the economic impact of Wal-Mart, Home Depot, and other retailers since the 1980s, calls a "zero-sum game." His studies have found that gains in sales at new superstores are invariably mirrored by sales losses at nearby businesses. Between 1983, when Wal-Mart opened its first store in Iowa, and 1993, when the company had expanded to 45 superstores, Stone found that the state lost 555 grocery stores, 591 hardware and building-supply dealers, 161 variety stores, 88 department stores, 291 apparel stores, 153 shoe stores, 116 drugstores, 111 jewelry stores, and 94 lawn and garden stores. And, of course, each of these store closures entailed job losses.[8]

The most extensive study to date of the effect of big-box stores on retail employment was done by David Neumark, an economist at the University of California at Irvine, and two researchers with the Public Policy Institute of California, Junfu Zhang and Stephen Ciccarella. Neumark and his colleagues conducted a sophisticated statistical analysis of counties across the United States where Wal-Mart had opened stores, looking at changes in employment and payroll. They found that the opening of a Wal-Mart store reduced a county's retail employment by an average of 180 jobs, or 3.2 percent. That is, Wal-Mart employed fewer people than the stores that closed or downsized following its arrival. This makes sense, given the efficiencies of big-box retailers and their tendency to understaff stores. The research also found that the opening of a Wal-Mart led to a drop in countywide retail earnings of 2.8 percent—a total payroll reduction of more than $2 million on average.[9]

Because the underlying market dynamics—the zero-sum game—are the same regardless of the name on the box, it's likely that all of the other chains—from Target to Barnes & Noble—also have no or even a negative impact on retail and wholesale employment when they open a new store (similar studies have not been done for these retailers). In fact, retail jobs as a percentage of total jobs nationally have actually declined slightly since 1990, despite the fact that large chains have opened thousands of new stores. Research in Britain has reached similar conclusions. One study, financed by major retailers, found, much to their embarrassment, that each superstore eliminates an average of 276 existing jobs.[10]

Still, the myth that a new big-box store or shopping center will expand job opportunities persists. Part of the problem is that, while the gains are visible and much touted, the job losses are not. They often happen a few employees at a time, and it may take several years for the impact to fully manifest. Local businesses may remain open for some time, appearing to have survived, when in fact they are running on little more than fumes. Nor are merchants likely to admit publicly that they are struggling, believing that the scent of failure will only further depress sales. Instead, most do what they were taught in business school: be upbeat and project success. The community may not realize anything is wrong until the day the business folds.

Some cities and towns also imagine that they can enlarge the pie, thus increasing retail sales and employment, by becoming regional shopping destinations that pull in consumers from surrounding communities. This rising tide will lift all boats, the thinking goes, including local businesses. The megastores reinforce this idea. In a new marketing campaign designed to improve its public image, Wal-Mart contends that "existing stores flourish as they take advantage of the increased customer flow to and from our stores." (This is the same company whose employees used to chant, "Sell 'em low, stack 'em high, make those downtown merchants cry!") But there are problems with this line of thinking. One is that big-box retailers' core strategy is one-stop shopping. No matter what their public relations materials say, their goal is to eliminate the need for customers to spend money at other businesses—thus their relentless expansion into new services. Wal-Mart is installing gas stations and banks in its stores. Home Depot and Lowe's are now doing some twenty-six thousand home-installations a day of windows, roofing, flooring, and other products, so their customers do not have to hire independent contractors. Maximizing spending at their own stores is part of the reason chains favor stand-alone boxes removed from established retail districts. But even under optimal circumstances big-box stores generate little spillover for other businesses. In Rutland, Vermont, where Wal-Mart built a superstore downtown, a survey found that 80 percent of its shoppers did not visit other downtown stores.[11]

Another problem is that, even if the majority of the business failures and layoffs that result from a new megastore occur in nearby towns, they are still losses that undermine the region's economic health and prosperity. Not only is it a rather unneighborly approach to economic growth, but maintaining dominance as a regional shopping hub is hard to do: it is only a matter of time before the same chains look to build stores in adjacent communities too. Economist Kenneth Stone's research in Iowa has shown that towns that gain a Wal-Mart store did show a jump in overall retail sales (at the expense of smaller towns nearby). But after a few years, sales leveled off and then begin to decline. Most of the host towns ended up with about the same level of consumer spending they had before Wal-Mart's arrival. About one in four dropped *below* pre-Wal-Mart levels. Stone has documented a similar pattern with Home Depot and other big-box home-improvement stores in metropolitan areas. He attributes his findings to the fact that chains expand by saturating markets; they build stores to fill in the gaps between their existing outlets until they reach a point where they are cannibalizing their own sales. In metro Atlanta, Wal-Mart is now opening supercenters less than three miles apart.[12]

CORPORATE COLONIES

The effect of mega-retailers on local economies does not end with shuttered local merchants and their laid-off employees. Most local retailers buy many goods and services locally: they bank at local banks, advertise in local newspapers, carry goods produced by local firms, and hire a range of professionals, from accountants to Web designers. Every dollar spent at a locally owned store sends a ripple of benefits through the local economy, supporting not only the store itself, but many other local businesses, which in turn provide jobs—often the sort of well-paid positions that form the backbone of a city's middle class and the core of its tax base. When chains displace local merchants, all of these economic relationships are severed. Money that used to flow through the community—from a local office-supply store that hires a local accountant, who in turn uses a local bank that lends money to a new entrepreneur, who stocks up at the local office-supply store, and so on—ceases to do so.

Communities dominated by global retail chains function in many respects like the colonial economies of the European superpowers, which were organized not to foster local development and prosperity but to enrich the colonizers. In Africa, the superpowers built railroads that, rather than forming links between cities, ran in single lines from the interior to the coast. The aim was to extract resources. So it is with today's corporate superpowers: they restructure local economies according to their own needs, not to spur internal development. They sever the webs of exchange that link local businesses with one another and with residents, and replace them with a single-track economy over which the community has little control and where wealth flows in only one direction: out.

Aside from their local payroll, which typically accounts for less than ten cents of every dollar spent at a big-box store, chains return very little of the revenue they take in back to the local economy. By design, they keep local spending on goods and services to a minimum. Among the many businesses that have been affected by this are newspapers and radio stations. The loss of independent stores and restaurants has destroyed one of their most important sources of advertising revenue, and that revenue stream has not been replaced by the chains, which direct most of their advertising budgets to national television spots and direct mail. "There's no doubt that Wal-Mart, and the whole big-box retailing approach, has had a negative impact on newspapers," said Frank Deaner, executive director of the Ohio Newspaper Association.[13]

One example is the *Review* in East Liverpool, Ohio. The *Review*'s advertising director, Lisa Ludovici, regrets not listening to the warnings of local merchants in 1992, when Wal-Mart proposed building a superstore in this town of thirteen thousand. "I thought they were worried for no reason, but they were right," she now admits. Today, about 70 percent of the storefronts downtown are empty—and they all represent lost advertising revenue. Meanwhile, the new Wal-Mart does not even come close to making up the difference. Once a month, the company gives the *Review* a glossy insert to stuff inside its pages. Because these inserts are produced elsewhere, they do not contribute nearly as much income as the paper once earned from designing and printing display ads for local retailers. While Ludovici insists that the paper still does a good job of serving the community, she acknowledges that less advertising revenue means fewer pages and less reporting—and ultimately, of course, fewer editorial and production jobs.[14]

Newspapers across the country have had similar experiences. Mike Buffington, editor of the *Jackson Herald* in Jackson, West Virginia, and chair of the National Newspaper Association, said that the impact of big-box retailers has become a leading topic of discussion at industry meetings. A recent report by Deutsche Bank Securities found an "extraordinary" correlation between declining newspaper revenue and the proliferation of big-box retailers. Those newspapers in cities most heavily blanketed with big-box stores are faring the worst, the report concluded, and the trend appears to be accelerating. Nationally, retail advertising makes up about half of newspaper revenue, but neighborhood weeklies and papers serving smaller cities and towns often depend on local stores and restaurants for as much as three-quarters of their income. Although big metro dailies are buffered to a degree by their more diverse advertising base, they, too, depend in part on locally owned businesses and have also lost key accounts as regional grocers and department stores have merged in an effort to survive competition from Wal-Mart and Target.[15]

Another group of businesses that have been squeezed by megachains are independent banks. "Small-business lending is the bread and butter of community banks across the country," said Ron Ence, vice president of congressional relations for the Independent Community Bankers of America. "If the businesses start folding up, the community bank loses customers, deposits, important accounts, and investment options. There's a debilitating effect all the way down the line." The chains themselves have little need for local banks other than to stash evening deposits that are wire-transferred to corporate headquarters the next morning. Even this little bit of business can be a money loser for a bank, noted Doug Krukowski, chief operating officer for the Independent Community Bankers of Minnesota. "Generally Wal-Mart will come in and negotiate very low or no fees on their deposit account," he said. When local banks fold, communities not only lose jobs, but local investment capital, especially for small businesses. Community banks have long been a critical source of financing for new entrepreneurs, because, unlike big banks, they make lending decisions through face-to-face relationships and have a much more intimate knowledge of local circumstances. The fate of local banks and local retailers are thus intertwined. "It's a symbiotic relationship that is very much threatened by big-box retailers," said Ence.[16]

The list of local professional services that independent retailers require and that chains do not is long. It includes attorneys, accountants, designers of Web sites and advertisements, printers, and marketing firms. Whether a local business is large enough to handle these tasks in-house through its own staff or it hires out, the work is usually carried out locally and the income earned accrues to someone who lives in the community. This is not the case with chains, which house these functions at their corporate headquarters. Indeed, the whole point of a chain is to consolidate as many operations as possible and to keep local spending to a minimum. Chain stores also carry almost no inventory that is produced locally. Small manufacturers and local artisans that might have made a viable living by selling their wares through a small number of independent stores are having a much harder time surviving in a chain store–dominated economy, where buying and distribution systems are highly centralized and global in scope. If a manufacturer is not large enough to supply thousands of outlets, the chains are generally not interested; adding one local product to the inventory system of a single superstore is a hassle.

By putting more of their revenue back to work in the local economy as compared with chains, independent retailers generate additional economic benefits for communities. Dan Houston and Matt Cunningham, cofounders of Civic Economics, an economic analysis and planning firm, have dubbed this added economic value the "local premium." Until recently, no one had measured it. Conventional economic analysis has always overlooked the differences in local spending and assumed that two similar businesses have the same impact on a city's economy, regardless of whether one is locally owned and the other part of a national chain. In 2002 Civic Economics started conducting case studies that quantified the local premium.[17]

The first one was done in Austin, Texas, after city officials approved the development of a twenty-five-thousand-square-foot Borders outlet at the same intersection occupied by BookPeople and Waterloo Records, two long-standing independent businesses. The city also offered to provide the developer with $2.1 million in public subsidies. Houston and Cunningham contacted Steve Bercu, who owns BookPeople, and John Kunz, who owns Waterloo, and volunteered to conduct a study that would examine the impact of the deal on Austin's economy. They needed the businesses to share their financial records. Bercu and Kunz readily agreed. The study found that, for every one hundred dollars in sales, the two stores were spending thirty dollars within Austin. Using a conventional economic multiplier, which accounts for indirect and induced spending, the study concluded that the direct input of thirty dollars resulted in a total local economic impact of forty-five dollars. To compare this with Borders, Civic Economics relied on numerous sources—including interviews with former employees, the chain's public financial records, and studies of similar stores conducted by Bank of America—to develop an estimate of what happens to dollars spent at a typical Borders. They concluded that every one hundred dollars spent at Borders results in a direct return of nine dollars and a total local economic impact of thirteen dollars.[18]

This means that shopping at Waterloo or BookPeople generates about three times as much economic activity within the city of Austin as shopping at Borders. The gap can be attributed to three factors. One is that all of the local stores' employees are on-site. "When people wonder why there's such a big difference, I tell them to go up to the fourth floor of BookPeople and look at all the professionals writing ad copy, buying inventory, and doing accounting," Houston said. Borders houses all of these functions at its headquarters in Ann Arbor, Michigan. Another factor is that Waterloo and BookPeople purchase more goods and services locally. Waterloo, for example, stocks a large selection of CDs by local bands that are recorded and produced locally. "The plastic case on the CD is about the only component that comes from out of state," noted Houston. (Although Borders stores do have sections featuring local bands, they only sell CDs from major labels, which return little of the sale price back to the local economy.) And because their owners live in Austin, most of the profits from the two businesses stay in the local economy.[19]

Because the local market for books and music was growing very slowly, Civic Economics concluded that the new Borders superstore would capture some of the sales currently flowing to BookPeople and Waterloo. Because a much larger share of the revenue diverted to Borders would leave the local economy, the study estimated that, for its $2.1 million in subsidies, Austin would suffer a net loss of $2.4 million in economic activity in the five years after Borders opened. Not surprisingly, that figure ignited a fierce public debate about not only whether the development should receive a major subsidy, but whether it should go forward at all. Four months later, Borders announced that it was pulling out of the project.[20]

Houston and Cunningham caution that their findings are specific to Austin and to those particular businesses. In 2004 they were hired to conduct a larger case study in a neighborhood called Andersonville on the north side of Chicago. A nineteenth-century Swedish village that was eventually engulfed by the expanding city, Andersonville today is a thriving urban neighborhood. Its main commercial corridor, Clark Street, is lined with local businesses, including a number of enterprises that reflect the neighborhood's Swedish roots, such as Wikstrom's Swedish Deli, along with hardware and paint-supply stores, clothing and home-furnishing retailers, a pharmacy, a seventy-year-old community bank, a toy store, several restaurants, and Women & Children First, the tenacious independent bookstore discussed in Chapter 1. But over the last few years, more chains have been moving onto Clark Street, and big-box stores and category killers have multiplied just beyond the neighborhood. Both trends are taking a toll on Andersonville's local retailers. Concerned, the Andersonville Chamber of Commerce commissioned Civic Economics to analyze the economic impact on the neighborhood and the city.

Cunningham and Houston examined the spending patterns of ten locally owned businesses. They included restaurants, like the eighty-year-old Swedish Bakery, which produces breads and sweets; retail stores, such as Chicago Aquarium, a twenty-year-old pet store whose owners are so local they live above the store; and service providers, like Visionary Eye Care. They compared these to ten corresponding chains, including Olive Garden and Petco. The study concluded that, for every one hundred dollars in sales, the locals generate sixty-eight dollars' worth of local economic activity and the chains just forty-three dollars. (The figures were higher overall than the Austin study, because of the inclusion of restaurants and service providers, which are more labor-intensive and have larger local payrolls.) Although many assume that chains have higher sales per square foot—this had been a common theme in the debate over chains locating on Clark Street—the study found that the opposite was true: Andersonville's local businesses had revenue of $263 per square foot, versus $243 for the chains. Because chains funnel more of this revenue out of the local economy, the study concluded that, for every square foot of space occupied by a chain, the local economic impact is $105, compared with $179 for every square foot occupied by an independent.[21]

Four factors accounted for the difference, according to Cunningham and Houston. One was labor. The local businesses spent 29 percent of their revenue on local employees, compared with 23 percent for the chains, which depend partly on staff at their corporate headquarters. Another was procurement. The local businesses spent more than twice as much buying goods and services locally. The independents also kept more of their profits in the city's economy and gave more money to local charitable causes.[22]

The ramifications of these studies for how cities approach economic development are substantial. They suggest that communities that can shift even a small percentage of consumer spending from chains to locally owned businesses stand to reap significant economic benefits. A study of three small towns in Maine by the Institute for Local Self-Reliance and Friends of Midcoast Maine concluded that a modest shift in spending to locally owned businesses could generate as much of an economic boost to the region as attracting a major factory or other big employer. Based on current growth rates, the study concluded that annual retail sales in the three towns would expand by $74 million over the following four years. If all of this additional spending were captured by new and expanding locally owned businesses, it would add $23 million more to the local economy each year than if all of the new spending were captured by chains.[23]

The local premium matters the most in small to midsize cities. While a big city might house the headquarters of a chain or other large companies, such as advertising firms, that count global retailers among their major clients, this is usually not the case for smaller cities, where most of the dollars flowing into a big-box store are unlikely to ever make their way back into the local economy. "The smaller cities and small towns that don't have those headquarters are really losing out," said Cunningham. But the local premium matters in big cities too, especially at the neighborhood level, where spending by local retailers on payroll and goods and services procured from other nearby businesses can be critical to the economic well-being and stability of the neighborhood.[24]

LIFELINES

Among those most threatened by the rise of corporate retailers are America's embattled family farmers. Supermarket chains have been merging left and right in an effort to bulk up against Wal-Mart, which in the space of little more than a decade has become the country's top grocer. In 2005, five chains controlled about half of grocery sales in the United States. This in turn has fueled further consolidation among food processors, as the grocery chains forge contracts with those companies that are large enough to supply all of their stores with a steady and highly standardized stream of meat, dairy, produce, and packaged foods. In 2001, for example, the nation's two largest milk processors, Dean Foods (which supplies Wal-Mart's store-brand milk) and Suiza, merged, in part to satisfy the needs of big retailers, according to Bob Cropp, a dairy expert at the University of Wisconsin. The processors' combined market power, he said, has pushed the price dairy farmers get for their milk down even further. Researchers from the University of Missouri have documented that most of our food supply is now controlled by a half-dozen "global food chain clusters," each made up of a few agribusiness giants tied to one or more mega-retailers. For family farmers, selling into these clusters is difficult, and getting a fair price is virtually impossible. The share of the consumer food dollar that retailers and processors keep for themselves has been rising along with their market power. It now stands at more than eighty cents of every dollar we spend on groceries, leaving less than twenty cents for farmers.[25]

"Trying to break the barriers of the supermarket chains has been a tremendous challenge," said Russ Kramer, a fifth-generation farmer in Osage County, Missouri. His farm is one of only fifteen hundred family hog farms left in the state, down from forty thousand in 1980. Farmers in his county used to sell their hogs through a market where several meat-processing companies would bid. Today, after a wave of mergers, the only buyer left at the market is the agribusiness giant Cargill, which has contracts with Wal-Mart and Kroger (owner of Fred Meyer and Ralphs, and the nation's second largest grocer). "You can imagine what that does to the price," said Kramer, noting that an Iowa study found that between 1994 and 2004, independent hog farmers lost an average of $3.70 on every hog they raised. To get by, Kramer holds down two jobs besides farming. "I live for getting back to the farm and doing it full-time," he said.[26]

A few years ago, Kramer and four dozen other family hog farmers found a way around Cargill. They formed the Ozark Mountain Pork Cooperative and raised $1 million to buy their own slaughterhouse. But it has been tough going. Although there seems to be plenty of consumer demand for their naturally raised pork, they have not been able to get their products into stores. Missouri has few independent grocers left, and the chains have refused to stock the co-op's pork. For now, the co-op is selling directly to local families and through a few natural-food distributors, but Ozark Mountain Pork needs to find more retail outlets to be a viable enterprise. Mega-retailers are destroying rural economies, Kramer believes. "Every small town had thriving local merchants, a thriving feed mill, and other businesses," he recalled. "Now you see this great decimation of rural communities." Kramer goes out of his way to avoid shopping at chains like Wal-Mart, but many Missouri farmers find it unavoidable; the state has almost twice as many Wal-Mart stores per capita as the national average. "Unfortunately folks in rural areas have no choices. Wal-Mart might be the only store within miles," he said. "Many people are forced to shop at the very place that put their family's farm out of business."[27]

Small farms around the world are facing the same plight, as global retail chains increasingly displace local merchants and food markets. Britain's apple growers, for example, are struggling to find outlets for their fruit. At the height of the season, when orchard harvests are yielding tens of thousands of bushels of fruit, the vast majority of the apples on sale at the country's top chains are imported, according to a study by the U.K. group Friends of the Earth. It's not that the local apples are too expensive or of poor quality. Quite the opposite. they are far fresher than the imports. But the United Kingdom's biggest food retailers, including Tesco and Wal-Mart-owned Asda, prefer to deal with a few foreign suppliers that can deliver a steady stream of fruit year-round. Meanwhile, in Latin America, multinational chains, which accounted for only 10 to 20 percent of food sales as recently as the 1990s, have grown to dominate grocery retailing across much of the region, marginalizing traditional open-air markets and driving untold numbers of family farmers, who are unable to supply sufficient volume for the chains, off the land. Even when chains do offer contracts to small farms, the deals are often transitory. When Wal-Mart first expanded into Canada, it purchased milk for each of its stores from nearby dairy farmers, like David Blackwell, who milks eighty cows on his century-old farm near Kamloops, British Columbia. But after a few years, Wal-Mart negotiated a national contract with Canada's largest dairy processing company to supply all of its outlets. Now the milk in the Kamloops Wal-Mart store comes not from Blackwell, but from a plant hundreds of miles away.[28]

The independent grocers that are left have become lifelines for some farmers, like Paul Buxman. A fourth-generation farmer in the Central Valley of California, Buxman very nearly lost it all. He began to struggle financially in the 1980s, and by the mid-1990s he was deeply in debt and in danger of forfeiting the farm he had inherited from his father and mortgaged to pay the bills. Buxman grows thirty varieties of fruit, mostly stone fruit like peaches and nectarines, on fifty-five acres. He used to sell directly to supermarkets, working with store buyers who were deeply knowledgeable about fruit and built long-term relationships with farmers like Buxman. But as the supermarkets consolidated and became part of larger regional and national chains, they ended their direct buying from farmers and hired third-party brokers to source their inventory. The reason for the change, according to Buxman, is that the people at corporate headquarters decided their stores could no longer afford to have relationships with farmers. "In a relationship you might have to actually be considerate. You might have to think of the farmer's point of view. You might have to end up caring about something other than the bottom line. And that is no longer acceptable as far as headquarters is concerned," Buxman explained.[29]

The brokers not only take 10 percent off the top of what farmers receive from the supermarkets, but they know almost nothing about what they are buying, brokering peaches one day and walnuts the next. "When you talk to a man in a cubicle, who has never tasted the fruit, who has never stepped on a farm ... there is no relationship. That is where 95 percent of the transactions occur now: a phone call from one cubicle to another," said Buxman. This distance enables brokers to drive a brutal bargain, demanding cutthroat prices and truckloads of identically sized fruit—the kind of perfect-looking but tasteless output that only industrial farms can supply. Buxman nearly lost his farm trying. Many of his fellow fruit growers did.

Then in the late 1990s, Buxman decided to try a radically different approach. He stopped selling to brokers for the big chains and went in search of independent grocers. Fortunately, there are still some left in California, like PW, a family-owned business with ten stores in San Jose, and Catalano's Market, a single-location grocer in Fresno that recently declined a buyout offer from a major chain. ("I don't know what it is about these Italians. They don't give in," said Buxman.) Now Buxman is back to having relationships with buyers. "The other day I called the buyer at PW and we didn't get around to talking about fruit for ten minutes. He wanted to talk about what we're doing on the ranch to preserve habitat for wildlife," said Buxman. "You tend not to break that kind of trust. You don't lie. You don't say the peaches are great if they're not. When I need help, they help me. When they need help, I help them."

Buxman spends several hours each week in the produce departments of his customers' stores, slicing fruit samples for shoppers and demonstrating how to make jam. His aim is not only to sell more fruit, but to help the independents differentiate themselves from the chains. The stakes are high. Catalano's Market, which sources from Buxman and about a dozen other local farmers, as well as an independent produce distributor, several local cheese makers, and a local beef producer, is one of just a few local grocers left in Fresno. About a half dozen others have closed, including the city's oldest, Hanolan's, which folded in 2001 after eighty-nine years in business. Michael Catalano, whose father started the market after returning from the Korean War in the 1950s, believes this connection to local farmers is critical to the store's survival. "It's a much better product. With Paul Buxman, it's picked that morning and here in the afternoon," he said. "It makes us shine." The market is doing well, but Catalano worries about the fact that Fresno keeps changing its zoning to allow in more chain supermarkets and recently a Wal-Mart. City officials believe they are creating jobs, he said, but they miss the fact that they are also causing layoffs as local stores downsize or close. Catalano's employs sixty-five people and, although the store is not unionized, it pays union-scale wages with full health benefits.[30]

As for Buxman, he is still a long way from paying down his debt, but he feels like he is on the right track. Recently he started helping other growers break away from the chains and their brokers, including a twenty-three-year-old man who inherited a fruit farm and $2 million in debt from his ailing father. Buxman likens the challenge facing independent farmers and retailers to that of the scattered survivors of a shipwreck: "The secret is to tie our inner tubes together. We'll all be more buoyant that way."[31]

SHAKEDOWN

In the spring of 2005, the power-tool manufacturer Black & Decker announced the closing of yet another factory. This time, 675 workers in Fayetteville, North Carolina, lost their jobs, forfeiting wages of about fifteen dollars an hour, plus health insurance and other benefits. They are unlikely to find work that pays as well. According to the state's Employment Security Commission, most of the new jobs in the region pay considerably less.

The layoffs continue a restructuring process that Black & Decker began in 2002. Pressured by Home Depot and Lowe's, which account for about one-third of the toolmaker's sales, Black & Decker has shuttered factories across the United States, laying off some four thousand people and shifting production to the Czech Republic, China, and Mexico, where wages are lower. The only alternative was to relinquish shelf space at the two megachains, both of which were turning more and more to lower-priced brands—including their own. Home Depot and Lowe's are not only top customers, but major competitors, both having contracted with foreign factories to make their own lines of power tools that compete directly with Black & Decker's.[32]

With mega-retailers combing the globe for factories that have the lowest wages, U.S. manufacturers have two options: they can either make their products in those factories or give up shelf space and market share to companies who will. In 1990 Levi Strauss made 90 percent of its jeans in the United States. But plummeting sales in the late 1990s convinced the company that it had to start producing jeans cheap enough to sell to Wal-Mart and Target. Levi's unveiled its bargain Signature line and shuttered all of its U.S. factories, laying off more than twenty-five thousand people. Today, the 150-year-old American icon does not even make jeans; it's purely a marketing and distribution company, contracting virtually all of its production work to factories in Asia and Latin America. Companies that produce everything from toys to toasters have done the same thing. Determined to stay on Wal-Mart's shelves by keeping its retail price under ten dollars, Etch A Sketch closed its Ohio plant in 2000 and contracted with a factory in Shenzhen, China, where workers earn twenty-four cents an hour. Maytag, maneuvering to meet the demands of major appliance sellers like Best Buy and Lowe's, recently fired sixteen hundred workers in Galesburg, Indiana, and moved their jobs to Mexico.[33]

Big retailers hold all of the cards in these relationships: not only can they opt to carry competing brands, but they can also choose to make the product themselves, by contracting directly with Asian factories. Many of the largest chains now have major sourcing offices in China. Best Buy opened one in Shanghai, from which it oversees factories producing its Insignia line of television sets and DVD players. Lowe's has a buying office in Shanghai as well, and is working directly with factories to produce a growing share of its merchandise. Home Depot sources flooring, lighting, and other products through two offices in China. The Gap and Target have major procurement offices there as well. Wal-Mart not only has its global sourcing headquarters in the fast-growing Chinese city of Shenzhen—from which the chain negotiates with factories to produce its own lines of clothing, consumer electronics, and other products—but in 2004 it convened its annual board meeting there.[34]

As challenging as these circumstances are for large manufacturers, they at least have the option of severing their domestic ties and becoming, as Levi's has done, nothing more than a brand name that sources from wherever the product can be made cheaply. But hundreds of small and midsize companies that used to produce parts for bigger manufacturers lack this mobility. They are being left stranded as their customers flee to low-wage countries. Pa-Ted Springs Co. of Bristol, Connecticut, which engineers springs that are used in a variety of appliances like irons and blenders, has had to close down one of its plants and cut its workforce at two others as its customers have moved their operations to China (where they buy springs locally). As a small, family-owned company, following appliance makers to the other side of the globe is not an option. But Pa-Ted Spring's prospects in the United States look grim. "The major retailers and big manufacturers are doing us in," said owner Fred Tedesco.[35]

After small-business owners, manufacturing workers are the second major pillar of the American middle class that has been decimated by megaretailers. Since 1990, U.S. manufacturing has hemorrhaged more than 3 million jobs. Most of these displaced workers have trouble finding new jobs and those that do often end up taking a substantial pay cut. According to surveys conducted by the U.S. Census Bureau and the Bureau of Labor Statistics, one-third of manufacturing workers who were laid off in the preceding five years had not found new work by the time they were surveyed. Of those who did land jobs, most took a pay cut, with one in four reporting a drop in earnings of 30 percent or more.[36]

Those who suffered the largest decline in income were those who ended up working in retail. Indeed, the outsourcing of manufacturing has not only benefited the chains by cutting their costs. It has also left a sizable pool of displaced workers desperate for jobs, as well as plenty of vacant urban industrial sites suitable for building big suburban-style boxes. Wal-Mart often shrugs off accusations of underpaying its store employees by pointing out that it's not uncommon for hundreds or even thousands of people to apply for work when a new superstore opens. But this is less an endorsement of the company's wages than a sign of desperate unemployment, for which Wal-Mart itself is partly to blame. Nor are cities that have undergone major plant closures likely to turn down a new superstore. In 1998, under pressure from Wal-Mart to cut costs, bicycle maker Huffy closed its factory in Celina, Ohio, laying off 650 union workers who made eleven dollars an hour plus benefits. Four years later, when Wal-Mart sought to build a massive supercenter in town, it was not only eagerly welcomed by local officials, but the company had no trouble finding employees willing to work for seven dollars an hour, or locating a site big enough for the store: Wal-Mart built on fifty acres once owned by Huffy.[37]

This transfer of manufacturing jobs might have an upside if it enabled people in poor countries to pull themselves out of poverty. But the chains' relentless drive to cut costs does not end with shipping jobs to low-wage countries. Even in places where the legal minimum wage is less than fifty cents an hour, retailers still press factories to lower their prices, often demanding that they make the same products for less than they did the year before—or lose the order to a factory that will. Inevitably this leads to working conditions and wages that are more akin to slave labor than they are an opportunity to work one's way out of poverty. In 2005 the NBC show *Dateline*, with the help of Charles Kernaghan of the National Labor Committee (NLC), a human rights organization that investigates working conditions in developing countries, traveled to Bangladesh to conduct an undercover investigation of factories making apparel for Wal-Mart, Kohl's, Kmart, Sears, and other retailers. Bangladesh exports over 900 million garments a year to the United States, nearly a third of which end up in Wal-Mart stores. Most of the country's 1.8 million garment workers are young women like Masuma, whom NLC and *Dateline* found working fourteen hours a day, seven days a week, sewing pants for Wal-Mart for just seventeen cents an hour. She lives in two small rooms with five other people, rarely eats meat or fish, and, after eight years of work, owns almost nothing.[38]

NLC and a number of investigative journalists have documented similar conditions around the world in factories making consumer goods destined for U.S. stores. In Nicaragua, NLC found workers logging sixty-nine hours a week sewing jeans for Target and Kmart and living in "utter misery" on sixty-five dollars a month. When they tried to form a union, twenty-three workers were fired. In China, workers making toys and consumer electronics, many of whom are migrants from rural areas, commonly live in crowded dormitories with poor food, little freedom, long hours, no earplugs or other safety equipment, and below-subsistence wages. China has laws setting a minimum wage and limiting hours of work, but they are, for the most part, not enforced—although laws that prohibit workers from forming independent trade unions are.[39]

For many of those who work in these factories, life is getting worse, not better. Since 2000, wages for garment workers in Bangladesh have fallen 8 percent, while the cost of living has risen 18 percent. Workers producing consumer goods have little chance of improving their wages, because, like U.S. workers, their jobs can easily be moved to some other low-wage country. The number of factory jobs in the maquiladoras along Mexico's northern border fell from 59,055 to 48,722 between 2000 and 2004 as companies shifted their focus to China, where wages are considerably lower. In the first two months of 2005, eighteen garment factories in Guatemala, Honduras, Costa Rica, and the Dominican Republic closed, putting some ten thousand people out of work. Virtually all of the production went to China. But even Chinese workers are vulnerable. A recent change in the value of China's currency, which is expected to push the cost of exports up slightly, has sent retailers scouring the globe for workers that can be had even cheaper. Rootless and unencumbered by commitments, the chains can turn on a dime: "Retailers could shift the fall season [of production] to India," Norbert Ore, chair of the Institute for Supply Management, told *Bloomberg News* in the summer of 2005.[40]

This mobility has the added advantage of making it easier for retailers to shrug off responsibility for the workers who produce their inventory. They own none of these factories and instead have short-term contracts with them or buy through manufacturers that do. Some chains have responded to criticism by establishing "codes of conduct" for suppliers and regularly inspecting their factories. But it seems in many cases that the big chains go out of their way to ensure that violations are hidden from their view. Li Qiang, who used to work at a toy factory in China's Guangdong province—which is home to more than four thousand factories producing goods for Wal-Mart—and now heads China Labor Watch, says that Wal-Mart gave his factory days of advance warning before an inspection so that the owners could clean up, coach employees on what to say, and create fake time cards to hide brutally long hours and wages below the legal minimum. That's standard practice according to NLC, which describes Wal-Mart's internal monitoring program as "an orchestrated farce and whitewash." Workers in the He Yi toy factory smuggled out a "cheat sheet" they were given in advance of a February 2004 inspection by Wal-Mart's monitors. The sheet included twenty-eight questions with answers they were required to memorize, describing a fantasy factory with five-day workweeks, limited overtime, legal wages, and regular fire-safety training. On the day of the inspection, the workforce in the factory was reduced from five hundred to one hundred. Those who gave correct answers to the inspectors were rewarded with a bonus equal to thirty-six hours' wages.[41]

Perhaps the best insight into Wal-Mart's approach to factory inspections comes from James Lynn, a loyal employee for eight years who worked his way up the ranks to become an executive in charge of inspecting factories in Central America. He lasted in that position for just six months before being fired. Lynn claims in a lawsuit pending against the company that he was let go because he actually believed that Wal-Mart wanted him to monitor and correct abusive working conditions. When Mike Duke, now second in command after CEO Lee Scott, visited Lynn's Costa Rica office, Lynn told him he found the same problems in factory after factory: mandatory pregnancy tests, padlocked fire exits, extreme heat, shifts that sometimes lasted twenty-four hours, and docking of two days' wages for a single sick day. Lynn also warned that Wal-Mart's practice of giving advance notice before inspections meant that he would never uncover cases of child labor or other extreme abuses. This was very different from Wal-Mart's quality control inspections, in which inspectors could drop in to factories unannounced (and inspectors were told not to document anything having to do with labor conditions). A few weeks after Duke's visit, Lynn got the ax, supposedly for having an affair with another Wal-Mart employee.[42]

This is one of the great tragedies of a far-flung system of production and distribution: the workers who make the things we buy are largely hidden from our view. They are not present in the all-American red-white-and-blue banners floating over racks of clothing at Wal-Mart or along the brightly lit shelves of television sets at Best Buy. The chains count on us to ignore the workers' plight. They portray their global sourcing practices as bargain hunting on our behalf. Some of the savings flow to consumers, to be sure, but the bulk of the benefits goes straight to the bottom line. Chains, especially the discounters like Wal-Mart and Target, cannot improve their profitability by raising prices, because they would lose sales. Their only option is to lower costs: thus the extortion of workers abroad. Gross profit margins on imported products can be many times the margins on domestic goods. One way that chains perpetuate the myth that they pass along every penny in savings to consumers is by setting very specific prices. Wal-Mart retails a denim long-sleeved shirt for $11.67, rather than $11.99 or $12.00, to suggest that it has whittled the price down as far as possible. But in fact Wal-Mart is making a killing on these shirts, marking the price up by more than 250 percent, according to NLC, which has traced the shirts back to a factory in Bangladesh that exports them for about $3.25 each.[43]

Although it is the big chains that are the driving force behind the shift to foreign production, virtually all retailers, including many independents, sell goods that are produced by low-wage workers in Asia and Latin America. But just as some small farms are forging mutually beneficial partnerships with local retailers, so too are some manufacturers. In 2005 Penofin Performance Coatings, which makes wood finishes, announced that it would no longer sell to big-box retailers. "We were forced to make a choice," Castle Newell III, president of Penofin, told *Building Online*. "Move our manufacturing overseas to continue to do business with one of the largest retailers in the nation, or say good-bye to this customer and keep these jobs from moving offshore." He added, "These giants want more rebates, more time to pay, added surcharges, and monetary demands for their bottom lines that have been forcing thousands of American businesses to take their jobs to foreign countries. . . . Our children, many of our employee's children, neighbors, and friends have worked here. For us this is not some abstract exercise in increasing the bottom line. Penofin is made in Ukiah, California, and we are not about to go overseas to make a buck at the expense of our employees." The company has since opened accounts with hundreds of independent retailers, who are eager to differentiate themselves by offering a product that cannot be found at Home Depot or Lowe's.[44]

A few years ago, Beka, Inc., a wooden-toy manufacturer in St. Paul, Minnesota, likewise decided to forgo selling to chains like Target. "We have in the past produced large volumes of product for large retailers, but we were invariably dissatisfied with the relationship," said Jamie Kreisman, who, along with two of his brothers, owns the business. "We decided we don't want a large organization telling us how to redesign our products to make them cheaper." Instead, Beka gets most of its design ideas from the locally owned toy stores that sell the company's wooden blocks, easels, and other products and that have a direct relationship with the parents and kids who buy them. Beka has no interest in moving production to China, Kreisman said, explaining that such an action would eliminate the two aspects of the business they most love: working with wood and the relationships they have with their suppliers, employees, and customers. "I know the people I order lumber from on a personal basis," Kreisman said. If you have something made in China, "you don't even see the product," he added. "You send the design to China, they make twenty thousand units and ship it to some warehouse. You contract out for the packaging and distribution. Then you get a bill." Kreisman currently serves as president of the American Specialty Toy Retailing Association, the group that represents independent toy stores. He is the only manufacturer ever to do so, explaining that independent retailers are crucial to his business: "Without them, none of us would be here."[45]

COGS IN THE CORPORATE WHEEL

In return for all the jobs they take away—in manufacturing and at small businesses—mega-retailers provide jobs in their stores. How good are these jobs? John Turner started working nights at the local Wal-Mart store in his hometown in Oregon in early 2003. He was young—twenty-two— and had a wife and two small children to support. There were few options; manufacturing and timber-industry jobs had disappeared in the 1980s and 1990s. "The main job market around here now is fast food," said Turner. His job at Wal-Mart was to restock the shelves on the overnight shift. He started at $7.65 an hour and became eligible for the company's health insurance plan after a few months on the job, but he could not afford the $240 monthly premium. His family relied instead on the Oregon Health Plan, a state health insurance program for low-income families.[46]

Inside the store, there was unrelenting pressure to cut costs and corners. "I usually ended up working at two or three departments every night. They'd keep telling me I wasn't working fast enough when I was doing an entire department by myself," said Turner. The store provided little or no training, even for workers assigned to positions with inherent dangers, like slicing meat in the deli or, in Turner's case, climbing ladders to reach top shelves. A coworker, recently recovered from a heart attack, died one night after falling backward off the top of a ladder. Nor were the ladders kept in good repair: "There would be damaged ladders, with really wobbly legs or they wouldn't stay straight. I'd take them to maintenance, but they'd be back on the floor [not repaired] the next night." Turner described the first store manager he worked for as a nice guy. He would come down to the store at night sometimes to help the restocking crew. He threw impromptu par-

ties for the staff every so often and signed off on employees' logging overtime during the busy holiday season. But not long after Turner started, Wal-
Mart forced the manager into retirement because, as Turner was told by a
lower-level manager, he was not doing enough to hold down costs.

The new store manager was much more aggressive. Overtime (for which
the company has to pay time-and-a-half) was strictly prohibited, even during the holidays when the store was desperately short-staffed. "Once I had
a few minutes overtime. They had me in the office and yelled at me and
threatened to fire me," Turner said. Management seemed to have a strategy
for keeping raises to a minimum: in the days leading up to a scheduled review, Turner said his supervisors would start finding things to criticize
about his performance. He would get a poor review and end up with little
or no raise. After two years, Turner was making nine dollars an hour, with
occasional bonuses consisting of a coupon for a free can of soda. Several
times he picked up his paycheck and found it was short quite a bit of money.
He would go down to the office and have the payroll people go back through
the records. "They'd be angry about having to sit down and go through all
of this stuff," he explained. Each time, they found that an entire day's work
had been mysteriously deleted.

Turner was a diligent employee. "I was one of the best people they
had. There were several people like me. We always came in and got straight
to work," he said. "But we were the ones who always got in trouble." This
theme surfaced repeatedly in conversations with big-box employees. It was
puzzling at first: wouldn't a company want to encourage those who were
striving to do well and who took pride in how competently they carried out
their work? But after a while it became clear: the megastores want the work
done, but they do not want employees to have any degree of self-confidence
or sense of their own worth, which only leads to costly problems, like demands for wage increases, independent thinking, and union-organizing
drives. "They like to put people down," Turner explained. One wonders
how many of his coworkers, especially those he described as the store manager's favorites, had also had entire days deleted from their paychecks, but,
rather than stand up for themselves, had opted to just let it go.

Trying to support a family on less than nineteen thousand dollars a year
became virtually impossible—an endless series of hard choices between
food and health care, electricity and rent. When Turner had to take time off
to care for the kids after his wife had surgery—daycare was too expensive—
Wal-Mart reprimanded him and gave him a "decision day," a one-day sus-

pension in which the employee is to contemplate whether he or she really wants to work at Wal-Mart. It's one step short of being fired. Eventually the stress undermined his marriage. Turner and his wife divorced. "We had a lot of stress in our life that led to that," he said. "A lot of it had to do with finances, with not being able to keep the bills caught up." In 2005 Wal-Mart cited Turner for two unexcused absences from work. He had called in sick but, without insurance, was unable to secure a doctor's note. He was fired. In August 2005 he was looking for work and had been unemployed for several months.

Retail has long been one of the lowest-paying occupations in the economy. But the rise of corporate chains and the enormous downward pressure they exert on labor costs has further constrained wage growth for those at the bottom. Between 1990 and 2001, as the top chains expanded exponentially, wage gains for retail workers lagged those of nonretail workers by 14 percent, according to data from the U.S. Bureau of Economic Analysis. That is, had wages for retail workers simply kept pace with the rest of the workforce, they would have been 14 percent higher by 2001 than they actually were. To make matters worse, in many communities the loss of manufacturing has left people more dependent than ever on retail jobs. Almost one in five Americans works in retail and, contrary to popular perception, only about 16 percent are teenagers. Nearly half are over the age of thirty-five. Almost one-third of those working in retail earn less than the federal poverty line (about fifteen thousand dollars a year for a family of three), compared with 16 percent of the overall population.[47]

Knowing exactly what employees of various chains make is difficult, because retailers generally do not disclose this information. Occasionally their spokespeople make statements about what jobs at a proposed store will pay, but they do not provide independently verifiable data on how much their current workers actually earn. A rare exception occurred when Wal-Mart was required to release payroll data as part of a class-action sex-discrimination lawsuit. According to the data, in 2001, nonsalaried, full-time employees, including everyone from cashiers to department heads, who had been on the job for at least a year, were paid an average of $9.35 an hour. The average across all workers—including part-time employees and those who have been at Wal-Mart less than a year—is probably quite a bit lower. Like many other big-box retailers, Wal-Mart has a high rate of turnover; almost half of those who take jobs at the company's stores either quit or are fired within a year. This keeps payroll costs down, because new hires come in at entry-level pay. In an internal memo leaked to the press, Susan Chambers, Wal-Mart's executive vice president for benefits, subtly suggests that the chain strive to keep turnover high, noting that "the cost of an associate with seven years tenure is almost 55 percent more than the cost of an associate with one year of tenure, yet there is no difference in his or her productivity." Wages and turnover at most other big chains appear to be roughly in line with Wal-Mart's. In the Minneapolis–St. Paul metro, Target pays entry-level wages of $6.25 to $8.00 an hour. In online forums, workers for Circuit City, Walgreens, Home Depot, Borders, and other major chains commonly report earning between $7 and $10 an hour.[48]

Most retail employees do not make enough to meet even basic needs. This threshold varies by region and the size of one's family, but according to the Economic Policy Institute, a single parent with one child would need to earn $12.60 an hour in Cedar Rapids, Iowa, to cover rent, transportation, food, and other basic items in a no-frills budget. For a two-parent family with two children in Portland, Maine, both adults would have to work full-time for $11.60 an hour. Even Wal-Mart admits the insufficiency of its hourly wages. In an interview with the *Wall Street Journal,* the company's vice president of communications said, "Hourly jobs like those offered by Wal-Mart . . . are generally not designed to support a family." Unfortunately, this is precisely what many of the company's employees are struggling to do.[49]

The chains respond by pointing out that employees have an opportunity to move into management and in fact many retailers do promote from within. But there are relatively few managers in a big-box store compared with the vast number of lower-level employees. Evidence also suggests that not all workers have equal access to the management track. Home Depot settled a sex-discrimination suit involving twenty-five thousand women in the late 1990s for nearly $90 million, one of the largest such settlements in history. A few years later, the Equal Employment Opportunity Commission filed new charges against the company, claiming that problems of bias in hiring and promotion had not ended. Target and Best Buy have been accused of age discrimination in several suits alleging that workers over forty (who are often more experienced and make more) are far more likely to be laid off. Costco and Wal-Mart are facing national class-action sex-discrimination lawsuits. While women make up half of Costco's workforce, they account for only 17 percent of its managers. At Wal-Mart, not only are women underrepresented in management, they earn significantly less than their male counterparts, in every job category from cashier to regional vice president. The 115 women who have testified in the case describe giving years of their lives to the company and getting little in return. Denise Mott started working at Wal-Mart in 1992 and was not only repeatedly denied access to management training while male coworkers advanced but, in 2002, after a decade on the job, she was making just nine dollars an hour.[50]

Health benefits are often as meager as wages. Although many chains offer coverage, their plans typically restrict eligibility and impose high out-of-pocket costs on employees. At Target, many part-time workers are not eligible for the company's health plan, and full-time employees must work for a year before they qualify. Some forgo coverage because they cannot afford the premium. "Anything you have to pay when you're making so little is tough," noted Bernie Hesse, an organizer with the United Food and Commercial Workers (UFCW) union in St. Paul, Minnesota. The monthly premium for an employee and his or her partner at Home Depot runs about $300 a month. At Wal-Mart, full-time employees must wait six months and part-timers one year to qualify, leaving almost 40 percent of the company's workforce ineligible for its insurance plan. Of those who are eligible, about one-third do not enroll, in many cases because of the high out-of-pocket cost. With a $350 deductible, the yearly premium runs about $2,500 for an employee and his or her spouse—hardly affordable on a wage of $9 an hour—and many basic services are not covered, including annual checkups, childhood immunizations, and routine screenings such as prostate exams.[51]

There are rare exceptions, chains that do provide decent wages and benefits. One is Costco, a descendent of Price Club, founded in the 1970s by Sol Price, whose father was a coal miner and who, in his entrepreneurial youth, read the *Daily Worker* more than the *Wall Street Journal*. At Costco, wages average seventeen dollars an hour, turnover is low, and workers pay only 8 percent of their health insurance costs. But the company faces perennial pressure from Wall Street analysts and some stockholders to bring compensation in line with Sam's Club and other big-box chains. Bill Dreher, a retailing analyst with Deutsche Bank Securities, contends that Costco's benefits are "overly generous" and shareholders "get the short end of the stick." Rather than spreading this high-wage model to other chains, it seems likely that Costco will continue to fight a lonely uphill battle, because, as Marjorie Kelly explains in *The Divine Right of Capital*, paying workers more violates the legal and financial structure of today's publicly traded corporations, which are legally obligated to maximize returns to shareholders.[52]

The other notable exceptions are unionized supermarkets. Groceries are the only segment of retailing in which a significant share of the workforce belongs to a union. (It varies by region; the UFCW has a strong presence at supermarkets in some states, but not others.) This has enabled many grocery store employees to earn middle-class incomes with benefits like pensions and health insurance. But they are losing ground as the supermarkets look to replicate the labor practices of big-box stores, like Target and Wal-Mart, that are rapidly expanding into groceries. The two megachains are now an invisible third-party presence in every contract negotiation with supermarkets, according to Bernie Hesse, an organizer with UFCW Local 789 in St. Paul, Minnesota. In 2003 California's top grocery chains—Kroger, Safeway, and Albertson's—used anticipated competition from Wal-Mart, which had not yet opened a store selling groceries in the state, to demand major cuts in their employees' wages and benefits. The demands precipitated a strike that involved seventy thousand workers and lasted nearly five months. In the end, the chains achieved their major demand: a two-tiered structure, whereby current workers would keep their wages and benefits —worth an average of eighteen dollars an hour—but all new employees would receive sharply inferior benefits and be paid according to a much lower pay scale. Normal turnover will result in most of the workforce being in the lower tier in a matter of years.[53]

The fierce drive to reduce labor costs has led many chains to cheat their own workers. Turner, the Wal-Mart employee in Oregon, is not alone in reporting hours deleted from his paychecks. Forcing employees to work off the clock, failing to pay them time-and-a-half for overtime, and deleting hours from their time cards have become pervasive practices. Dozens of lawsuits have been brought against mega-retailers in the last few years. In a case against Home Depot in New York, former bookkeeper Dora Hernandez said her management ordered her to alter computer payroll records to show that employees had taken unpaid breaks when they had not. Target Corp. reached a $7.3 million settlement in a suit involving workers who were pressed into working overtime without pay. Petco, Taco Bell, CVS, RadioShack, and the supermarket chain Albertson's have all settled cases involving unpaid overtime. In 2005 a California court ordered Wal-Mart to pay $172 million in damages to 116,000 current and former employees who had worked off the clock. The company lost another suit in Oregon involving workers at two dozen stores. Among those who testified in the case was Carolyn Thiebes, who worked in personnel and said that she was ordered to systematically delete hours from employees' time cards. Similar cases are pending against Wal-Mart in about thirty other states. In a class-action suit involving sixty-five thousand former and current Wal-Mart employees in Minnesota, plaintiff Debbie Simonson said her supervisor often assigned her tasks, like retrieving shopping carts from the parking lot, after she had punched out for the day. In another case involving forty thousand Wal-Mart workers in Washington state, plaintiff Georgie Hartwig said her manager regularly gave her more work than she could complete in one shift. Because overtime was not allowed, she would work through meal breaks and stay after her shift to finish, donating two to five hours of free labor to Wal-Mart each week.[54]

"Off-the-clock work is just part of doing business for these companies," said Cathy Ruckelshaus of the National Employment Law Project. After an internal audit (which was leaked to the media) found more than seventy-five thousand instances where employees had worked through breaks and meals at 128 stores over a period of just seven days, Wal-Mart changed its policy so that employees are no longer required to punch out for breaks—essentially eliminating the paper trail of evidence rather than correcting the problem. Because of several factors—limited government enforcement, employees who are too afraid of losing their jobs to complain, and the fact that attorneys will not bring private suits unless they are likely to become successful class-action cases—violators end up saving more on payroll than they incur in fines and settlement fees, according to Ruckleshaus. This transfer of wealth from those who can least afford it to some of the most profitable companies in the world not only cheats workers. Law-abiding businesses, which pay their employees fairly, are at a competitive disadvantage.[55]

Other tactics major chains have used to keep labor costs down include firing the highest-paid workers in the store and replacing them with new hires who make less; using undocumented janitors who are paid less than minimum wage to clean stores at night; violating child labor laws by having low-paid teenagers put in long hours or man forklifts and other dangerous machinery; and aggressively contesting workers' compensation claims. When accused, retailers invariably insist that the problems are limited to isolated incidents involving a few "bad apple" store managers. It's similar to the excuse they use to deny responsibility for exploitation in foreign factories: the fault lies with some third party, either a rogue store manager or a subcontracting supplier. But any lack of awareness on the part of corporate headquarters is only because they have chosen to look the other way; after all, these companies maintain precise control over sales and inventory at every store. It is hard to believe that Wal-Mart, which controls the thermostats and lights of all of its U.S. stores from Bentonville, does not know that thousands of its employees are working off the clock.[56]

Just as they effectively guarantee abuses at overseas factories by insisting on prices that are too low to legitimately produce goods, big-box retailers ensure that store employees will be cheated, by giving each store manager a payroll budget that is below what is actually needed to run the store. Having spent years working their way up the ladder, putting in sixty to eighty hours a week, store managers are understandably eager to hold on to what they have achieved. Those who find some way, licit or otherwise, to meet the budget, earn substantial bonuses that can double or triple their base pay; those who do not are either demoted or fired. Moreover, annual increases in a store's sales are expected to exceed the rate of growth in payroll costs—so every year, the screws tighten.

Above all, it is the store manager's responsibility to snuff out any attempts by workers to form a union. Organizing a retail store is already extremely difficult, due to the high rate of employee turnover and the vulnerability of a workforce that is easily replaced. Sporadic organizing drives at stores operated by Home Depot, Target, and other chains have collapsed, often amid allegations that union supporters were illegally intimidated or even fired by store managers. Federal law does little to deter such union-busting tactics. Since 1995, the National Labor Relations Board has issued some sixty complaints against Wal-Mart for illegally threatening, spying on, and firing workers who support unions. The violations continue year after year, because the penalties are minuscule—paying a few thousand dollars in back wages to a fired employee, for instance—and do not increase for repeat offenders. Breaking the law ends up being less costly than the wage increases a union might obtain. Should intimidation fail, Wal-Mart has developed a last-ditch "nuclear option" for keeping out unions. After workers at a superstore in Quebec succeeded in forming a union in 2004, Wal-Mart announced that it would close the store, laying off all two hundred employees. Just to be sure its message was heard, Wal-Mart enclosed a copy of a press release with every Canadian employee's paycheck, explaining that the closed store was "not meeting its business plan" and that

the "labour situation" was "proving detrimental to improving the performance of the store."[57]

No wonder retail workers have been losing ground relative to workers
in other sectors. Are employees at small businesses any better off? There are
plenty of local retailers who offer the same rock-bottom wages common at
the chains. But they lack the massive market power that Wal-Mart and other
top chains have used to unilaterally drive wages in the retail sector lower.
And the chains have used their considerable political power as well—in the
form of lobbyists and campaign donations—to fight minimum wage increases and "living wage" laws. In Florida, top retail and restaurant chains,
including Outback Steakhouse, Olive Garden, and Publix supermarkets,
spent well over $1 million in 2004 trying to persuade voters to reject a bal-
lot measure to raise the state's minimum wage to $6.15 an hour. Meanwhile,
a number of small-business owners championed the increase, which ultimately passed. It's not uncommon for independent businesses—including
many of those interviewed for this book—to opt to pay more. Employees
at Hot Lips Pizza in Portland, Oregon, earn $10 an hour, plus tips and paid
vacation. Jim Amaral, owner of Borealis Breads, a retail bakery in Portland,
Maine, pays all of his employees a living wage with health insurance. Many
say that this makes their businesses stronger, but most are also motivated
by a conviction that employees deserve to make at least a basic living. While
Costco must forever justify its labor policies, local owners do not have to
answer to the stock market; they can and do have motivations beyond the
bottom line.[58]

Extracting every penny possible from workers boosts profits, but the
practice comes with a huge hidden cost to taxpayers. Unable to meet even
basic expenses, many employees of chain retailers and restaurants rely
heavily on public-assistance programs, including food stamps, subsidized
housing, and health insurance plans like Medicaid. In 2006 Massachusetts
officials reported that the state was spending $212 million a year providing
health care to employees of some of the world's largest corporations. Of the
twenty companies that had the most employees enrolled in either Medicaid or another state health care program, thirteen were retail and restaurant chains, including Wal-Mart, Stop & Shop, McDonald's, CVS, Burger
King, Home Depot, Walgreens, and Target. Together these thirteen chains
had more than thirty-two thousand workers and their dependents relying
on the programs, at a cost to taxpayers of $45 million a year. More than
twenty states have also reported that employees of corporate chains are

swelling the ranks of welfare programs. In Arizona, officials released data showing that twenty-seven hundred Wal-Mart employees receive health insurance through the state. Other companies near the top of the list include Target, Kroger, Safeway, Walgreens, and Home Depot. In Arkansas, nearly four thousand Wal-Mart employees and twelve hundred Target employees rely on Medicaid or food stamps.[59]

THE SPRAWL TAX

Taxpayers end up footing the bill for big-box retailers in other ways as well. Although many cities assume that converting farmland and open space to shopping centers will yield a financial windfall and reduce levies on home owners, the tax benefits promised by developers in many cases prove to be as illusory as the employment gains. Focused on only one side of the equation—growing the tax base—many cities have lost sight of the fact that development also creates costs. These costs are quite high in the case of sprawling big-box stores—so high that they can reduce the tax gains to a negligible trickle or even result in a net loss for the city.

One frequently overlooked cost is the effect big-box stores have on existing property values. Nearby homes may lose value due to the added traffic and noise, but more significant are the effects on commercial property. As downtowns and older shopping centers lose sales, they also decline in value and ultimately produce less tax revenue. In an analysis of the impact of Wal-Mart's arrival on several Iowa towns, Thomas Muller and Elizabeth Humstone found that most of the superstores' revenue (84 percent) came at the expense of other businesses, many of which closed. They concluded, "Although the local tax base added about $2 million with each Wal-Mart, the decline in retail stores following the opening had a depressing effect on property values in downtowns and on shopping strips, offsetting gains from the Wal-Mart property." These dead downtowns and derelict strip malls—thousands of which now litter the country—also represent a tremendous waste of public investment in the form of roads, water lines, utilities, and the like that are sitting idle or underutilized while taxpayers build still more infrastructure to serve new big-box complexes.[60]

Cities that rely heavily on local sales taxes, as opposed to property taxes, generally reap more revenue from new shopping centers, but these gains are offset by lost revenue elsewhere and can be short-lived. In California, strict caps on property tax rates have forced cities to rely primarily on a local sales tax, sparking fierce competition to attract big-box stores, shopping malls, and auto dealerships. But despite the proliferation of sprawling retail centers throughout much of the state, the total amount of sales tax revenue that California cities are raising has remained about the same (on a per capita basis, adjusted for inflation). This is because consumers have only so much to spend; sales gains in one location are mirrored by losses elsewhere. Some cities may become tax winners by playing host to a new shopping center that siphons customers from stores in nearby cities. But these gains are usually fleeting: it's only a matter of time before that center is eclipsed by new retail development elsewhere in the region. Some evidence suggests that big-box stores may not even produce a temporary revenue bounce. One study of 116 cities in northern California found that, in all but two cases, the presence of stores operated by Wal-Mart, Target, Costco, Kmart, or Sam's Club did not in fact correspond to increased local sales tax revenue. Yet in surveys, officials still profess a strong preference for big-box stores over other kinds of development—even high-wage industries—because of the perceived tax benefits.[61]

Big-box development also creates substantial direct costs. Every time a cornfield or a forest succumbs to a new shopping center, the local government incurs new expenses for maintaining roads, water and sewer lines, and police and fire services. The more spread out and auto-intensive the development, the more costly it tends to be. Compared with traditional, compact neighborhoods and downtowns, suburban housing subdivisions and big-box stores generally require longer roads, more road maintenance, additional miles of utilities, and larger fire and police departments that are capable of covering bigger land areas. Indeed, many land-use experts blame sprawl for much of the rise in the cost of local government.[62]

To put this another way, the local downtown and neighborhood businesses that once supplied the bulk of our retail needs are efficient users of public infrastructure and services. Sprawling megastores are not. As these giants take over more of the economy, the public cost of retail is growing. Although there have been no large studies of this, there are noteworthy case studies. In 2002 the city of Barnstable, Massachusetts, a community of about fifty thousand people, hired TischlerBise, a firm that specializes in the fiscal (tax) impact of development, to analyze various land uses in the city, such as single-family homes and office buildings, and to determine how much each generates in tax revenue and how much each requires in public services. The study found that specialty retail, a category that includes small businesses in downtowns and neighborhood centers, costs the city less than any other type of retail development—$786 per one thousand square feet in road maintenance, police, and other services each year, compared with $1,023 for big-box stores, $1,248 for strip shopping centers, and a stunning $7,284 for fast-food outlets.[63]

Road maintenance costs accounted for part of the difference. Downtown and neighborhood business districts are scaled for pedestrians and often situated within walking distance of surrounding homes and apartments, while big-box stores, strip shopping centers, and fast-food outlets are designed and located in areas that encourage and even necessitate driving. As consumers drive more, they create more wear and tear on roads and more work for public works departments. (In Barnstable, fast food generated the largest number of car trips per one thousand square feet and thus the greatest impact on the city's budget.) Although developers may offer to upgrade the infrastructure—paying for new turn lanes and signals, for example—the real issue here is ongoing operational costs. Another study by traffic expert Rick Chellman suggests that downtowns are roughly twice as efficient as outlying stores in terms of their burden on roads. Chellman applied standard suburban trip-generation rates to downtown Portsmouth, New Hampshire, and found that the busy town center was generating half as many car trips as one would expect from the same amount of retail space in a suburban shopping format.[64]

Police expenses are another factor. This is partly because, as traffic increases, officers must spend more time patrolling roads, issuing traffic citations, and responding to accidents. But some big-box stores also generate an exceptionally large volume of police calls for crimes like shoplifting and check fraud. Many cities are unprepared for this. In Royal Palm Beach, Florida, the arrival of Home Depot, Lowe's, Wal-Mart, and other chains along a state highway resulted in fifteen hundred additional police calls each year, forcing the town to hire more officers and build a new police station near the retail strip. In East Lampeter, Pennsylvania, district justice Ronald Savage had to add two more days to his monthly court calendar just to deal with crimes at the local Wal-Mart, which accounts for nearly one-third of the area's nontraffic criminal violations, criminal misdemeanors, and felony complaints. Since the mid-1990s, the small town of Pineville, North Carolina, has attracted some 6 million square feet of new retail, including a major shopping mall, big-box stores, chain restaurants, and gas stations. The mayor expected the stores to be a financial boon, but they are costing the town a fortune in police time. Pineville finally had to raise its property tax rates in 2002. Big cities are also reporting problems. When Wal-Mart proposed building another superstore in Dallas, the police department sent a memo to the city council warning that the store would increase officers' workload and result in longer response times in the surrounding neighborhoods.[65]

Why does a superstore generate so many more police calls than a downtown? The answer lies partly in strict chain store policies that mandate prosecuting bad checks and suspected shoplifting violations to the fullest extent of the law. While a downtown merchant who catches someone trying to walk out with an inexpensive item might let him or her go with a warning never to come back, at a big chain the police are automatically brought in. A stolen item with a price tag of three dollars can end up costing the city hours of police time in responding to the call, filling out paperwork, and appearing in court. Big-box stores, especially those that are open twenty-four hours and situated along a highway, also seem to be more attractive targets for criminals. Perhaps it is the anonymity afforded by the long aisles of some faceless superstore, as opposed to the more intimate environment of a place like Joe's Hardware, where Joe himself is greeting you from behind the counter.

Once these added costs are factored in, retail development can end up costing a city more than it's worth. Such was the case in Barnstable. The study concluded that big-box stores produced an annual loss of $468 per 1,000 square feet—meaning that a 125,000-square-foot superstore cost about $59,000 each year beyond what it contributed in revenue. Shopping centers came in at a net loss of $314 per 1,000 square feet. Among the retail categories, only Main Street stores produced a net surplus ($326 per 1,000 square feet). These stores not only required less in services, but they generated more revenue than the big boxes, because they occupied nicer buildings with higher property values. Although fast food produced more tax revenue than any other type of retail, it also placed the heaviest burden on city services, resulting in an annual loss of $5,168 per 1,000 square feet. "This study shatters the common misperception that any sort of growth creates revenue," said Christopher Cullinan of TischlerBise.[66]

These findings are specific to Barnstable. Whether a big-box store will be a net loss or gain for a particular city depends on its tax structure and what services it has to provide. In areas where roads are maintained by the state, a big-box store might be a financial gain for a town, but only because the additional road costs are borne by all of the state's taxpayers. Cities that rely on local sales taxes, like those in California and Arizona, are more likely to find big-box stores a financial plus, at least in the short-term, but only if the costs to neighboring jurisdictions and the region as a whole are ignored. In states where cities derive the majority of their revenue from property taxes, as is the case in Massachusetts, sprawling retail centers are more often financial losers for local governments. The same is true for cities that depend on local income taxes, as communities in Ohio do. Case studies in Dublin, Delaware, and other Ohio cities have found retail development to be a net drain, because its low-wage jobs produce little revenue relative to its high public costs.[67]

LOSING GROUND

The rise of corporate retailers has propelled a disturbing trend in the American economy: the middle class is losing ground. Since 1985, the share of the nation's income flowing to families in the middle 60 percent of the income distribution has fallen from 52 to 48 percent—meaning that the broad middle now takes in less than half of all income. And they are working more for it too. Middle-income couples with kids are putting in four hundred hours a year more on the job than they did in 1985. They have also become less financially secure. Year-to-year income for many middle-class families now fluctuates dramatically, according to an analysis by the *Los Angeles Times*. Problems once reserved for the poor—lack of health insurance, bankruptcy, and long-term unemployment—are becoming increasingly common among the middle class.[68]

The poor have fared even worse. The share of the nation's income going to the poorest 20 percent of families has fallen even faster, from 5 to 4 percent since 1985. (Meanwhile the richest 20 percent saw their share rise from 43 to 48 percent.) Poverty is no longer confined to the under- and unemployed; many people who work full-time do not earn enough to cover housing, food, and other basic needs. Today, one in four workers, or 30 million Americans, makes less than $8.70 an hour. Nor does the future hold much hope. In all but two of the states, the jobs being created today pay less than those being lost. In New Hampshire, new jobs pay 35 percent less. In West Virginia, they pay 33 percent less. Studies are also finding that social mobility is on the decline; those at the bottom of the income ladder, as well as their children and grandchildren, are more likely to stay at the bottom.[69]

Mega-retailers have contributed significantly to these trends by pushing down wages for those at the bottom, driving out manufacturing jobs, destroying family-owned (and family-supporting) businesses, and leaching wealth from local economies. The most insidious—and ingenious—aspect of their business model is that it is self-reinforcing: underpaid and overworked, many Americans find the prospect of a bargain and the siren call of one-stop shopping irresistible.

But we are shopping ourselves out of decent jobs with good wages. The chains want us to measure our standard of living solely by how much we pay for a pair of jeans or a coffeemaker (more on chain store pricing in Chapter 5). But these savings must be weighed against diminished job opportunities and stagnating incomes, which are making it harder for many Americans to afford the things most crucial to their economic well-being: housing, health care, and education. Although mega-retailers, especially Wal-Mart, portray themselves as allies of the poor—helping them buy more for less—in fact no group has suffered greater losses. In a nationwide study, Penn State University researchers Stephan J. Goetz and Hema Swaminathan, after controlling for other factors that influence poverty, found that counties that gained Wal-Mart stores between 1987 and 1998 fared worse in terms of family poverty rates than those that did not—and those that gained two Wal-Mart stores fared even worse. Among likely explanations for their findings, Goetz and Swaminathan point to Wal-Mart's tendency to replace better-paying jobs with lower-wage jobs and to siphon dollars out of local economies. They also cite the loss of social capital that occurs when locally owned businesses fail, rendering a community less capable of tackling complex problems like poverty and of nurturing high-quality economic development.[70]

DEPENDENCE

As the chains have expanded, our communities have become less economically self-reliant and ever more dependent on a handful of corporations. This dependency carries risks. Unlike economies composed primarily of locally owned businesses focused on meeting local needs, which affords a measure of insulation from outside forces, those dominated by a few global corporations are highly vulnerable and can be affected by a wide range of events that have little to do with local conditions: a downturn in the stock market, a currency crisis on the other side of the planet, a change in corporate strategy handed down from a distant board of directors. Communities that rely on a few big boxes for much of their tax revenue, employment, and shopping options are at the mercy of absentee decision-makers that might raise prices, lay off employees, demand tax breaks, or even close altogether.

When the small town of Saukville, Wisconsin, undertook a townwide property reassessment in 2002, almost every homeowner and business saw their tax bills go up. But the town's largest taxpayer, Wal-Mart, balked, demanding a $1.1 million reduction in its assessed value that would cut its property taxes by twenty-one thousand dollars. The cut would take more than eleven thousand dollars from the local school system, an amount that "far exceeds the value of the store's well-publicized Teacher of the Year award," wrote Bill Schanen, editor of the local newspaper. "No matter how hard the store tries to give the impression that it is a concerned member of the business community, the truth is it is part of a chain whose interest in Saukville is, at best, fleeting." With Wal-Mart threatening a lawsuit, Saukville officials negotiated a deal to reduce the company's assessment.[71]

Lafayette, Colorado, was the victim of a similar extortion when Wal-Mart threatened to move to a neighboring town, taking with it about one-seventh of the city's tax revenue. In a panic, the city council offered Wal-Mart $2.3 million in subsidies and persuaded the company to build its new supercenter in Lafayette. Although the city averted immediate financial catastrophe, it has only dug itself in deeper: the new supercenter is larger than Wal-Mart's old store and, as it squeezes out competing grocers and other businesses, it will likely end up accounting for an even larger share of the local tax base.[72]

Lancaster, a city of about 125,000 people in California's Antelope Valley, also went to extraordinary lengths to appease a big-box retailer—in this case Costco, which had threatened to abandon its Lancaster store to build a slightly larger store with a gas station in nearby Palmdale. Determined to hang on to the big box and its tax revenue, the city first tried to help Costco expand at its existing location by using eminent domain to condemn an adjacent business. But when that tactic was struck down by a federal court, Lancaster officials instead forfeited one of the city's parks, cutting down dozens of trees, for the new Costco warehouse and topped off the deal with a tax break worth an estimated $8 to $9 million.[73]

Independent businesses are not only much more rooted, by virtue of their local ownership, but communities that are home to a wide diversity of small businesses enjoy the same resiliency and other advantages that species diversity confers on ecosystems. Trading this for one or two big boxes is the equivalent of growing a monocrop that can be wiped out by a single pest. Corporate retailers are notoriously footloose. When Wal-Mart built a store in Nowata, Oklahoma, it decimated most of the town's locally owned businesses and then abandoned the community, shuttering its store and opening a supercenter thirty miles away. The small farming community of Bunkie, Louisiana, went through much the same thing when Wal-Mart came in, forced twenty local stores to close, and then left to build a supercenter twenty miles away. Mayor Gerard Moreau campaigned to convince the company to stay, presenting Wal-Mart with a petition signed by some five thousand people, but, he said, "They didn't give a flip."[74]

Urban neighborhoods are vulnerable, too. Richard Lipsky, head of New York City's Neighborhood Retail Alliance, recalls that when the city was going through hard times in the 1970s, chain retailers pulled out of many neighborhoods, leaving residents without access to groceries and other basic goods and services. "As soon as things got a little dicey, they closed up and moved out to the suburbs," said Lipsky. Now that New York is on an upswing, chain retailers—from Target to Starbucks—are back in force, offering landlords high rents and pushing out countless independent merchants, many of whom took a major risk by investing in the city's neighborhoods during those rougher years. But Lipsky warns that the chains' rekindled interest in New York is fleeting and will undoubtedly be snuffed out when hard times come again.[75]

Cities overrun by chain stores may have trouble attracting other kinds of investment and economic development. In today's economy, where technology has enabled a growing number of businesses to operate virtually anywhere, a community's quality of life matters more than ever in attracting entrepreneurs and new investment. In an increasingly sprawl-ridden and homogeneous landscape, communities that have preserved their unique identity and the vitality of their commercial centers have a rare advantage. Research has found that vibrant and distinctive downtowns, open space, walkable neighborhoods and commercial districts, and natural amenities are important factors in many business-location decisions. Conversely, the consequences of big-box development—traffic congestion, sprawl, and a dead downtown—tend to undermine a city's appeal and can even drive businesses away.[76]

THREE

COMMUNITY LIFE

IN THE MID-1940S, Walter Goldschmidt, a sociologist with the U.S. Department of Agriculture, embarked on a remarkable study of two farming communities in the fertile San Joaquin Valley of California. The two towns, Arvin and Dinuba, had much in common. They were the same size, possessed the same rich soil and balmy climate, and produced an identical volume of agricultural crops. Both were about the same distance from major cities, and they were similarly served by highways and railroads. Both relied primarily on agriculture; neither had large factories or other sources of income. The two towns differed in only one major respect: Dinuba's economy was composed of many small, family-owned farms, while Arvin's was dominated by a handful of large agribusinesses. The average farm in Arvin was nine times the size of the average Dinuba spread, and most of Arvin's farms were owned and operated by interests outside the community.[1]

Goldschmidt discovered that Dinuba, with its family-farm economy, enjoyed a better standard of living. Not only was the median income higher in Dinuba, but there was less income inequality as compared with Arvin. That is, extremes of poverty and wealth were less common. More people belonged to the broad middle class and more of those employed in Dinuba controlled their own livelihoods, working either as farmers, small-business owners, or independent professionals. Goldschmidt also found that Dinuba possessed far superior community infrastructure. The town's paved streets, sidewalks, and garbage services exceeded those in Arvin in both quality and quantity. While Dinuba maintained four elementary schools and one high school, Arvin had but one elementary school and no high school. Dinuba likewise contained three sizable public parks, while Arvin had only a meager playground, which was not even publicly owned but had been lent by a corporation. Perhaps the most significant difference that Goldschmidt discovered was that Dinuba had a richer civic life. Dinuba had more than twice the number of civic and social organizations as Arvin. It supported two newspapers, each larger than Arvin's single newspaper. And Dinuba's citizens were much more engaged in public affairs. They exercised a greater degree of local democratic authority than their counterparts in Arvin, which lacked structures for political participation and had largely surrendered decision-making to county bureaucrats.

At about the same time that Goldschmidt was working in California, two other sociologists—C. Wright Mills and Melville J. Ulmer—were undertaking a similar study of three pairs of manufacturing communities in the Northeast and Midwest. Like Goldschmidt, they chose pairs that were similar in virtually every respect—population, climate, distance to major urban centers, and so on. The first set each had a population of 150,000; the second, 60,000; and the third, 30,000. All had manufacturing economies and none was the site of a state capitol or major public institution. The main difference within each set was that one city's economy was composed of many small, locally owned businesses, while the other's was controlled by a few large, absentee-owned firms.[2]

Mills and Ulmer found that employment in the small-business cities was more diversified—that is, they contained a wider variety of jobs than their big-business counterparts. They also had a history of greater economic stability. While all of the cities were subject to downturns in the business cycle, the troughs for the small-business cities were not as deep. This was due partly to their greater economic diversification and partly to the fact that their local businesses did not shed employees as readily as big companies did during hard times. Mills and Ulmer found, just as Goldschmidt had, that the income gap was not as wide in the small-business cities and that a larger share of residents belonged to the middle class. The small-business cities had a greater rate of home ownership and more of their homes were served by electricity and telephones. These communities also maintained more robust parks, libraries, and public schools, devoted more resources to public health, and reported much lower levels of infant mortality than their big-business counterparts. Indeed, the small-business cities outscored the big-business cities by a wide margin on an index of community well-being composed of some three dozen measures, including literacy, support for the YMCA, acreage of parks, value of schools versus jails, rarity of extreme poverty, households with radios, rarity of car accidents, and teachers' salaries.

What Mills and Ulmer and Goldschmidt had demonstrated with these studies is that ownership matters. Communities that possess a degree of economic self-reliance more competently care for themselves, while concentrated economic power threatens civic participation and democracy. One might expect such findings to have had a powerful influence on public policy. Indeed, both studies were commissioned by federal agencies for the very purpose of informing policymaking at a time of growing corporate consolidation. But in fact the studies were ignored and even actively suppressed. In the case of Mills and Ulmer, the two researchers had been put to work by the Smaller War Plants Corporation, an agency concerned with the increasing marginalization of small manufacturers and the rapid growth of what President Eisenhower would later dub the "military-industrial complex." Their study was published by the U.S. Senate's Special Committee to Study the Problems of American Small Business. Hearings were held, but that was all that came of their work. Congress seems to have ignored their findings. Instead, postwar policy was built on the idea that big business was more efficient and therefore would provide higher incomes and thus improved social welfare. In the following decades, a wide range of government policies would work to facilitate and promote the concentration of capital and the rise of big industry.[3]

Goldschmidt, meanwhile, met with a more overtly hostile reaction. His research came at a time when the federal government, under intense pressure from agribusiness giants, was weighing whether to lift a policy that supported small-scale agriculture by limiting access to public irrigation to farms of 160 acres or less. Goldschmidt's research provided strong support for keeping the limit. Agribusiness interests tried first to suppress his study and then to discredit it. They had powerful allies in Congress who put pressure on Goldschmidt's employer, the U.S. Department of Agriculture. Although the USDA had initiated the study, the agency not only declined to publish it, but eventually fired Goldschmidt and even abolished his department, the Bureau of Agricultural Economics. Goldschmidt's study did find its way into print thanks to the same Senate committee that had published Mills and Ulmer (and it would subsequently be included in textbooks used by Harvard, Columbia, and other leading universities), but his methodology was impugned publicly by California senator Sheridan

Downey and by a media campaign led by large landowners. While the 160-acre limit was never formally lifted, the federal government essentially stopped enforcing it and massive farms came to dominate much of the arid West.[4]

Today it is hard to imagine Congress or any federal agency even considering the question of whether big corporations might affect democracy and community well-being. Fortunately, a handful of sociologists are. They have rediscovered Goldschmidt and Mills and Ulmer, and picked up where this earlier research left off. Their findings are equally as provocative. After a colleague gave him a copy of the Mills and Ulmer study, Dr. Thomas Lyson of Cornell University started designing large-scale statistical studies that would test the relationship between small businesses and social welfare. In one analysis, he examined more than two hundred manufacturing counties nationwide and compared those dominated by one or more large factories with those home to many small firms. He found that the big-business counties had greater income inequality, lower housing standards, more low-birth-weight babies (an indicator of overall health), more worker disability, lower educational outcomes, and higher crime rates. The small-business counties not only scored better on all of these social welfare measures, but their residents belonged to more civic organizations and voted more often.[5]

Lyson and colleagues Charles Tolbert of Baylor University and Michael Irwin of Duquesne University conducted another analysis of some three thousand counties, looking at the prevalence of locally rooted economic and social institutions, including small manufacturing businesses, small farms, community gathering places (e.g., coffee shops and taverns), churches, and associations. They found that counties that are home to a large number of these local enterprises and institutions generally have higher median incomes, less income inequality, and lower unemployment. The three researchers, along with Troy Blanchard of Mississippi State University and Alfred Nucci, with the U.S. Bureau of the Census, also examined rootedness, finding that counties that have a larger number of long-standing local businesses and community gathering places tend to retain their residents—and the longer people live in a community, the more they participate in local affairs and civic organizations.[6]

In 2005 Tolbert, chair of Baylor's sociology department, began to analyze the civic and social value of locally owned retail businesses in particular. He found that states in which a larger share of the retail activity is captured by locally owned businesses rank higher on a wide range of social, economic, and civic measures. Poverty, crime, and infant mortality are all lower in local-retail states than in those with a greater share of chain stores. The local-retail states scored higher on an index of social capital developed by Robert Putnam, author of the seminal book *Bowling Alone: The Collapse and Revival of American Community* and a professor of public policy at Harvard. The index measures the strength of local social networks and the degree to which people are involved in the community (it includes, for example, how often people volunteer and attend city council or school board meetings, and whether they belong to a neighborhood group or social club). Tolbert also found that "where there are relatively larger proportions of locally oriented retail establishments, voter turnout is higher." The positive effect that local retail has on community life carries even when other factors that influence a person's level of participation are considered. Tolbert found, for instance, that young adults—the age group with the lowest level of civic engagement—participate in local affairs to a much greater degree if they live in states with a high proportion of locally owned retail businesses.[7]

WHY OWNERSHIP MATTERS

What accounts for these findings? How is it that locally owned businesses strengthen community life and democracy? Or, conversely, what is it about having one's local economy colonized by the likes of Wal-Mart and Walgreens that undermines the social fabric and makes people less likely to get involved in local civic organizations and even to vote?

The answer lies partly in the fact that local owners are both financially and personally vested in their communities. To a chain, a town or a neighborhood is little more than a place that can be milked for profits. For a local business owner, the community is much more than that: it's home. Relationships with customers, suppliers, and employees are face-to-face. They are personal and often multifaceted: a customer is also a neighbor; an employee, the mother of a child who goes to the same school as your child; a supplier, a fellow member of a city committee. These community roots and personal connections influence business decisions, which often reflect a broader range of concerns than simply maximizing the bottom line. Local ownership serves to narrow the distance between those who make the decisions and those who feel the impact. While a corporate retail chain has nothing to lose and much to gain by lobbying for a cut in local property taxes, a local owner must weigh the financial benefit to her business against the impact the loss of city revenue will have on the quality of the schools her children attend.

In field research, Tolbert and his colleagues have repeatedly encountered local merchants who behave in ways that are not economically rational, but that generate tangible community benefits. "One business owner explained to us, 'I can't lay this guy off, because he lives down the street. So instead we're all going to cut back on our hours and no one has to lose a job,'" said Tolbert. He pointed to another town where, during recessions, a local gas station owner switched from self-service to full-service and hired ten more people to work the pumps. Although he had to charge more, most of his customers continued to buy gas at his station, because they understood what he was up to.[8]

The primary allegiance of most chain store managers is to the parent corporation, not to the local community. Indeed, climbing the store management ladder at a big-box retail chain often means relocating every year or two as job opportunities arise at other outlets. This severely limits a manager's roots and connections within the community, which is good for the bottom line. As we have seen, any sort of camaraderie with store employees or suppliers, or concern for their needs, is frowned upon and can result in termination. Corporate managers derive much of their social status and sense of worth from their position and accomplishments within the company. In contrast, local retailers are "inward-looking rather than outward-looking," notes Cornell's Lyson. Unlike larger corporations, which are focused on how to operate and compete in a global market, the fortunes of independent business owners are very much tied to the prosperity and future prospects of their communities. Local merchants derive much of their social standing from their accomplishments within the community; they win recognition and status from such things as taking the lead in addressing a local problem, organizing a fund-raiser for a local cause, or restoring a landmark downtown commercial building to its full glory.[9]

Local business owners often take on the role of what Jane Jacobs, author of the monumental *Death and Life of Great American Cities,* calls "public characters." These are people stationed in public places who carry out a wide range of informal community tasks. Public characters talk to many people in the course of a day and, through this contact, serve to spread news and information and to strengthen the web of ties that bind communities together. Jacobs describes the activities of one public character in her own New York City neighborhood:

> One ordinary morning last winter, Mr. Jaffe, whose formal business name is Bernie, and his wife, whose formal business name is Ann, supervised the small children crossing at the corner on the way to P.S. 41, as Bernie always does because he sees the need; lent an umbrella to one customer and a dollar to another; took custody of two keys; took in some packages for people in the next building who were away; lectured two youngsters who asked for cigarettes; gave street directions; took custody of a watch to give the repair man across the street when he opened later; gave out information on the range of rents in the neighborhood to an apartment seeker; listened to a tale of domestic difficulty and offered reassurance; told some rowdies they could not come in unless they behaved and then defined (and got) good behavior; provided an incidental forum for half a dozen conversations among customers who dropped in for oddments; set aside certain newly arrived papers and magazines for regular customers who would depend on getting them; advised a mother who came for a birthday present not to get the ship-model kit because another child going to the same birthday party was giving that; and got a back copy (this was for me) of the previous day's newspaper out of the deliverer's surplus returns when he came by.[10]

When was the last time a chain store lent you a dollar or an umbrella? Although each of these tasks is rather trivial on its own, the sum of their value to the community is not. Most of these tasks could not be formalized, nor feasibly carried out by a chain. If Rite Aid or Barnes & Noble were to take custody of people's keys or broken watches, surely the companies would have to purchase insurance. They would have to develop policies. There would be forms to fill out and, undoubtedly, fees to pay. It would become a formalized service and thus thoroughly unsuited to fulfilling a very informal neighborhood need. Unlike the public character who is present, with his eyes on the street, the staff at a chain's corporate headquarters are far removed and unable to identify the varied and particular needs—such as helping schoolchildren cross the street—that exist in the vicinity of each of their thousands of stores, and have no reliable way of meeting those needs, even if they were so inclined.

Local retailers help to sustain a network of informal relationships that nurture community. It's not only the connections that local business owners themselves have with residents, but the fact that their businesses provide a setting for casual social engagement, not only within their stores but along the streets that those stores occupy. Local businesses fulfill this purpose because they are generally humanly scaled and embedded within traditional neighborhood business districts or, in smaller cities and towns, along Main Street. People tend to get around on foot in these settings, and they not only interact with store owners, but there's a high likelihood of chance encounters with one's neighbors—in line at the bakery, perhaps, or lounging in the coffee shop or walking along the sidewalk. Much like the informal tasks that public characters undertake, these interactions are rather insignificant on their own, but together they add up to a valuable social asset. "The sum of such casual, public contact at a local level—most of it fortuitous, most of it associated with errands, all of it metered by the person concerned and not thrust upon him by anyone—is a feeling for the public identity of people, a web of public respect and trust, and a resource in time of personal or neighborhood need," observed Jacobs.[11]

These networks of exchange are part of what sociologists refer to as "social capital," and they yield important dividends. For one, they enable people to have a wide range of casual acquaintances. While people are selective in choosing their intimate friends, they are much less so with casual sidewalk acquaintances. So, in places that nurture informal interaction, residents are apt to know a much more diverse range of people, which helps to reduce social divisions and to foster empathy, camaraderie, and a sense of responsibility for one another. It's not surprising, then, that people who live in places that sustain a vibrant informal public life are far more likely to volunteer, join a club, or run for local office. These social networks yield economic benefits as well: through the grapevines of exchange, job openings are advertised and filled, innovative ideas hatched, skills shared, business partners matched, and investors found. Communities with reserves of social capital are also more resilient in times of adversity or disaster; the web of connections among people becomes a source of mutual aid and a means of pulling together. The community continues to exist, even if the physical structure of the town or neighborhood has been destroyed.

One of the most important social benefits of local ownership is that it enhances a community's problem-solving capacity. This stems partly from the fact that communities that manage a fair share of their own economic affairs are more enterprising; faced with a problem or an opportunity, they are more likely to have, and to believe they have, the wherewithal to tackle or embrace it themselves. "If local business is viable, it's indicative of an environment where people feel like they have some control over their future and feel like they can succeed in solving their own problems," explained

Tolbert. "In those places, we find local politics to be more intense and people to be more engaged." Another factor is the presence of a large number of small-business owners whose ambitions are tied to the community and who often devote their energy and considerable skills to local projects and causes. The strong social networks that emerge from locally owned economies also function as a safety net for families who fall on hard times. They nurture a sense of neighborliness and foster a greater willingness to commit private resources to collective endeavors (by, for example, accepting a tax increase to fund a new park or donating to a charity that provides healthcare to low-income residents).[12]

Conversely, the greater the degree of outside ownership of the local economy, the less control people have over the forces that affect their lives and their communities. This feeling of powerlessness tends to infect civic and political life: people become more passive as citizens and stewards of a democracy. It's a vicious cycle: the less involved people are, the more their elected officials are likely to fall sway to corporate influences. Without a robust civic discourse, communities struggle to solve local problems and marshal their resources for collective goals.

Chains fail to foster informal social networks the way local businesses do in part because their overworked, high-turnover employees are unlikely to become "public characters." Nor do they create the sort of civic spaces that nurture interaction. For one, big-box stores and malls are built at a regional scale; the likelihood that the person ahead of you in line is someone you know or someone who lives in your neighborhood is slim. Unlike traditional business districts, which support a fluid mix of public and private uses and afford plenty of opportunities for meaningful loitering, corporate retail developments are designed for ruthless efficiency. The sole aim is to maximize the dollars spent per square foot. Observe a busy Main Street and you are apt to see at least a few people chatting, strolling leisurely, or sitting idly on stoops and benches. But such behaviors are rare in big-box parking lots, where the vast majority make a beeline from their cars to the entrance. Big-box shopping does afford a certain kind of convenience; many people, especially women juggling children and work, cite the ease of being able to buy everything under one roof, rather than going from store to store. But the price is a loss of community cohesion; it's much like the family that forgoes sitting down to dinner together for the expediency of grabbing supper on the run.

Unfortunately, all of these issues are largely absent from the public debate about corporate retail chains. As these companies displace independent businesses, we are inadequately equipped to even articulate what's at stake for our communities, much less to defend them. And year after year, there are fewer people who have their own experiences of a strong local economy to draw from. "We have a whole generation of people who may not have grown up around local businesses," said Tolbert. He and his colleagues hope to continue their research, but it depends on funding and, while other sociologists have been supportive of their grant proposals, economists often give them a negative review. "They refer to us as crackpots and nostalgists," said Tolbert, explaining that, "if you can't assume efficiency is and should be the only driving force, then the whole neoclassical economic model starts to unravel."[13]

COMMITMENT

Long before the earthquake hit, Neal and Candy Coonerty's bookstore had earned the nickname "the living room of Santa Cruz." With its big, overstuffed chairs and central location, Bookshop Santa Cruz was a place where residents could count on running into old friends or catching up with their neighbors. It was a common spot to meet before heading off to see a movie or out to a play. Hours could be spent browsing the aisles or reading postcard book reviews tacked up on the "people's review" board. It was a good place to find out what was happening around town and even to buy a ticket: the store sold tickets for every kind of local event, from nonprofit fundraisers to community theater productions, with no markup. Opened in 1966 and purchased by the Coonertys in 1973, the store had evolved into a key downtown anchor and community-gathering spot in this city of fifty-five thousand people, about an hour and a half south of San Francisco.[14]

On October 17, 1989, Neal Coonerty mailed a check for one thousand dollars to a fellow bookseller in Charleston, South Carolina, whose store had been ravaged by Hurricane Hugo. A few hours later, Santa Cruz was rocked by a 7.1 magnitude earthquake. Most of the nineteenth-century buildings lining the downtown, including the one housing the bookstore, were destroyed or severely damaged. A wall dividing the bookstore from its neighbor, the Santa Cruz Roasting Company, collapsed, killing two of the coffee shop's employees. The city cordoned off what remained of Bookshop Santa Cruz and determined that the building was unsafe to enter and would have to be demolished with the store's inventory inside. With upward of

$1 million in inventory at stake, Neal Coonerty knew that demolition would be the end of the business; there would be no way to recover. He and John Livingston, who owned Logos, a local used-books store in the same predicament, went to court and asked that they be allowed to have their own engineers shore up the structures so that they could retrieve their inventory. The judge agreed. Later that night Coonerty went on a local radio show and asked for volunteers to help move the store's stock. He explained that they would have to sign city release forms affirming that they understood the danger and were aware that the city would be under no obligation to send in rescue workers in the event of the building's collapse, because of the risk to emergency crews.

Coonerty went to bed that night hoping against the odds that forty people would show up to help the next day. "In the morning, my wife and I went downtown and there were four hundred people lined up," he said, a sense of wonder and gratitude evident in his voice even after sixteen years. People felt that the store was theirs, he explained, an important part of who they were as a community, and they were not going to let it go. The volunteers formed a chain snaking through the plywood tunnels erected by the engineers and, working in four-hour shifts throughout the day, removed some two hundred thousand books, along with critical financial records. A local frozen-foods company donated thousands of boxes, others lent pickup trucks, and a team of six librarians cataloged and organized the stock. Aid arrived from other quarters as well: independent bookstores across the country donated to a fund set up by the Northern California Independent Booksellers Association, which paid the salaries of employees of Logos and Bookshop Santa Cruz for weeks following the disaster. "That was critical," Coonerty said, "because it enabled us to keep our team together," including five managers who had been with the business for more than a decade.

The next challenge for the community was figuring out how to keep the local businesses going while the downtown was rebuilt—a process expected to take eighteen months but that in actuality took three years. Should Santa Cruz lose the roughly fifty businesses operating downtown, it would mean not only the loss of tax revenue and hundreds of jobs, and perhaps a permanent shift in shopping patterns to outlying malls, but also, in a very real sense, the end of the community itself. Without its downtown and local businesses, there would be no place for residents to gather. There would be little tying people to Santa Cruz and to one another, and all the more reason for residents to give up on rebuilding and simply move elsewhere. The community decided to set up large tents in an empty parking lot on the edge of downtown to house the local businesses during the rebuilding. Word spread through local unions that the stores were desperate to reopen by the day after Thanksgiving, the critical start to the holiday shopping season, and, over the course of one November weekend, more than 150 volunteer carpenters, electricians, plumbers, and others erected the steel framing, secured the tents, rolled out temporary flooring, and installed electricity and telephone lines.

About three dozen businesses moved into the seven tents. Others found their own ways to reopen: a shoe repair shop set up in a parked van, while the local deli moved into a trailer. It was hard going; the gray tents were dull and unappealing from the outside and customers had to navigate streets littered first with debris and later with construction activity. "The tents were not very good places for retailing. They were dusty. When it was warm out, it was hot in the tents. When the weather was cold, it was freezing inside," recalled Coonerty. "Yet our customers kept coming and keeping us alive. We felt like they gave us this great gift—the gift of their patronage. We did that for three years."

The year after the earthquake, Neal Coonerty ran for city council to help lead the community's rebuilding effort. He won, and three years later presided as mayor when the downtown celebrated its grand reopening. As it turned out, the willingness of the local businesses to stay and operate out of the tents was crucial to the city's resurrection: without their lease commitments, Santa Cruz would have been hard-pressed to secure the financing necessary to reconstruct the downtown. The business owners made many personal sacrifices along the way. With college tuition looming on the horizon for their two teenagers, Coonerty and his wife, Candy, who died of a stroke in 1999 at the age of forty-nine, put their home up as collateral for a loan to buy new fixtures and equipment, and to rebuild the store itself. Neither hesitated to take the risk—even though it would take more than a decade to pay off the loan and the suppliers who had extended credit after the earthquake. Today, Bookshop Santa Cruz is once again the community's living room and, with forty employees and twenty thousand square feet of floor space, a major anchor for the downtown business district. Coonerty has made hearing the story of the earthquake a standard part of every new employee's training. "I want them to understand that this store is about more than the exchange of money for books," he said.

Among the dozens of retailers who stuck it out in the tents or some other makeshift arrangement during those three long years, there was not a single chain. It was not that Santa Cruz was devoid of chains; there had been several downtown. But after the earthquake, "they basically closed their doors and left," said Coonerty. Years later, when the downtown had been rebuilt and brought back to life again, national chains once again became interested in Santa Cruz. In 2000, despite vigorous opposition from many residents, Borders opened down the street from Bookshop Santa Cruz. Coonerty's sales took a hit. While longtime residents remained loyal, Bookshop Santa Cruz lost two significant segments of the market to Borders: tourists and university students. "We always thought that tourists would want to see what's unique in town, but that's not actually true. They want what is familiar," explained Coonerty. Much the same is true of students, he said, especially those from the suburbs who have no experience of independent bookstores and have grown up thinking of Borders as "a cultural oasis." Coonerty believes that the Borders is not doing any more in sales than his store and may not even be profitable, but it has skimmed off enough revenue to make it hard for Bookshop Santa Cruz to stay in the black. "The grand theory of the marketplace is that the best operator is going to win, but that's not true. The chains have deep pockets. They can wait you out. That makes it very difficult," he said. It is especially hard after having gone through the worst of times with the community and knowing that Borders' allegiance to Santa Cruz is tenuous and will last only as long as the town remains an easy source of revenue.

There is nothing like a crisis for bringing into stark relief true loyalties. Unlike corporate retailers, local business owners are rooted. Their investment in a community is both financial and personal, and it often spans decades and even carries through multiple generations. This commitment influences the way they run their businesses and the kinds of choices they make. For decades, as the city of Cleveland suffered population loss and the collapse of its industrial economy, Burt Saltzman and his two sons not only kept their family's seventy-five-year-old grocery business in the city, but they expanded into underserved, struggling neighborhoods, becoming a catalyst for revitalization. Saltzman still remembers the strangers who hugged him on the street back in 1997 when Dave's Supermarket opened in Ohio City, a neighborhood with double-digit unemployment and few businesses. The store brought both access to groceries and nearly one hundred union jobs to the area, and helped spark other new investment.[15]

"Dave's is the kind of business that's supposed to be impossible nowadays," said Bill Callahan, who was the head of a redevelopment organization in the Stockyards neighborhood when Dave's came to that area. "They hired dozens of local residents, brought in a badly needed commercial bank branch, created space for a family practice clinic, supported community activities," he recalled. "And they ran—still run—a very classy mid-sized store that pays attention to its poor and blue-collar customers." Although Dave's now has outlets in seven Cleveland neighborhoods, Burt Saltzman and his two sons, who have recently taken the helm, still spend much of their time in the stores, talking with employees and customers and even bagging groceries. But even though they are beloved by residents, the Saltzmans are now worried that they may have to pull out of two neighborhoods. Wal-Mart and Target are planning to open supercenters as part of a massive 127-acre suburban-style big-box development in the heart of Cleveland. The Saltzmans believe the low-wage giants could skim off enough of the city's grocery sales to force Dave's, which pays a union wage with full health benefits, to consolidate down to five stores. "If that happens," Burt Saltzman said, "then we'll be back to square one in some of these neighborhoods with housing but no businesses."[16]

Local entrepreneurs often take chances on depressed neighborhoods because they believe in their communities and see the possibilities in a way that no executive hundreds of miles away looking at demographic and market data could. In the early 1990s, when Mary Allen Lindemann and her husband, Alan Spear, started looking for a space to open a new coffeehouse and roastery in Portland, Maine, real estate brokers would not even show them locations along upper Congress Street, an area that, at the time, was nearly half vacancies. But that's where they decided to put their store. "We thought the neighborhood needed a place where people could come together," recalled Lindemann. "It's not that we didn't do our marketing homework. Alan would spend hours sitting on the corner counting foot traffic." The coffeehouse opened in 1994 and was an immediate success. "People were so glad to have someone who believed in the neighborhood," said Lindemann. Coffee By Design inspired others and today the storefronts along upper Congress are filled with local businesses. Lindemann and Spear have gone on to open coffeehouses in two other neglected Portland neighborhoods.[17]

Coffee By Design donates 10 percent of its profits to local causes and both Spear and Lindemann are involved in a variety of committees and community organizations. But their most important contributions have been made in their efforts to address local problems that they encounter in their day-to-day business. One early challenge involved mental illness. About the time they opened their first store, the state of Maine had decided to move patients with mental health issues out of a state hospital and into smaller facilities embedded in neighborhoods like upper Congress Street. Some of the newly arrived patients began to frequent Coffee By Design, and interactions with staff and other customers were not always good. "When they were in distress, we didn't know how to handle it," recalled Lindemann. But rather than trying to keep these neighbors out of the shop, Lindemann and Spear called state health officials and asked them to design a special training program for their staff. It was a huge success: employees learned how best to respond to patients and now the training is provided for merchants throughout the city. Coffee By Design has been honored by the governor and others for this initiative, but Lindemann shrugs off the attention. "That's just being part of the community," she said.[18]

That personal connection influences every decision a small business makes, according to Judy Wicks, owner of the White Dog Café, a twenty-three-year-old restaurant in Philadelphia. "I make decisions from the heart as well as the head, because I have personal relationships with the people affected, whether they are employees or customers or suppliers," she said. One example was her decision to pay a "living wage"—a wage higher than the minimum that reflects what someone actually needs to meet basic expenses in Philadelphia. "When I first heard about that, I thought, that sounds great for other businesses, but how could you make it work with a restaurant?" Wicks recalled. "Then one day I went down to the kitchen and there just happened to be these three prep cooks and they looked up at me at the same moment. I suddenly thought to myself, what am I thinking? Of course I want these three young men to be able to pay the rent and to buy food." These personal relationships have influenced many other decisions, including initiatives to help local farmers, train high-school students interested in the restaurant business, and even a marketing program that encourages White Dog customers to support other local restaurants, particularly the city's minority-owned eateries. "I've had many opportunities to grow White Dog into a chain," said Wicks. "But what you lose are the relationships."[19]

LOST IDENTITY

Unlike local business owners, mega-retailers' profit drive is not tempered by any personal or community considerations. Their decision-making is governed by a single, overriding purpose, and the directors and executives who make the decisions do not have to live with the effects of their actions. If they opt to pave a wetland and pollute the groundwater, it is not their families who end up with compromised drinking water. If they leave one of their stores sitting vacant or inundate a neighborhood with traffic, it is not their own property values or quality of life that suffers. Invariably, chains marshal their considerable political might and resources to block any initiatives that may increase their costs for the benefit of the community—such as a tax levy to renovate the library or new regulations to curb polluted runoff from parking lots.

They also routinely sacrifice valuable community assets, such as a beautiful view or the quiet of a neighborhood, in pursuit of their own expansion and profitability. Many chains exhibit a remarkable disregard for the places where they operate. Wal-Mart, Home Depot, and other big-box retailers have been fined for repeatedly violating rules that govern the storage of hazardous materials, such as solvents and lawn chemicals, and thereby creating a risk of dangerous fires or, when the materials are left outside, groundwater contamination. Connecticut attorney general Richard Blumenthal described the violations at twenty-two Wal-Mart stores in his state as "irresponsible and reprehensible." Noise is another issue. For those who live near big-box stores, excessive noise that interferes with sleep and keeps families indoors has become a chronic problem. Complaints include semi-truck deliveries, beeping forklifts, and idling engines at all hours of the night (when most superstores do the bulk of their restocking)—in many cases in violation of local noise ordinances and even promises made by the companies themselves. In November 2005, a frustrated Reno city council ordered its staff to begin proceedings to force the closure of a Home Depot store that, despite repeated warnings, failed to comply with city rules governing early-morning truck deliveries, outdoor storage, and other issues affecting the neighborhood.[20]

Among the more blatant illustrations of this disregard for local assets is the staggering number of landmark historic buildings that chain retailers have demolished to make way for their cookie-cutter outlets. Gone are buildings that have stood for generations, replaced by structures that may

not last much more than a decade (more on the short life of chain store outlets and shopping centers in Chapter 4). Chain drugstores have a particularly extensive track record of destroying historic buildings. Several years
ago, having saturated suburban strip malls, the nation's top drug chains—
Walgreens, CVS, Rite Aid, Brooks, and Eckerd (the latter two are owned by
the same company)—announced that their new preferred location was
"the corner of Main and Main." They aimed to open stores that would tap
markets in downtowns and older neighborhoods. But rather than adjusting their stores to fit into these historic areas, they decided instead to bring
in their most profitable suburban format—a freestanding outlet of about
fifteen thousand square feet that operates as both a pharmacy and a miniature grocery and variety store, and comes complete with a generous swath
of parking in front and a drive-through window. Creating enough space to
accommodate such an outlet in a traditional business district often requires
razing one or more historic structures.[21]

In 1995, despite a vigorous campaign by the Citizens Downtown Improvement Council to save a massive and magnificent century-old post
office building in Dekalb, Illinois, it was demolished to make way for a new
Walgreens pharmacy. The Beaux-Arts-style building was made of Indiana
limestone, with marble floors and an elaborate rotunda under a thirty-
foot-high copper dome. It had anchored one end of the town's Main Street,
serving as a gateway into the downtown. Today, the footprint of the old post
office is not even occupied by the Walgreens building, but rather by the
chain's sixty-two-space parking lot. "The sense was that this Walgreens
would be a key to downtown revitalization," said Steve Kapitan, a leader in
the effort to save the building, who recently won a seat on the city council.
"But ten years later, there are very few people who would say that the
Walgreens has been the savior that was promised." Because of their high
visibility, major gateways into downtowns are commonly targeted by the
chains. In Lancaster, Pennsylvania, CVS tore down the Baumgardner
Brothers Tobacco Warehouse, an imposing 1881 brick building that had
served as a dramatic landmark along an important entryway into the town
center. Age and historic significance seem to matter little to corporate retailers. In Whitpain, Pennsylvania, CVS razed a two-hundred-year-old tav-
ern and inn, known as Mr. Ron's Publick House, that likely witnessed lively
democratic debate in the earliest days of the Republic. "They would tear
down Independence Hall if it were on a busy intersection and the public
wasn't looking," remarked one outraged local resident.[22]

Sometimes entire blocks are demolished. In Pawtucket, Rhode Island, Walgreen purchased and razed one whole block of the town's eight-block Main Street. Numerous two-story attached brick buildings came down, including the 1915 Leroy Theater. Today, a large parking lot occupies much of the block, with a standard Walgreens set back from the street. With four CVS outlets, a Brooks, another Walgreens, and a few independents, Pawtucket hardly needed another drugstore. In Hartford, Connecticut, a turn-of-the-century three-story brick building housing two small businesses and several apartments was demolished to make way for a Brooks diagonally across the street from a CVS and two blocks from a Rite Aid. In Salem, Indiana, CVS purchased and demolished five homes in the middle of a historic district to make way for a new outlet just half a mile away from one it had closed in a strip shopping center. "It got kind of ugly," said Greg Sekula of the Historic Landmarks Foundation of Indiana, explaining that CVS secretly bought all but one of the homes before the neighborhood learned what was happening. The sellers, who were paid above market value for their houses, then became advocates for CVS, pitting neighbor against neighbor. The owners of the last house held out for a time, but finally gave in when the CVS developer threatened to turn their house into an island in the middle of the parking lot.[23]

In 2001, under intense pressure from a media campaign launched by the National Trust for Historic Preservation, the pharmacy chains pledged to stop razing structures listed on the National Register of Historic Places. Unfortunately, many historically significant buildings eligible for the National Register have not yet been officially listed, and those continue to be torn down for corporate drugstores. One of the greatest recent losses was an imposing two-story granite bank building that occupied the main intersection in the town of East Chicago, Indiana. Built in 1929, the bank was the scene of a holdup by John Dillinger in 1934, and its ornate stone and brass interior had changed little in the years since. "It was such a large and significant presence," lamented Erica Taylor of the Historic Landmarks Foundation of Indiana. Walgreen demolished it in the fall of 2005 to build a drive-through outlet just one block from an existing Walgreens.[24]

Although the pharmacy chains have been responsible for the demolition of a particularly stunning number of historic structures, other corporate retailers have also been quick to sacrifice the history and architectural assets of local communities for their own immediate gain. Just outside of Albany, New York, Target, unwilling to settle for a smaller store and parking lot, leveled an 1834 brick Greek Revival house that had played a major role in the region's Anti-Rent Rebellion, a watershed nineteenth-century event when farmers threw off a two-hundred-year-old feudal land-management system. In Hillsboro, Oregon, an old county hospital likewise fell to a sprawling Lowe's outlet.[25]

Inner-city historic sites, particularly early industrial structures, are increasingly under threat as big-box retailers look to bring their massive suburban outlets into urban areas. Providence, Rhode Island, has lost several historic mill buildings to Home Depot and other big-box retailers, including the Narragansett Brewing Company complex. "That was a tremendous loss," said Jack Gold of the Providence Preservation Society. "[The chains] strong-arm municipalities. Once they decide on a location, it's like a battleship armada approaching a foreign country. They are determined to have their way." In Red Hook, a waterfront area of Brooklyn, New York, with narrow cobblestone streets bearing Dutch names, a developer for the global furniture giant Ikea, which was determined to build a three-hundred-thousand-square-foot superstore, snuck in on New Year's Eve and demolished part of a Civil War–era warehouse before neighborhood activists could intercede. Ikea lacked a permit for the demolition—which is surprisingly common. In the fall of 2005, a Home Depot developer bulldozed a 1794 house in Nashville, Tennessee, that had a stop-work order from the city taped to the front door.[26]

Everywhere, it seems, corporate identity is trampling local identity. Ornate commercial buildings, designed to reflect local character and last for centuries, are being gutted—economically and even physically—for cheap retail outlets that evince none of the same pride of place and will be obsolete in as little as ten or twenty years. Mega-retailers are homogenizing the United States, and now the global, landscape. Ironically, many small towns and urban neighborhoods believe that the entrance of a major national chain somehow confers a degree of geographic legitimacy—that it puts them on the map. But dropped blindfolded into the parking lot of Wal-Mart Store #2178, one would have little clue, other than the seagulls along the roofline, as to the location. Starbucks—which, it should be noted, is one of the few chains that has a record of preserving and reusing historic buildings—has nevertheless, through its relentless multiplication, made the world a more uniform and less interesting place. The chain, which has 223 outlets in London and 49 in Bangkok, recently opened its ten-thousandth store—at the Great Wall of China.[27]

PUBLIC SPACE

Fast disappearing under the big-box influx are the kinds of public spaces that nurture a vibrant, informal public life. One of the best places in Portland, Maine, to bump into a neighbor or catch up with an old pal is Videoport. A singular and very Portland institution, Videoport fills a large basement space on Middle Street in the heart of downtown. Like many independent video stores, its library is deep, with a good deal of locally produced fare, foreign films, and worthwhile but obscure documentaries. Titles are not always shelved according to protocol: some films meant as serious dramas are put in the comedy section—a not-so-subtle commentary by the staff. The Julia Roberts and Brad Pitt vehicle *The Mexican* has been shelved in a section called "Incredibly Strange Films." Throughout the day and evening, people can be found browsing Videoport's shelves. It's a rare visit that does not involve running into a neighbor or friend. There are often clusters of people chatting in the aisles or with the staff, most of whom have been there for years and are encyclopedias of both movies and Portland. If you have lost touch with someone, the best place to ask after them is at Videoport.

Videoport is part of a complex of local businesses that share a nineteenth-century brick building. On the same basement level as the video store is Anthony's Italian Kitchen, another good local hangout, and Bull Moose Music, where many residents make weekly pilgrimages to check out new releases and flip through the bins of newly arrived used CDs. Upstairs is Casco Bay Books, a bookstore café that is a favorite place to lounge, and, across the hall, Casablanca Comics, which serves as a second home to a crowd of comic book aficionados.

This cluster of local businesses constitutes what sociologist Ray Oldenburg has dubbed a "third place"—a place where people can put aside the concerns of home and work (the first and second places) and find good company and lively conversation among their neighbors. Third places are the bars, coffeehouses, bookstores, and barber shops at the heart of a community's informal public life, its social vitality and democratic spirit. To function as a third place, a business must be relatively modest in scale, be embedded in a neighborhood or small downtown, and provide space for loitering and casual interaction. These essential characteristics mean that third places are almost always locally owned.[28]

The personal and civic benefits of third places are numerous, Oldenburg argues in his book *The Great Good Place*. Third places engender a feeling of belonging that contributes to a person's well-being. They nurture the web of connections that knit communities together, and act as "levelers" by bridging differences of background and social rank. They cultivate the habit of association: those who frequently engage in casual socializing with their neighbors are more apt to start and join formal civic and community organizations, which in turn encourage greater participation in the political process. Casual gathering spots facilitate collective undertakings: neighbors learn of problems or opportunities, hatch ideas, find out who among them has special skills, and recruit one another for various activities. This is the essence of grassroots democracy. It explains why totalitarian governments are loath to accommodate informal gathering spots; in conversing with their neighbors, people may not only find fault with their rulers, but realize their collective power. The American Revolution, after all, took root over cups of ale in local taverns. Third places, Oldenburg argues, are a crucial—though increasingly rare and embattled—democratic antidote to the shortcomings of mass media. They are, he writes, "a source of news *along with* the opportunity to question, protest, sound out, supplement, and form opinion locally and collectively" (emphasis in original).[29]

Whether they serve as third places or not, many independent businesses sustain another valuable kind of public space: the sidewalk. Local retailers inhabit and animate our downtowns and neighborhood business districts. Although one would never suspect as much from current planning and development patterns, it is hard to overstate the value to community life of well-trod sidewalks. When people walk, they become custodians of their neighborhood; their sense of their own territory begins to extend beyond their front doors. The neighborhood is a different, more intimate place at three miles per hour than it is at thirty. Something happening on a street regularly patrolled on foot is of much greater personal concern than anything sped past in a car. As a result, walkers tend to be more involved—to call the police if they spot something suspicious, keep a watchful eye on the neighborhood kids, and show up at planning-board meetings about projects and issues that affect their turf.

How much people walk depends on both the quality of the local walking environment and whether there are worthwhile destinations within a short distance of home. Dr. Hollie Lund, professor of urban and regional planning at California State University, has found, not surprisingly, that people who live in neighborhoods with grocers, coffee shops, video stores, pharmacies, and other businesses close at hand walk much more than those who inhabit residential-only areas. And the more people walk, the more they interact with their neighbors and the wider their network of casual acquaintances. A trip to the corner bakery might involve nodding hello to an elderly resident sitting on her front porch, passing another neighbor who reminds you of an upcoming meeting, and exchanging news with the store owner. In her study, Lund found that those who live in older neighborhoods with stores a short walk from homes engage much more frequently in "supportive acts of neighboring"—providing and receiving assistance from their neighbors—than those who live in car-bound areas where running an errand entails driving to the nearest big-box.[30]

Spaces that support informal public life are no longer common in America. They are almost entirely absent from today's suburbs and corporate retail developments. Unlike traditional business districts—where the streets and sidewalks are publicly owned and support commerce as well as a variety of other uses, from libraries to public gatherings—chain retail parking lots are private and reserved for the sole purpose of facilitating spending. Most of these stores and shopping centers are scaled not for a neighborhood or small town center but to serve a wider region, and thus most of the other shoppers are strangers. One cannot stop by Old Navy or Panera Bread in a big suburban retail center and reliably find neighborhood pals—which is why corporate retail outlets almost never function as third places. Nor do these areas support a lively sidewalk scene; getting to the store entails driving, and daily errands offer little in the way of casual social exchange.

In the suburbs, life takes place in a series of fragmented, single-purpose zones—home, office, shopping—that stretch indefinitely toward the horizon, with no obvious geographic center or outer boundaries. This lack of a well-defined community has a powerful negative influence on civic participation, according to *Bowling Alone* author Robert Putnam, as does the amount of time one spends in the car each day.[31]

Mega-retailers have not only produced landscapes that are remarkably inhospitable to community life, but they have also severely compromised the vitality of our downtowns and older, "mixed-use" neighborhoods by undermining the local businesses that were once their lifeblood. Walking is no longer appealing if most of the worthwhile destinations have closed and the streets are a dreary series of vacant and half-used storefronts. "I can remember in the weeks before Christmas the sidewalks were packed," recalled Karl Knudson, an attorney in Decorah, Iowa. "Now there's no one. The storefronts downtown are still occupied, but it's antique shops and tattoo parlors." Wal-Mart opened a store on the outskirts of Decorah in the 1980s, and then in 2003 vacated that store to build a larger supercenter in an undeveloped area on the other side of town. "You used to have a middle class that lived in the community and belonged to the Chamber and raised money for local causes and ran ads in the newspaper and so forth," lamented Knudson. "Now these people are associates at Wal-Mart and are just trying to get by."[32]

Even downtowns that manage to refill their storefronts often do not recover their role as community centers. In many cases, the spaces become filled with low-overhead businesses, like nail salons, highly specialized stores that have a narrow market, or offices for attorneys and other professionals—all uses that most people do not need on a daily or weekly basis, rendering the town center irrelevant to everyday life. Rather than getting by on the economic margins, other downtowns and neighborhood business districts have recovered by going upscale and offering high-end shopping, dining, and entertainment. While their economic turnaround may be laudatory, these Main Streets have also ceased to be genuine community centers. They do not satisfy day-to-day needs and offer nothing at all for poor and working-class families. Such a conversion also reduces walking as a routine form of transportation and exacerbates car traffic: nearby residents have to drive elsewhere to buy basic goods, while the shops downtown need to pull from a much wider area in order to find enough buyers for their high-end goods. (To see how this works, consider that the average household spends about $3,800 a year on groceries. A twenty-thousand-square-foot grocery store therefore needs to serve about two thousand households to be viable. In a historic neighborhood, that many households can be found within a radius of one-quarter of a mile—easy walking distance. But average household spending on high-end goods such as jewelry is much lower, so a much larger number of households are needed to support such a store.) These upscale districts are no longer mixed use in any meaningful sense; they have become another specialized zone in the larger, suburbanized, and auto-dependent region.

Still other downtowns and neighborhood business districts are being overtaken by the chains themselves. Along Broadway north of Columbus Circle in Manhattan, hundreds of small businesses have been replaced by a series of superstores that each occupy an entire city block: Staples, Bed Bath

& Beyond, CVS, Victoria's Secret, Circuit City, and so on. Gone is the finely woven fabric of the neighborhood, where there were many different types of goods and services on a single block. Here and there, remnants of the former streetscape remain. "That gives me hope that some independents can survive, but then I realize that it's just that they had a longer lease and it hasn't come up yet for renewal," lamented Virginie-Alvine Perrette, a neighborhood resident whose film *Twilight Becomes Night* chronicles the consequences of the city's disappearing local stores. Not only do neighborhoods lose the economic and social contributions of local owners, but chains are rootless and unreliable. They often arrive in a wave and can leave just as quickly. In the 1990s, numerous chains set up shop in downtown Boulder, Colorado, driving up rents and displacing independent businesses. Now most are pulling out and moving to new shopping centers in surrounding towns. "Abercrombie & Fitch, Ann Taylor, The Gap, Banana Republic—they've all left," said David Bolduc, owner of the Boulder Bookstore. "As soon as things changed, they were out of here."[33]

FAKING COMMUNITY

Corporate retailers have responded to the unease many Americans feel about our increasingly anemic community life by brashly asserting that their stores are the cure, not the culprit. The doublespeak begins with the names of their developments. In Memphis, one can visit The Commons, a standard big-box complex with Home Depot, Circuit City, Old Navy, and other chains. Wal-Mart and Best Buy are part of New Hope Commons near Durham, North Carolina. "Village" is another popular corporate retail term, as in Erskine Village, a superstore development in South Bend, Indiana. Wal-Mart has described itself as "the gathering place of the community." Some developers have gone so far as to adopt the term "town center" and arrange their stores to mimic the real thing. Just outside of Charleston, South Carolina, is Mount Pleasant Towne Centre, with chains like Barnes & Noble, Bed Bath & Beyond, and Chili's set along a faux Main Street, which is surrounded by parking lots with easy access to the highway. Corporate retailers have so eroded our sense of community that they have even managed to sell it back to us in the form of a superficial design concept.[34]

To overcome opposition on the part of city planners and elected officials, corporate retailers often make a big show of redesigning their original store plans "to better fit the community." In Fishkill, New York, Home

Depot offered a revised design that featured a standard big-box store dressed up with "cultured stone and a gabled roof." Sometimes chains include amenities, like pockets of "green space" or pedestrian walkways that snake alongside parking lots and add a suggestion of walkability to a project built entirely for cars. These revisions are always presented as major concessions and meant to make the city planner feel as though she is doing her job by holding a tough line with the developer and even forging a legitimate compromise with citizens who oppose the project.[35]

Countless communities have been sold on the idea that they are getting a "unique" Wal-Mart or "the best" Home Depot. In Centerville, Utah, city manager Steve Thacker threw his support behind a controversial Wal-Mart after being persuaded that the store would be "the nicest one in Utah." Although bricks are better than concrete, and earth tones may be superior to Target red and Home Depot orange, these are minor improvements that serve mostly to obscure the real issues. Dan Burden, executive director of Walkable Communities, takes a particularly dim view of the so-called pedestrian features that some big-box developers incorporate into their sprawling plans: "It's like that saying about putting lipstick on a pig. You can't put cosmetics on a bad concept and expect it to work."[36]

One of the more potent methods that corporate retailers employ to depict themselves as responsible and involved members of the community is donating to various local causes and charities. This is not to say that gifts to schools and food banks are bad, but in the case of the big boxes they are rarely motivated by altruism and often manipulated to further the corporation's growth. Target has been extensively advertising its good works in New York in advance of proposing multiple superstores in the city. Strategically timed gifts are even used to overcome opposition to particular development proposals. In Arlington, Texas, just weeks before officials were scheduled to decide the fate of a controversial plan to build a Wal-Mart supercenter, the company gave a much-publicized twenty thousand dollars to local charities. As the industry magazine *Chain Store Age* counseled, "Cause programs can help operators in their ... dealings with local zoning boards."[37]

Grand openings are another common time to make donations. When Target opened a store in Humble, Texas, it donated grants of two hundred to five thousand dollars to thirteen organizations. Local residents accepting oversize checks not only garnered free advertising for the new store in the form of headlines in the *Houston Chronicle,* but put a local face on a global corporation that might otherwise be perceived by its potential customers as an outsider taking over the local economy. Sometimes donations can even make friends of natural enemies. Randall Gross, an economic development consultant with Development Economics, once visited the offices of a Main Street revitalization program in a small community that had had its downtown destroyed by Wal-Mart. "They were so proud," he recalled. "They had one of those blown-up checks from Wal-Mart for $500. That Wal-Mart store was doing upwards of $100 million in sales, a big chunk of it stolen from the downtown."[38]

The latest trend in corporate retail giving is "cause branding," in which a chain uses a particular cause to embed certain feelings about its brand in the minds (and hearts) of consumers. "We believe that brands should be vital to people's lives and the values they advocate," explains the Web site of Cone Inc., a cause-branding firm that advises Home Depot, Starbucks, Target, and other chains. Cause branding, Cone says, can "forge strong emotional and practical bonds with customers." In its simplest form, cause branding involves "transactional campaigns," in which chains urge consumers to spend by donating a portion of the purchase price to a cause, as Starbucks is doing by giving to clean drinking water programs in other countries every time a customer buys a bottle of water. Target is both the most generous of the chains, giving 2.5 percent of its profits every year, and the most sophisticated cause brander. The chain has a credit card program that donates 1 percent of a customer's purchase to the local school of her choice, which cleverly associates Target with the feelings she has not just about schools generally, but about a particular school, perhaps the one educating her child.[39]

Home Depot has adopted the local-school strategy as well. Steve Coffin was horrified when his seven-year-old daughter came home from school wearing a Home Depot shirt and singing the Home Depot song. The company had donated materials to help the girl's school build a new playground. Volunteer parents did the work, decked out in Home Depot orange, while the children were taken out of class to watch the activity and practice the song. Home Depot also got its logo emblazoned on the school's four-foot "welcome" sign. Rather than sharing Coffin's concern, many of the parents seemed eager to thank the chain by shopping at its newly opened superstore a few miles away. As *Marketing Management* magazine explained, cause branding can "create experiences" for consumers and evoke "a sense of community."[40]

But the most critical question about corporate retailers' charitable giving—and the one rarely asked—is whether their donations actually make up for the contributions lost when locally owned businesses close in their wake. It's easy to develop a sense that chains donate a great deal, partly because many advertise their giving and also because the dollar amounts are large. Wal-Mart donated $170 million in 2004. That's no small sum, but it is not as generous as it might appear at first. It works out to less than one-tenth of 1 percent of revenue—the equivalent of someone who earns $35,000 a year giving $21 to charity. Indeed, Wal-Mart's own low-wage employees are much more generous; one study found that those with annual incomes of $10,000 to $20,000 donate an average of $209 a year to charity. Some evidence indicates that the megachains give substantially less than the local stores they replace. One survey of eight independent retailers found that their annual cash donations totaled 0.4 percent of revenue, or about seven times as much as Wal-Mart gives, eight times as much as Home Depot, and twice as much as Target.[41]

A much larger study of charitable giving compared large and small businesses and found that the firms with fewer than one hundred employees donated more than twice as much per employee as those with more than five hundred employees—$789 a year versus $334. The study's author, Dr. Patricia Frishkoff, former director of the Austin Family Business Program at Oregon State University, said the findings suggest that corporate consolidation may be undermining community programs both by removing the hands-on involvement provided by local business owners and shrinking the available funds. "I have significant concerns about the loss of community dollars when local businesses close," she said. The way local retailers donate is different too. Collectively, they give to a much broader and more diverse range of organizations than the chains do. They often donate to community causes in which they are personally involved, so their contribution includes time and skills as well as money. And while obtaining a donation from a local business can be as simple as walking in and asking the owner, with corporations, the process tends to be longer and may require approval from corporate headquarters.[42]

We are drifting ever more toward living in the Arvin of Walter Goldschmidt's study. Our communities lack lively public spaces; our local infrastructure is shabby and underfunded. We have a diminishing sense of connection to our neighbors. As we make our way between work and home, car and superstore, daily life affords little opportunity for social interaction and developing a rich informal public life. This estrangement affects not only our own personal well-being and happiness, but has contributed to the atrophy of every aspect of our civic life—from participation in public meetings and community groups to voting rates and the quality of our local media. There are undoubtedly many causes behind the decay of community, but the collapse of our local economies is a significant one. Although ignored as a matter of public policy, there is a tremendous civic value to doing business with our neighbors and vesting economic capacity and decision-making locally. In 1831 the Frenchman Alexis de Tocqueville toured the United States in a quest to uncover the secret of our robust democracy. In his two-volume *Democracy in America,* he concluded that it was to be found in the vitality of our local enterprises and institutions. "The strength of free peoples resides in the local community," he wrote.[43]

FOUR

BLIGHTED LANDSCAPE

AT FIRST BLUSH, LEGACY VILLAGE looks like a traditional town center. Its narrow two-lane streets are lined with buildings of varying heights and architectural styles. Street-level storefronts are filled with shops and restaurants. The wide brick sidewalks accommodate old-fashioned lampposts, trees, and park benches. But Legacy Village is not a real Main Street; it's an imposter. The buildings are not the work of many different hands over many decades. They were erected by a single developer in a few months' time. Like on an elaborate movie set, they sport false facades and architectural details meant to look like wood or stone, but molded out of plastic. Even the flower baskets are fake.

No one lives in this "village." It houses none of the functions one would expect to find in a town center: there's no school, post office, or town hall. Rather than local businesses, the storefronts are filled with the same chains that inhabit countless malls and shopping centers across the country: Crate & Barrel, Home Depot's Expo Design Center, Restoration Hardware, Talbots, Starbucks, Chipotle, The Cheesecake Factory, California Pizza Kitchen. While the sidewalks might give the impression of people arriving here on foot—maybe strolling downtown from a nearby neighborhood— the only way anyone actually gets to Legacy Village is by car. Pan back from this little snow-globe scene and the entire development is surrounded by asphalt, more than twenty-six hundred parking spaces in all.

Located in the western suburbs of Cleveland, Legacy Village debuted in 2003 with much fanfare and quickly became the region's hottest shopping destination. Its simulated town center represents the latest trend in shopping center design. Dozens of these faux Main Streets have been built around the country and many more are in the works. Developers call them "lifestyle centers" or "town centers," but they're not really the center of anything. The only geography governing the location of Legacy Village is its proximity to Exit 32 off Interstate 271. Much like Disney World, lifestyle centers employ a carefully crafted hucksterism designed to lull patrons into a warm nostalgia that induces spending. They are enormously successful. Legacy raked in $225 million during its first year, drawing shoppers from the entire Cleveland metro and well beyond.[1]

The troubling irony is that, not far from Legacy Village, there are many genuine Main Streets that are barely functioning. Each of Cleveland's old neighborhoods once had its own commercial center—blocks of buildings lined solidly with businesses that supplied most needs, within easy walking distance of home. Unlike Legacy Village, these districts were shaped by many different people and supported more than just commerce, incorporating apartments over the stores and public buildings like libraries and post offices. Today, almost all of these neighborhood Main Streets are struggling, having been crippled economically by wave after wave of suburban retail development. First there were the strip shopping centers, built on wide boulevards radiating out into the suburbs. Then came the first enclosed malls, followed by a series of ever-larger regional malls. Big-box stores came next, first as single outlets and anchors in strip shopping centers, and then grouped with category killers to form massive retail conglomerations known in the industry as "power centers." Now these same developers and retail chains have taken the very thing they destroyed, Main Street, and are selling it back to people in the form of lifestyle centers.

Hardest hit have been inner-city neighborhoods. In many of these areas, the few small businesses that remain are surrounded by vacant storefronts. But excessive retail development on the outer suburban fringe has also taken a toll on the city's older, first-ring suburbs, which were built along streetcar lines in the early twentieth century. Even relatively prosperous commercial districts like Coventry in Cleveland Heights have been affected. Customer traffic is down, according to Steve Presser, who owns the local toy store Big Fun. Key anchors have closed, notably a landmark three-screen movie theater unable to survive as more multiplexes opened in the outer suburbs.[2]

The trouble, Presser explains, is that none of the new suburban shopping centers were built in response to population growth. In fact, the metro's population has been declining since the 1970s. "It's the exact opposite of musical chairs," he laments. "Every round, instead of taking away chairs, they keep adding more. There are just not enough bodies to fill those seats." Sales have dropped at Big Fun, which, despite being celebrated in both local and national publications as one of the country's best toy stores, is now losing money. Across the street, Tommy's Restaurant, in business for more than thirty years, reports that bookings fell after the debut of Legacy Village, which added two thousand seats to an already oversaturated dining market. "When you couple that with the effect of big-box retailers, it's a one-two punch to older business districts," said Tommy's owner, Tom Fello.[3]

Each new shopping center not only undercuts older business districts and local retailers, but siphons sales from earlier generations of suburban retail. The Cleveland metro is now littered with the carcasses of bygone stores. Vacant strip malls haunt old commercial corridors. Abandoned big-box stores sit idle and decaying. Most staggering in scope are the dying malls. The metro is home to several. Euclid Square, Westgate, and Southgate are in various states of demise. Perhaps the most startling is Randall Park Mall. Built in the southeastern suburbs in 1976, Randall Park reigned as one of the largest malls in Ohio, a seemingly invulnerable fortress of retailing, with 1.6 million square feet spread over two floors. It began to fall apart in the late 1990s. Two of the mall's four anchors, JC Penney and Dillard's, left as part of a companywide downsizing triggered by big-box competition. Many of the smaller stores soon followed. Today Randall Park is half vacant. To save money, the mall's owners have turned off the lights and fountains in the mall's dead half, leaving eerily dark corridors. Stores in the other half limp along. Recently, management installed a Baptist worship center, apparently hoping that spiritual uplift would produce a corresponding upturn in the mall's finances.[4]

In 2000, alarmed by all of these vacant shopping centers, Jim Kastelic, then the deputy director of the Cuyahoga County Planning Commission, which encompasses Cleveland and some of its suburbs, launched a major study of the problem. "I was amazed at how much retail was being developed," he said. "There were all these vacancies in the city and inner suburbs, yet building continued on the outer edges." The study, which covered the seven counties that make up the Cleveland metro, counted 88 million square feet of retail stores, most built within the last few decades on open land farther from the city center. Although there had been plenty of development, the metro's population had not grown in decades; it had only dispersed. Stagnant consumer spending combined with extensive development had left the region with a staggering 10 million square feet of vacant retail space. And the problem was getting worse. At the time of the study, developers had put forward plans for dozens of new shopping centers and big-box stores. Together these projects totaled over 10 million square feet of new retail space—an amount identical to the region's existing vacancy. "We determined that the market was already oversaturated," Kastelic said, "yet there was 10 million square feet of retail on the table to be built."[5]

Much of it would in fact be constructed. In 2003, the year Legacy Village opened, greater Cleveland added 2.7 million square feet of new stores and shopping centers. And there is no end in sight: the region's municipalities have zoned more than seventy-seven square miles of land for retail development, enough to accommodate three hundred megamalls or more than four thousand new big-box stores.[6]

Despite the bird's-eye view provided by the study and the ample evidence on the ground, the region's communities continue to approve new retail projects. Lured by the prospect of a boost in tax revenue, most local officials mistakenly believe that these new shopping centers will somehow escape an obsolescence that is both inevitable and often shockingly fast in coming, or at least they assume that it will not happen on their watch. Nor do many give much consideration to the regional implications. "We keep duplicating infrastructure and services. Dollars are being diverted from the inner core to these outer areas to build water and sewer lines and roadways," explained Kastelic. "There's no concern about the common good of the region," concurred Julie Langan, director of Future Heights, which works to revitalize local business districts in Cleveland Heights, a task made more difficult each time a new shopping center opens.[7]

Citizens meanwhile are blind to what's really happening, contended David Beach, director of EcoCity Cleveland, a nonprofit organization that advocates for more sustainable land-use patterns. "They see all this new stuff going up and think it's growth and progress." But in fact it's nothing more than a retail merry-go-round that ultimately benefits no one save developers and corporate chains. "What is so hideous to me about it is that the dynamics are driven by national corporate retail strategies," Beach explained. "They come up with a new store or a new format that they want to unroll across the country. It has nothing to do with local needs. Much of it is driven by the pressures of Wall Street to grow, grow, grow."[8]

Communities ultimately pay the price. Some are obvious losers: the older city neighborhoods that must try to survive an outwardly sprawling and overbuilt retail market. But in this game, even the winners eventually become losers. Many suburbs that developed downtown-killing shopping malls thirty years ago are now themselves under siege as newer formats like superstores and lifestyle centers undercut mall revenue. Spend enough time in places like Randall Park Mall and it becomes hard to walk around Legacy Village without fast-forwarding to the time when it, too, will become a ghost town, its sidewalks devoid of people and its plastic architecture dingy and dated. Whether that time will come in twenty years or ten is anyone's guess. But it certainly will come. By then, the developer will have long ago sold off the property, and the chain stores and restaurants, having no ties to the community or to the place itself, will have moved on to newer developments in other suburbs. Already, Legacy Village is facing competition from Crocker Park, a bigger lifestyle center that opened on the metro's west side about a year after Legacy's debut.

Locally owned businesses are at a significant disadvantage in this fluctuating retail market. The very characteristics that make them so important to the stability and vitality of neighborhoods—their long-term roots and ongoing reinvestment in a particular location—are severe handicaps in a system of land use and development that strongly favors mobility over place. Many have failed by virtue of their location in historic business districts that have been repeatedly undercut and compromised by a glut of sprawling shopping center development. Even the best local retailers can be pulled under by a downward cycle of diminished traffic, increased vacancy, and disinvestment. Meanwhile, the development industry generally excludes independent businesses from new shopping centers. (Although they are welcome to lease space in old strip malls that have been abandoned by the chains). Even when local retailers are offered space in new developments, community ties may make them reluctant to move. Steve Presser declined an invitation to relocate Big Fun to a new suburban shopping center, because both his business and his family are deeply rooted in the neighborhood. "I live two blocks from my store. My kid goes to school up the street. The library is on the corner," he explained.[9]

But perhaps the greatest toll of all is the impact on the environment. Mega-retailers are consuming land and habitat at a stunning pace. The construction of strip centers, malls, big-box stores, and now lifestyle centers has devoured roughly nine thousand acres of land around Cleveland since the 1960s, even as the region's population declined slightly. Wetlands have been filled; forests have been cut down, including the sixty-seven acres of woods that is now Legacy Village; and vast tracts of the eastern Ohio Till Plain, some of the richest and most valuable farmland in the world, have been lost.[10]

As development has spread out into the countryside in all directions, sprawl has eclipsed power plants and factories as Cleveland's biggest polluter and most significant environmental threat. Driving has increased substantially, with the amount of road miles logged for shopping rising much faster than for other kinds of trips, such as commuting to work. Even basic errands, like picking up a carton of milk—once a short trip to a neighborhood store—can require miles of driving: wending out of the residential-only subdivision, merging onto a multilane "collector" road, and pulling into the parking lot of a large chain store. Residents of the Cleveland metro now drive 5.6 billion miles a year just for shopping, generating 2.7 million tons of carbon dioxide, a leading contributor to global warming, and emissions of other pollutants that rival or exceed the region's largest industries. Emissions from Cleveland's Ford Motor Company plant, for example, are dwarfed by the volume of air pollution associated with the metro's eleven regional malls. Designed to draw shoppers from miles around, these malls together account for eight times the nitrogen oxide, nineteen times the hydrocarbons, and fourteen times the carbon monoxide of the Ford plant.[11]

Sprawl has also surpassed industry as the greatest menace to Ohio's lakes and rivers. In 1969 the Cuyahoga River, which runs through Cleveland and empties into Lake Erie, was so full of industrial effluent that it caught on fire. Captured in photographs published in *Time* and *National Geographic,* the incident caught the nation's attention and helped propel passage of the Clean Water Act in 1973, which required factories to clean up their discharges. Over time the law led to significant improvements in water quality, but today, according to Jim White, director of the Cuyahoga River Remedial Action Plan, the river faces a new and more pernicious threat: runoff from rooftops, parking lots, and roadways. Maps developed by White's team show dramatic increases in the amount of developed land in the river's watershed since 1990. During storms, rainwater no longer soaks into the ground or trickles into streams and rivers, but instead rushes across paved areas in torrents that erode riverbanks, cause flooding, and destroy critical habitat. Much of this runoff is loaded with toxic pollutants generated by automobiles and deposited onto parking lots and roads. In the Cleveland metro, big-box stores and shopping centers alone are responsible for almost 900 million cubic feet of runoff each year. Unlike factories, when these stores cease to function economically, they still pollute. "We've left this giant inner ring of abandoned buildings," laments White. "The businesses are gone, but the parking lots and the rooftops are still there."[12]

LAND CONSUMPTION

Cleveland is not alone. Retail sprawl has engulfed much of the country, plundering both the built and natural environment from coast to coast. As mega-retailers have gained market share, the amount of land devoted to shopping has grown exponentially. In 1960 the United States had four square feet of retail store space per person. The construction of shopping malls and strip centers pushed the figure up to nineteen square feet by 1990. Then, over the next fifteen years, as big-box retailers multiplied, the amount of retail space doubled to thirty-eight square feet for every man, woman, and child. This growth did not come in response to increased demand. Consumer spending has expanded at a much more modest rate. Since 1960, median family income, adjusted for inflation, has increased by about 80 percent, while the amount of retail space has grown 850 percent.[13]

Compared with other high-income countries, Americans are retail gluttons. Great Britain, for example, has less than seven square feet of store space per capita. But our land binge is even worse than that. About two-thirds of the retail space in Great Britain is located in town centers. Downtown retail is far more land-efficient, because the need for parking lots and roadways is substantially reduced and buildings that house stores commonly include one or more upper stories of housing or offices. In the United States, the vast majority of retail development in recent years has been in the form of single-story big-box stores and other conventional shopping centers, which, by virtue of their design and location, require parking lots several times the size of the stores themselves, plus extensive networks of arterial roads and highways. "What concerns me the most is the accelerated consumption and fragmentation of open land," said Ed McMahon, senior fellow with the Urban Land Institute. "If you had two hundred thousand square feet of retail in 1960, the footprint of the building was about one acre, because it was in a four-story building downtown. Today, it's a one-story building that covers four acres and requires another dozen acres of parking."[14]

Erecting single-story boxes on vacant land is relatively cheap and easy.

Each chain has one or two standard store formats, the design and layout of which have been carefully engineered to maximize efficiency and drive sales. The most profitable way to expand is not to build unique stores that are adapted to the local area, but to unroll these identical outlets everywhere, from northern Maine to southern California. This means forcing the location to accommodate the store, not the other way around. Bulldozing undeveloped land is therefore infinitely preferable to adjusting the model to fit an empty downtown lot or, worse, an existing building. Even when big-box retailers enter cities—a market that many chains are now pursuing aggressively—their first objective is not to adjust their approach to a fundamentally different built environment, but to suburbanize the city by finding enough land to construct a standard superstore surrounded by parking. In New Orleans, for example, Wal-Mart took advantage of the demolition of a large public-housing project to drop one of its single-story supercenters into the heart of the city.

No place is too beautiful or environmentally sensitive to escape the designs of big-box retailers. For years, Wal-Mart has been trying to pave the Penjajawoc Marsh in Bangor, Maine. Identified by state officials as "the single most significant emergent marsh for waterbirds in Maine," the Penjajawoc is home to numerous rare and endangered birds. So far Wal-Mart's plans have been blocked by a tenacious citizens group and an alert state agency. But often the big chains get their way. In Covington, Louisiana, 103 acres of pine savanna wetlands were filled for a shopping center anchored by Target and Best Buy. In Austin, Lowe's is building a superstore on highly sensitive land within the recharge zone for the Edwards Aquifer, which is one of the most prolific artesian aquifers in the world and supplies drinking water to tens of thousands of people. In Decorah, Iowa, Wal-Mart built a store in the upper Iowa River floodplain, dumping 120,000 cubic feet of fill onto the site. But more significant than the places that make the headlines are the cumulative losses: the few acres of wetlands, the small streams, the bits of woodland that succumb to the relentless push by mega-retailers to open more stores.[15]

Retail sprawl is fueled in part by the drive to build ever-bigger outlets. Stores and shopping centers have their own gravitational pull and, like planets and stars, the bigger they are, the greater the attraction. This was first observed in the 1920s by William J. Reilly of the University of Texas. Although Reilly's concern was the relationship between the size of a town and the geographic extent of its trade area, his law of retail gravitation applies quite well to suburban shopping centers and is codified today in the Urban Land Institute's *Shopping Center Development Handbook*. Essentially it says that people will travel farther to reach bigger stores, driving about twice the distance for a store that is twice the size of a closer alternative. "All other things being equal, a bigger store or shopping center will always outpull and, hence, outperform a similar store or shopping center of smaller size," explained architect and town planner Seth Harry. For retailers, the imperative is clear: find a large parcel of undeveloped land, easily accessible to a highway or major road, and build a structure that is bigger than everything it competes with. This has set off a kind of development arms race—a never-ending quest to outsize competitors.[16]

Facilitating this arms race, of course, is our extensive road and highway system. Indeed, had the United States not opted for a primarily car-oriented development pattern beginning in the 1950s, the occasional large store would still exist, but big-box retailers as we know them would not. While size is everything in the suburbs, in traditional towns and cities, where neighborhoods are more compact and people depend less on the automobile, a business's proximity to its customers and its central location (whether that's downtown or the center of a neighborhood) is more important to its success than its size. Road networks in traditional cities are made up of a broad hierarchy of streets—from small neighborhood roads to larger avenues and subarterials and so on, all fully interconnected—and this hierarchy in turn supports a wide range of store sizes, each matched to its place within the urban fabric. A neighborhood street might house a small corner store and Laundromat that serve a few hundred households. The intersection of two larger streets might support a twenty-thousand-square-foot grocery store and a pharmacy that serve multiple neighborhoods. Everything converges downtown, which hosts the biggest stores and the largest overall concentration of retail.[17]

In suburbia, there are no central locations, and the value of being proximate to one's customers has been rendered largely irrelevant by the regional road network. "In the suburbs, the whole middle range of that road hierarchy went away," explained Harry. "Once you leave that local street network [of a housing subdivision], you go immediately to a four- or six-lane arterial." Once you are on this high-capacity road network, traveling at speeds that allow large distances to be covered in minutes, "size becomes the predominate determinant of a store's pull." In this setting, most people will bypass a small hardware store near their neighborhood for a big-box home-improvement center that may be several miles away but adds only a few minutes to the journey. If an even bigger big-box opens a little farther away, they'll start shopping there. This explains why neighborhood-size businesses—twenty-thousand-square-foot grocery stores, say—are virtually nonexistent in the suburbs. Although many retail experts flatly contend that grocery stores of that size are simply no longer viable, in fact they are— there are numerous examples—provided they are situated in a more traditional built environment, where a well-run business in the right place can succeed even if it's not the size of several football fields.[18]

Sprawl severs the relationship between a business and the community it serves, and creates, in the words of Harry, "a regional population of carborne, free-ranging consumers—easily aggregated at major intersections in sufficient quantities to sustain virtually any size retail box imaginable." Provided they can find a spot anywhere along a major road—and such sites, of course, are not only abundant, but most are already zoned for commercial development—retail chains have every incentive to keep building newer and bigger shopping centers that have greater pull and can grab market share from competing outlets anywhere else on the regional road network. In suburban sprawl, there's nothing to check overdevelopment. Back when downtowns were the place to be, "you had to wait until a space became vacant," noted Richard Knitter, a commercial real estate appraiser with Great Realty Advisors in Chicago. "Now you just go down the road and find additional vacant land and build the next round of big boxes." If the highways are large enough and linked to a sizable regional population, then the population of the local community hardly matters. In the small town of Deptford, New Jersey, which already has a 1.2-million-square-foot mall and numerous big-box stores, Wal-Mart recently proposed not one, but three new supercenters. Only twenty-eight thousand people live in Deptford, but the town hosts the confluence of Interstate 295 and four state highways.[19]

It is no surprise that our already bloated supply of stores and shopping centers has doubled since 1990 and shows no signs of slowing. Megaretailers are consuming a great deal of land, but their influence on our landscape does not end there. It extends far beyond their own acreage. About one in three of the trips Americans take each day is related to shopping. Indeed, the journey to the store counts for much of the way we experience the places we live. What was once a short trip through the neighborhood to a local grocer now more often involves traveling a major arterial to visit a supercenter. These shifting travel patterns in turn influence all sorts of other land-use decisions. Post offices and government buildings have been leaving downtowns in droves, moving out to where the big boxes are. Many schools and churches have not only relocated to the fringe, but they themselves have become huge, isolated compounds surrounded by parking and accessible only by car.[20]

Although developers like to say, "Retail follows rooftops," meaning that the chains only colonize areas where houses have been built, in fact big retailers today often form the front lines of sprawl. They locate on the far outer fringes, anticipating and, by their presence, catalyzing the construction of houses and other development nearby. "One thousand housing units are to be built in this area over the next ten years," explained Kiffi Summa in 2003, standing outside a new Target supercenter on the outskirts of Northfield, Minnesota, a community of eighteen thousand people on the rolling prairie about an hour south of Minneapolis. Summa moved to Northfield with her husband, Victor, after retiring in the mid-1990s. They live on a tree-lined street in one of Northfield's old Victorian neighborhoods, where the houses are relatively close together and the downtown is a short, pleasant walk away. Kiffi and Victor chose Northfield in large measure for its lively downtown, which, at the time they moved here, was home to a locally owned grocery store, Patrica's; a department store owned by three generations of the Jacobsen family; and numerous other businesses that met the everyday needs of the town's residents.[21]

Then in 1999, the Summas learned that Target wanted to build a 126,000-square-foot superstore on a state highway two miles outside of the downtown. Together with hundreds of their neighbors, they formed the Main Street Defense Fund to fight the proposal. They argued that Target would undermine the downtown and trigger an avalanche of sprawl around Northfield, which until then had remained a fairly compact town surrounded by open space. But when the plan was put to a townwide referendum, opponents of the supercenter lost by a margin of just ninety-four votes. Five years after Target opened, the downtown is not what it was. Both Patrica's and Jacobsen's have closed. Several other downtown businesses have relocated to be near Target. Smaller chains and strip shopping centers are now sprouting up next to the supercenter. Bulldozers are making way for a new drive-through bank surrounded by parking. The first crop of new houses is visible in the fields behind Target. These houses are quite different from those in the Summas' neighborhood. They are widely spaced on winding, dead-end roads, not in walking distance of communal locales. Downtown Northfield is miles away, and although Target is close at hand, it's hard to imagine that anyone with other means of transportation would walk from here out along the highway to shop at the superstore.

ON THE ROAD

As corporate chains have come to dominate retailing, Americans are logging more road miles each year for shopping and errands. Driving in general has been expanding rapidly, but driving for shopping has been growing more than twice as fast as driving for any other purpose, including commuting to work. Between 1990 and 2001, the number of miles driven by the average household for shopping increased by more than 40 percent. Shopping-related driving for the country as a whole rose by almost 95 billion miles in just eleven years. It's not that we're taking more shopping trips, but rather that more of those trips are by automobile and the journeys are longer. As the chains build ever-bigger stores, each outlet depends on a greater number of households spread over a wider geographic area. Thus the distance between home and store continues to grow. By 2001 the average length of a shopping trip had climbed to nearly seven miles, from five miles a decade earlier.[22]

Driving has become less about choice and more about necessity. In much of America, walking or taking public transit to the store is no longer an option. Most families have moved to suburban subdivisions that, by virtue of both zoning codes and convention, are strictly residential and lack the small neighborhood shops common in older communities. Not surprisingly, families that live in the suburbs rely much more on their cars than those who live in more traditional neighborhoods. Researchers at the University of California recently tracked shopping trips in two San Francisco Bay Area communities, Lafayette and Rockridge, which are similar in many respects. Both are about the same distance from downtown San Francisco. Both have comparable income levels and are served by the same regional freeway and rapid-transit line. They differ significantly in only one regard: Lafayette is a typical postwar suburb with low-density housing served by auto-oriented strip shopping centers, while Rockridge is an older Oakland neighborhood centered on a traditional Main Street lined with dozens of small businesses. This difference has dramatically affected driving rates. The researchers found that, while Lafayette residents make just 2 percent of their shopping trips by a means other than the automobile, residents of Rockridge walk, bike, or take public transit for one in five of their shopping trips. Moreover, Lafayette residents travel almost twice as far as those who live in Rockridge.[23]

Corporate chains have a strong preference for locations and store designs that encourage and even necessitate traveling by car. The kinds of landscapes that cars create—vast, homogeneous, highly mobile, and divorced from the constraints of place and community—are ideally suited for footloose and fast-growing chains. They in turn design their stores in every respect for driving, offering luxurious expanses of parking while creating an environment so hostile to pedestrians that people commonly drive between big-box stores located in the same shopping plaza, rather than traverse the asphalt on foot.[24]

It's not just the design of the buildings and the parking lots but, more fundamentally, the nature of the shopping experience that necessitates driving. Picking up a few things after work every day—which is fast and easy if you have a few good small stores in the neighborhood—is not at all convenient when you have to navigate a superstore the size of several football fields and then wait in line behind families buying a week's worth of supplies. Superstores encourage people to do big shopping trips, stocking up once or twice a week, and that requires having a car to get everything home. This is why efforts to reduce driving by building superstores along light-rail lines or adding pathways and other pedestrian amenities to their parking lots are doomed. Even regular walkers and public-transit users are unlikely to visit a big-box store without their cars, because that's what the shopping format demands. University of California researcher Ruth Steiner found that residents of El Cerrito, another Bay Area community, walk to the store one-third as often as those who live in Oakland's Rockridge neighborhood, despite the fact that El Cerrito has nearly the same housing density and plenty of retail within a short distance of residents' homes. The essential difference is that, while Rockridge has small stores along a traditional Main Street, El Cerrito has a 1960s shopping plaza flanked by a big parking lot and filled with large chain stores. The format calls for driving and so people drive.[25]

All of these extra miles constitute one of the hidden costs of big-box retail. Part of the price we pay is in lost time: the average adult under the age of sixty-five spends 426 hours each year behind the wheel, including more than 100 hours of driving just for shopping and errands. And they are the fortunate ones: some 80 million Americans are too old, too young, or too poor to drive. As neighborhood and downtown retailers are displaced by sprawling big-box stores along highways, these nondrivers are having an increasingly difficult time gaining access to basic goods and services.[26]

Driving is also a major financial drain. Transportation expenses account for one in five dollars that the average American household spends. That's more than healthcare and food combined, and double what the previous generation spent, when transportation consumed only 10 percent of the average household budget. Add to these private expenses the additional public costs (not covered by the gas tax) of maintaining roads, and the total bill comes in at close to $2 trillion annually. That's 14 percent of our gross domestic product and almost twice what other developed nations spend on transportation. This counts only direct costs. Indirect costs, such as time wasted in traffic and accident-related costs not covered by insurance, add perhaps another $1 trillion.[27]

But the greatest cost of all is the threat that our dependence on cars poses to the planet and human health. The United States, with only 5 percent of the world's population, consumes 25 percent of the world's oil. Nearly half of this, or 8.7 million barrels a day, is used to fuel passenger vehicles (cars, SUVs, and light trucks). Passenger vehicles emit the lion's share of the pollutants (nitrogen oxide and reactive hydrocarbons) that create ground-level ozone or smog. They contribute significantly to acid rain (by emitting nitrogen oxide) and are a major source of carbon dioxide, the primary greenhouse gas causing global warming. As mega-retailers sprawl and driving increases, such activities as buying clothes and picking up groceries are becoming ever more polluting. The extra 95 billion road miles that Americans are logging for shopping (over 1990 levels) account for 40 million metric tons of carbon dioxide, 300,000 tons of hydrocarbons, and 150,000 tons of nitrogen oxide released into the atmosphere each year.

The rise of big-box retail has not only spurred more driving and increased air pollution at the national and global level, but it has also created local hotspots of dirty air. As Cleveland has found, big-box power centers and other retail clusters often rank among a region's biggest air polluters. A 220,000-square-foot Wal-Mart supercenter generates on average more than ten thousand car trips a day, producing a high concentration of exhaust in the immediate area and annually contributing about 25 tons of nitrogen oxide, 65 tons of volatile organic chemicals (VOCs), 360 tons of carbon monoxide, and 6,500 tons of carbon dioxide to the atmosphere.

These localized clouds of carbon monoxide and ozone are hazardous, especially for people with respiratory or heart problems. Sprawling retail—from big-box stores to drive-through pharmacies and fast-food outlets—ranks as one of the worst ways to develop land, from an air-quality standpoint. Offices or light industry covering the same land area produce only one-eighth to one-fourth the volume of traffic and pollution.[28]

High volumes of car and truck traffic, and the associated noise and pollution, are among the main reasons that no one wants to live near a mega-retailer. The chains have managed to transform businesses that were once neighborhood amenities into nuisances. Consider the difference between a traditional corner store—the kind with a front door that opens onto the sidewalk and an apartment on the floor above—and a corporate convenience store like 7-Eleven. Or between a neighborhood eatery and a typical chain restaurant. The former are mostly welcome neighbors. They offer useful services and social interaction in a format that actually enhances surrounding property values. The latter, with their acres of parking and glowing signs, are noisy, congestive places that reduce the appeal and market value of nearby homes. The unpleasantness of living near most chains has only furthered our dependence on cars. Big-box stores are typically insulated from adjacent subdivisions by large walls and plantings, so that even those living next door often have to drive a quarter mile or more to reach the store. Attempts to alter suburban zoning to allow small retail outlets to open within residential neighborhoods usually meet with fierce resistance, not because people are opposed to a place like Joe's General Store, but because they fear living next door to a 7-Eleven.

LONG-HAUL GOODS

The world's big retailers have increased not only the distance traveled by customers, but the distance that goods are transported. One place where this is especially apparent is off the coast of Southern California. Cargo-ship traffic jams have become common here since the 1990s as ships arriving from Asia line up to unload at the twin ports of Los Angeles and Long Beach. Cargo volume at the ports, already among the largest in the world, has been growing by more than 10 percent annually and is expected to triple by 2020. Consumer goods manufactured in China and destined for superstore shelves account for most of this flood of new cargo. Wal-Mart is the shipping terminal's top customer. The ports accommodate not only incoming ships, but fleets of outgoing trucks and railcars. All of these engines burn vast quantities of fuel and together make the port complex the single largest source of concentrated air pollution in the region. The ports account for one-quarter of the area's diesel exhaust and emit more nitrogen oxide than Southern California's 350 largest factories and refineries combined. The human toll includes high rates of asthma and respiratory illnesses and a cancer risk twenty times greater than federal clean air standards for those living in neighborhoods adjacent to the ports.[29]

Each year, we ship, truck, and fly more goods around the world and across the country. Global shipping has been expanding faster than the world's economic output, while domestic shipping is one of the fastest growing industries in the United States. Ton-miles of freight transported within the country rose 24 percent between 1993 and 2002 (a ton-mile equals one ton of freight moved one mile). Trucking, which is more polluting than rail or water transport, expanded even faster, by 55 percent, and now accounts for 16 percent of U.S. greenhouse gas emissions. There are many factors behind this growth. One is the rise of corporate retailers. While many independent retailers source some of their wares locally— small grocers may carry foods produced on nearby farms, or home-furnishings stores might feature items made by local manufacturers—big retail chains source virtually all of their goods through global distribution channels. They deal with giant global manufacturers or contract directly with factories to produce items in sufficient quantities to stock thousands of stores. All buying decisions are made centrally and inventory is tracked and managed companywide. It is simply not practical for chains to purchase goods on a store-by-store basis from tens of thousands of local venders and producers.[30]

The result is not only a highly standardized array of products that varies little from store to store, but the distance consumer goods travel from factory to store shelf is greater than ever. Even goods readily and cheaply available locally are commonly not found on chain store shelves. In Iowa, as farmers struggle to sell their meat and produce through farmers' markets and a dwindling number of local and regional grocery retailers, large supermarket chains are importing the same foods from other states. Researchers found that ingredients for a traditional heartland meal of beef, potatoes, and vegetables purchased at a big chain had been transported an average of sixteen hundred miles, even as the same foods were being grown and raised less than an hour from the store.[31]

Orchestrating these massive flows of goods from distant factories to thousands of stores is the primary activity that mega-retailers are engaged in. It is the core of their day-to-day operations. Wal-Mart's genius, what boosted it to the top of the industry and made it a revolutionary force in re-tailing, is that it developed the most sophisticated distribution system in the world—a marvel of modern technology capable of moving more goods around the planet with more precision and efficiency than ever before. Its methods have since been widely imitated by other chains. But these exten-sive distribution networks are efficient only to the degree that one ignores their huge cost to the environment and human health. The long supply lines behind every superstore, category killer, and fast-food outlet rely on combusting vast quantities of fossil fuels, the effects and costs of which are borne, not by the chains, but by society as a whole.

TOXIC PARKING LOTS

While many people recognize the connection between sprawl and air pol-lution, few are aware that sprawl—or, more precisely, pavement—is now the leading threat to our rivers, lakes, and estuaries. After years of steady improvement following passage of the 1973 Clean Water Act, which limited industrial discharges, many water bodies are once again in decline. This time the culprit is polluted runoff from roads, driveways, and parking lots. Runoff now ranks as the nation's leading source of water pollution, affect-ing more than 40 percent of U.S. lakes and streams and leading to fifteen hundred beach closings and advisories since 1998, according to the U.S. Environmental Protection Agency. Every corner of the country has been affected. In Ohio, as we have seen, sprawl is fast becoming the largest contributor of pollution to the Cuyahoga River. In Washington, the once pristine Skykomish River, beloved for fishing and recreation, has seen a startling decline in wild steelhead and salmon numbers. The cause, ac-cording to the nonprofit group American Rivers, which in 2005 listed the Skykomish as one of the nation's ten most endangered rivers, is runoff from poorly planned development, especially big-box stores, strip malls, and parking lots. In Vermont, the waters of northern Lake Champlain, which borders the fast-sprawling region around Burlington, have become dan-gerously dirty, afflicted by toxic algae blooms caused by runoff.[32]

Big-box stores, strip shopping centers, and malls are by far the worst type of development from a water-quality standpoint. No other use of land generates a larger volume of contaminated runoff. This is because of the vast amount of parking these stores require—a two-hundred-thousand-square-foot supercenter typically has a twelve-acre parking lot—and the volume of car and truck traffic they generate, which coats the asphalt with a range of contaminants. "From an environmental standpoint, parking lots rank among the most harmful land uses in any watershed," explained Tom Schueler of the Center for Watershed Protection. "Simply put, there is no other kind of surface in a watershed that produces more runoff and delivers it [to a local water body] faster than a parking lot."[33]

After a field or forest is converted into a big-box store, rainwater that would normally soak into the ground instead washes in torrents across the parking lot and driveways. As it does, it becomes warmer and picks up a nasty stew of toxic pollutants, including phosphorous, nitrogen, road salt, sediments, hydrocarbons from motor oils and fuels, heavy metals, pesticides, and herbicides. When this runoff flows into a nearby river, it not only delivers a concentrated load of pollutants, it raises the river's temperature, which harms fish like trout and changes the watershed's hydrology. Because the ground can no longer act as a sponge—soaking up water during storms and releasing it slowly during dry spells—the river will run very high when it rains, destroying stream-bank vegetation and crucial spawning habitat, and very low at other times, further stressing plants and fish. Scientists have found that lakes and rivers become impaired when the amount of impervious surface (pavement and rooftops) in a watershed reaches as little as 10 to 15 percent of the total land area. New research also suggests that pavement, which heats up in the sun, is not only contributing to localized "heat islands," but to global climate change.[34]

Federal runoff regulations are too mild to control the problem, and some of the nation's biggest retailers have failed to comply even with these measures. In 2000 the EPA fined Wal-Mart $1 million for violating storm-water regulations at seventeen store construction sites. The rules are designed to prevent the erosion of sediments into nearby water bodies during building. At the time, Wal-Mart pledged to reform its practices, but four years later the EPA again found widespread violations. Wal-Mart was fined $3.1 million, the largest penalty ever assessed for storm-water violations (although it's a mere drop in the bucket for a company with more than one-quarter of a trillion dollars in annual revenue). Wal-Mart is not the only one. Lowe's was fined by the EPA for failing to adequately control runoff from a construction site in Massachusetts, while investigations of other big chains are reportedly under way.[35]

With their voracious appetite for land and affinity for locations that increase car dependence, mega-retailers have become some of the nation's largest water polluters. The losses happen incrementally—one new shopping center or superstore at a time—but the cumulative effects are staggering: the nineteen square feet of store space per capita that retailers have developed since 1990 translates into 125,000 acres of rooftop and 375,000 acres of parking lot. That's an area about half the size of Rhode Island. Meanwhile, thousands of older shopping centers and big-box stores are being left vacant, even as their parking lots continue to deliver runoff to nearby streams and rivers.

BLIGHT

Much of the country is now strewn with the wreckage of excess retail development. Not only are many downtowns and neighborhood business districts struggling with underutilized and vacant storefronts, but a staggering number of strip centers, malls, and big-box stores have gone dark. Dark stores have become so common, they have earned an official name ("greyfields"), spawned numerous Web sites, and inspired everything from art exhibitions to competitions for designing viable reuse plans. No one knows exactly how much retail space currently sits idle, but the tally is somewhere in the neighborhood of several hundred million—perhaps approaching 1 billion—square feet. That's not even counting the acres of parking that surround many of these lifeless properties. Retail vacancy is a fast-spreading epidemic and, in the absence of intervention, it will only get worse.[36]

Even investment advisers are sounding the alarm about this new suburban blight. Annual "Emerging Trends in Real Estate" reports produced by PricewaterhouseCoopers, in partnership with Lend Lease Real Estate Investments and later the Urban Land Institute, have included increasingly dire warnings about the dangers of investing in retail property. (City officials weighing zoning and development decisions might do well to heed their advice.) "America is overstored—too many formats cannibalize each other," the 2002 report read. "Dead and dying malls litter the nation's suburbs.... Most power centers are risky propositions, as category killers and discounters battle amongst themselves in submarket-by-submarket survival contests. The only sure thing is that owners will be challenged to release empty boxes abandoned by the losers." The 2003 report bluntly stated: "The most overretailed country in the world hardly needs more shopping outlets of any kind." The 2004 report predicts even more fallout: "The best locations today 'can quickly morph into weak ones.'. . . Neighborhood centers have been overpriced, given the risk of supermarket chain failures and the threat of Wal-Mart incursions. . . . Only the top one or two grocery chains in each market will survive. . . . Expect major mall owners to step up their courting of discounters and big boxes. They need fallbacks if anchors go under. That could set off a turbulent round of retailer musical chairs."[37]

Colossal in both their physical and psychological impact, dead malls have attracted the most attention. A 2001 study by the Congress for the New Urbanism and PricewaterhouseCoopers conservatively estimated that 140 malls are either dead or nearly so, and an additional 250 are vulnerable to collapse. This represents one in five malls. The researchers found that another 570 malls have annual sales of between $200 and $250 per square foot, enough to remain viable, at least for now, but far below the revenue of big-box retailers like Wal-Mart and Home Depot, which generate about $400 per square foot. Other analysts paint an even starker picture. "Only a small percentage of malls are successful today—perhaps 25 percent. Another 25 percent are limping along. Probably 50 percent are getting killed," contended Robert Antall, CEO of the retail consultants group LakeWest. The malls that continue to draw crowds and post strong sales are typically the largest malls—what the industry calls superregional centers or fortress malls. Many of these have managed to pull big-box stores into their orbits, becoming epicenters of massive retail conglomerations.[38]

But second-tier malls face a bleak future. Many are hemorrhaging sales. They can no longer count on their department store anchors, which have been downsizing, merging, or entering bankruptcy reorganization in an effort to survive competition from Wal-Mart and Target. Like rats on a sinking ship, some, including Sears, are fleeing the malls to build their own freestanding box stores. Almost every state in the Union is now home to at least one dead mall: Dixie Square in Harvey, Illinois; River Roads in Jennings, Missouri; Osceola Square in Orlando; Beloit Mall in Beloit, Wisconsin; Mall of Memphis in Memphis, Tennessee; Wonderland Mall near Detroit; Myrtle Square Mall in Myrtle Beach, South Carolina; Town and Country Mall in Houston; Cinnaminson Mall in South Jersey; and Eastland Mall in North Versailles, Pennsylvania. By far the most poignant are the dying malls built on the remains of historic downtown buildings razed to make way for what would turn out to be a fleeting shopping trend. Santa Maria, California, bulldozed its downtown in the 1970s for a shopping mall that is now almost half vacant. Columbus, Ohio, built a downtown mall in 1989 that died a decade later after three competing malls opened on the edge of the city. [39]

Having trounced the malls, the big-box stores themselves are now going dark, victims of competing chains and their own upsizing. Cavernous shells of defunct superstores now number in the thousands. Many metro areas are overrun. A 2001 report counted thirty-one vacant big-box stores in Charlotte, North Carolina. Columbus, Ohio, is home to sixty-nine empty boxes. As of 2003, Kansas City had thirty-nine dark stores, totaling 2.3 million square feet, even as another 3 million square feet of new stores and shopping centers were under construction. The Chicago metro reports more than 10 million square feet of vacant big-box retail, while Dallas–Fort Worth has nearly 15 million square feet of empty stores. Many small towns have been hit, too, with one or more crumbling superstores now lurking on their outskirts. Sitting idle in Joplin, Missouri, for instance, are three supermarkets, two mall-based department stores, a Kmart, and a Wal-Mart.[40]

Some of these empty stores are the remains of retail chains that have gone belly-up, including Ames, Bradlees, Builders Square, Caldor, Grand Union, HomeBase, Montgomery Ward, Service Merchandise, and Zayre. Before Kmart emerged from bankruptcy in 2003, it cast off 600 of its stores, 370 of which were still vacant in early 2005. JC Penney, Sears, Albertson's, and Toys "R" Us have all shuttered stores in recent years. A remarkable number of vacant big-box stores, however, are not the result of failure, but of success. Lowe's, for example, which has some 30 vacant stores across the country, recently vacated a 98,000-square-foot store in Prince William County, Virginia, to build a 177,000-square-foot outlet less than a mile away. The idle Lowe's became Prince William's third shuttered box. In Athens, Georgia, Target abandoned a fifteen-year-old, 90,000-square-foot store to open a larger outlet one mile down the highway, leaving the eighth empty big-box in this community of one hundred thousand people.[41]

Always an industry leader, Wal-Mart is one of the worst offenders when it comes to vacating stores. In 2005 the United States was home to more than three hundred empty Wal-Mart superstores—almost all of them discarded as the company built bigger stores in the same local markets. A map of these vacant stores would show heavy concentrations in the Southeast and Midwest, where Wal-Mart first expanded and has now completed at least one or two rounds of upsizing. As of March 2005 the company's list of available properties included twenty-eight superstores in Georgia, thirty-six in Texas, eighteen in Arkansas, nineteen in Tennessee, and fifteen in Louisiana. Much like a contagious disease, vacant Wal-Mart syndrome is spreading steadily north and west as the company abandons its first round of superstores to build supercenters that are twice the size and include full grocery departments. The company commonly vacates stores that are little more than a decade old. In Albert Lea, Minnesota, Wal-Mart abandoned an eighty-thousand-square-foot building that was just eleven years old. Four years later, it was still sitting empty. While Wal-Mart occasionally expands an existing store, more often it's cheaper and easier to colonize new land. In Auburn, Maine, Wal-Mart's new supercenter sprawls across some twenty-five acres just a stone's throw from the carcass of its original store, built in 1992.[42]

With the specter of vacant boxes beginning to make cities nervous about approving new supercenters, Wal-Mart's community relations people have crafted several statements designed to soothe local officials. Responding to concerns by a member of the Sacramento City Council, company spokesperson Amy Hill declared, "We have never closed a supercenter anywhere in the country." Not yet anyway. Supercenters are Wal-Mart's most recent format. Like earlier generations of Wal-Mart stores, supercenters will undoubtedly be eclipsed by some newer format down the road. It's an endless cycle. Some communities have already gone through more than one cycle of Wal-Mart supersizing. Bardstown, a small Kentucky town of about ten thousand people, is now on its third Wal-Mart. The first one went dark in 1984, when Wal-Mart built a larger store on the opposite side of town. It sat empty for fifteen years before the county finally put up funds to have it torn down. Now Wal-Mart has vacated the second store, moving back to the east side of town to build a supercenter about a mile from its first location. Wal-Mart plans to vacate many more stores in the future. The company's 2004 annual report affirmed that about 150 of its stores would be converted to supercenters in 2005. Some of these conversions involve expanding an existing store, but most are what Wal-Mart euphemistically calls "relocations," meaning that the existing outlet would be abandoned.[43]

Big-box stores often remain vacant for years. The structures deteriorate rapidly and they can become magnets for crime and vandalism, and a source of blight that can pull down surrounding property values and deter new investment in the area. While communities pay a high price for these idle properties, the retailers responsible incur virtually no penalties. Nor do the developers. While it was once common for developers to build and then own shopping centers, today most cash out almost immediately. They make money on the initial development and are long gone, often developing new retail projects, by the time the property goes dark. "If a [national] retailer agrees to a lease, the developer can get the loan and do the project and sell it. They don't really care if the project goes broke down the line," said Chicago real estate appraiser Richard Knitter.[44]

What can a community do with a vacant box? "It's one of the toughest challenges in real estate," said retail consultant Chris Boring. While Main Street buildings have an inherent and lasting value, and can be adapted and reused for centuries, big-box stores are cheaply constructed and designed for only one thing: big-box retail. But installing another chain in an empty store is not easy. Most are not interested in adjusting their own store formats to fit some other company's discarded box—especially with plenty of open land zoned for retail development. Nor are the former occupants inclined to let their stores fall into the hands of competitors. In fact, if they do not own the building, many chains insist on clauses in their leases that bar the owner from renting the store to a competitor should it be left vacant. As mentioned previously, they often even continue to pay rent on an empty store in order to control the property. "That's not always apparent to the public. You might drive by and wonder why the owner hasn't done anything with a building that's been sitting empty for years," Boring explained.[45]

Some empty big-box stores have been converted to nonretail uses: roller rinks, flea markets, county offices, and even churches. (In 2002 Calvary Chapel in Pinellas, Florida, left its home in an old Winn-Dixie supermarket and took over a vacant Wal-Mart store.) But these kinds of unusual adaptations are relatively rare; there are far more empty boxes than potential users. Vacant malls are also difficult to rehabilitate. Some are in such good locations that they can attract a developer willing to level the structure to build something else. But razing an old mall is costly and few are located in areas that warrant such an expense.

Often the burden of dealing with these vacant stores falls to the local government. Many have spent a great deal of money and time marketing, razing, or redeveloping blighted retail properties. They feel that they have no choice: the alternative is to leave an eyesore that can be a drain on the economy and ultimately tax revenue. Stuck with a derelict Kmart, the town of Port St. Lucie, Florida, finally bought the building and had it torn down. In 2005 Trotwood, a suburb of Dayton, Ohio, announced that it would spend $60 million redeveloping the defunct Salem Mall. The city of Charlotte, North Carolina, has been heavily involved in trying to address several persistent pockets of vacant big-box retail, such as Independence Boulevard, home to a number of empty superstores, including Barnes & Noble, Circuit City, and Kmart. Recently the city agreed to provide a $10 million subsidy to build a Target store on the site of a dead mall—despite the fact that Target is very much part of the problem, having abandoned two stores elsewhere in Charlotte. "Target has become as devastating to these neighborhoods as Wal-Mart has been to small towns," noted former planning commissioner Mary Hopper, who has been active in efforts to address retail blight.[46]

Although a long-term solution will require addressing sprawl and not zoning so much land for retail development, some communities are beginning to look at intermediate measures, such as requiring developers to post demolition bonds to pay for the cost of razing a store should it go dark. But retailers, developers, and many elected officials have fought such proposals, arguing that cities should opt for a "carrots" rather than a "sticks" approach. The International Mass Retailers Association, which represents most major chains, has said that cities should provide financial incentives to encourage retailers to find new tenants for their empty buildings. Cities are urged to view vacant shopping centers as "opportunities" and to undertake "public-private partnerships"—which translates into taxpayers picking up the tab for this merry-go-round, while developers and chains run off with the profits. Meanwhile, older neighborhoods and locally owned businesses are penalized for their stability, left to sink or swim in a sea of shopping center excess, often with little public attention or investment.[47]

COMMUNITIES VERSUS LIFESTYLES

Anxiety about sprawl is on the rise, whether it's frustration at the number of hours we spend in our cars, the loss of yet another farm or forest, the dead mall on the edge of town, or the sense that we live, work, and shop in artificially generated landscapes that bear no connection to place or community.

The cumulative impact of sprawl is probably the greatest environmental threat we face. It is certainly a major contributor to air and water pollution, and to global warming. Although critically important, addressing the symptoms of sprawl and not the underlying cause will only get us so far. Improvements in automobile fuel efficiency, for example, would have to be fairly dramatic to outstrip the rate of growth in driving. Likewise, new regulations are expected to lead to cleaner trucks and diesel fuel, but if shipping continues to expand at its current rate, these gains will be more than offset by increases in cargo volume. Better parking lot design and storm-water treatment techniques can reduce the impact of runoff, but again, even if every existing parking lot were upgraded, the rate at which land is currently being paved would soon overtake these gains.

Nor do these approaches address the considerable community costs of sprawl. Sprawl is poisonous to independent businesses and local economies. It has sucked the life from traditional neighborhoods and town centers, which are not only home to many established independent businesses but are, by virtue of their density and human scale, ideally suited to nurturing new entrepreneurs. The collapse of these commercial centers has greatly impeded the creation of new small businesses. Meanwhile, there are few opportunities for independent retailers in the suburbs. Housing subdivisions that spring up virtually overnight require instant retail. Only corporate chains can provide this: a big-box shopping center can be built and fully stocked in a matter of months. Putting down roots and growing with the community, as local businesses tend to do, is not an option on the fast-expanding suburban fringe. The financing behind most of these shopping center projects further ensures that not even small spaces will be available to independents.

There are many reasons, then, why we might reconsider our current approach to transportation and land development. There would be substantial benefits to leaving behind the suburban model, where big-box stores and highways reign, and moving toward a more traditional settlement pattern—characterized by neighborhoods where the houses are nestled more closely together, cars are not the only means of getting around, and local stores that provide the basics of daily life are close at hand.

Keen to capitalize on the sense that we should be building better communities, but loath to change the underlying dynamics of auto-oriented retail that have proven so profitable, developers and national chains have come up with places like Legacy Village. Dozens of these faux Main Streets have been built in the last few years and have been repeatedly hyped as a means of reconstructing the urban fabric and bringing town centers to the suburbs. But their resemblance to traditional communities is only skin deep. Even those that incorporate some housing or offices still function very much like regional malls. Easton Town Center outside of Columbus, Ohio, for example, includes stores built around a town square, along with upper-story offices and nearby apartments. But the 1.5 million square feet of retail dwarfs the office and housing space. All of these stores and restaurants—Williams-Sonoma, Abercrombie & Fitch, Brio Tuscan Grille, and so on—are not intended to primarily serve the few dozen households that live in the immediate area. They are designed to draw shoppers from the entire region. Indeed, Easton, which is located at the confluence of Interstates 270 and 670, attracts 18 million visitors a year—making it at once a kind of celebration of walkable places and a major inducement to more driving.

FIVE

SOMETIMES LOW PRICES

SHOPPERS ARE DRAWN TO CHAIN STORES for many reasons, chief among them the predictability of the experience and the prospect of saving money. Not all chains compete on price, of course. The Gap sells plenty of pricey apparel. A frothy cappuccino from Starbucks will set you back as much or even more than one from a locally owned coffeehouse. An informal survey of Blockbuster stores and competing independents in five cities found that the chain charged more for a DVD rental in every case, by an average of 29 percent. But for the big-box stores, low prices are their primary selling point. Most people, including many critics, take it for granted that they deliver on this count. After all, global retailers have all the advantages of scale: they buy in volume, have highly efficient distribution systems, and exert powerful downward pressure on costs, especially wages. But how much do these retailers actually save shoppers? Not nearly as much as many imagine, the evidence suggests.[1]

Consumers' perceptions of prices and actual prices are not necessarily the same thing. Mega-retailers employ sophisticated marketing and merchandising strategies to create and sustain an image of low prices. The science of influencing shoppers' price perceptions is well developed and touches on every aspect of how these stores operate, from the way they display products to their interior decor. (Researchers have determined, for example, that combining certain colors, like orange, with bright lighting produces an expectation of very low prices.) According to Duncan Simester at MIT's Sloan School of Management and Northwestern University marketing professor Eric Anderson, most consumers are not particularly well informed about prices. "Remarkably," the researchers reported, "they rely on retailers to tell them whether they're getting a good price."[2]

The big-box retailers do an exceptionally thorough job of informing us that we are indeed getting a good deal. Target's slogan is "Expect more. Pay less." Best Buy has chosen a name that says it all. No company does this better or more relentlessly than Wal-Mart. "Always low prices. Always," is emblazoned on every superstore, every truck rolling down the highway, and every advertisement. (In the United Kingdom, "Permanently Low Prices Forever" is literally carved in stone outside Wal-Mart's Asda stores.) A frequent TV ad features Wal-Mart's smiley face rolling back prices. We see several price signs spinning backward like reverse odometers. The actual numbers are entirely meaningless, though, because these prices are not attached to any products. But that hardly matters; the ad is about reinforcing an idea. Once inside the store, the message repeats with large "Low Prices" signs hanging in every section. Perhaps by design, Wal-Mart spokespeople almost always mention low prices in interviews with the media, regardless of the subject of the story. The chain has also cultivated a powerful mythology of cost cutting. Many people know, for example, that, when traveling, Wal-Mart employees share motel rooms—even CEO Lee Scott bunks up with another executive, saving the company $150 a night, while taking home millions of dollars a year in compensation.

The manipulation of consumer perceptions continues with the way big-box retailers price and display products. Many people assume that retailers set prices according to an old-fashioned formula whereby they take what they paid for an item and mark it up by a set margin to cover their costs and provide a profit. But in fact markups vary dramatically from one item to the next. All big-box retailers employ a fine-tuned pricing strategy that relies on "signposts" and "blinds." Signposts are items, such as milk and lightbulbs, for which most shoppers know the going price. Less than 5 percent of the items in a big-box store are signposts. "Customers use the prices of signpost items to form an overall impression of a store's prices. That impression then guides their purchase of other items for which they have less price knowledge," explained Simester and Anderson.[3]

Home Depot is a master of this technique, according to Bill Lee, a sales and management consultant who has advised hardware and lumber dealers, including Home Depot. "They'll advertise products at or below cost to get your attention and get you in the store. And once you are in the store, there are thousands of other products that you are likely to buy that have much higher margins." These other products are known as blinds—items for which consumers do not know the going rate. Blinds account for the bulk of a store's inventory and all of its profit. This approach to pricing recognizes that what matters is not how much a retailer makes on any one item, but the overall profit margin on everything in a customer's shopping cart. "I once heard Home Depot founder Bernie Marcus give a speech in which he called it 'islands of losses amid seas of profits,'" said Lee.[4]

Both Home Depot and Lowe's further reinforce the perception of low prices through a "low price guarantee" that is prominently displayed in stores. Should a shopper find a lower price, both companies promise to match the price and beat it by 10 percent. Considerable research has found that consumers find price guarantees very reassuring, according to Simester and Anderson. Shoppers are more likely to trust that companies offering such guarantees do in fact have the lowest prices in town. They assume that the manager, wishing to avoid the 10 percent penalty, is shopping the competition and making sure that his store beats it. But price guarantees require enforcement, and the reality is that, once reassured, most shoppers tend not to look elsewhere. While there are those vigilant few who do bring higher prices to the attention of management and receive the discount, other customers do not necessarily benefit. Although a low-price guarantee seems to imply that, once aware of a discrepancy, the store will lower its price to beat the competition, that's not actually part of the policy. Indeed, it's not uncommon for Home Depot and Lowe's to satisfy the vigilant shopper but leave the store price unchanged.[5]

There are, however, limits to how much a chain's price image can diverge from reality. Even if consumers perceive prices at Home Depot and Lowe's to be lower than they actually are, that does not mean that they are not saving something. The empirical evidence, though, is surprisingly scant. Two case studies have produced mixed results. One compared prices at a local hardware store in California with a newly opened Home Depot and found that, on a basket of ten items, the big-box was 15 percent cheaper. Another study in Idaho price-shopped forty items and found that the local hardware store beat Home Depot by 5 percent. Many independent hardware stores insist their prices are competitive. Almost all belong to three large buying and distribution cooperatives—Ace, True Value, and Do It Best. These co-ops operate at sufficient scale to buy and deliver products to member stores with a degree of efficiency that comes fairly close to Home Depot and Lowe's. After that, it's up to the individual owner to run a tight ship. Under the advice of their co-ops, many local hardware stores have adopted signpost pricing themselves—although some are reluctant both to accept no margin on some items and to substantially mark up others. But otherwise, they say, consumers will compare signpost items at the big chains and assume the smaller stores are price gouging across the board.[6]

"We really feared their pricing at first," said Steven Tanner, owner of Tanner Paint in Tampa, Florida, referring to a Home Depot that opened nearby a few years ago. "They did a great job of lowballing in the beginning. They would advertise and cherry-pick items.... The general feeling was that it was a much better buy," he said. "But I have become much more confident after seeing more of their prices that the image is really a fallacy of sorts." Tanner's grandfather started Tanner Paint in 1933. His wife, Jett, works at the store, as does their son Walker, who is twenty-three and left college two years ago to join the business after his father had a stroke. Seniority among the store's employees—including the talented color specialists who match paint color by eye with more accuracy than a computer —ranges from seven to thirty years. After Home Depot opened, Tanner Paint was able to pick up business from competing local paint stores that closed and, as a result, has not seen a drop in sales. But the business has stopped growing, even as Tampa's population mushrooms. New residents, bombarded by Sunday advertising circulars featuring Home Depot, rarely try the local store. "Home Depot has the protection of people having that mentality that they are the low-price leader," Tanner said. But he pointed to the many contractors who watch costs closely and continue to frequent his business: "If they had seen genuine savings at Home Depot, I think they would have gone there in some numbers."[7]

Other big-box retailers, including Wal-Mart, also employ the signposts and blinds approach to pricing. Wal-Mart considers about fifteen hundred of the one hundred thousand items it carries to be especially price-sensitive, according to Dr. Kenneth Stone, an economist at Iowa State University. About half of these items are in the grocery aisles—bananas, milk, bread—while the others are things like diapers and four-packs of lightbulbs. "These items they display on kiosks, end caps, or dump bins in the middle of the aisle," said Stone. "You see them in prominent places and you start assuming that what they've been telling us for years in their ads is true: that their prices across the board are lower." Wal-Mart excels at offering spectacular loss leaders (though the losses are often financed by manufacturers, not Wal-Mart) that function like bright neon signposts—a gallon of milk for a quarter or a massive jar of pickles for $2.97. Nothing makes a better, or more prominent, signpost than gasoline prices, which is in part

why Wal-Mart has been adding filling stations to the parking lots of its supercenters. In several states, the company has lobbied aggressively to overturn laws that prohibit retailers from selling gas for less than what they paid
for it. (These laws are designed to prevent big oil companies from forcing
independent stations to close, reducing competition and raising prices.)[8]

"But they have to make a profit somewhere," Stone said of Wal-Mart.
Those who look closely, he said, will find examples of the other end of their
bipolar pricing strategy. They might price a basic four-pack of lightbulbs
very low, he said, but charge more than the competition for single bulbs and
unusual wattages. Jon Lehman, a former store manager and seventeen-year
veteran of Wal-Mart described the strategy in an interview with the PBS
show *Frontline:* "So you go to Wal-Mart, and you're looking for a lawn
mower, and to your delight, you walk in, and you see this $99 lawn mower.
You may not want a cheap, basic lawn mower, but you see that price point
on an end cap or a big display stack base, and you say, 'Wow, what a great
price.' And it draws you in. It lures you into the department, and you form
the perception immediately that 'Hey, Wal-Mart's got the lowest prices in
town. Look at this item right here. How could they sell it for $99?... But as
you walk into the department and look for that $269 power-drive lawn
mower that you really are after, they're not losing money on that item. And
it may not be the lowest price in town."[9]

Wal-Mart excels at using these opening price points to manipulate
consumers' perceptions, according to Race Cowgill, principal with Zenith
Management Consulting. In 2005 Zenith checked the prices of thirty-eight-
hundred items at Wal-Mart, Target, Kmart, chain drugstores, and chain
supermarkets in sixty cities. (Unfortunately, the survey did not include independent retailers.) On more than 80 percent of these items, Wal-Mart did
not have the lowest prices. Zenith then presented its findings in small focus
groups to 180 frequent Wal-Mart shoppers. "There was a sense of betrayal,
first at us and then at Wal-Mart," said Cowgill. "When someone positively
identifies with a store and you present information that contradicts that,
the defensive reaction is that [the presenter is] wrong and dishonest."
Cowgill and his team urged participants to verify the findings themselves.
Most came to accept the data, and subsequent surveys revealed that these
shoppers cut by more than half the number of shopping trips they took to
Wal-Mart each month. Cowgill believes that exposing Wal-Mart's pricing
tactics is critical to preventing the company from completely dominating
the retail sector.[10]

Most consumers do not regularly shop around and compare prices. (Those who do are known in the industry as "cherry pickers," and they account for only 18 percent of households, according to one study.) "The research is very consistent about the low levels of consumer search," said Donald Lichtenstein, a marketing professor at the University of Colorado. "The perception that a store has lower prices is such a powerful advantage. If consumers think that Wal-Mart has the lowest prices, they go there first and they tend to go ahead and buy and not do further searching." People tend to be particularly routine about grocery shopping; they pick the store that offers good value and go there week in and week out. This is one of the reasons Wal-Mart has been so keen to add grocery departments to its stores: shoppers picking up a bag of low-margin groceries might also buy an appliance, not realizing that another retailer may offer a better deal.[11]

"Think big-box stores and bargains are synonymous? Think again," declared a report on buying appliances in the September 2005 issue of *Consumer Reports.* "None of the major retailers outpriced the independents for ranges, refrigerators, and other large appliances, and only two were clear winners for small ones such as grills and vacuums. What's more, readers found Wal-Mart no cheaper than other stores overall, despite its low-price slogan." The report compared prices, service, selection, product quality, and checkout ease at independent appliance dealers, Best Buy, Costco, Home Depot, Lowe's, Sears, Target, and Wal-Mart. Overall, the local stores outscored their big competitors by a significant margin. Not only were they price-competitive—only Costco and Target beat them on price for small appliances and none of the chains did better on large appliances—but they offered a broader selection and better service. "Seventy-five percent of small-appliance buyers thought independent-store staffers were pleasant, informed, or helpful; five percent or fewer felt that way about Costco, Target, or Wal-Mart workers," noted *Consumer Reports.* Wal-Mart ranked the lowest in terms of quality and selection; 40 percent of those who bought appliances at the chain had to settle for a different brand than they had planned to buy.[12]

This raises yet another challenge in trying to determine how much big-box retailers save consumers: differences in product quality. While some products are uniform across stores, others are not. Under pressure from the chains to reduce costs, some manufacturers have redesigned their products with lower-quality components or developed special lines to sell exclusively at big-box stores, as Levi's has done with its Signature line of jeans, which are not nearly as sturdy as its traditional line. Further muddying the waters, many retailers now manufacture their own products; both Best Buy and Wal-Mart, for example, produce television sets and other consumer electronics. "That's one of the biggest advantages Wal-Mart has: the vendors have bent over backwards to do what Wal-Mart wants," said Stone. "They may ask for a different switch, one that's cheaper, or a different belt on a vacuum cleaner. The manufacturer will give it a new model number. It can't be compared with what anybody else has. But in the eyes of most people, it would look like the same product."[13]

John Reny, who comanages his family's chain of thirteen small department stores in rural Maine towns, recalled the day he first learned that suppliers were not always providing his stores and Wal-Mart with identical products. A salesman from Intercraft frames had come by to go over orders for the coming year and Reny asked him how Wal-Mart had the same eight-by-ten-inch frame for a lower price. "He said, 'John, they're not the same frames. They want that frame at this price, so we had to come up with a way to do it. The glass is thinner and the molding around the edge is not the same,'" recalled Reny. "Unless you put them side by side, you would never notice." Quality differences obviously complicate price comparisons: if you pay 25 percent less for something, but it lasts half as long, then you have paid more, not less, for it.[14]

Whether this practice is widespread or not is unclear. Rick Karp, who owns Cole's Hardware in San Francisco and serves on the board of the Ace cooperative, does not believe such stealth product variations are common in the hardware sector. What has happened, he said, is that the chains have sought out cheaper factories overseas, other retailers have followed suit to keep their prices in line, and the market has been left with predominately lower-end products. Indeed, the lifespan of many products has been falling. We discard clothing at a much faster rate than ever before. Between 1979 and 1999, the average lifespan for appliances, including electric shavers, vacuum cleaners, toasters, irons, blenders, clothes washers, and dishwashers, dropped 10 to 50 percent, according to data supplied by *Appliance Magazine*. These figures do not necessarily reflect durability; they indicate how long the owner kept the product before discarding it for any reason, including nothing more than the desire to buy a new one. Still, one way or another, we are becoming more of a throwaway society and that itself has a hidden cost: the amount of trash generated by Americans has doubled since the mid-1980s.[15]

Yet another complicating factor is that chains charge different prices at different outlets depending on the level of local competition. Recognizing the power of first impressions, many offer especially low prices when they first enter an area, only to raise them as competitors disappear and consumers become accustomed to shopping at the big box. There is no commonly agreed upon term for this in the United States, but British antitrust authorities have dubbed the practice "price flexing," and documented its use among several superstore chains. Known price flexers in the United States include Target, Wal-Mart, Rite Aid, CVS, and Staples. While consumers expect that higher labor and real estate costs in some regions will be reflected in a store's prices, most are unaware of the degree to which chains vary prices within the same region based on their degree of market dominance. Indeed, price flexing seems to violate the tacit promise of "always low prices" that big-box retailers have made to consumers.[16]

One study in Nebraska compared the cost of a basket of fifty-four grocery items at eleven Wal-Mart supercenters across the state and found the total varied by more than 13 percent. At the high end were supercenters in McCook ($79.37), North Platte ($78.89), and Beatrice ($76.15). At the low end were those in Omaha ($70.00) and Bellevue ($72.19). No obvious differences in operating costs can explain the divergence. Indeed, North Platte is home to a Wal-Mart distribution center, so its shipping costs should be minimal. The study instead suggested that the difference may reflect the decline of competing retailers in the high-priced communities. "The supercenter in Beatrice is well on the way to becoming the sole retail provider in that area," the study noted.[17]

Other evidence comes from surveys of prescription drug prices conducted by government agencies and consumer groups. The Maine Department of Human Services, for example, checked the cost of fifteen frequently prescribed drugs at ninety-one pharmacies across the state in 2003 and found wide differences in the prices charged by outlets of the same chain. The highest-priced Rite Aid was 15 percent more expensive than the lowest, while prices at different Wal-Mart outlets varied by 16 percent. The survey found that the ten lowest-priced pharmacies in the state were all locally owned and beat Wal-Mart's prices by an average of 13 percent and Rite Aid's by 14 percent. (Like hardware stores, most local pharmacies belong to regional buying groups.) Similar price surveys conducted in seven major metropolitan areas in 2004 by *Consumers' Checkbook* likewise found that many chains were charging widely different prices within the same metro.

Moreover, the magazine discovered that, "in most areas the mom-and-pop independent stores were, on average, less expensive than the big chains." Another study by the Sutherland Institute found that drug prices varied by 7 percent at Wal-Mart stores in Utah. The state's independent pharmacies were less expensive on average than Albertson's supermarkets, about the same as Wal-Mart and Walgreen's, and somewhat more expensive than Costco.[18]

One of the more striking examples of chains using discounts to build market share, only to raise prices later, occurred in the book industry. As Barnes & Noble and Borders multiplied across the country during the 1990s, the two chains offered substantial discounts on most books. Barnes & Noble discounted almost all hardcovers by 20 percent and half of its trade paperbacks by 10 percent. In 1999—at the end of a decade that saw nearly three thousand independent bookstores close and Barnes & Noble and Borders rise to dominate the industry—the two chains quietly put an end to most of their discounts. Today, they discount a select list of about twenty of their own "bestsellers"—these are self-selected, not *New York Times* bestsellers—and a handful of other books. "It is one of the most successful marketing tricks that has ever been pulled on the American consumer," said Oren Teicher, chief operating officer of the American Booksellers Association. "Lots of consumers will tell you that every book sold at the chains is discounted. That hasn't been true for years."[19]

Wal-Mart has pursued a similar strategy as it has expanded into new categories. In the 1980s, when Wal-Mart was opening superstores in small towns across the heartland, its primary competitors were drugstores and five-and-dime variety stores. To take their business, Wal-Mart sold up to one-third of the products in its health and beauty department at a loss, according to evidence presented in a court case brought by independent pharmacists in Arkansas, who accused the chain of violating antitrust laws. In a 4–3 vote, the Arkansas Supreme Court ruled that Wal-Mart's below-cost pricing tactics were legal. The company has since gone on to use the same strategy to capture a dominant position in other product categories. In 2003, for example, it sold many of the items in its toy department below cost, sending Toys "R" Us and other toy retailers into a tailspin. While Wal-Mart can recoup these losses in other departments, locally owned retailers and chains that specialize in one product category do not have that option.[20]

Wal-Mart's most significant category expansion of late has been its move into groceries. More than half of its outlets now feature full grocery departments, and the chain has managed to seize one-fifth of U.S. grocery spending in little more than a decade. Several studies have found that Wal-Mart's food prices are substantially lower. A study coauthored by Jerry Hausman of MIT and Ephraim Leibtag of the U.S. Department of Agriculture found that Wal-Mart "offers many identical food items at an average price about 15%–25% lower than traditional supermarkets" and provides "a significant overall benefit to consumers." These studies show Wal-Mart at its low-priced best: when it's expanding into a new product category and is working aggressively to win over shoppers.[21]

The unanswered question is what will happen to Wal-Mart's grocery prices over time. Hausman and Leibtag offered a troubling clue. They noted that Wal-Mart has been able to undercut prices at other supermarket chains to such a large degree in part because grocery prices became inflated in the 1990s. Between 1991 and 2001, consumer prices rose by 28 percent, while the producer price index for groceries, which approximates the wholesale price paid by supermarkets, increased by only 14 percent. The culprit was likely the massive wave of mergers that occurred during the 1990s, as a few supermarket chains came to dominate the industry. Consumers ended up paying more for food, while operating profit margins for the top chains, including Kroger and Safeway, increased substantially. But rather than diversifying the market, we are now digging ourselves in deeper. Wal-Mart's entry into the grocery business has only fueled more consolidation as independents and smaller chains fold and larger supermarket companies merge in an effort to compete against the world's largest corporation. In the Dallas–Fort Worth metro, where Wal-Mart has more than one hundred stores, just four chains now capture 71 percent of grocery spending.[22]

Some argue that the megachains will offer sufficient competition to one another to protect consumers from exorbitant prices—that Target and Costco will keep Wal-Mart honest and Lowe's will provide a check on Home Depot. Perhaps. But our experience with other industries that were dominated for a time by just three or four companies—remember having just three television stations and three big auto makers—is not reassuring. Few would describe these periods as providing anything but exceptionally low levels of product innovation and poor overall value. Nor would it be easy for a new entrant to challenge the dominant chains, particularly if the wholesale and distribution network that currently supports independent retailers were to collapse—and there is nothing to prevent Wal-Mart from temporarily dropping its prices to fend off a new competitor.

So where does all of this leave the question of chain store prices? It's hard to imagine that mega-retailers, especially Wal-Mart, given its size and distribution efficiencies, are not capable of delivering both profits and some level of consumer savings. But those savings are probably more modest than many shoppers imagine, because of the sophisticated pricing strategies these companies employ and differences in product quality. We know that the big boxes are not always the low-price leaders and that, thanks in part to buying cooperatives, independents are more competitive in some categories (pharmacy, appliances, books, video, hardware) than many might assume.

Most importantly, it is worth keeping in mind a basic tenet of market economics: consumers are best served when there are many businesses vigorously vying for their patronage. While the chains often say they bring more competition to local markets, in fact their growth has substantially reduced competition in most retail categories. There are already troubling signs that this consolidation could harm consumers over the long term.

SIX

MONOPOLIZED CONSUMERS

IN THE SUMMER OF 2005, the *Arkansas Democrat-Gazette* reported that Wal-Mart, which sells nearly 1 billion pounds of beef a year, had ordered suppliers to start breeding smaller cows that would yield smaller rib eyes. Had Wal-Mart, with its vast data systems tracking shoppers from coast to coast, detected a shift in consumer tastes? Had Americans suddenly lost their passion for big steaks? No, the article explained, the move had nothing to do with consumers. Wal-Mart had calculated, based on the size of its meat cases, that if it could fit four, rather than three, steaks into a package, it could substantially increase its revenue. "With cattle that big, we only get three rib-eyes in a tray. If we could get another steak in, the tray would have been [priced] $2 more," said the company's meat buyer, Ken Stettmeier.[1]

As Wal-Mart's shrinking steaks make clear, the chains' allegiance is not to shoppers, but to stockholders. Meeting consumer needs is incidental to the primary enterprise, hitting growth and profit projections. Given this underlying dynamic, it's alarming that we have turned over so much of this sector of our economy, upon which we depend in a very immediate and day-to-day way, to a handful of corporations. Contrary to their rhetoric, mega-retailers have dramatically reduced consumer choice. The pressure they place on manufacturers to lower costs has sharply curtailed investment in product research and development. Centralized buying by a handful of gatekeepers has further narrowed the range of products that reach consumers, a fact camouflaged by the apparent abundance on big-box shelves. In a consumer environment largely defined by the way corporate retailers operate, the added value provided by independent businesses—many of which possess a degree of expertise and passion for what they sell unmatched by the chains—is commonly overlooked.

ILLUSORY CORNUCOPIA

One of the paradoxes of big-box retail is that superstores provide a greater selection while at the same time actually reducing the range of products available. Take bookstores. For people who love to read, one of the pleasures of shopping at Barnes & Noble or Borders is the sheer number of books they carry. Each of their superstores stocks about one hundred thousand titles in twenty-five thousand square feet of selling space. While some independent bookstores rival or even exceed these numbers—Tattered Cover in Denver and Powell's in Portland, Oregon, for example—most local stores are smaller and have only twenty thousand to forty thousand books on hand (though they can order virtually anything). One might suppose, then, that the growth of the chains has been a boon to authors and publishers, vastly expanding the amount of shelf space devoted to selling books and putting more titles within reach of more consumers.

But, curiously, the opposite has occurred. Sales of books have not increased since the advent of the superstores. Overall consumer spending on books has remained stagnant and, more troubling, a larger share of that spending now flows to a handful of bestsellers at the expense of the tens of thousands of other titles released each year. "The most persuasive explanation for this is the runaway growth of the chains," contended David D. Kirkpatrick, who produced a report on the decline of "midlist" books for the Authors Guild in 2000 and then took a job covering the book industry for the *New York Times*. Midlist books include literary fiction and serious nonfiction titles that are not earmarked by publishers as likely bestsellers. They make up a significant portion of the new titles released each year and, while some do become surprise hits, publishers generally expect that they will post modest sales of perhaps five thousand to ten thousand copies.[2]

Midlist books are suffering, Kirkpatrick found, not because their authors cannot get them into print. Indeed, publishers are turning out more titles than ever before. (Because author advances for midlist books are small, they can be profitable even with low sales.) But midlist books are losing readers. The reason, Kirkpatrick's report concluded, is that "chain-store merchandising policies help turn consumers' attention away from midlist titles and toward an elite of books that are backed by heavy marketing budgets." Sales patterns at the two chains, according to Kirkpatrick, reveal that "most titles they stock serve essentially as wallpaper." Their presence on the shelves creates a rich ambiance that appeals to readers, but most people who enter a superstore are drawn to the books stacked on the tables in the center aisle or those displayed face out on the end of each row of shelves. Watch people entering a Borders or Barnes & Noble and even those intending to browse the biography or science sections usually stop at the center-aisle tables. This narrowing of the customer's attention also tends to focus more of their spending on those featured books.[3]

Many shoppers undoubtedly assume that the books selected for these tables—and each of the two chains display almost identical sets of titles at every one of their outlets nationwide—are chosen for no other reason than someone at corporate headquarters thought they were worthwhile. In fact most of these books have landed at the front of the store in part because their publishers paid Borders and Barnes & Noble to put them there. The two chains have designated the space at the front of the stores as high-rent real estate. Although both have some promotional spots that run as low as fifteen hundred to three thousand dollars, securing two or three weeks of "power-aisle placement" for a new title at one of the chains costs a publisher from ten thousand to twenty thousand dollars, depending on the time of year. (Amazon.com also charges publishers for prominently displaying books on its site.) Publishers are willing to spend this much only on titles they think will sell in large numbers. Those by authors that are already well known are much safer bets, while such spending is out of the question for most new authors and other midlist books. The chains' merchandising policies thereby further concentrate resources and attention on big-name authors and books that are already positioned to do well—while new novelists and important works of nonfiction that need the most help getting noticed are left with a diminished marketing budget and banished to the back shelves. Kirkpatrick described this as a "reverse Robin Hood effect."[4]

Fortunately, writers still have another avenue for reaching readers: locally owned bookstores. "Virtually every time a midlist book succeeds," Kirkpatrick reported, "its editor credits independent bookstores with having gotten it going and kept it alive." Without independent bookstores, many wonderful and beloved books would have gone unnoticed and unread, quietly in and out of print. Like the chains, local bookstores draw their customers' attention to particular books featured at front tables or along walls of "staff picks." Determined to level the playing field financially, some independents also now apply for "co-op" money—the funds that publishers offer for prominently featuring a title. Because the fees flowing to the chains gave them an unfair advantage—effectively boosting their revenue at the expense of competing bookstores—the American Booksellers Association, which represents the independents, demanded (and, indeed, U.S. antitrust law requires) that publishers make these funds available to all retailers in proportion to their contribution to publicizing a particular book. Today, an independent bookstore might be eligible for fifty dollars in co-op fees for featuring a book in its newsletter. But the decisions about which books to display prominently in the store are not centralized in the hands of a few buyers as they are with respect to the chains. Thousands of local bookstore owners and their employees make their own choices about what books to feature. Independents also commonly feature books that are not backed by publisher money. As a result, even though independent bookstores are generally smaller than their big competitors, collectively they stock—and, more importantly, promote—a vastly wider array of books than Barnes & Noble and Borders.

"We sell books we like and we try to match books to people," explained Betsy Burton, who opened The King's English bookstore in Salt Lake City in 1977. It is one of just two general independent bookstores left in the region, down from a high of eleven. As Borders and Barnes & Noble multiplied across Salt Lake, "there was a ten-year period when we struggled with whether we should close our doors," she said. "Staying open was an act of supreme stubbornness." Burton and her staff select books for the store first by reading the initial galleys sent by publishers. Some get tossed aside, others they like and decide to carry, and still others they love and opt to feature prominently in the store and in their newsletter. "We all do this together," she said. "There are two things that are crucial to our hiring. One is that they know a lot about books and the other is that they are very good with people." In addition to promoting books in the store and in the newsletter, The King's English introduces writers to readers by hosting author events, more than one hundred each year. "We do a lot of first-time authors. This gives them a chance at an audience and some media attention," said Burton, explaining that the staff works the local media on behalf of visiting authors and routinely turns out large crowds for readings. "We put our hearts into these things. We don't just strand some author at a table in the middle of the store."[5]

Even with independents eligible for co-op dollars from publishers, the playing field remains far from level, according to the ABA's Oren Teicher. "The publishers have created these very convoluted rules and regulations for co-op dollars," he said, explaining that the paperwork can be arduous for relatively small sums. "The system is devised, given the time and effort involved, so that you have to have a certain scale to make it worthwhile. The independents generally won't go after it. The chains will, because in their world it adds up to a lot of money. It's one of the inequities in our business." Those independents that do apply for co-op fees—and The King's English is one—insist that their process is the reverse of the chains: they pick books first and then ask the publishers for support. "Whether we get it or not has no effect on whether we feature the book," said Burton.[6]

"It's very clear to me that I owe my career as a writer to independent booksellers," said novelist Barbara Kingsolver. "I saw it happening when my first book came out. My local bookseller and, as it turns out, other independent booksellers around the country, were pressing this book into their customers' hands. It was so heartening to have these advocates . . . at a time when no corporate entity really cared." Today, Barnes & Noble and Borders care a great deal: Kingsolver's new books are often among those piled high at the front of the superstores. But she doubts she would have gotten to this point had it not been for independent booksellers, and she believes the growth of the chains in the years since her first book, *The Bean Trees,* was published in 1992, has made it even harder for today's first-time authors. "I don't have statistics, but I have a strong hunch based on being in this business for a long time and talking to lots of people, especially publishers, who will tell you it's harder to take a risk on an unknown author or an edgy book today," Kingsolver said. "Publishers now have to put all of their resources into a few items. They can't afford to lose money on things they think no one is going to hear about." Independent booksellers know their customers and they pay attention to what's important at the local level, Kingsolver said. "Are you ready to let someone far away make these decisions about what books will appear on your horizon?" she asked. "That seems so un-American to me."[7]

Other authors tell similar stories of their first books. Richard Howorth, who owns Square Books in Oxford, Mississippi, still remembers getting a call in 1989 from a young writer named John Grisham, whose first book, *A Time to Kill,* had just been released by an obscure publisher and was not doing well. Send us copies, Howorth advised, and contact other independent bookstores. Grisham hit the road in his station wagon, stopping at local bookstores throughout the South. "He didn't really break out until his second book, but perhaps we gave him enough encouragement to write that second book," said Howorth. Today, Grisham limits his signing appearances to Square Books and four other independent bookstores that supported that first book. For every superstar like John Grisham or Barbara Kingsolver, there are dozens of lesser-known authors who have managed to produce modestly successful, and perhaps important, books and make a living as writers thanks to support from independent bookstores.[8]

"Amid all the books that are published, they find the gems that would otherwise go unnoticed," said Karen Torres, vice president and director of marketing at Time Warner Book Group. "Independent booksellers have a special talent and a special passion that's unique. It's connecting to readers—something that you can't put dollars to." Craig Popelars of Algonquin Books concurred: "When you are bringing in a strong debut novel that you know has potential, one of the first things on your marketing plan is getting independent booksellers to read it." Independent stores enable a book to succeed, he said, without "buying its way into a consumer's mind." Recent Algonquin titles that did well largely because of support from independents include *Candy Freak: A Journey through the Chocolate Underbelly of America* by Steve Almond and the novel *The Last Girls* by Lee Smith. A small number of stores can sometimes get a new book rolling. Popelars sent Bob Gray at Northshire Books in Manchester, Vermont, a copy of *Ursula, Under* by Ingrid Hill. "He read it and fell in love with it. They sold close to five hundred copies of that book," said Popelars. News of a book often spreads from one bookstore owner to another, propelling a title to nationwide success first at the independents and then at the chains. "I think Borders, Barnes & Noble, Amazon—they all benefit from the enthusiasm for a book that is created in the independent community," said Popelars.[9]

He and other publishing executives interviewed for this book were quick to emphasize that the book buyers at Borders and Barnes & Noble are passionate about books and do a good job of supporting and selling the titles they feature. While most of the books the two chains display prominently are backed by publisher dollars, that's not true in every case. "Every once in a while you get a position because the buyer loves the book," said Popelars. With hundreds of outlets, that's a huge break for an author.[10]

Still, consolidation has made it harder for most new writers to succeed. "There are fewer gatekeepers, fewer entries into the market. If the main fiction buyer at Barnes & Noble is not interested in your book, that can have a huge impact on your sales," said Paul Aiken, director of the Authors Guild. "When there were more independents, there were lots of individual choices being made about what books to buy." Aiken noted that this is particularly important for fiction. While there are other ways readers might learn about a nonfiction book—it could be mentioned in a news story on the topic, for instance—that's not the case with fiction. "The best way for a fiction writer to be discovered, barring a drop-dead review in the *New York Times*—and even that may not be worth as much—is word of mouth and independent booksellers," said Aiken. One top publishing house executive remarked that he did not concur with the findings of Kirkpatrick's report when it came out in 2000, but does now. "I've watched it come true," he said. "I always felt that a really great book would find its audience. But, for the first time in my twenty-five years in this business, I despair about literary fiction. It's really tough."[11]

Part of the problem is that books are now expected to "break out" much like Hollywood movies during opening weekend. Given the high cost of store placement and the advertising that typically goes along with it, most books are given only a short window to demonstrate their potential. Yet it can take months for a novel to catch the attention of readers, spread by word of mouth to their friends, and begin to sell. Such patient nurturing of a book occurs only at the independents. "Surprise blockbusters such as *Cold Mountain, Angela's Ashes, A Civil Action,* or *The Perfect Storm* did not have any significant momentum until more than three months after publication date, according to their editors," noted Kirkpatrick. "Without the publishers' long-term support and a steady building of sales through the independents, the chains would have returned most copies, and banished the ones they kept to back aisles." More recent examples of this phenomenon include Khaled Hosseini's *Kite Runner,* which finally began to sell in large numbers at the chains and hit the *New York Times* bestseller list after months of gathering speed at locally owned stores like Book Passage in Corte Madera, California, where co-owner Elaine Petrocelli had been advising her customers to read it, and the Pulitzer Prize–winning *The Known World* by Edward P. Jones, which was originally championed by independents such as Washington, D.C.'s, Politics & Prose.[12]

"Little by little, they get picked up," explained Chuck Robinson, owner of Village Books in Bellingham, Washington. "There's a saying among publishers that independents sell the first printing of a book and the chains sell all the rest." Village Books spans ten thousand square feet over three floors, stocks about seventy thousand titles, and does 250 author events every year. "Good sellers for us often start with someone on our staff getting excited about the book," said Robinson. "Right now, in our store, we have a 'picks' shelf for each staff member—all thirty of us—and on the main floor there's a wall of books with written recommendations from our staff." Allowing the staff free rein to decide what books to promote is fairly common among independent bookstores and it helps ensure that the books featured reflect a range of interests as diverse as the store's customers. "People working on the floor make decisions about where books are placed," said Howorth of Square Books. "We give them the authority to run with their ideas. That's what creates this inspiration that expands the market. It's about one reader connecting to another reader."[13]

Although the chains allow for some variation in what their stores stock, their centralized purchasing has made it much more difficult for publishers to succeed with books that have a local or regional appeal. "Six of our top ten books two Christmas seasons ago were by local people," recalled Neal Coonerty of Bookshop Santa Cruz, the independent that survived the 1989 earthquake. "There's a guy here who distributes them. He approached [the staff of the local] Borders about carrying them, but their response was that they don't take anything except what was purchased through corporate headquarters." After seeing the success Bookshop Santa Cruz had with these titles, the Borders outlet started stocking them too. But Coonerty wonders what would become of locally produced books in a world without independents to give them a chance.[14]

He also worries about the influence that Borders and Barnes & Noble have over what gets published in the first place. Although Kirkpatrick believes that concerns about the chains dictating what publishers decide to print are "overblown," Coonerty is not convinced. He pointed to Azar Nafisi's *Reading Lolita in Tehran,* which became a bestseller. "When Random House first took that around, one of the major chains took zero on it [i.e., declined to order any copies]," he said. "Random House went ahead and published it, because of the interest they had from other booksellers. The thing we don't know is how many books are killed before they make it into print." Indeed, there were a number of well-documented incidents in the late 1990s in which lukewarm receptions from buyers at the chains led publishers to drop books that they had planned to publish.[15] (Publishers may also self-censor books they believe the chains would dislike. More than one publisher rejected this book on those grounds. "I thought this was an excellent proposal," one editor replied by e-mail. "Genuinely fascinating, and there was interest in the meeting but the problem is the obvious one: the exposure of Barnes & Noble and Border [*sic*]. Our publisher shut it down immediately—didn't want to bite the hand that feeds it, etc. I hope you're able to find someone willing to tough this out; as I say, it seems like a fine and important book.")

Local buying also better matches an independent store's selections to the interests of the community. Malaprop's Bookstore in Asheville, North Carolina, is a good example of this, according to Algonquin's Popelars. "Her shelves are dictated by her community's interest," he said of owner Emoke B'Racz. "There are larger sections that speak to segments of the community, like outdoors, backpacking, and organic farming. When Emoke buys books, she is representing her customer base." Popelars noted that independents often take the lead in promoting new authors from their own regions. He pointed to *The Highest Tide,* a debut novel by Olympia, Washington, native Jim Lynch. Booksellers in the Pacific Northwest "carried that book on their shoulders," he said. "They just felt, we're the ones that have a responsibility for introducing this writer."[16]

FINDING AN AUDIENCE

Independents play much the same role in the music industry as they do in publishing. As with books, the challenge is not so much getting your music recorded and reproduced—today's technology has put that within reach even for those who do not get signed by a record label. "The challenge becomes how do you let the fans know about it. That's where the independent store excels," said John Kunz, who worked at a record store part-time while attending the University of Texas, and in 1983 started his own store in Austin. Waterloo Records & Video has since become a major landmark on the nation's music landscape, with seventy-five employees and an in-store stock of about fifty thousand albums. The store's staff, Kunz said, is crucial to introducing people to new artists. "We've got our experts in just about every genre there is and they've got people coming in to talk to them looking for advice," he said. "That's a strength to any indie music store: there's a fan working in the store who is going to do everything they can to tell people about the album." Waterloo allows local musicians to sell their albums, many locally recorded and reproduced, on consignment in the store. "We do a couple hundred thousand dollars worth of consignment each year," Kunz said. One of the store's biggest all-time sellers is Bob Schneider's *Lonelyland.* Waterloo has moved more than twenty thousand copies, the first ten thousand of which were sold on consignment. "[Schneider] got signed based on the success here to Universal Records," said Kunz.[17]

Waterloo also hosts about five hundred in-store concerts and CD-release parties every year, often using its connections to local radio stations to get the album airtime as well. "It's a chance to really shine a light on a band," explained Kunz. He recalled inviting Norah Jones to play in the store when her first album, *Come Away with Me,* was released in February 2002. At the time, few had heard of her. "It was the largest audience she ever performed before at that point," he said. As with bookstores, news of an artist often spreads from one independent store owner to another. "Those early smoke signals are legendary in the industry," Kunz explained.[18]

More than thirteen hundred record stores, most independently owned, have closed in the last few years. The casualties include long-standing stores like Repo Records in Charlotte and In Your Ear in Providence. By 2005 the share of the market captured by independents had fallen to just 8 percent. Music specialty chains, like Tower Records, which filed for bankruptcy in 2004, are likewise shrinking. Online merchants and other nontraditional channels have picked up some of the market, accounting for just under 8 percent of sales. But by far the biggest gains have been posted by mass merchandisers, such as Wal-Mart, Target, and Best Buy, which climbed from less than 14 percent of album sales in 1995 to more than 50 percent ten years later. Wal-Mart is now the largest seller of CDs on the planet.[19]

Many in the industry believe this shift is devastating music by curtailing the cultivation of diverse sounds and the development of new artists. "Of those three thousand Wal-Marts, how many would put someone in their music department until they had a name people were looking for?" Kunz asked. "Music is a life-affirming force. I don't think a few gatekeepers at a few chains trying to satisfy a national directive and their stockholders can fully deliver on all of music's possibilities." While independent music stores average roughly thirty-five thousand albums in stock (though there's quite a range from one to another), according to Don VanCleave, president of the Coalition of Independent Music Stores, the mass merchandisers carry fewer than five thousand chart toppers.[20]

Wal-Mart has refused to stock CDs with parental guidance stickers or songs that deal with abortion, homosexuality, its own business practices, or other topics that the company deems objectionable. In order to have their albums in Wal-Mart's stores, many artists, including Willie Nelson,

Nirvana, and John Mellencamp, have had to alter their cover art or song lyrics, or issue a second, sanitized version of the CD. (Wal-Mart polices the content of other products too, including books, movies, and magazines. Nor is it the only chain to do so. Blockbuster insists on sanitized versions of movies deemed objectionable and does not stock those rated NC-17 or those that are unrated, a category that includes many foreign films.) Such censorship by one retailer would not be a big deal except for the fact that Wal-Mart is the only purveyor of music in a growing number of communities.[21]

Best Buy, Circuit City, Wal-Mart, and Target not only reduce music to a commodity no different from toothpaste, but they use albums as loss leaders, hoping that someone who comes in for the latest Keith Urban CD will also buy a DVD player or a refrigerator. "It's frustrating to see something we have to pay eleven fifty or twelve dollars for advertised below ten dollars," said Kunz. While the mass merchandisers can make up the losses in other departments, stores that sell only music lack this option.[22]

More ominously, the chains are increasingly using their market power to cut exclusive deals with record labels. R & B star Usher's new three-CD set was available only at Best Buy for the first four months following its 2005 release. The Rolling Stones and Elton John have cut similar deals with the chain. For several months, Target was the only place fans could find a new CD from Rob Thomas, the lead singer of Matchbox Twenty, or a special edition of a Sara Evans album that contained four bonus tracks. Bob Dylan and Alanis Morissette sold recent releases exclusively at Starbucks for several months. Garth Brooks cut a deal to make his entire catalog, past and future, available only through Wal-Mart. Even longtime establishment critics Public Enemy, whose front man Chuck D has been a strong advocate of independent record labels, forced fans to patronize Best Buy if they wanted a copy of New Whirl Odor during its first month on the market.[23]

"It's very shortsighted on the part of the manufacturers," contended Ed Christman, senior editor covering retail for Billboard. The record labels are harming the retail segment that they rely on to help them develop new talent and the next generation of megahits, he said. The mass merchandisers cannot fulfill this role. Moreover, Christman said, the impulse purchases of consumers who go to an independent store for a new album are likely to be other CDs; at Target, those impulse buys might be drinking glasses or throw rugs. Some executives see the pitfalls of steering consumers to the mass retailers, he said, but they cannot help themselves when offered the chance to harness the advertising and merchandising muscle of one of the chains to pump up sales of a particular album. Independents have tried to fight back by temporarily pulling albums by the artist or the label from their racks. "We managed to raise our voices against it and stick our finger in that hole in the dike and hold it back for a while, but it's increasing," said Waterloo's Kunz. He believes exclusives are more about the chains trying to grab market share from one another, but in the process, "we get hit by a lot of the shrapnel." It's particularly frustrating with bands like U2, he said, which rose to stardom with lots of help from independent music stores and then became one of the first groups to cut an exclusive deal with Best Buy.[24]

Although chain store executives often talk about bringing more competition and choice to consumers, in fact the chains' rise to market dominance has reduced consumers' choices, both in terms of the range of products found on store shelves and the shrinking number of retailers competing in each category. Exclusive control of the sale of a particular product represents an extreme manifestation of this narrowing of choice, and is on the rise not only in the music industry, but also with other goods, including, alarmingly, books and movies. Barnes & Noble is publishing a growing number of its own books, including both classics that are in the public domain and new works that the chain has acquired from current authors. "They have made a strategic decision that to be competitive and to get their margins up, they have to produce their own product," said the ABA's Oren Teicher. "One of the nightmares in this business is that authors will get branded by particular chains."[25]

Exclusive access to certain new releases has also been cropping up in the video-rental business. Netflix, the fast-growing online mail-order rental company, has been cutting deals to gain sole rights to rent films for up to ninety days after their release. In 2005, for instance, director Hal Hartley, whose films include *Henry Fool*, released his new movie, *The Girl from Monday*, exclusively through Netflix. "This is one of America's preeminent independent filmmakers," said Tod Herskovitz, who owns Box Office Video, a neighborhood video store in St. Paul, Minnesota. "It's painful to think that you spent fifteen years collecting his filmography at your store and putting his films in your customers' hands, and now he's going to deny you access to his latest film." Not only are filmmakers and studios supporting Netflix, but PBS has also been giving the Web retailer ninety days of sole access to a growing number of new documentaries, including the Academy Award–nominated *Daughter from Danang*.[26]

That's particularly frustrating to Herskovitz, who has long been a strong advocate of documentary films. He not only stocks hundreds of them, but has devoted the best real estate in his store to documentaries. Located in a nineteenth-century brick building on St. Paul's Selby Avenue, Box Office Video is less than half the size of a typical Blockbuster or Hollywood Video outlet, but it stocks more than twice as many films—about fifteen thousand titles, compared to the seven thousand carried by the average Blockbuster. Rather than burying the documentary section at the back, Herskovitz, who coaches high school soccer and augments his already extensive knowledge of film by watching half a dozen new movies a week, shelved documentaries opposite the front door, so they are the first films people see when they walk in. He and his staff spend time talking with customers about what they like and regularly make recommendations, often suggesting films that customers might not have heard of. "Someone comes and they don't know what to rent, so you put three or four titles in their hands. They go home with something they never would have thought of," Herskovitz explained.[27]

He believes that Blockbuster and Hollywood Video, which capture more than half of all rentals nationally, have steered customers more and more toward big-budget Hollywood movies, at the expense of a broad range of other films. It's not only what they choose to stock, but their basic merchandising strategy: the chains will carry dozens of copies of a major Hollywood release, no matter how poor the movie, but will have only one or two copies of a well-done small-budget or independent film. This affects people's perception of the relative value of movies. "Customers are subconsciously being told that the movie [with only one or two copies] isn't really worth their while," Herskovitz said. Both chains do carry some independent films, but they typically keep them on their shelves for only a few months before moving them out, and they also routinely cull older films that have stopped renting as frequently. There's a brutal logic to this, in terms of the profits per square inch of shelf space, but independent video store owners argue it's not good for consumers or film in general, because the chains end up with major holes in their libraries. "I have Blockbuster customers coming in here for *The Color Purple*," said Herskovitz. Although they seem grateful to find such films at Box Office Video, many still continue to rent the bulk of their movies from the Blockbuster outlet a mile away, not making the connection between their regular patronage and Herskovitz's ability to keep his business, with its broad library of films, afloat.[28]

THE LONG TAIL?

How have online retailers like Amazon.com and Netflix, which stock large numbers of titles, changed these dynamics? An idea that has caught fire in some circles is the notion of the "long tail." It refers to the basic demand curve governing many products, which starts high and then drops steeply once you move beyond the top sellers, petering out and flatlining across a large number of items (books, albums, or whatever) that sell in relatively small numbers. This last bit of the curve—all of the niche products that post modest sales—is the tail. The tail is only as long as the total number of titles sold by the store; hence online retailers can develop much longer tails than physical stores. *Wired* magazine editor in chief Chris Anderson argued in "The Long Tail," an article that appeared in the October 2004 issue, that Web retailers are helping to move our economy and culture away from a focus on hits and toward a broader range of products that appeal to much more varied interests.[29]

We have long suffered "the tyranny of lowest-common-denominator fare," Anderson wrote, because of both the physical limits of store shelf space and the underlying economics that make it more profitable for Barnes & Noble to heavily promote a few big books and for Blockbuster to decline a film that might only appeal to a handful of people in each local market and instead stock yet another copy of the latest big-budget action flick. Online retailers are free of these constraints; warehouse space is not nearly as expensive as store space, and because their customers are nationwide or even global, they can easily amass enough people with a particular niche interest to make it worthwhile to carry that album, book, or film.

While it's certainly true that the Web has enabled us to easily locate obscure goods, it's not at all clear that the giants of online retailing are achieving the sort of revolution in diversity that Anderson attributes to them. He cites a variety of statistics on how much of the revenue stream at online retailers comes from titles outside of those typically carried by physical stores. The trouble is, he lumps all physical stores together for these comparisons and treats the chains as representative, which has the effect of exaggerating his findings. "A fifth of Netflix rentals are outside of its top 3,000 titles," he wrote, referring to the number of movies he says the average Blockbuster stocks. Blockbuster officials assert that it's closer to 7,000, but either way, Blockbuster's anemic offerings are hardly a reasonable yardstick.[30]

Videoport, in Portland, Maine, stocks some forty thousand titles in its two thousand square feet of store space and derives a significant share of its revenue from those beyond the top three thousand. Videoport has deliberately opted not to have a section for new releases; as they come in, they are shelved by genre as a way of encouraging people to browse the library. Moreover, the store has been making its complete inventory available via mail rental to all of rural Maine for years. It's far from alone. Video Station in Boulder, Colorado, has a library of fifty-four thousand films, more than Netflix had at the time of this writing. When asked about how she selects which titles to carry, owner Sheri LaPres replied, "We order pretty much everything that comes out." She rarely culls titles from the library (although she admits to recently chucking *Regis Philbin: My Personal Workout*). For music, Anderson reported that Rhapsody, the online purveyor of digital music files, "had 28 percent of its sales outside of its top 55,000 tracks (roughly equal to the inventory of a typical Wal-Mart)." But Wal-Mart's five thousand CDs are just a small fraction of the albums found at independent record stores.[31]

The choiceless tyranny that Anderson describes is not, as he writes, long-standing, but rather a much more recent consequence of the corporate takeover of the cultural landscape. The economic constraints he highlights are true enough; the drive to maximize revenue per square foot does indeed lead Blockbuster and Wal-Mart not to devote space to anything but the top sellers. But independent retailers largely ignore these profit parameters, which may reflect badly on them as business owners—except in the one respect that arguably ought to matter most to consumers: many have a passion for books or film or music and, while they must pay attention to the bottom line, their passion often trumps profits when it comes to inventory decisions. ("If you love documentaries," Anderson wrote in "The Long Tail," "Blockbuster is not for you. Nor is any other video store—there are too many documentaries, and they sell too poorly to justify stocking more than a few dozen of them on physical shelves." He has clearly not visited Box Office Video or any of the hundreds of independent stores nationally that stock and rent large libraries of documentaries, often because the owner happens to be a fan.) This passion has a real value in the marketplace—certainly to creators and fans, but also to those who have a casual interest, as well as to the overall vitality of our culture and ultimately our democracy, which, after all, derives its sustenance from the free flow of ideas.

Another problem with the long tail argument is that the challenge for people who produce creative works is less about access to customers than it is about getting their attention. "I remain skeptical [of the long tail theory]," said David Kirkpatrick, who wrote the report on midlist books. "In my experience covering the book industry for the *New York Times,* the crucial ingredient is not the availability of a book; the crucial ingredient is getting public attention for a book. That game is not changed by Amazon." While Amazon.com does highlight certain titles via lists that are created by humans, these lists have the effect of steering users to a relatively small number of titles. Customers are directed deeper into the stacks through links that are created by computer algorithms ("Customers who bought this book also bought..."). These are at least partly sales-driven and customers are therefore not necessarily led off the beaten path. "When I go on Amazon to look at virtually any business book, they'll recommend [the international megahit] *Liar's Poker.* That's the counter long-tail effect," said Kirkpatrick.[32]

Fiction particularly can have a tough time finding its way in the world of Boolean searching and algorithms, but even in the case of nonfiction, independent booksellers often introduce their customers to books on topics they did not realize they had an interest in. "It's true that the online bookseller has a huge inventory of books, but to become informed about books you didn't know you even needed, you really need a person—someone who sees you often and who knows you and who can say, this is something you ought to look at. That's what you are giving up if you let your local bookstore close," said Barbara Kingsolver, who regularly orders titles from the local bookseller in the small southern farming town where she lives and is often able to pick them up just two days later. (Hundreds of local bookstores also offer their customers the option of ordering online through their own e-commerce sites, which have a database of some 2 million titles powered by Booksense.com. More on this in Chapter 9.) Plus, Kingsolver said, there is the joy of browsing the aisles and the community gathering space provided by the store. And when was the last time Amazon.com hosted an author event or a CD-release party in your town?[33]

There is no doubt that, for people who love movies and live in places that lack an independent video store, Netflix is a godsend, and downloading tracks of music or searching Amazon.com's sprawling Web site for books on an obscure subject provides an indisputable convenience. But can a few online mega-retailers nurture and sustain a truly diverse marketplace of books, film, music, and other works? This seems doubtful. The passion of thousands of independent owners making their own decisions about what to carry and promote adds up to so much more than a centralized system and a set of computer algoritl.ns could ever deliver. Nor does the issue of diversity end with the range of products sold. Other kinds of diversity are at stake, too: namely the diversity of the retail environment and the storefronts that animate our streets, as well as the diversity of ownership in our economy.

•

KNOWLEDGE AND EXPERTISE

David Rochefort knows most of the people who walk into his pharmacy by name. Sullivan Drugs has been operating on Main Street in the small northern New Hampshire town of Lancaster since 1856. Rochefort's father, Rich, a pharmacist, and his mother bought the business in 1972. Rochefort started working in the store as a teenager and then decided to train as a pharmacist. "I never looked at my dad as having a job—not in the sense of something that you have to get up and go to that you don't like," Rochefort explained. "He'd go to work and he'd love it. He'd come home and have a big smile on his face. When I was in high school, I realized that was a pretty good way to be." After college, Rochefort moved to Vermont and took a job with a chain pharmacy, but it turned out to be a far cry from his father's drugstore. On one of his first days on the job, his district manager reprimanded him for spending too much time with a customer who was looking for the right cough medicine for her husband. "They can read the boxes on their own," the manager told him. Rochefort suddenly realized he'd been hired not for his training as a health care provider, but because he had a license to dispense drugs. "It was a real eye-opener for a naive kid out of college," he said. "That was the beginning of the end for me at the chains."[34]

Rochefort eventually moved back home and began to take over his father's business. Now he can spend time with patients, talking not only about their prescriptions, but also about what they are taking over the counter and how their lifestyle choices might be affecting their health. Like a growing number of independent pharmacies, Sullivan Drugs has developed a compounding practice, which involves preparing medications by hand in customized dosages, forms, or combinations. "One of the problems with manufactured drugs is that it's one-size-fits-all," Rochefort explained.

"We had a woman, for example, who couldn't tolerate a particular blood pressure drug, but her doctor really wanted her on this medication. We were able to compound a smaller dosage." He has made pain medications that are absorbed through the skin for hospice patients who are unable to swallow, ultra-low-dosage forms for babies, and even special preparations to help ailing family pets.

Sullivan Drugs is not an anomaly. Most independent pharmacies provide a level of personal attention and health care that goes well beyond dispensing drugs, according to a yearlong study conducted by *Consumer Reports* in 2003. So superior were the independents to their competitors, the magazine's report opens by bluntly advising readers to abandon the chains and seek out one of the nation's twenty-five thousand locally owned pharmacies instead. On a variety of measures—from the knowledge of the pharmacist and the quality of the information provided to the speed with which prescriptions are filled—the independents outscored all other types of pharmacies (including chain drugstores, supermarkets, mass merchandisers, and mail-order suppliers) by "an eye-popping margin." The independents were far less likely to be out of a drug, according to the study, and, when they were, they were able to obtain it within a day 80 percent of the time, compared to 55 to 60 percent of the time for other pharmacies. "Chains typically made readers wait longer, were slower to fill orders, and provided less personal attention," *Consumer Reports* found. And most independents offered health care services not provided by other pharmacies, such as disease-management education, in-store screenings for high cholesterol and other conditions, and home delivery.[35]

But for Sullivan Drugs and many other local pharmacies, spending time with patients and providing additional health care services is becoming increasingly difficult. Drug manufacturers are charging more, even as insurance reimbursement rates drop, leaving a shrinking margin—often less than two dollars per prescription—for pharmacists, who must fill more prescriptions in less time in order to stay in business. Worse, a growing number of insurance plans, as well as large companies such as IBM and unions like the United Auto Workers, are mandating that employees use mail-order services for their prescriptions. Some plans flatly require it; others create a significant financial incentive to do so by charging the same co-pay for a thirty-day supply acquired from a retail pharmacy as for a ninety-day supply ordered by mail. "We've been really hit hard in the last year and half," said Rochefort, explaining that longtime customers keep stopping by to say that they can no longer use his pharmacy because their plans will not allow it.[36]

Mail order has expanded rapidly since 2000 and now accounts for 19 percent of the prescription market. Whether this represents a more efficient health care delivery system is the subject of fierce debate, with independent pharmacies arguing that the shift to mail order is bad for patients. They note that the top four pharmacy benefit managers (PBMs)—the companies that administer prescription drug benefits for HMOs—own their own mail-order companies and thus profit from pushing their clients to use mail order. These four companies, which capture 77 percent of the mail-order market, also receive kickbacks from drugmakers for filling prescriptions with brand-name drugs and, as a result, only about 30 percent of the drugs they dispense are cheaper generics, compared to 40 percent at retail pharmacies. Moreover, mail-order pharmacies do not provide the same counseling and other health care services that local pharmacists do, forcing patients to rely more heavily on doctors—a far more expensive option.[37]

Pharmacists are at the far end of what might be called the knowledge-intensive wing of the retail sector. While many of the things we buy are self-explanatory—we can generally select towels or orange juice without assistance—other categories of goods require a degree of expertise. Having a knowledgeable retailer to help sort through the options and determine what will best suit our needs can be extremely valuable. This expert assistance has generally been provided for free—or, more accurately, it has been built into the price of the product. Today, in this era of big-box stores and Internet retailers, which have conditioned consumers to focus almost exclusively on price—often even to the point of ignoring differences in product quality and levels of service—knowledge-intensive retail businesses are having an especially difficult time surviving.

"People will come in and try on the waders, try on the boat shoes. They'll cast the rods and ask our advice, and then they go get it on the Internet," said Rich Youngers, a fly-fishing guide with thirty-five years of experience who owns Creekside Flyfishing in Salem, Oregon. "You can't blame them for looking for the cheaper price," he said, but his store—with its expert advice, fly-tying and casting classes, and guided trips—provides a service many shoppers clearly value that will no longer be there if they continue to spend elsewhere. Indeed, Creekside is now Salem's lone independent fly shop; two others have closed since 2003, unable to weather competition from online retailers and a growing number of chains, like Sportsman's Warehouse, that have moved into the region.[38]

Local outfitters across the country tell much the same story. Mountain State Outfitters in Charleston, West Virginia, is one of hundreds that have closed. "I hated to close it down, but my wife and I were working long hours for no money. By the end, I was paying my employees and my bills and that was it. You can't go on working for free," said owner Bill Murray, who bought the business in 1991 and shuttered it in 2005. Sales had steadily eroded as competitors, including Internet dealers, the chain Dick's Sporting Goods, and mass merchandisers Wal-Mart and Target, which offer some fishing and outdoors gear, came into the market. Murray contends that the chains were no match in terms of expertise. "All of my employees had already been involved in the industry before they started working at the store," he said. "If you go out to Dick's or Wal-Mart, they just hire people who need a job." As a result, the chains, he said, would sell people things they really did not need or that were ill-suited to their particular outdoor pursuit.[39]

Recognizing the gulf in knowledge, some customers turned to Mountain State for advice but then shopped elsewhere. "They'd say, 'I don't know which one of these I need.' We'd tell them and then they'd go somewhere else, either online or to the big boxes, where they thought they could get a better price," Murray said. Frequently the store was left to deal with the fallout of bad purchases made online: "We'd have people come in with something they'd bought on the Internet that they couldn't get to work. They'd ask us to fix it or help them figure it out. Half the time, they'd bought the wrong thing." Many relied on Mountain State as a backup option, seemingly unaware that it would cease to exist without their regular patronage. "People would come in and say, 'I went to Dick's, but they couldn't answer my questions.' I always thought, yeah, but you went to Dick's first," said Murray, his voice still filled with frustration.

He was finally forced to close the business and cancel its busy calendar of fly-fishing classes and hands-on kayak and boat demonstrations, none of which are offered by the chains. Murray feels bad about leaving his good customers without their local fly shop, but at least knowledgeable outdoor enthusiasts can fend for themselves. He worries most about people who want to try fly-fishing but no longer have the easy entrée into the sport that Mountain State Outfitters, with its expert guidance, provided. He also misses the camaraderie and community the store fostered. "The high point

of my week was working on the weekends," he recalled. "All my fishing bud-
dies would come in. We'd have customers looking to try something out. We
might have kids getting ready to go to Outward Bound and they'd have lists
of things they needed. Or people who'd come back from their big trip with
pictures to show."[40]

Virtually every kind of local retailer with specialized expertise faces
the same challenge. "I call them BSOs—bicycle-shaped objects," said Mike
McGettigan, owner of Trophy Bikes in Philadelphia, referring to the bicycles people buy at Wal-Mart and bring to his shop when they break. There's
not much he can do to repair them. "Your brakes have to work; they can't
just kind of work," he explained. "Wal-Mart bikes are heavy, because they
are made of crummy materials. They have fake things like dual-suspension
springs, front and back, but they are not adjustable to the rider's weight, so
they are essentially useless." Spending $80 on a bike might seem like a good
deal, but McGettigan insists that such bikes are neither durable nor safe. Indeed, Wal-Mart has been sued by the families of children who were severely
injured when the front wheels of their bikes, all made exclusively for the
chain under its house brand, fell off. At Trophy Bikes, bicycles start at $249,
but, McGettigan said, with regular tune-ups and the occasional replacement part, one of his bikes will last a daily rider a decade or more. But it's
a tough sell. Mass merchants now retail three out of every four bikes, while
the number of specialty bicycle shops dropped from over six thousand in
2000 to less than five thousand five years later.[41]

"People will come to us because something's gone wrong and the Pet-
Smart people don't really know what to tell them," said Harold Ellis,
co-owner of Chicago Aquarium, a twenty-five-year-old pet store. He has
become accustomed to a small but steady stream of customers who purchased aquariums at PetSmart, but come to him when the fish die or other
problems arise. "We did not benefit from any of the profit, but we go ahead
and help them anyway. We don't send them back to PetSmart," he said.
Some become loyal customers of Chicago Aquarium; others return to regularly shopping at PetSmart, apparently unconcerned about a future retail
landscape that lacks the local store's expertise. As pet chains have prolifer-
ated in the city, Ellis and his life and business partner, Ken Riley, have had
to stop carrying birds and turtles and focus exclusively on fish in order to
survive. Few shop owners are more accessible to their customers: Ellis and
Riley live above the store and report that people often come around to the
backyard or knock on their front door when they're not behind the counter.

"That's a big part of the draw—the relationships with people, knowing them for years and watching their kids grow up," said Ellis. "We're both getting older and thinking about retirement, but it's hard to imagine not going down to the store and seeing our customers every day."[42]

"They are a little cheaper—not across the board, but on some items," said Jeff Franklin, who is apprehensively watching the construction of a Target across the street from his toy store, Be Beep, in Annapolis, Maryland. Franklin and his wife left teaching twenty-seven years ago to found their toy business. They pride themselves on having well-trained employees who have played with every toy and game in the store; knowing many of their little customers well enough to help friends find the right birthday gift; and doing more than simply selling toys. Be Beep organizes reading groups for children, brings storytellers and performers into the local schools, and hosts regular family game nights. "That's one of the kinds of play that families still do together. We think those are rich experiences," explained Franklin. Needless to say, Target, which is one of the fastest-growing toy sellers in the country, offers none of these extras. Franklin believes his customers will still identify Be Beep as their favorite toy store, but he worries that they may start to pick up more toys at Target while shopping for other things. A loss of just 20 percent of sales can be enough to close a store, he points out. "I don't expect them to buy every toy here...but we're all so busy and sometimes you don't stop and think about that in making a decision about where to buy something."[43]

As an educator, Franklin also worries that mega-retailers are strangling the development of innovative toys. He is not alone. "I don't think that consumers realize how serious this is," said Maria Weiskott, editor in chief of the industry publication *Playthings*. A few chains now largely dictate what toys are produced, and the pressure they put on manufacturers to lower costs has sharply curtailed the development of new products. The chains are also increasingly manufacturing their own private-label toys—often knockoffs of popular sellers—but with no investment in long-term R & D. Most breakthrough toys, Weiskott said, are coming from a handful of small toymakers that do not sell to Target and Wal-Mart, but rely instead on locally owned toy stores. "If the independent retailers and the small manufacturers do not survive," she said, "then someday what we can buy is going to be decided entirely by some guy in Bentonville."[44]

The power relations are evident at the industry's annual trade shows. The first one takes place in October, when manufacturers present prototypes to the toy buyers for Wal-Mart and other major chains. A thumbs-down from one of these buyers is enough to nix production of a toy and ensure that it will not be on display at the industrywide show in February. "The buyers do not have the mind-set of a [local] merchant. They are dollar-oriented, not product-oriented. For them it's about maximizing the dollars per square foot," said Tom Murdough, who founded Little Tikes in 1969, sold it to Rubbermaid in 1984, and then created another toy company, Step2, which he runs today. "It use to be that we had a broader customer base, so we could design great products with more features and find an outlet for them," he said. Now a handful of retailers dominate his sales. "Innovation is suffering terribly. It's an enormous problem. You don't do things the way you'd like to. Either it won't fit on their shelves the way they want it to or it doesn't hit the right price point." Murdough is surprised that there has not been more of a backlash from consumers. But, he said, consumers do not always know what they want—or what they are missing. "You have to design something that's going to excite them," he said.[45]

Unfortunately, control over the design, development, and distribution of products is less and less in the hands of a broad array of manufacturers and retailers, and is instead concentrated among a few global retailing giants. While this trend might be most alarming in the context of books, music, and other works of expression, its effects on product innovation and diversity apply with equal force to everything else we buy. Home Depot determines what paint colors will be available this year; Wal-Mart dictates the size of steaks. Meanwhile, small producers, no matter how original or ingenious their products, are having an increasingly difficult time finding shelf space for their wares.

As locally owned retail businesses disappear, what we are losing as consumers are people who are, in many cases, enthusiasts for whatever it is that they sell. This enthusiasm influences their decisions about what products to stock and the quality standards they expect from manufacturers. It means they often possess a valuable level of expertise and provide a variety of extras—from family game nights to lessons on managing diabetes—that cannot be found at the chains.

PART TWO

SEVEN

UNCLE SAM'S
INVISIBLE HAND

IT WAS EARLY 2005 WHEN KEVIN OHM, who owns the thirty-three-year-old Ohm's Appliance store in Brookings, South Dakota, first learned that city officials were planning to grant Lowe's nearly $3 million in public subsidies to build a superstore in town. "Surprise would be an understatement," he recalled. "I was aghast." Ohm was not alone. Brookings, a community of just under twenty thousand people on the eastern edge of the state, contains a remarkable number of independent businesses selling the same kinds of products Lowe's offers, including hardware stores, carpet dealers, lighting shops, plumbing-supply stores, lumberyards, and, by Ohm's count, half a dozen other appliance dealers. Many have contributed to the local economy for decades. They were outraged that the city intended to hand their tax dollars over to a powerful competitor. "None of us were given these kinds of incentives when we invested in Brookings," said Kevin Nyburg, owner of Nyburg's Ace Hardware, which employs twenty-five people.[1]

Dozens of local business owners, along with many other residents, started attending city council meetings and arguing against the plan, which involved the city buying a vacant Kmart site for $3.1 million, demolishing the building at a cost of about $250,000, and selling the improved property to Lowe's for $618,000—giving the chain a subsidy of $2.7 million. (Because the city would have to issue bonds to finance the deal, taxpayers would also incur about $650,000 in interest payments.) But despite their arguments—that the subsidy was unfair and that it would help Lowe's take sales from existing businesses, resulting in job and tax losses that would leave Brookings worse off—opponents of the deal were unable to win over the city council, which voted 5–2 in favor of the plan. Lowe's had the council, which was enamored with the idea of a "major player" coming to Brookings, convinced it would not build without a handout, according to Ohm. Nyburg added: "They think there's going to be this pot of gold at the end of the rainbow, but they have no clue how it is going to hurt the people who gave their blood, sweat, and tears to this community."[2]

Opponents of the giveaway decided to take their case to voters. They formed Citizens Against Retail Subsidies, and collected enough signatures to put the issue on the ballot. They raised $7,000 to get their message out and ran newspaper ads featuring pictures of local business owners with the text, "Good neighbors pay their own bills." But they were heavily outspent by Lowe's, which poured $67,000 into a slick radio and newspaper ad campaign that accused opponents of the subsidy of being antigrowth. Lowe's targeted its ads to the community's young voters, many of whom have been left behind by the global economy and face an uncertain future. The strategy worked. On election day, Lowe's won its subsidy by a margin of just ninety-four votes—2,212 to 2,118.[3]

The reigning assumption is that mega-retailers have attained their market dominance solely because of consumer choices. But corporate chains have been aided and abetted in no small part by public policy. Federal, state, and local policies have created an uneven playing field. It began in the late 1950s with accelerated depreciation, which fueled the explosion of shopping malls, and picked up speed in the 1980s and 1990s, as policymakers funneled billions of dollars in development subsidies to big retail chains, opened up tax loopholes that gave large retailers a decided edge over local competitors, and failed to adequately police abuses of market power. This favoritism has been driven in part by the political power of the chains and the retail development industry, and by the persistent myth that big-box stores boost employment and tax revenue. But it also flows from a double standard pervasive among policymakers, who insist that small businesses be subject to the rigors of the free market, while granting their biggest competitors a leg up in the name of the public good.

GOVERNMENT HANDOUTS

Many of the big-box stores and shopping centers that open each year are built with the help of public subsidies. These giveaways take many forms: free or reduced-price land (as in Brookings); property tax breaks; sales tax rebates; free infrastructure and other site improvements; low-interest, tax-free loans; and job training credits, to name a few. Most of these subsidies are provided locally by cities and towns, and occasionally counties, though state and even federal tax dollars may be involved. Together they constitute one of the most substantial, and certainly the most overt, means by which government policy fuels corporate retail expansion.

Recent examples include over $7 million in sales and property tax breaks provided to a Target store in Fort Worth, Texas; $2 million in tax incentives given to Home Depot by the town of Mokena, Illinois; and $9.5 million for a shopping center anchored by a Lowe's in Maplewood, Missouri. Not surprisingly, the world's biggest corporation has been especially aggressive at securing public funding. Evergreen Park, Illinois, granted Wal-Mart $5.25 million in sales tax rebates for a superstore that opened in 2005. State and local giveaways valued at $1.7 million were used to fund another one in Olive Branch, Mississippi, while some $10 million was pledged to support a Wal-Mart and Sam's Club in North Charleston, South Carolina.[4]

One would be hard-pressed to find a major chain that had not financed part of its growth with public subsidies. Costco was given $1.6 million in tax incentives to open a store in Lake in the Hills, a town just outside Chicago. Spokesman Michael Stratis said the company had received subsidies for three of its ten stores in the Chicago region and that such deals were necessary to ensure Costco's expected rate of return on investments. It's not just the big boxes, either. In 2004 Little Chute, Wisconsin, appropriated $361,000 for a Walgreens drugstore. In 2002 California funneled $4.6 million in federal tax dollars allocated to the state under the Community Renewal Tax Relief Act to Borders to open a store in San Diego.[5]

Some chains have based their entire expansion strategy on government handouts. The upscale department store chain Nordstrom has rarely opened outlets without massive incentives. The company has been courted by so many cities that it even coyly declined lucrative deals offered by Pittsburgh ($28 million) and Cincinnati ($48 million). The hunting and outdoors retailer Cabela's—which builds colossal megastores featuring waterfalls, aquariums, and wildlife displays—has relied so heavily on public funding, its 2004 prospectus explicitly warned investors that, should the government cash run dry, its growth would likely suffer. The company picked up $32 million for a store in Pennsylvania; $57 million for one in Texas; and a jaw-dropping $92 million in grants and tax breaks in West Virginia, where state officials also spent $13 million building Cabela's its own exit off I-70.[6]

Many shopping centers, particularly the hot new "lifestyle center" projects, are also heavily subsidized. West Des Moines, a fast-growing suburb of Des Moines, footed the bill for $60 million in infrastructure and other site improvements to help a developer convert more than two hundred acres of farmland into Jordan Creek Town Center, home to dozens of chain stores, including Barnes & Noble, Best Buy, and Pottery Barn, and restaurants, like The Cheesecake Factory and PF Chang's. In Garland, Texas, a similar retail complex called the Firewheel Town Center, which opened in 2005 and features stores such as Dillard's, Circuit City, and Barnes & Noble, received nearly $24 million worth of sales tax rebates and infrastructure from the city.[7]

The logic behind these giveaways is that the new stores will generate enough new tax revenue to more than cover the cost of the subsidy. "Sometimes you have to spend a nickel to make a quarter," explained Gary Klaphake, city administrator for Lafayette, Colorado, which in 2005 agreed to $2.3 million in subsidies for a Wal-Mart supercenter that was expected to produce $18 million in sales tax revenue for the city over the next decade. But such cost-benefit calculations only work if one ignores the full range of costs, notably lost sales and property tax revenue from local business districts, as well as competing shopping centers. Just two years after one of its anchors closed in response to competing big-box stores, a Rhode Island strip mall's assessed value fell from $36 million to $20 million. A dead mall in Wisconsin sold for less than $4 million in 2001, after having an assessed value of over $100 million when it was fully occupied in 1990. Combine these forgone taxes with the cost of the subsidy itself and the added expense of providing services to the new big-box store, and it becomes a net loss to taxpayers. Cities sometimes escape this negative bottom-line by offloading the costs onto their neighbors. A subsidized shopping mall, for example, might cause sales losses and vacancies not in the host community, but in the next town over. The region as a whole is worse off, but the host city benefits—at least in the short-term. As we have already seen, today's winners in the retail development race often become tomorrow's losers, eclipsed by even bigger stores in other towns.[8]

This competition for tax base has been adroitly exploited by the chains, which excel at playing neighboring cities against one another to exact bigger subsidies. Indeed, it's now common for cities to provide incentives not only to lure new outlets, but to keep the ones they already have. When Target threatened to abandon its store in the small town of Parker, Colorado, and relocate to an adjacent community, the town council quickly approved a $6.2 million subsidy to persuade the company to stay. In 1993 Belleville, Illinois, put up $6 million to convince Wal-Mart to expand at its existing site, rather than build a bigger outlet in a nearby town. Thirteen years later, Belleville okayed another tax break, valued at $11.3 million, to finance yet another Wal-Mart expansion (along with a Lowe's), again under threat of losing the retailer and the $900,000 in annual tax revenue it generates.[9]

Subsidies have fueled the massive overdevelopment that has left much of the nation littered with dead malls and vacant big-box stores. It's a self-perpetuating cycle: faced with an empty box, cities are even more desperate to entice any sort of development. Costco "may be riding to the rescue," the *Dallas Morning News* reported when the town of Duncanville—which had suffered a crushing decline in its finances after Wal-Mart, Kmart, and Circuit City all closed their doors—agreed to pay $4.4 million in incentives to land one of the chain's big warehouse stores. Birmingham, Alabama, has been engaged in a tragicomic game of exchanging vacant boxes. In 2002 the city paid Wal-Mart $10 million to build a store on the site of an empty Kmart. Wal-Mart soon closed one of its other stores about a mile away, which was still vacant three years later. Undeterred by this experience, Birmingham put together another $10 million bid for Wal-Mart to build on the grounds of the city's nearly empty Eastwood Mall.[10]

Ironically, one of the incentive programs that is most often used to subsidize big-box stores was originally intended to spur revitalization of older urban neighborhoods. Forty-seven states allow cities to set up tax increment financing—or TIF—districts. These laws, most of which were enacted in the 1970s and 1980s, recognized that redeveloping crumbling urban areas was more expensive than building on the outskirts of town and, on this basis, allowed cities to provide financial assistance to make urban redevelopment more attractive. Typically the way it works is that a city establishes a TIF district and issues bonds to cover part of the cost of redeveloping the site. The city then uses the bonds to pay for site improvements or, in some cases, gives the money directly to a developer. Once the site is redeveloped and the property's assessed value rises, all of the new tax revenue generated by the site is diverted from the public coffers and used instead to pay off the bonds. This diversion may last as long as forty years, during which time schools and other public services receive no benefit from the project. TIF essentially allows tax-exempt, low-interest public capital to be used for private development, and further subsidizes that development with future tax dollars.[11]

Initially, most TIF laws ensured that these subsidies flowed only to projects that produced real community benefits and that were infeasible without public assistance. Cities had to determine that an area was "blighted" before it could be designated a TIF district. But over the years, TIF rules have been loosened to the point where terms like "blight" can be applied to anything and where the subsidies more often flow to big-box stores in well-to-do suburbs than to struggling urban neighborhoods. In 2003 Allegheny County, Pennsylvania, for example, deemed a wooded hillside blighted and negotiated a $6.7 million TIF deal to fund a shopping center with Target, Sam's Club, and Sportsman's Warehouse. An analysis by 1000 Friends of Wisconsin found that nearly half of the state's 661 TIF districts involved development of open space. Many were being used to subsidize chain retailers. The town of Baraboo, for example, declared a cornfield and an apple orchard blighted in order to finance a Wal-Mart superstore. "This misuse has exacerbated the state's property tax crisis," said John Goldstein, president of the Milwaukee County Labor Council.[12]

Rather than lessening disparities as originally intended, TIF subsidies aggravate them: they favor sprawl over urban redevelopment, wealthy over low-income areas, and global chains over locally owned businesses. In the St. Louis metro, 57 percent of total TIF-captured tax-base lies beyond I-270, the region's outer ring road. Much of it consists of chain retail development. The wealthy suburb of Des Peres declared the thriving West County Shopping Center blighted—although it was almost fully leased and generating $100 million in revenue a year—in order to provide $30 million in TIF subsidies to bring Nordstrom and Lord & Taylor to the center. Another St. Louis suburb deployed $17 million in TIF to fund a Target-anchored strip mall. Similar deals have financed Costco, Home Depot, Lowe's, Bass Pro Shops, and other big-box stores throughout the suburbs. In some cases, the repayment period on TIF bonds is as much as thirty or forty years—longer than many of these stores are likely to last.[13]

Some argue that TIF is not really a subsidy, because the future tax dollars diverted to pay off the bonds would not have been generated without the development. The idea that suburban households might lack places to spend their money without TIF-supported development is absurd. But even in cities, it appears that many TIF subsidies may have been unnecessary. An analysis of thirty-six TIF districts in Chicago by the Neighborhood Capital Budget Group found that more than 80 percent of the $1.6 billion in new revenue generated by these districts (and diverted to pay back the bonds) would have been created anyway.[14]

Subsidies for chain retailers are particularly rampant in states like Missouri, Arizona, and California, where cities are heavily dependent on local sales taxes, often because of legal or political restrictions on their ability to raise revenue through other means, such as property taxes. In Arizona, cities derive much of their revenue from local sales taxes that typically range from 1 to 3 percent (state and county sales taxes add another 6 to 7 percent), and they compete fiercely to attract retail stores and auto dealerships. Since 2000, cities in the Phoenix metro have given hundreds of millions of dollars to massive retail projects, such as the Chandler Fashion Center ($42 million), home to chains like Barnes & Noble, Pottery Barn, and The Limited; the Tempe Marketplace ($40 million), which includes Target, Best Buy, Old Navy, and so on; and Mesa Riverview ($84 million), featuring Wal-Mart. "We've got bidding wars going on among cities out here," lamented Kimber Lanning, owner of Stinkweeds, a local music store in Phoenix. "The chains are having a feeding frenzy."[15]

They are busy at the public trough in California too. "Superstores now line our freeways, decimating local businesses and cannibalizing customers from older retail areas," said Ventura city manager Rick Cole, who has been an outspoken advocate for reform. "Short of betting in Las Vegas, it would be hard to devise a worse way to fund city services." In addition to undermining local businesses, the scramble for sales tax dollars has led to what would otherwise be irrational land-use decisions, as cities forgo development of much-needed housing and high-wage enterprises in order to devote land to still more big-box stores and shopping malls. Critics have dubbed this problem "cash box zoning." A survey in 1999 confirmed its distorting effects, finding that more than three-quarters of California cities ranked retail as their top priority both for vacant land and areas needing redevelopment, and they identified maximizing sales tax revenue as their main motivation. Yet despite the liberal application of subsidies and the proliferation of stores, Californians are not spending more. Sales tax collections per person have remained relatively constant since the 1980s.[16]

Government handouts have also helped large retailers build their distribution warehouses. Wal-Mart has received subsidies for eighty-four of its ninety-one distribution centers, according to an analysis by the policy research group Good Jobs First. Many of these giveaways topped $10 million, including those in Sharon Springs, New York ($46 million), Arcadia, Florida ($24 million), Ottawa, Kansas ($19 million), and Lewiston, Maine ($16 million). Other chains also rely on subsidies. Best Buy received $12.9 million for a warehouse in Tioga County, New York, while Target landed $9.6 million in tax breaks for one in DeKalb, Illinois. Unlike stores, distribution centers are often funded with state, rather than local, tax dollars, because state officials tend to see these warehouses as job creators. (Chain store executives learn how to sell states on this notion by attending workshops such as "Turning Your State Government Relations Department from a Money Pit into a Cash Cow," sponsored by the accounting firm Ernst & Young.) But spending tax dollars on distribution centers makes as little sense as subsidizing the stores. As big-box retailers gain market share, other retailers lose business—and so do the distributors they rely on.[17]

What is the total value of all of these subsidies? No one knows. They are authorized on a piecemeal basis, often at the local level, and no state or federal entity tracks them. Researchers at Good Jobs First compiled a list of development incentives given to Wal-Mart since the early 1990s and found that the chain had received at least $1 billion. Because they had to search newspapers to find these subsidies and because not all subsidies are reported and not all newspapers have electronic archives, the researchers concluded that this figure "may very well be the tip of the iceberg." Indeed, a Wal-Mart official said the firm seeks subsidies for about one-third of its stores, suggesting that as many as sixteen hundred U.S. outlets may have been taxpayer supported. Add the missing Wal-Mart subsidies, plus all of the dollars that have gone to other corporate retailers since the early 1990s, and what's the total—$3 billion, $5 billion, $10 billion?[18]

Subsidizing chain retailers deals a double blow to independent businesses. Not only are independents rarely given any sort of public funding but, as taxpayers, they end up shouldering the cost of financing the expansion of their biggest competitors. Their employees pay a price, too. "All it has done is put a lot of good people out of work in the downtown," said Maine state senator Peter Mills of a big-box subsidy in the town of Waterville. Cities that subsidize big-box stores not only harm local retailers, they may undermine their prosperity in other ways as well. Subsidies may deplete city budgets, forcing cutbacks in spending on schools and public infrastructure—the bedrock of long-term economic development. In Utah, for example, school districts are currently losing $49 million a year in tax revenue that has been diverted by a subsidy program similar to TIF, with most of it flowing to big retail projects.[19]

There have been a growing number of attempts to reform state laws governing TIF and other incentive programs. Big retailers, developers, and some cities have lobbied heavily against these reforms, and so far, at least, they have prevailed. In Missouri, a coalition of small businesses and labor unions pushed for the adoption of a bill that would limit TIF to economically depressed areas and prohibit its use for projects that are primarily retail or that involve building on open space. But with developers and many suburban cities strongly opposed—and millions of dollars at stake—they lost. In California, lawmakers did pass a measure that prohibits cities from using incentives to steal stores from adjacent towns, but they have declined to enact bills that would bar big-box subsidies and halt the bidding wars for new shopping centers. In Arizona, Senator Jack Harper thought he had enough support for a bill to curtail retail subsidies until "lobbyists for Westcor [a major mall developer] and Wal-Mart started peeling off my votes." The bill died in the Arizona House.[20]

Some cities have gone even further to help retail chains build new stores; they have used eminent domain—the power governments have to seize property for public purposes—to divest people of their homes and businesses in order to clear land for developers. Traditionally, land seizure was reserved for public uses, such as roads and schools, but cities have increasingly used it to transfer property from one private owner to another. They argue that expanding the tax base is a public purpose as legitimate as building a road. Often cities need not even go through the legal procedures; simply the threat of condemnation is sufficient to convince owners to sell. Such was the case in the Utah town of West Bountiful. In 2005 the city declared an area occupied by thirty local businesses blighted and strong-armed the owners into selling their properties to make way for Costco. Although the city provided some assistance with relocation, two of the businesses soon folded, while others, including Barton's Scooters and All Seasons Pool and Spa, have reported a sharp drop in sales at their new locations. Such seizures are remarkably common and have benefited many big retailers, including Wal-Mart, Target, Home Depot, CVS, Walgreen, and Stop & Shop. Fortunately, the public outcry over a recent U.S. Supreme Court decision upholding eminent domain for private development may lead cities to reconsider this tactic in the future.[21]

There's nothing wrong with cities being actively engaged in local economic development, and there are situations in which subsidies, and perhaps even eminent domain, may be warranted. Rehabilitating historic commercial buildings may be cost prohibitive without some public assistance, for example. Incentives may be needed to help develop retail in low-income neighborhoods that lack basic goods and services. But in both cases, subsidies will yield much greater pubic benefits if they are directed at local business creation rather than chain retail expansion. And these are the rare exceptions; the vast majority of retail subsidies are very poor public policy, both grossly unfair to small businesses and harmful to taxpayers. It's even unfair to those businesses in regions where development subsidies are uncommon, because the chains, after all, are global companies. A dollar saved by Wal-Mart in Alabama or Arizona is a dollar that can be spent building stores elsewhere.

Subsidies are an extreme manifestation of a much broader favoritism that pervades many city governments. When a corporate retailer unveils plans for a new store, local officials often bend over backward to accommodate the project, meeting with company representatives, expediting procedures, and granting exceptions, known as variances, to local zoning laws. They may even go so far as to alter their comprehensive plan or change the zoning code to allow large-scale commercial development in an area that had been reserved for homes, agriculture, or recreation. Independent retailers looking to open or expand rarely receive similar treatment; usually they are left to navigate the bureaucracy on their own and are required to comply with the strict letter of the law.

THE GEOFFREY LOOPHOLE

It's commonly referred to as the Geoffrey Loophole, named after Geoffrey the Giraffe, the trademarked mascot of Toys "R" Us. The chain was one of the first to discover the loophole and use it to escape paying its full share of state corporate income taxes. Today, almost every chain takes advantage of this scheme, including Burger King, Circuit City, The Gap, Home Depot, Ikea, Kmart, Kohl's, Limited Brands (the owner of Bath & Body Works, Victoria's Secret, and others), Lowe's, May (the parent company of a bunch of department store chains now owned by Federated), Payless ShoeSource, Sherwin-Williams, Staples, and Wal-Mart. Although closing the loophole is relatively simple, only seventeen states have done so. Most of the others have left it wide open, letting large corporations sidestep billions of dollars in state tax obligations each year. This gives them a major competitive advantage over locally owned businesses, virtually none of which are able to utilize the Geoffrey Loophole.[22]

The way it works is that a chain sets up a subsidiary in Delaware or Michigan, two states that do not tax profits earned from trademarks and other intangible corporate assets, or in Nevada, which does not tax any corporate income. It then assigns ownership of its name and other trademark slogans to this shell company. Kmart, for example, has a Michigan subsidiary that owns such trademarked phrases as "Blue Light Special" and "At Home with Martha Stewart." Home Depot has a similar holding company in Delaware called Homer TLC Inc. Kmart and Home Depot stores in other states, such as New York and Virginia, then pay these subsidiaries hefty fees to use the name and phrases. These payments are deducted as business expenses on their New York and Virginia tax returns and are not taxed. Nor are these transfers taxed in Delaware and Michigan, which do not tax earnings attributed to corporate trademarks. Profits shifted in this manner are thus sheltered from all state corporate income tax liability. Some chains go further: they have their Delaware subsidiary "loan" money to the main company, which then can deduct the "interest" it pays on the loan.[23]

Because corporations are not required to publicly disclose these transfers, or even to reveal the existence of a Delaware holding company, no one knows exactly how much profit is being sheltered in this manner. Court cases brought by states against a few retail chains have shed light on the scope of some of the transfers. Over a three-year period in the early 1990s, Kmart moved more than $1 billion in profits into its Michigan subsidiary. Limited Brands likewise used its Delaware subsidiary to shield about $1.2 billion in earnings from state tax liability between 1992 and 1994, a period during which the retailer posted a total of $1.8 billion in profits. State corporate income tax rates are generally in the 6 to 8 percent range, meaning a company saves $60 to $80 million in state taxes for every $1 billion sheltered. The Multistate Tax Commission reports that the Geoffrey Loophole is one of several major corporate tax-sheltering schemes that together cost states an estimated $8.3 to $12.4 billion a year.[24]

Although other kinds of firms can take advantage of this loophole, the users of trademark holding companies are overwhelming retail chains, according to Michael Mazerov, a senior fellow at the Center on Budget and Policy Priorities and an expert on state business taxes. Setting up one of these subsidiaries is not difficult. There are dozens of accounting firms that are happy to handle the details. PriceWaterhouseCoopers, for example, markets its services under the title "Utilization of an Investment Holding Company to Minimize State and Local Income Taxes." The cost can be as little as one hundred thousand dollars, a tiny fraction of the potential savings. Although trademark holding companies are entirely paper creations, in order to pass legal muster they do need at least a thin veneer of physical existence. Delaware Corporate Management Inc. is one of several firms that supply this veneer by providing a mailing address and phone service to trademark holding companies. Its twenty-story office building in Wilmington houses some 670 such companies.[25]

While relatively inexpensive for a large retail chain, setting up a Delaware subsidiary is beyond the reach of the vast majority of local businesses, who have little choice but to pay state corporate income taxes on all of their earnings. Indeed, small-business owners and other taxpayers ultimately end up shouldering a larger share of state costs as corporations duck their responsibility. Corporate tax revenue has plummeted since the 1990s, according to several studies. Since 1992, for example, the share of Connecticut's revenue derived from corporate income taxes has dropped from 10.6 to 4.2 percent, according to University of Connecticut tax law professor Richard Pomp, who attributes much of the decline to the Geoffrey Loophole and other tax-sheltering strategies. In Pennsylvania, Governor Ed Rendell has said that closing the Geoffrey Loophole would recover enough revenue from tax-avoiding firms to cut the state's corporate income tax rate from 9.99 percent—the third highest in the nation—to 7.9 percent, saving small businesses tens of millions of dollars.[26]

Closing the Geoffrey Loophole is relatively simple. Seventeen states have done so by adopting combined (also known as unitary) reporting, which requires companies to add together all of their income from related subsidiaries before determining their tax liability in each state. In effect, combined reporting says that, if a portion of the profits made by an out-of-state subsidiary were derived from a company's in-state operations, then those profits are taxable in that state. Of the remaining thirty-three states, five do not have a corporate income tax. A few others have enacted some restrictions on tax-avoidance strategies based on trademark holding companies, but Mazerov contends that most of these limits are a poor substitute for combined reporting. "They have exceptions that you could drive a truck through," he said. The rest of the states—more than twenty in all—are fully vulnerable to the Geoffrey Loophole.[27]

Almost all of the states with combined reporting adopted it decades ago, long before big retail chains discovered and began to exploit the Geoffrey Loophole. (California originated the idea in the 1930s to counter various schemes by Hollywood movie studios to escape state income taxes.) Since 2000, bills to enact combined reporting have been introduced in many states but, with one exception, all have failed under intense pressure from corporate lobbyists. Despite his offer of an across-the-board tax cut, Governor Rendell has been unable to win over staunch opponents of combined reporting, such as the Pennsylvania Chamber of Business and Industry, which counts many large multistate corporations among its members. Pleas by New Mexico state legislator Peter Wirth for fairness have likewise gone unheeded. "Local New Mexico businesses pay their fair share of the corporate tax," he has argued. "Why should the Wal-Marts of the world be allowed to pay little or no corporate tax on the money they make in New Mexico?" Big-business interests in Connecticut have also succeeded in blocking legislation to require combined reporting, even though the recovered revenue would be used to cut the tax rate that all businesses pay.[28]

In 2004 Vermont became the first state in more than two decades to adopt combined reporting. Governor Jim Douglas led the effort. In his 2004 State of the State address, he said, "Huge companies pay only a minimum $250 tax, while our homegrown Vermont businesses, particularly our small businesses, pick up the rest of the tab." He later gave an example of three multistate companies (which he did not identify) that had $6 billion in combined revenue in Vermont in 2003, but paid only $250 each in state income taxes. Meanwhile, the governor reported, a group of locally owned businesses with combined revenue of $700 million paid $7 million in state income taxes. Vermont lawmakers endorsed his proposal and combined reporting took effect at the beginning of 2006.[29]

It is hoped that other states will soon follow. Allowing big retail chains to skirt their tax obligations not only deprives states of needed revenue, forcing other taxpayers to shoulder more of the load, but it creates an uneven playing field that disadvantages locally owned businesses against their largest and most powerful competitors. While the Geoffrey Loophole ranks as the most significant type of chain store favoritism embedded in state tax codes, it is not the only way that large corporations escape tax obligations. "There are just a host of ways that multistate corporations can avoid paying taxes on far less than 100 percent of their income," said Mazerov. "Small business cannot."[30]

SALES TAX FREE

Buy a book at Book Passage, a lively bookstore in the town of Corte Madera in northern California, and the clerk by law must charge you 7.75 percent in state and local sales tax. Purchase the same book at Amazon.com and, although technically you still owe the tax, Amazon is not required to collect it from you. Unless you are one of the rare people who opt to report such purchases to your state's tax authorities, the book will be yours tax free. "It's astonishing," fumes Bill Petrocelli, who owns Book Passage and has been lobbying lawmakers for years to apply sales tax equally to all retailers. "It's one thing to compete against a dot-com. But when you add that extra 7 to 8 percent advantage on top, it's awfully hard."[31]

The disparity stems from two Supreme Court decisions in 1967 and 1992, in which the Court concluded that states could not require remote sellers—mostly catalog and Web retailers—to collect sales taxes. Complying with the varied rates and rules established by each state and by the thousands of local taxing bodies would impose too heavy a burden on these companies, the Court said. Retailers are only required to collect sales taxes from customers in states where they have a physical presence, such as a store or a warehouse. In its 1992 ruling, the Court did note, however, that the issue was not a constitutional one; Congress was therefore free to ignore its ruling and mandate that catalog and Web retailers collect the taxes.[32]

Congress has not done so. The consequences for state governments, some forty-six of which rely on sales taxes for at least one-quarter of their revenue, have been substantial—and they mount with each passing year, as online shopping grows. In 2001 states forfeited an estimated $13 billion in sales taxes that were not collected by mail-order and online retailers. Not only has this given Web retailers like Amazon.com a competitive advantage, but for many years big national chains, including Wal-Mart and Barnes & Noble, did not collect sales taxes online, either—despite the fact that their physical presence in every state is undeniable. The chains set up their online operations as separate companies, distinct from their physical stores—except, of course, in the minds of shoppers—and therefore, they claimed, free of the obligation to collect sales taxes (a trick known among tax experts as "entity isolation"). But increasingly concerned about the potential liability, in 2003 most of these sales-tax evaders cut a deal with thirty-seven states, under which they were forgiven all of their back taxes—a giveaway of undisclosed value—in exchange for collecting sales taxes from that point forward. Although most of the big chains now collect taxes online, there remain stragglers, including, at the time of this writing, Sports Authority and Cabela's.[33]

The states have also banded together and adopted legislation to bring their sales tax regulations into alignment, thus greatly simplifying tax collection and removing the burden that troubled the Supreme Court. But Congress still has not moved to authorize states to require Internet retailers to collect sales taxes. In the early days of the Web, lawmakers often justified this unequal policy as a way of nurturing fledgling e-commerce, but Book Passage's Petrocelli notes that he has now been competing against Amazon.com for more than a decade and his store's sales are dwarfed by those of the online retailer, which took in $7 billion in 2004. Petrocelli believes that states do not have to wait for Congress to act to remove this competitive disadvantage. He argues that Amazon's hundreds of California affiliates—companies and organizations that, in exchange for a commission, feature products on their own Web sites and link visitors to Amazon to purchase these goods—constitute a physical presence sufficient for the state to require the company to collect sales taxes. But in a state where the dot-com industry dominates politics, Petrocelli has not been able to persuade the state's tax authority, the Board of Equalization, to adopt this stance. "If we make one mistake on our paperwork or we are a day late [paying sales taxes], they are all over us with penalties," he said. "At the same time, they let the big guys slide."[34]

POLICING ABUSES OF MARKET POWER

When U.S. antitrust laws were first enacted, and for many decades following, they were infused with both an economic and a civic purpose. The goal of antitrust policy was not only to protect consumers from monopoly pricing, but to foster an economy compatible with democracy. Concentrated market power amounted to "a kingly prerogative, inconsistent with our form of government," said Senator John Sherman, author of the first major piece of antitrust legislation in 1890. "If we will not endure a king as a political power we should not endure a king over the production, transportation, and sale of the necessaries of life." Nearly half a century later, Franklin Roosevelt echoed this sentiment when he noted, "The liberty of a democracy is not safe if the people tolerate the growth of private power to a point where it becomes stronger than their democratic state itself." Dispersing ownership and maintaining a decentralized economy of numerous small businesses would both ensure healthy competition and be accordant with democratic self-governance.[35]

This broad civic purpose faded from antitrust policy in the second half of the twentieth century, as courts and federal enforcement agencies began to interpret antitrust laws with a much more narrow focus on consumer welfare. Delivering the lowest possible prices to consumers became the single overriding goal of antitrust policy. Concerns about the dangers that concentrated market power posed to democracy were eclipsed by the conviction that bigness conferred economies of scale and that these efficiencies could lead to lower prices. The two major federal enforcement agencies— the Antitrust Division of the U.S. Department of Justice and the Federal Trade Commission—grew reluctant to constrain the scale of business and to limit predatory tactics that could lead to lower prices, even at the risk of reducing competition over the long term. The agencies were further hamstrung by severe budget and staffing cuts during the 1980s, from which they have yet to recover. Meanwhile, the U.S. Supreme Court repeatedly raised the bar for proving certain kinds of antitrust violations.[36]

The result is an antitrust environment today in which corporate retailers can use their size and market power to undermine smaller rivals and tilt the playing field to their own advantage with little fear of prosecution. The presiding assumption is that chains are aggressive competitors; if they overstep the line and use their power to damage smaller rivals, it is of little concern, because consumers are benefiting from lower prices. Enforcement is limited, and independent retailers who feel they have been harmed by anticompetitive practices have a difficult, if not impossible, time seeking relief through private lawsuits.

The two types of antitrust violations of most concern in the retail sector are predatory pricing and buyer power. Predatory pricing occurs when a company sells its products below its own cost, taking a temporary loss in order to drive competitors out of business and reap the rewards of having a dominant market position. Independent retailers are especially vulnerable, because they lack the financial reserves to withstand a sustained predatory pricing assault, while their competitors can operate individual outlets (or departments) at a loss for some time. Determining at what point beneficial price competition becomes predation has always been a challenge and the subject of much debate. But in the 1970s, scholars identified with the influential Chicago school of economics began to question the very idea of predation. They argued that firms were highly unlikely to achieve and sustain a dominant market position long enough to recoup the money they lost selling below cost. Since predatory pricing did not make bottom-line sense, it was irrational and therefore very unlikely to occur.[37]

In two crucial decisions in 1986 *(Matsushita)* and 1993 *(Brooke Group)*, the U.S. Supreme Court embraced this view, concluding that "there is a consensus among commentators that predatory pricing schemes are rarely tried, and even more rarely successful." On this basis, the Court established an almost impossibly high standard for proving predatory pricing violations, ruling that the evidence must demonstrate that the defendant priced goods below actual cost for a sustained period of time and had a "dangerous probability" of driving competitors out of business and recouping the losses through future profits gained in a monopoly market. In *Brooke Group,* a case involving a cigarette manufacturer, the Court noted that there was extensive evidence of the defendant's intent to crush the plaintiff through predatory pricing. But the Court still acquitted the defendant, concluding that intent did not matter unless the plaintiff could show that there was a strong likelihood that the predator would actually succeed and be able to recover its lost profits. Such a showing is immensely difficult, requiring extensive economic analysis—so much so that, at the time, many believed that the ruling would "prove fatal to all future predatory pricing claims." Indeed, a review in 2000 found that, since *Brooke Group,* "no predatory pricing plaintiff has prevailed on the merits in the federal courts."[38]

Later scholarship, however, has contradicted the Supreme Court's assertion that predatory pricing is irrational and therefore rare. Even if a predator is unable to recoup all of its losses in the aftermath of driving a rival out of business, predatory pricing may still confer a competitive advantage that is well worth the investment. This is especially true of companies that operate in multiple markets, where aggressive, competitor-crushing behavior in one local market or product category can send a strong signal to other markets. Selling below cost is thus an investment "in building a particular kind of reputation that is thought to have strategic value in the overall business of the firm," explained Albert Foer, president of the American Antitrust Institute. Such a reputation can confer many benefits; it may, for example, deter a new competitor from entering the market (or cause banks and investors to be unwilling to finance the venture). Moreover, a failed predatory pricing scheme (one that does not result in a single firm gaining enough market share to raise prices) still leads to market distortion and the destruction of one or more rival businesses.[39]

"It is now the consensus view in modern economics that predatory pricing can be a successful and fully rational business strategy," reported two economists and a leading antitrust scholar in a paper published by the *Georgetown Law Journal* in 2000. "In addition, several sophisticated empirical case studies have confirmed the use of predatory pricing strategies." Yet, the "extreme judicial skepticism" of the existence of predatory pricing continues to be the law of the land, with federal courts following the dictates of *Brooke Group* and enforcement agencies highly reluctant to pursue cases given the monumental evidentiary requirements. "By making it extremely difficult for a plaintiff to succeed in a predatory pricing case, the Chicago school has taken away one of the most important tools for protecting small businesses' ability to compete on a level playing field," contended Foer.[40]

Just four months after the *Brooke Group* decision, in November 1993, a state court in Arkansas ruled against Wal-Mart in a suit concerning predatory pricing. The case had been brought on behalf of three local pharmacies in Faulkner County. The decision rocked headlines. Not only had a successful lawsuit been carried out against this giant company—in its own home state no less—but the ruling, coming as it did on the heels of *Brooke Group,* generated sudden interest in state antitrust laws. Observers wondered if states might step into the void left by the federal government and start policing predatory pricing. Many states have unfair trade laws on the books that prohibit selling below cost with an intent to injure competitors. Most were adopted in the 1930s, during a period of strong populist sentiment in favor of small businesses, and they generally have a much simpler and more attainable standard for proving a violation. But Wal-Mart appealed the decision and two years later, in a 4–3 vote, a divided Arkansas Supreme Court overturned the lower court and ruled that Wal-Mart's tactics had been legal.[41]

Evidence presented in the case showed that Wal-Mart had been selling up to 30 percent of its health and beauty products below its own acquisition costs—a point never contested by the retailer. The lower court had inferred an intent to injure competition from the extent and duration of below-cost sales, the fact that store employees regularly checked prices at the local pharmacies, and evidence showing that Wal-Mart charged different prices in other parts of the state for the same products. The Arkansas Supreme Court, however, concluded that loss-leader pricing was not illegal on its own and that the evidence was insufficient to prove that Wal-Mart employed below-cost pricing for the purpose of destroying competition and dominating the market. In effect, by establishing a much higher bar for proving predatory pricing, the court brought Arkansas state law into alignment with federal antitrust policy under *Brooke Group*. It was a troubling ruling. If Wal-Mart can sell whole categories of goods at a loss, while making up the difference by charging more in other departments, it's hard to see how that constitutes fair competition to retailers that operate in only one category.[42]

Although states could theoretically pursue a tougher line on predatory pricing than the federal government does—they have the authority to do so—in reality, most state courts tend to follow the precedents set by federal courts and very few states devote more than meager resources to antitrust enforcement. "The difficulty is that there are only a few states that have more than a few employees and that can take on more than an occasional case," especially against a big company, said Foer. "Until we get some better precedents and a more aggressive vision at the federal level, I don't think we are going to see a lot of state cases."[43]

One state that has taken action against predatory tactics by a retailer in recent years is Wisconsin. In 2000, the state's Department of Agriculture, Trade, and Consumer Protection filed a complaint against Wal-Mart for selling products below cost in five communities, with an intent to put competing grocery stores and pharmacies out of business. The case provides an insight into Wal-Mart's attitude toward antitrust laws. Over the course of more than a year, state investigators repeatedly wrote to the company asking for a response to the evidence, according to Bill Oemichen, who was head of the trade and consumer protection division at the time, but Wal-Mart never wrote back. Finally, Oemichen threatened to file formal charges. Wal-Mart soon agreed to a meeting, arriving with several newly hired Wisconsin attorneys, including the state's former deputy attorney general. "It was a very short meeting," recalled Oemichen. "Their primary defense was that the law was a stupid law."[44]

He filed the complaint. But rather than go to court, Oemichen, who now works for the Wisconsin Federation of Cooperatives, ultimately agreed to a settlement, under which Wal-Mart promised not to sell goods below cost in Wisconsin. Oemichen said he moved to settle because he was leaving the agency and feared his successors would not have the appetite to mount a major court case against such a powerful company. "It takes a lot of resources to take on a company the size of Wal-Mart," he said. Oemichen hopes that the state has continued to monitor the chain, but he noted that budget cuts have shrunk his old department by about 40 percent.[45]

Wal-Mart, meanwhile, has been lobbying to dismantle part of the state's antitrust laws. Wisconsin is one of about sixteen states that not only prohibit predatory pricing generally, but specifically outlaw selling gasoline below cost under any circumstances. These provisions were adopted to prevent oil companies from undercutting independent gas stations, driving them out of business, and then raising prices. Intent on expanding its share of the gasoline market by selling at a loss, Wal-Mart has been working to repeal these laws, or prevent the adoption of them, in several states. It has powerful allies, including the Federal Trade Commission, which has been outspoken on the issue, espousing the idea that predatory pricing is virtually nonexistent and, therefore, that outlawing below-cost sales will only serve to chill legitimate competition. Also weighing in on Wal-Mart's side are many state legislators, who argue that these laws protect small businesses at the expense of consumers. They make the case—compelling in its simplicity—that these policies block big chains from selling gas for less.[46]

Those who support bans on below-cost selling contend that protecting small businesses helps, not harms, consumers. They point to a 2005 study by three academics at the University of Wisconsin and Georgia State University, who tracked gas prices beginning in the early 1980s in states with and without these laws, paying particular attention to those that either adopted or repealed a measure on below-cost gas sales during this period, and concluded that these policies work just as intended: they increase the number of competing gas stations and lower the pump price. While the view that a market with numerous competitors serves consumers better than one dominated by a few larger businesses still has traction within a handful of states' policy debates, the argument has largely been lost, at least for now, at the federal level, where potential efficiency gains tend to trump other concerns. As a result, there has been little investigation of Wal-Mart's pricing practices, even though below-cost selling appears to be a core part of its strategy, perhaps most visible in 2003 when the company was widely reported to have crushed competing toy chains by selling toys at a loss.[47]

Other countries have taken a different tack. In 2002 Germany's highest court decided against Wal-Mart in a predatory pricing case brought by the

Federal Cartel Office, which determined that the chain was harming independent retailers and overall competition by selling key products, such as milk and butter, at a loss. Germany's strict stance on predatory pricing, along with the fact that its retail workforce is largely unionized and better paid, probably at least partly explains why Wal-Mart has not come to dominate the country's market as it has in other parts of the world. Since the chain first entered Germany in 1997, its financial performance has been lackluster. In 2003 Wal-Mart scuttled plans to open fifty new superstores in the country. By 2006 the situation had not improved and the chain moved to close several existing stores.[48]

POWER BUYERS

The other major antitrust issue for retailers has to do with the exercise of buyer power—that is, the ability of big retailers to use their clout to bully suppliers into providing special discounts and favorable terms that are not made available to local businesses. A 1936 federal law, the Robinson-Patman Act, makes it illegal both for suppliers to offer discriminatory deals and for retailers to induce such discounts. The law was enacted following the rapid growth of chains like Woolworth and A&P in the years following World War I. Concerned about the power these firms exercised in their dealing with manufacturers and farmers, Congressman Wright Patman, a Democrat from Texas, held hearings on chain store buying practices in the summer of 1935. Patman, who served in the House for nearly fifty years and was a supporter of the New Deal and an advocate for the rights of workers and small businesses, summed up his concerns about large chains when he wrote, "The wide distribution of economic power among many independent proprietors is the foundation of the nation's economy. Both Franklin and Jefferson feared that industrialization would lead to a labor proletariat without property and without hope. Small-business enterprise is a symbol of a society where a hired man can become his own boss."[49]

Patman's hearings revealed that the chains were indeed receiving special deals—for instance, some $8 million in promotional fees, no small sum at the time, flowed from food manufacturers to A&P in a single year—that were not available to independent retailers. The next year, Congress overwhelmingly passed the Robinson-Patman Act, which makes it illegal for suppliers to "discriminate in price between different purchasers ... where the effect of such discrimination may be substantially to lessen competition," and for buyers to "knowingly [receive] the benefit of such discrimination." Giving favored buyers other kinds of advantages denied to their competitors—such as special terms, secret incentive payments, or co-op advertising fees—is also prohibited. The law does, however, preserve the benefits of increased efficiency; it allows suppliers to charge some companies less than others to the extent that those lower prices are justified by actual cost savings. (If, for example, it costs less for the supplier to ship bulk quantities to a large firm, then the price can reflect that difference.)[50]

The Robinson-Patman Act fundamentally differs from other antitrust policies. While proving a violation of most antitrust laws requires evidence that the anticompetitive tactic in question diminished overall competition in that market, under the Robinson-Patman Act, plaintiffs only need to show that a particular business was injured by the discriminatory discounts. In structuring the law this way, Congress intended not only to foster a competitive market for consumers, but to maintain an even playing field for small businesses. Its purpose was to restore "equality of opportunity in business" and to protect both consumers and "independent... businessmen," according to a House Judiciary Committee report that accompanied the legislation. "Congress was convinced that, by protecting small businesses, it was also protecting the operation of a competitive economy," explained federal appeals court judge Abner Mikva in 1988.[51]

Since the 1970s, the Robinson-Patman Act has been, in the words of the American Antitrust Institute's Foer, "dissed, cussed, and otherwise condemned" by antitrust enforcement agencies and many scholars, who see its goal of a level playing field for small businesses as inconsistent with the appropriate role of antitrust policy, which is to foster efficiency and lower prices. While some argue that the courts should essentially negate the law by requiring plaintiffs to meet the same strict standards established in *Brooke Group*, the courts have declined to do so, in large part because the act's explicit language and legislative history leave no doubt as to Congress's intention. Attempts to repeal the law have so far failed—although opponents are even now gearing up for another push. Stuck with a law that does not concur with their worldview, the Department of Justice and the Federal Trade Commission have taken the only option left: they have ignored it. The DOJ stopped enforcing the Robinson-Patman Act in the 1970s, while the FTC has been, at best, highly reluctant to investigate buyer power and pursue possible violations. "Essentially the federal government has ceded the field to private litigation," said Bruce Spiva, an attorney who has represented plaintiffs in Robinson-Patman Act cases. Given the expense of bringing these lawsuits, which require gathering extensive evidence and economic analysis and may entail years of legal fees, leaving small-business owners to file suit on their own hardly substitutes for federal enforcement.[52]

One group of retailers has, however, managed to use the Robinson-Patman Act to demand fair treatment. In 1998, twenty-six independent bookstores and their trade group, the American Booksellers Association, filed a lawsuit alleging that Barnes & Noble and Borders had marshaled their considerable market power to exact "secret, discriminatory, and illegal" discounts from publishers. According to evidence presented in the case, the two chains were able to buy books through a major wholesaler for 3 to 5 percent less than independents were charged under the same circumstances. Publishers further rewarded the chains with a 2 percent discount if they paid their invoices within twenty-five days, but allowed independents only ten days. Publishers also gave Borders volume discounts when it ordered less than the minimum carton quantity that independents had to buy to qualify for the same discounts. Additional evidence suggested that the chains knew about and actively solicited the illegal advantages. One Barnes & Noble employee wrote that the terms reached with a publisher "CANNOT be put in writing for legal reasons." Perhaps most chilling of all, in a company memo, a high-level Borders executive wrote that, although one publisher "claims to have leveled the playing field, what they don't realize is that in a couple of years there may only be a couple of players left who will dictate the game on their own terms."[53]

The roots of the case stretch back to 1979, when the FTC launched an investigation into whether publishers were favoring bookstore chains with sweetheart deals. The leading chains at the time were Waldenbooks (later purchased by Borders), B. Dalton (bought by Barnes & Noble), and Crown Books. The inquiry proceeded at a snail's pace. Nearly a decade after the investigation began, in 1988, the FTC formally issued complaints against six leading publishers, outlining evidence that they had given the chains special deals not available to independents, even on orders of the same size. Their published pricing schedules also provided steep volume discounts at very high-quantity levels (e.g., more than forty-two hundred books) that appeared to be unrelated to actual cost savings—especially since they often had to break down the orders and ship the books separately to each of the chains' outlets. But then the case slipped back into slow motion. Four years later, in 1992, the FTC reached tentative consent agreements with the publishers, the terms of which were not made public. Then the matter was tabled. Four more years passed and finally, in 1996, with the commission reportedly deadlocked over how to proceed, the case was dropped and the complaints dismissed.[54]

Tired of waiting for the government to take action, in 1994 the American Booksellers Association initiated its own lawsuit, reaching a settlement three years later with six major publishers that was to establish flatter pricing schedules and give independent bookstores proportional access to cooperative advertising fees. The publishers covered legal expenses, but the ABA did not seek further damages. A few months later, Penguin USA was found to have violated the terms of the deal and settled with the ABA for $25 million. But the favoritism persisted, according to many independent booksellers, who traced it to the coercive power of Barnes & Noble and Borders. Larger than the top ten publishers combined and controlling a substantial share of the nation's shelf space, their bargaining power was immense and hard for publishers to resist. "Addressing the real issues of inequity in our industry meant that we would have to address the coercive practices of these corporate retailers," explained ABA executive director Avin Domnitz.[55]

"The stories we heard [from other booksellers] were the same. This was not just a matter of competition. We were not being treated fairly," explained Carla Jimenez, co-owner of Inkwood Books, which occupies an old 1920s house on the south side of Tampa, each of its many cozy rooms filled with books. Jimenez left her law practice in 1991 to join friend and business partner Leslie Reiner in opening the store. A few years later, the chains began to roll out stores across the region. Soon there were seven superstores within a ten-mile radius of Inkwood. In a market suddenly oversaturated with bookstores and paying what they felt certain were higher wholesale prices than their chain competitors were getting, Jimenez and Reiner teetered on the brink of failure and came close to shuttering the business in the mid-1990s. But they pulled through and, with twenty-five other stores across the country, decided to challenge the chains in court.[56]

Before their case went to trial in 2001, however, the booksellers suffered a major setback. The case had drawn a judge, William Orrick, who indicated that he saw little problem with the chains using their size to exact special deals. Isn't that "what capitalism's all about?" he asked one witness. Although evidence linked declining sales at Inkwood and the other stores to discriminatory pricing, Orrick ruled in a pivotal pretrial decision that expert testimony had not completely ruled out every other possible cause for the revenue losses. The decision meant that the ABA could seek only an injunction, not damages. This had two crucial consequences: the case would be tried by a judge instead of a jury, and the focus would be on the chains' current practices, rather than the evidence of price discrimination going back to 1994 that the ABA had gathered. By the time of the trial, the special discounts and discriminatory terms had lessened considerably, largely as a result of the lawsuit. The ABA felt that Orrick's ruling was reversible on appeal—it set an exceptionally high bar that was inconsistent with other federal courts—but an appeal would have required several more years of litigation and the group had already spent $18 million on the case.[57]

Instead the ABA pursued a settlement. The chains agreed to pay $4.7 million, but admitted no wrongdoing and required that all evidence not yet made public in the suit be destroyed. Both sides declared victory. Barnes & Noble and Borders called the settlement a "vindication," while the ABA said that, while the suit had fallen short of expectations, it had succeeded in achieving its main goal, namely pricing schedules and terms that are much fairer to locally owned stores. "Things had changed significantly as a result of bringing the suit," said Jimenez. Although the case might be seen as an indication that private litigation can be sufficient to enforce a fair market, most independent retailers do not belong to a trade association that has the capacity or the resources to bring such a suit. Jimenez also worries that, without government attention, the discriminatory deals might start to creep back into the book business. "The feds are not interested in enforcement and have not done oversight over the years, and, as a result, this industry and others do not feel that this is serious."[58]

Given the limited attention that buyer power has received from government agencies, it's anyone's guess as to whether discriminatory deals have been confined to the book trade or are in fact common across retail. Occasional lawsuits in the United States and investigations by foreign governments suggest that the chains may routinely use their power over suppliers to put smaller rivals at an unfair disadvantage. Wal-Mart and other big chains have obtained rates from Visa and MasterCard that are less than half the 1.5 to 3.0 percent of the purchase price that local stores remit to the card companies when a shopper pays with plastic. David Balto, an attorney with Robins, Kaplan, Miller, and Ciresi, a law firm representing independent businesses in a case aimed at ending the disparity, contended that the rates are driven by market clout, not cost differences: "It costs exactly the same for Visa to have a link with the merchant processor for a small retailer as for it to have a link with the processor handling Wal-Mart's transactions." Other evidence comes from the movie industry. Independent theaters have taken legal action against top movie theater chains, claiming that the chains use their clout to coerce the studios into denying independents access to first-run blockbuster movies.[59]

In Britain, a yearlong investigation by the Competition Commission documented more than a dozen ways in which the country's top chains, including Tesco and Wal-Mart-owned Asda, have exploited their market power to squeeze suppliers and undermine independent retailers. The commission found that the chains were charging suppliers fees for access to shelf space, requiring them to contribute financially to the cost of opening new stores, and inducing them to provide volume discounts even on small orders. Some of the chains even demanded retroactive discounts when sales of a supplier's product did not meet their expectations. So intimidated were the suppliers, particularly small producers and farmers, that, even with guarantees of anonymity, many were reluctant to share information with investigators. Suppliers were not the only ones injured. Local stores are "doubly disadvantaged," the commission concluded. Not only do they lack the muscle to obtain the same favorable discounts, they often end up paying even higher prices as suppliers seek to recover losses incurred dealing with the chains. Consumers, too, are suffering as the range of shopping choices shrinks. But rather than taking strong action to halt the tactics, the Competition Commission opted instead to negotiate a "Code of Practices" for big retailers to follow. The toothless code has done little to curb the abuses, according to Break the Armlock, a coalition of farming, consumer, and small-business groups, as well as to the government's own reviews in 2004 and 2005. Yet the authorities have not taken further action.[60]

Back in the United States, opponents of the Robinson-Patman Act are gearing up to once again push for repeal of the law. In 2002 Congress established the Antitrust Modernization Commission, charging it with reviewing antitrust laws and recommending any needed changes by 2007. Although the legislation that created the commission requires that its twelve members, who are chosen by Congress and the president, include "equitable representation of various points of view," it is in fact dominated by people who have primarily been engaged in defending companies against antitrust charges. None of the AMC's members represent consumers, small businesses, or the states. The AMC has identified the Robinson-Patman Act as a priority issue, and many observers believe it is likely to recommend either outright repeal or revisions that effectively negate the act, removing the only significant restraint on buyer power in U.S. law. In testimony before the commission, the Business Roundtable, an association of corporate executives, urged repeal, describing the Robinson-Patman Act, with its focus on a level playing field, as an "anachronism"— even as the unprecedented clout of global retailers has made concerns about powerful buyers more relevant now than ever before.[61]

Opponents of the Robinson-Patman Act characterize its protection of small businesses as being at odds with consumer welfare. They argue that powerful retail buyers ultimately benefit consumers by passing on some of the lower prices they wrest from suppliers. This is certainly true in some cases, particularly when there is excessive market concentration among suppliers. The Visa and MasterCard case is a good example. Lack of competition has enabled the two companies to charge retailers (and, indirectly, consumers) exorbitant rates. Wal-Mart has the power to bring the card companies in line and demand a fairer price, which it may pass on to its customers. But this is a poor solution to the real problem, as it further disadvantages competing retailers that continue to be gouged by Visa and MasterCard, as well as their customers. A different approach was taken by the European Union, which responded to the card companies' market power by capping their rates at 0.7 percent, thereby fostering both lower prices and greater retail competition.[62]

Moreover, there are a number of scenarios in which the tactics of power buyers directly harm consumers, according to John Kirkwood, a former FTC lead attorney who now teaches at Seattle University School of Law. Should a power buyer succeed in using discriminatory deals to drive out competitors, it could attain sufficient market share to raise its prices. By undermining other retailers, power buyers deprive consumers of a robust array of choices in the marketplace. Their death grip on suppliers may also lead to a reduction in product research and development, resulting in less innovation.[63]

Beyond the consumer issues, the debate over the Robinson-Patman Act is about whether a fair playing field should be a goal of antitrust policy. If not, then we are consenting to a distorted marketplace in which companies can succeed not by being better, but simply by being bigger. Such unbridled power would serve neither the interests of a truly competitive economy, nor, as the original authors of our antitrust laws understood, those of a democratic, self-governing people.

Subsidies, tax loopholes, and lax antitrust enforcement rank as some of the more significant policy advantages chain stores enjoy. But the favoritism is pervasive and shows up in a host of government decisions. Many states, for example, do not require health plans to treat all pharmacies equally. As we saw in Chapter 6, some prescription drug coverage coerces consumers into using an affiliated mail-order service by allowing them to make only one co-pay for a ninety-day mail-order supply, but blocking local drugstores from dispensing more than thirty days' worth of drugs with each co-pay. Another example can be found in New York, where the city council recently transferred ownership of some three hundred independent newsstands to a single corporation. The former owners will be permitted to continue on as managers for now, while the new corporate owner plans to make a fortune selling advertising on the outside of their stands. The move effectively turns independent businesspeople, such as Mary Whalen, whose family has had a newsstand at the corner of William and Wall Streets since the 1920s, into "some kind of serfs," said Robert Bookman, an attorney representing the dispossessed owners. Other examples can be found at the federal level. In 2005 Congress appropriated $35 million to expand a road connecting Wal-Mart's headquarters in Bentonville to I-540. Normally, federal road funds are given out only if cities ask for the money and agree to come up with at least 20 percent of the project's cost. But in this case, the city never requested the grant—Wal-Mart did—and Congress voted to cover the full bill.[64]

Earlier that year, the U.S. Department of Labor gave Wal-Mart an even more valuable gift: the agency agreed to provide the company fifteen days' notice before investigating any alleged labor-law violations at its stores. The deal—which was reached after the department found that the chain had violated child labor laws by having teenage workers use chain saws and other dangerous equipment—also gave Wal-Mart ten days to correct any violations before penalties would be imposed, and stipulated that Labor Department officials could not talk publicly about the agreement without permission from the company. In exchange for this generous treatment, Wal-Mart agreed to pay a $136,000 fine and abide by labor laws. A subsequent investigation by the U.S. inspector general determined that the deal was legal, but unprecedented in the department's history, and found that it had largely been written by Wal-Mart's attorneys and adopted wholesale by federal officials. With its lengthy rap sheet of wage-and-hour and right-to-organize violations, Wal-Mart had managed to get itself appointed as the fox guarding the henhouse. In 2006, as criticism of the deal mounted, the Labor Department opted not to continue the arrangement. But the deal remains a striking example of the lax attitude that federal officials seem to take toward enforcing labor laws at Wal-Mart and other offending chains, which has not only harmed workers but put businesses, both large and small, that do comply with the law at a competitive disadvantage.[65]

The ugly truth is that the decline of independent businesses and the rise of the big boxes has been fueled by government policy, which has championed, fostered, and financed chain store expansion. In a country that values fairness and independence, this is a troubling realization. It is, however, in one respect good news: it suggests that locally owned businesses are not the inherently antiquated and obsolete entities that some make them out to be. In fact, given the uphill terrain they have faced, we might well conclude that the remarkable wonder is not that so many have failed, but rather that so many have been skilled and scrappy enough to survive. It's good news too in the sense that policy is something we control. We can opt to end the favoritism and instead enact policies that better reflect the economic and community value of locally owned businesses. Indeed, across the country, there is a growing grassroots movement afoot to do just that.

EIGHT

COMMUNITIES UNCHAINED

ON A CRISP SATURDAY MORNING IN JANUARY 2006, a big crowd had gathered, spilling out onto the sidewalk, at Waltz Pharmacy in downtown Damariscotta, Maine. They were there to save their small coastal community, a village of just two thousand people, from a megastore. This was the big kickoff event for the final two-month leg of a campaign to enact a law limiting stores to thirty-five thousand square feet. Should voters endorse the size cap, it would put an end to Wal-Mart's plans to build a supercenter several times that size. People were picking up signs and fliers to distribute, and signing up to volunteer to go door-to-door and turn out the vote. Most everyone had donned a red baseball cap with "Yes" printed boldly across the front.

At the center of all this activity were two women, Eleanor Kinney and Jenny Mayher, who had sparked the effort almost a year before, when Wal-Mart's plans were no more than speculation. Neither had much experience with political campaigns, but both had the same reaction when they heard the rumor that Wal-Mart had expressed interest in coming to town. "It was like a punch in the gut," recalled Mayher, whose roots are in Maine but who lived in Mississippi for four years before settling in Damariscotta. "I was so aware there of dead downtowns. The architecture is beautiful, but every storefront is boarded over, because every town has a big-box strip." The experience left Mayher all the more appreciative, and fiercely protective, of Damariscotta's lively downtown and many local businesses, like Waltz Pharmacy, Yellowfront Grocery, Damariscotta Hardware, Maine Coast Books, and Reny's department store.[1]

Kinney and Mayher began by circulating a simple petition. "We didn't know anything. We didn't know what land-use laws were on the books. We didn't know about citizens' initiatives. We just thought [town officials] should know how the community felt. It was sort of naive, but we were trusting in the best spirit of the democratic process," said Mayher. They left the petitions on the counters of various downtown stores. Within five days they had over a thousand signatures. "There was an outpouring of support. It just bubbled up like a spring from the ground," said Mayher. "People were thanking us. We got identified as those two women who were doing something." In May 2005 they presented their petition to the select board (similar to a city council). By then, Wal-Mart was still a rumor, but a more defined one. The chain was eyeing a piece of property along Route 1B for a store of either 109,000 or 186,000 square feet, the size of two to three football fields. The land was zoned for commercial use. But rather than take immediate action, as the petition urged, the board set up a study committee.

Months passed before the committee's first meeting in September, by which time Kinney and Mayher had learned much more about big-box retailers and how little protection Damariscotta's existing zoning code afforded. "We realized the best thing to do was to get out in front of it," said Kinney. Rather than wait for the committee, they drafted, with the help of an attorney, a formal legal petition to put a thirty-five-thousand-square-foot size cap before the voters. They soon gathered the necessary signatures and submitted the petition in November. They had gotten in front of Wal-Mart, but just barely: the day that they filed the documents, Wal-Mart executives arrived in Damariscotta on a private jet to present their plans. Rumor suddenly became reality. (Under Maine law, local land-use measures that win approval from voters are retroactive to the date the referendum petition was filed.)

Now the work of persuading their fellow citizens to prohibit big-box stores was under way. Fortunately, Kinney and Mayher, both stay-at-home moms with young children, were not alone. At a community meeting on the cap, nearly sixty people stepped forward to help. Damariscotta's downtown turned out to be one of their greatest assets, providing an easy way to spread information and enlist support. "You go downtown to do your errands and everywhere you go you stop and talk to people," said Kinney. They named their group Our Town Damariscotta and set up a Web site and an e-mail list. They split into committees—research, letters to the editor, visibility, and fund-raising—to carry out different aspects of the campaign. Meanwhile, seventy business owners formed their own committee to support the cap. One of the campaign's smartest moves was to urge residents of neighboring communities—Newcastle, Nobleboro, and Edgecomb—who offered help to instead start similar efforts in their own towns. Soon, size-cap petition drives were under way across the region. The multitown strategy neutralized one of Wal-Mart's more potent threats. "Wal-Mart told our selectmen, 'If we don't build here, we'll build next door,'" said Kinney.

To counter the grassroots campaign, Wal-Mart hired a top-flight PR firm, ran newspaper ads, and sent several rounds of slick, full-color mailers touting consumer choice and lower prices to every household in town. Company representatives phoned voters and pushed the idea that the size cap would stifle economic development. Kinney and Mayher kept their campaign focused on protecting Damariscotta's future and ensuring economic development at a scale that would benefit the community. Their strategy worked. In March, voters endorsed the size cap by a 62 to 38 percent margin. It was the highest turnout in the town's history, with over 80 percent of voters participating. The neighboring towns of Newcastle and Nobleboro adopted similar store size-caps that month and several other nearby towns took steps in that direction.

Citizens campaigns have succeeded in blocking chain retail projects in hundreds of communities across the country. Where once Wal-Mart and Home Depot could multiply with little or no resistance, now they face organized opposition on as many as one out of every three of their proposals. These efforts have arisen in every region of the country and in a wide range of communities, from small towns to cities and suburbs. Wal-Mart has been defeated in towns similar to Damariscotta as well as in places that would seem to share little in common with that community. In 2004 voters in Inglewood, a working-class city of 112,000 people, mostly African American and Latino, in the Los Angeles metro, soundly rejected a Wal-Mart proposal by 61 to 39 percent. The company had spent over $1 million on the campaign. But in the end, the issues motivating Inglewood residents were much the same as those at play in Damariscotta: local control, small business, and community. Big-box stores are not the only projects facing opposition. Citizens groups have fought strip malls and power centers, chain pharmacies and Starbucks outlets.[2]

"Local opposition has successfully squashed numerous plans among the big-box players in different parts of the country," noted Bernstein Research, a firm that advises institutional investors, in a report on opposition to Wal-Mart, Target, and other big-box retailers. The report warned, "Heightened resistance could negatively impact these retailers by slowing their square footage growth rates." Between 2000 and 2004, at least 132 big-box projects were blocked by citizens groups, the firm found. Others had been significantly delayed or altered. Even Wal-Mart admits that grassroots resistance to its stores is widespread. In a remark often repeated by opponents, founder Sam Walton once commented, "If some community, for whatever reason, doesn't want us in there, we aren't interested in going in and creating a fuss." Asked about this in 2005, Wal-Mart real estate manager Jeff Doss replied, "Were that the case, we'd never build a store anywhere."[3]

Despite the increasingly successful grassroots opposition—in fact because of it—retail developers usually unveil their projects to the public as though they are already done deals. They talk about any necessary approvals—a site-plan review, a storm-water permit—as though they are simply routine formalities to be checked off before breaking ground. Their aim is to foster a sense of inevitability. But communities in fact have a great deal of authority over development within their borders. Even those that have not adopted specific big-box policies may have any number of laws on the books that give elected officials the power to reject a retail project. The developer may need to get the property rezoned from, say, agricultural to commercial, or acquire a variance from certain zoning code provisions. City officials are under no obligation to change established policies to accommodate a developer, especially if they have been persuaded that the project would harm the community—or at least that it's unpopular with their constituents. Even projects that do not require rezoning land may need to undergo a traffic study or an environmental-impact review. Given the amount of traffic these stores generate, that alone is often sufficient for cities to conclude that a project would not be in the best interests of public safety and welfare. If state roads are involved, or wetlands or impaired waterways, then the project may also require permits from various state agencies.

Even if the land is zoned correctly and the traffic study presents no obstacles, a project may not comply with the city's comprehensive plan, a document that puts forth the community's broad policies and goals with regard to land use and development. The plan may state, for example, that it is the city's intention to maintain the downtown as the center of commercial activity, ensure that development is compatible with its surroundings, or foster locally owned businesses. In most states, the failure of a proposal to fit the comprehensive plan obligates, or at least provides a legal basis for, the city to reject the project. Cities are understandably nervous about being sued over such rejections, but they should be heartened by the fact that, while the developer's attorney may make threats, such suits are usually futile. On land-use matters, the courts generally defer to city officials, presuming their decisions are legal if they followed reasonable logic and the process was fair.[4]

While developers and even city officials commonly tell citizens that municipal land-use decisions may take into account only a narrow range of planning issues, such as traffic and building design, in fact a project's impact on the community and its local economy are entirely relevant factors. That these central issues ought to be considered makes common sense, and has been endorsed by the courts. In 1995 the Idaho Supreme Court upheld the town of Hailey's decision to reject a big-box project on the grounds that its comprehensive plan called for the downtown to remain "the primary commercial center of the community." The court concluded, "Preserving ...the economic viability of a community's downtown business core can be a proper zoning purpose." The Vermont Supreme Court similarly endorsed the rejection of a Wal-Mart store because of the economic ramifications. The court ruled that the "project's impact on market competition was a relevant factor" for officials to consider. When Lawrence, Kansas, denied approval for a shopping center that would harm the downtown, both state and federal courts upheld the decision. The rulings affirmed that preserving the vitality of the downtown "constitutes a legitimate concern of the governing body."[5]

The bottom line is that chain retail projects are done deals only if the community opts not to contest them. One recent example of a seemingly done deal that collapsed under the weight of citizen opposition was a proposal by Wal-Mart to build a 156,000-square-foot superstore in Charlevoix, a small town in northern Michigan. Wal-Mart intended to put the store just beyond the city limits in another jurisdiction known as Charlevoix Township. At first there appeared to be no obstacles. The permits seemed easily attainable and roughly two-thirds of the residents supported the plan, according to Bob Hoffman, an accountant who moved to Charlevoix from Detroit in 1987. But he and several other residents were deeply concerned about the project's impact on local businesses and community life. They began to meet and strategize. "It was the funniest group of people," said Marell Staffel, owner of a photo and frame shop, who joined the campaign early on. "You would never put this bunch together." Politically, they ranged from Hoffman, a self-described "independent on the Republican side," to a Green Party activist. Socially the group was even more eclectic, encompassing both a millionaire and a welfare recipient, business owners and hippies. "We probably didn't agree on anything else," said Hoffman.[6]

At one of their first meetings, one participant cut to the core of what everyone was feeling with the comment, "This is our town, not Wal-Mart's." The remark provided the group with a name and slogan, emblazoned on signs, bumper stickers, fliers, buttons, and advertisements. Their strategy was straightforward. "We knew that we had two goals to accomplish. One was to inform the public about the impacts of these stores. The second was to put up as many roadblocks as we could," said Hoffman. Having a few business owners—including a bookseller, the owner of the local hardware store, and Staffel—on board was crucial to giving the campaign legitimacy and visibility early on. When Hoffman was asked how he recruited business owners and what he said to those who hesitated to take a public stand on a controversial issue, even one that would directly affect their livelihoods, he quoted from a speech Ronald Reagan made on behalf of Barry Goldwater's presidential run in 1964: "If some among you fear taking a stand because you are afraid of reprisals from customers, clients, or even government, recognize that you are just feeding the crocodile hoping he'll eat you last."[7]

Members of This Is Our Town began a steady stream of letters to the editor, using the most-read section of the newspaper to highlight major concerns about big-box retail. They organized a town hall meeting on the issue that drew some three hundred residents and circulated a petition that ultimately attracted more than four thousand signatures. They did their research and stayed on message. To give people a sense of the sheer scale of the development, they took a large map of Charlevoix and overlaid an outline of the superstore, showing how it would dwarf the downtown—and, by inference, economically devour it. Hoffman observed that their information campaign really started to gain momentum after a group of high school students were required, as part of a class, to attend a city council meeting. Wal-Mart was discussed at the meeting and the students took an interest and started reading up on the issue. "All of the sudden all the high school students were wearing buttons and talking to their parents about Wal-Mart," said Hoffman. Within months, public opinion had reversed; now about two-thirds opposed the megastore.[8]

Meanwhile, This Is Our Town assembled the ammunition that elected officials would need to turn down the project. Members highlighted how the proposal was at odds with various sections of the comprehensive plan. They detailed concerns about traffic and researched the impact of polluted runoff on Stover Creek, a registered trout stream running through the property. Then they won two crucial victories. Although the site was outside of the city of Charlevoix's boundaries, the city would still have to run water and sewer lines out to the development. At the urging of This Is Our Town, the city council passed a resolution requiring that all projects beyond the city limits pass an economic-impact review before being granted water and sewer access. Given that such a review would likely show Wal-Mart significantly affecting existing businesses and jobs, this posed a major obstacle to the retailer's plans. Then the Charlevoix Township Planning Commission, which had jurisdiction over the site, voted to grant This Is Our Town standing. This meant that the group would not be subject to a three-minute time limit at the public hearing on the proposal, but would have ample time to present its research and even arrange for expert testimony. "Wal-Mart's people went through the roof," recalled Hoffman. Not long after, the chain decided to drop the deal and walk away from Charlevoix.[9]

Knowing that it was only a matter of time before Wal-Mart or another big-box returned for a second try, This Is Our Town began a new campaign to persuade both the township and the city to enact laws prohibiting large stores. In the city, the group won a store size-cap of forty-five thousand square feet—the size of Charlevoix's largest supermarket and less than one-third as big as Wal-Mart's proposed store. For its part, the township revised its zoning code to require proposals for stores over fifty thousand square feet to pass an economic- and community-impact review in order to obtain approval and established an absolute size limit of ninety thousand square feet. A voter referendum in November 2005 endorsed the new measures by 61 to 39 percent, confirming the potency of This Is Our Town's educational campaign. Today, Hoffman, who had never before been involved in anything like this, travels around Michigan helping citizens groups contest big-box projects. His advice: "First, it's worth the fight. Don't let them tell you that they can't be stopped. Look at all the different approaches." Better yet, he said, strengthen your city's policies now so as to avoid such battles in the future.[10]

This Is Our Town did virtually everything right, according to Al Norman, who advises grassroots groups fighting big-box projects nationwide and whose book, *Slam-Dunking Wal-Mart: How You Can Stop Superstore Sprawl in Your Hometown*, is an indispensable guide for these campaigns.

Norman says that, like many people who become involved in this issue, he is an "accidental activist." He'd never thought much about superstores until Wal-Mart showed up on the doorstep of his hometown of Greenfield, Massachusetts, in 1993. The town council approved Wal-Mart, but a group of residents managed to get an initiative on the ballot to overturn its decision. They asked Norman, who has a background in running political campaigns, to help them win the referendum. He took the gig, still wondering how a store could be such a big deal. Two months later, after a roller-coaster campaign, Greenfield voters rejected Wal-Mart and Norman emerged as a passionate opponent of big-box sprawl.

The vote made headlines nationally; it was one of the first times that a citizens group had challenged and blocked Wal-Mart's expansion. Soon Norman was getting calls from people across the country looking for his help. These days, Norman, who is in his late fifties and by day runs an organization advocating for home health care for the elderly, spends his evenings advising grassroots groups by phone and his weekends traveling the country to help them plan and execute effective campaigns. He jokes that his wife has become a "Wal-Mart widow." More than a decade after becoming an activist, Norman has been involved in dozens of successful grassroots campaigns. A savvy campaign tactician, he has a gift for compelling messages. "They don't sell small-town quality of life on any Wal-Mart shelf, and once they take it from you, you can't buy it back from them at any price," he says.

There are four ingredients needed to beat a big-box retail project, according to Norman. One is a citizens coalition. It need not be huge—the core group may be as small as a dozen—but it should be as broad a cross-section of the community as possible: civic leaders, business owners, environmentalists, labor union members, religious leaders, and ordinary citizens. A diverse group will not only connect with more people, but it can't be tagged as a "special interest" (e.g., just a bunch of small-business owners out to protect their profits, or labor unions angry with Wal-Mart). The second ingredient is a land-use attorney. Having an attorney, Norman explained, tells city officials two things: that you are serious, and that they may face a lawsuit should they approve a project that harms public welfare or violates the city's comprehensive plan. Other experts who can undertake relevant traffic, environmental, or economic-impact studies are also helpful in refuting the rosy scenarios presented by the developer. A third ingredient is fund-raising to pay for the attorney and the campaign materials. Rather than having bake sales, Norman advises, grassroots groups should ask for sizable contributions from local merchants and other major donors.[11]

The final ingredient is visibility. To overcome a big-box retailer's spending on advertising and direct mail, grassroots campaigns have to find ways to get their message out. Lawn signs, letters to the editor, radio ads, and T-shirts are staple tools. Creative, high-visibility events can work wonders both in pressing home the campaign's message and in energizing those involved. In Greenfield, Norman set up three giant bulletin boards in the middle of the town green, where residents could tack up messages expressing their feelings about Wal-Mart. It became the campaign's most powerful symbol and a favorite subject of news photographers and television cameras. In Hood River, Oregon, a grassroots group called Citizens for Responsible Growth organized an event one afternoon in which two hundred people linked arms to form a giant circle around the downtown. The event was designed to demonstrate community support for local businesses and to illustrate just how large and economically overwhelming a proposed Wal-Mart supercenter would be. It was one of the high points in a successful campaign that eventually led the county commission to reject Wal-Mart's application to build.[12]

CHALLENGING GOLIATH

Even well-organized campaigns face a tough fight against big-box expansion. Mega-retailers are experts at this game. The deck is stacked in their favor. While citizens groups struggle to raise money and fit meetings into participants' already busy lives, the chains have deep pockets, extensive experience, and scores of attorneys and public relations people working full-time to expand their empires. They have an arsenal of effective tactics. One is stealth. The chains typically operate in secret for as long as they can, scouting locations, negotiating an option on a piece of property, and developing a site plan, all the while concealing their identity by working through a local real estate broker or other representative. Once everything is lined up, they go public, formally filing an application, at which point citizens typically have only a limited window of time in which to respond and are already several steps behind.

Another tactic is hubris. Mega-retailers act as though they will eventually have their way, a strategy that helps wear down the opposition. In Decorah, Iowa, Wal-Mart built a superstore in the floodplain of a local river even though the city's approval of the project was being contested in the courts and was ultimately deemed illegal. But by the time the Iowa Supreme Court issued its ruling, opponents were exhausted and the building was already complete. Rather than ordering it torn down, a settlement was negotiated. In Central Point, Oregon, Wal-Mart similarly spent $6 million on a piece of land *after* the city denied the chain a permit to build a supercenter on the site. In a statement to the local newspaper, the chain's attorney explained, "The fact that Wal-Mart is willing to purchase the property at this stage of the game tells the community that they're willing to do whatever is necessary to be able to have a store there."[13]

Still another tactic is intimidation. Mega-retailers often threaten local officials with a lawsuit if they vote against a proposal. Even a suit that has no merit and is eventually decided in the city's favor can be extremely costly. Small towns especially cannot afford protracted legal battles with some of the world's largest corporations. Often these threats are not overtly stated, but dramatically implied. Several big chains recently began to bring their own court reporters to city council and planning board hearings. As the reporter sits at the front of the room transcribing everything local officials say, the message to those inclined to scrutinize or vote against the project is clear: we're already gathering evidence for a lawsuit.[14]

By far their greatest advantage is financial. While ballot initiatives have long been a last resort for grassroots groups that fail to persuade their local officials to reject a big-box project, mega-retailers are increasingly turning to this tactic themselves, either to overturn a city decision denying them approval or to sidestep the process altogether by going straight to voters. The chains like ballot initiatives because they know that money confers a huge advantage in these campaigns. Yet they also want to avoid looking like global giants trying to buy the vote, so the chains have become adept at setting up fake grassroots groups (critics call them "Astroturf" groups) to campaign on their behalf. In Aberdeen, South Dakota, Wal-Mart created the Committee FOR a Vibrant Aberdeen to advocate for zoning changes that would allow it to build a supercenter. Although the committee's ads gave the impression that it was a genuine effort by ordinary residents seeking to bring a supercenter to town, it was in fact run by a Wal-Mart attorney and funded almost entirely by a $105,000 contribution from Wal-Mart. Residents were paid $50 to attend one of the committee's "information" sessions. Those opposed to the supercenter, Concerned Citizens for Aberdeen, managed to raise $32,000 from residents and business owners, but proved no match for Wal-Mart's Astroturf campaign. They lost the vote.[15]

This storyline has played out many times across the country. In the tiny town of Lake Geneva, Wisconsin, Home Depot set up the Lake Geneva Good Neighbor committee and spent $66,000 on a referendum involving a total of 1,412 voters, who approved the superstore by 53 to 47 percent. In Augusta, Maine, a developer for Target and Lowe's spent $174,000 to win voter approval for the stores. Wal-Mart funded a group called Protect Flagstaff's Future and spent nearly $400,000 convincing voters in this northern Arizona city to change their zoning laws to allow for the building of supercenters. It was by far the most ever spent in a Flagstaff election and made the difference, according to Becky Daggett, the director of a ten-year-old, bona fide citizens organization, Friends of Flagstaff's Future, which opposes big-box expansion. Even with the help of a local union, Daggett's fund-raising and volunteers were unable to match Wal-Mart's barrage of glossy mailings and advertisements, including one print ad that likened those who supported the zoning restrictions to Nazis. Wal-Mart won by just 365 votes.[16]

Big-box retailers have adroitly exploited race and class tensions in cities like Chicago, San Francisco, and Brooklyn, dividing neighbors to win approval for their outlets. In an African American neighborhood on the West Side of Chicago, Wal-Mart portrayed the members of unions opposed to its store as racist whites trying to protect their turf, an idea that gained traction even as a number of prominent black community leaders spoke against the development. Ikea worked a similar angle in Red Hook, a waterfront neighborhood in Brooklyn, where black and white residents have united in the past to fight garbage-transfer stations and waste-processing facilities, but split over the furniture giant's plans for a massive store that would funnel more than eight thousand cars a day through the area's narrow streets. "Their message to African Americans was that we were out to stop them from getting jobs. That became their driving drumbeat," said John McGettrick, a longtime resident and co-chair of the Red Hook Civic Association, who contends that the store will harm the area's prosperity by strangling much-needed mixed-use housing and job development with traffic snarls. The tactic can even work in relatively homogeneous communities, like Bennington, Vermont, where Wal-Mart and its local developer derisively referred to opponents as "doctors' wives and all those trustee people"—

even as the chain outspent them ten to one in a successful bid to overturn a law that capped store sizes and barred Wal-Mart, which already had one store, from building an even larger one.[17]

Citizens who oppose big-box projects sometimes find that they are up against not only the developer but their own elected officials. Many people pay little attention to local elections, only to discover, once a big-box project is on the table, that their planning board is stacked with people from the development industry, and the city council does not reflect most residents' views. The results can be disastrous. The local newspaper in Grand Island, Nebraska, reported that the city council "violated the public's trust by meeting with Wal-Mart officials . . . behind closed doors" and then threw "the city's comprehensive plan out the window" by approving the super-center. In Westminster, Colorado, the mayor and several city council members actively campaigned on Wal-Mart's behalf during a referendum on its proposed store. Only after the vote, which Wal-Mart won, did voters learn that, in secret meetings more than a year earlier, city officials had pledged to provide the chain with $5 million in subsidies. "The city council ran roughshod over the public interest," said resident Michael Melio. In Westbrook, Maine, residents concerned about a Wal-Mart coming into their neighborhood were told that they could not mention Wal-Mart at planning board meetings, because the company had not yet submitted an application—although the city's own economic development director had corresponded extensively with Wal-Mart about the project.[18]

But despite all their advantages, these goliaths are still routinely beaten by citizens groups. It's a testament both to how compelling the case against mega-retailers is for those who look beyond the dominant job and tax myths and to the fact that a dedicated group of ordinary people can still rally their neighbors and change their community's course. Emily Simon, an attorney and community activist in Portland, Oregon, first learned that a big-box store was slated for her neighborhood when a representative of the Portland Development Corporation (PDC) came to her door and said, "I have great news. We're going to put a Home Depot in Burnside." Simon replied, "Over my dead body," and immediately began contacting neighborhood associations and local business owners. The PDC, a quasi-public agency that uses tax dollars to catalyze redevelopment, planned to redevelop a five-block area at the base of Burnside Bridgehead on the east side of the Willamette River. Two developers had submitted proposals for mixed housing and commercial projects, each dominated by a big-box store. One was working with Lowe's; the other Home Depot. By the time the project became public, the wheels were already in motion.[19]

But citizen reaction was swift and potent. Word spread through Portland's numerous civic organizations. A coalition formed to fight the project, made up of eight neighborhood associations, scores of residents, and over one hundred local business owners, such as Anne Kilkenny, owner of the ninety-seven-year-old Winks Hardware, one of several hardware and building-supply stores within blocks of the site. People flooded the PDC with over eight hundred e-mails, turned out in droves at public hearings, and became so noisy that the city's elected leadership started to pressure the PDC to reconsider. "The PDC was flabbergasted," recalled neighborhood activist M'Lou Christ. With the writing on the wall, the developers resubmitted their proposals—this time calling for mixed residential and small-business spaces and no big-box stores.[20]

"Many did not have any clue as to how this would impact the community," said Sydney Yuan, who helped lead a campaign to block a Home Depot in Frisco, Colorado. "We did a lot of research and boiled it down into straightforward facts we could present to the voters. We really opened a lot of eyes." On election day, voters nixed the store by 57 to 43 percent—despite the fact that Home Depot spent nearly thirty thousand dollars on radio and newspaper ads, promised to give the town money for a new ball field, and had the active support of the city council. "One of the key elements of our success was our ability to get off the mark early and fast," said George Sherman, a retired diplomat and co-organizer of Citizens against Home Depot. Their slogan was, "Frisco can do better," which they put on yard signs, bumper stickers, and buttons. They bought a list of registered voters and set up phone banks and even mailed handwritten postcards. They wrote dozens of letters to the editor.[21]

They also worked to recruit business owners to their cause. "People didn't realize what a broad range of goods Home Depot sells," said Don Sather, who owns a local lumberyard. They contacted over fifty businesses, such as pet stores and banks, many of which were unaware that Home Depot, which sells pet food and finances construction, might affect their livelihoods. They asked the owners to join the campaign, make a donation, and talk to their employees, many of whom are Frisco voters. By raising numerous small donations, they managed to turn Home Depot's big spending into a liability. Colorado law requires that parties in an election disclose their donors. Shortly before the vote, the local newspaper ran a long list of community members who had made small contributions to the anti–Home Depot campaign, while the pro–Home Depot side listed only one donor. That made a huge impression on voters, said Sherman. Now with the vote behind them, the group is launching a new effort to replace three pro–big box city councilors in the next election.[22]

While these grassroots efforts have done much to advance public education and engagement, they are still fingers in the dike, each consuming lots of energy to stop a single development. Fortunately, many of these citizens groups have opted not to disband once the immediate fight before them is over, but to continue working to change local and state laws. The fruits of their efforts can be found in the growing number of cities and towns (and, increasingly, regions and states) that have enacted policies that limit big-box development, shift the burden of proof regarding a project's impacts from citizens to developers, and foster the kind of built environment in which locally owned businesses can thrive.

THE FIRST ANTI-CHAIN STORE MOVEMENT

Before examining what these communities are doing to stop chain store sprawl, it's worth taking a look at the first anti–chain store movement, which swept the nation in the 1920s and 1930s. Today, who prevails in a big-box fight often hinges on how local residents conceive of themselves. Opponents of these projects appeal to people's broad sense of being citizens and stewards of their community, which is why they often choose names like "Our Town." Chain retailers, on the other hand, win by getting people to assume the narrow role of consumer and to see the issue as simply a matter of shopping options. Although dominant today, this consumer identity is a relatively recent invention; it only became a powerful force in American politics in the years after World War II. Its origins are many, but one of them was the massive public relations campaign that chain retailers undertook in response to the first anti–chain store movement.[23]

Chain stores first began to multiply in large numbers in the years following World War I. During the 1920s, the number of chain stores climbed from about 30,000 to 150,000. By the end of the decade, they were capturing 22 percent of all retail sales nationally. Leading the pack was A&P, with some 15,000, mostly small, outlets that accounted for 11 percent of the country's grocery sales and generated over $1 billion in annual revenue. A&P was the Wal-Mart of its day—although it was, in relative terms, significantly smaller, accounting for 2.5 percent of all retail sales, compared to Wal-Mart's 10 percent share today.[24]

As the chains expanded, so too did opposition to their presence. It was a cause embraced by populists, Progressives, unions concerned about wage pressures, farmers fearful of chain store buying power, wholesalers, and, of course, local business owners. By the late 1920s, more than four hundred local organizations had sprung up around the country to counter the chains. These "home defense leagues" and "better business associations" were varied in their approaches. Some, like the Community Builders in Danville, Virginia, never mentioned the chains, but instead promoted the idea, through billboards and radio programs, that money that stayed in town helped to build the community and its institutions. Other groups attacked the chains directly and exhorted people to boycott them. A campaign in Springfield, Missouri, urged, "Keep Ozark Dollars in the Ozarks," and ran newspaper ads describing chain store managers as "mechanical operators" whose duty was to "get Springfield's money and to send it to the Home Office." The anti-chain cause was the focus of at least forty newspapers and a dozen radio programs, including a broadcast by the popular and foulmouthed W. K. Henderson, forerunner of today's shock jocks, whose show, out of KWKH in Shreveport, Louisiana, was heard throughout the South and West. In 1930 the Reverend J. M. Gates, a prolific African American preacher who sold tens of thousands of his recorded sermons, including such hits as "Are You Bound for Heaven or Hell?" and "Kinky Hair Is No Disgrace," recorded one calling on people to "stay out of the chain stores."[25]

By 1930, "the chain store problem" had entered the national political debate in full force. The *Nation* ran a four-part series titled "Chains versus Independents," while the *New Republic* asked, "Chain Stores: Menace or Promise?" That year, the nation's high school and college debate teams argued the proposition, "Resolved: that chain stores are detrimental to the best interests of the American public." Several U.S. senators and congressmen ran on anti-chain platforms, while Progressive gubernatorial candidates in Wisconsin and Minnesota made the chains a central issue in their campaigns. A former governor of Texas reportedly "received a revelation from God to get back into politics and save his people from the chain-store dragon."[26]

Opponents argued that the chains threatened democracy by undermining local economic independence and community self-determination. As they drove out the local merchant—a "loyal and energetic type of citizen"—the chains replaced him with a manager, a "transient," who was discouraged from independent thought and community involvement, and who served as "merely a representative of a non-resident group of stockholders who pay him according to his ability to line their pockets with silver." Many believe, wrote Supreme Court Justice Louis Brandeis, author of *The Curse of Bigness* and a strong advocate of vesting both economic and political power in local communities, that "the chain store, by furthering the concentration of wealth and of power and by promoting absentee ownership, is thwarting American ideals; that it is making impossible equality of opportunity; that it is converting independent tradesmen into clerks; and that it is sapping the resources, the vigor and the hope of the smaller cities and towns." Chain stores drained money from communities, drove down wages, and squeezed producers. In a study of forty-five chain and independent grocers in ten cities, two writers for *The Nation* found that prices at the chains were 7 percent lower, but their wages were 20 percent less. At a time when Americans had not yet defined their role in economic and political life as primarily that of consumers, but still thought of themselves as independent producers, workers, citizens, and custodians of local communities, these arguments found widespread support.[27]

Those opposed to chains sought not only to change people's shopping habits but to implement legislation that would retard the big retailers' growth. In the mid-1920s several state legislatures debated bills that would impose a special tax on chains. In 1929 Indiana became the first state to adopt such a tax. It was a graduated business license fee that increased according to the number of outlets a retailer operated, ranging from three dollars a year for a single store up to twenty-five dollars per store for chains with twenty or more outlets. The law was immediately challenged as a violation of the equal protection clause of the U.S. Constitution. Two years later, it was upheld by the Supreme Court in a 5–4 ruling; the Court had concluded that the distinction between chains and independents was reasonable enough to justify different tax rates.[28]

Between 1931 and 1937, twenty-six states adopted chain store taxes. Dozens of cities did, as well, led by Portland, Oregon, in 1931. Others, including Cleveland, Louisville, and Phoenix, soon followed. Some of these taxes, such as Indiana's, were nominal enough to have little impact on the chains. Others were more severe. Texas assessed a $750 per store tax on chains with fifty or more outlets; Pennsylvania collected $500 on stores in chains exceeding five hundred units. To put this in perspective, the grocery chain Kroger, which had 4,000 outlets in 1938, posted profits of about $1,000 per store, while Walgreens, with 1,900 units, earned about $4,000 per store. When figuring the tax, most states counted only the number of outlets within their borders, but Louisiana based its levy on the total number of stores the chain had nationally.[29]

Although the U.S. Supreme Court upheld these taxes in several cases, including one challenging Louisiana's law in 1937, it defined the scope of state authority very narrowly and somewhat arbitrarily. Variations on the standard chain store tax—the graduated license fee—were struck down by the Court, including laws in Kentucky and Iowa that taxed a retailer's revenue, increasing the rate according to the volume of sales. The majority concluded—with Brandeis and two other justices dissenting—that these laws treated national retailers differently from other retailers, violating their rights under the Fourteenth Amendment, which was adopted after the Civil War to ensure all people equal treatment under the law. The decision was built on rulings going back to the 1880s, when the Supreme Court had greatly expanded the power of corporations by extending to them the same protections granted to citizens under the Bill of Rights. It was a radical departure in thinking from the first century of U.S. history. Where once corporations had been subordinate to the public will, now they were given equal footing and potent legal rights. This expansive notion of corporate "rights" hindered states' ability to regulate chains. It endures to this day and explains why mega-retailers have been allowed to initiate ballot referenda and engage in political campaigns: despite their superior financial resources, they are deemed to have the same rights as citizens to free speech and participation in the political process.[30]

As cities and states continued to test the reach of their authority to regulate chain stores, Congress took up the issue, passing the Robinson-Patman Act and then, in 1938, turning its attention to another proposal by Representative Wright Patman, who sought to levy a national tax on chain stores. Cosponsored by seventy-five congressmen from thirty-three states, the bill would have dealt a deathblow to most national chains. For those with more than five hundred outlets, the base rate was $1,000 per unit. This was then multiplied by the number of states the chain spanned. Had the tax been in place in 1938, A&P would have owed $472 million in taxes on earnings of $9 million, while Woolworth's would have been assessed $81 million on $29 million in profits. Patman's bill phased in the tax over several years; the intent was to give the chains time to sell most of their stores to local owners.[31]

By the time Congress considered Patman's bill, however, the political terrain had begun to shift. The chains had mounted a massive public relations effort. It began in California in 1936, when the chains hired the Lord and Thomas advertising agency to gather signatures to force a referendum on the state's newly enacted chain store tax and to wage a campaign against the measure. Lord and Thomas advised the chains that they had three natural allies: their employees, suppliers, and customers. Under the ad firm's counsel, the chains started calling employees by name rather than number, raised their salaries, and lessened their workload. They curried favor with farmers by absorbing a bumper crop of peaches. They tried to improve their community image by ordering store managers to join local chambers of commerce. Lord and Thomas dispatched an army of speakers, who extolled the chains' virtues before any civic group or club that would listen. Two months before the vote, they unleashed a barrage of radio and newspaper advertising. They sidestepped the issue of community self-determination and reframed the debate instead around consumers. "Vote NO and keep prices low," they urged. Early opinion polls had shown strong support for the tax, but on election day, it was trounced by a two-to-one margin.[32]

The chains took their public relations campaign national, forming the American Retail Federation. They ran advertisements touting their consumer benefits and attacking the Patman tax in every daily newspaper in the country. They won over key constituencies, notably farmers and organized labor. Support from farmers came as the chains continued to buy up surplus crops, saving citrus growers in Florida, walnut growers in Oregon, and turkey farmers in New York. In 1938 and 1939 A&P, which had previously fought unionization, permitted its stores to be organized and signed a series of collective-bargaining agreements. The company's change of heart came "under the guidance of their public relations council." In meetings with the president of the American Labor Federation, they cut a deal: unionization in exchange for labor's opposition to Patman's bill. Most important, the chains continued to cultivate the consumer identity. The more people saw themselves as consumers—not producers, workers, or citizens—the less concerned they were about the impact on their livelihoods and community life, and the more inclined they were to see the chains as satisfying an essential need for "quality, price, and better buying information." In 1939 *Business Week* reported that the chains had "reversed the trend against them."[33]

Patman's tax failed in 1940. The following year, Utah voters rejected a chain store tax. No other chain store taxes were enacted after that point. Over the years, those on the books were either repealed or rendered irrelevant by inflation. The postwar years saw the triumph of the consumer as the primary way in which Americans identified themselves and articulated their economic and political interests. The notion that the structure of the economy ought to embody and support democratic values faded from view. Economic policy was no longer seen as an instrument for nurturing self-reliance and self-government, but for furthering efficiency and consumer welfare. Brandeis's stance in favor of decentralizing both economic and political power disappeared as a working policy position. Liberals instead resolved the problem of concentrated economic power by embracing a strong federal government that would regulate corporate America's worst excesses and establish a social welfare system to absorb the fallout. Today, while liberals and conservatives may argue about the size and scope of the federal government, support for breaking up and dispersing economic power finds expression in neither of the major parties.

COMMUNITY SELF-DETERMINATION

Unease about corporate power and a desire for greater community self-determination has, however, emerged once again as a potent issue at the local level. It's evident in the rising interest in locally grown food and other products, and in the many communities that are setting their own economic policies, enacting such measures as living wage laws and bans on factory farming. A growing number of cities are adopting policies that curb the proliferation of large retailers and support small-scale local business districts. Most of these laws fall within the framework of land-use policy. There are two pieces of local land-use policy: the comprehensive plan and the zoning code. The plan is essentially a community vision statement, laying out broad policies for development. As noted above, plans that articulate support for the downtown and local businesses can provide crucial—and in many states legally mandated—guidance to decision makers. But the real teeth of a town's land-use policy are found in its zoning code, which sets out specific rules regarding allowable uses, scale, and so forth.[34]

"It came down to two issues. One was the scale of enterprises that we felt

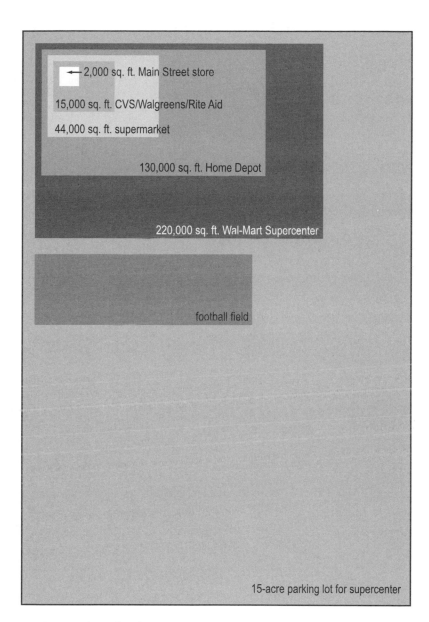

2,000 sq. ft. Main Street store

15,000 sq. ft. CVS/Walgreens/Rite Aid

44,000 sq. ft. supermarket

130,000 sq. ft. Home Depot

220,000 sq. ft. Wal-Mart Supercenter

football field

15-acre parking lot for supercenter

Average sizes of various stores.

we wanted in the city, and the second was conserving land," said Brent Thompson, who served on the planning commission in Ashland, Oregon, in the early 1990s when the town enacted a law that limits retail stores to no more than forty-five thousand square feet. At just over an acre, the cap allows for supermarkets and other fairly large stores, but is about one-fifth to one-third the size of a typical big box. Cities across the country have enacted similar laws. In the mid-1990s, in response to interest by Kmart in building on the edge of town, Hailey, Idaho, capped stores at thirty-six thousand square feet (an area equivalent to one-half of a platted downtown block). "I don't see any evidence that economic development is slowing down whatsoever. We've got many mixed-use buildings going up in the downtown," said city planner Kathy Grotto, explaining that the law has given small businesses more confidence to invest in Hailey's downtown because they know it will not be undercut by big-box development on the fringe.[35]

Lisa Rother, who was the planning director in Rockville, Maryland, when the city decided to cap stores at sixty-five thousand square feet in 2000, explained that the immediate impetus was a Costco proposal. The city had recently begun working to transform its auto-oriented commercial strips into more pedestrian-friendly areas and realized that big-box stores would frustrate that goal. Today, the proposed Costco site is a multistory residential building with small stores and restaurants on the first floor. Both the town and county of Hood River, Oregon, acted in concert in 2002 to cap stores at fifty thousand square feet, putting an end to Wal-Mart's interest in building a supercenter in town and its threat, if denied a permit, to locate just beyond the town line on unincorporated county land. The northern New Mexico town of Taos adopted an eighty-thousand-square-foot limit in 1999 and reaffirmed it in 2003, after a Wal-Mart developer funded a campaign to have it overturned. Polls found that support for the cap had actually increased from about half in favor when it was first enacted to over 60 percent. Both of the town's two main business groups —the Taos County Chamber of Commerce and the Hispano Chamber of Commerce—endorsed the measure.[36]

Other communities that have passed retail-store size limits include Madison, Wisconsin; Bozeman, Montana; and Santa Fe, New Mexico. (Some European countries have enacted nationwide size limits or tightly restricted where superstores may locate. Ireland, for example, bars stores over thirty-eight-thousand square feet in all areas of the country except for a handful of sites in Dublin and eight other cities.) Sometimes these laws are enacted after one or more superstores opens, when cities become aware of the hidden costs and decide to curtail further big-box development. While most of these caps apply citywide, they can also be adopted on a neighborhood basis. Several neighborhoods in San Francisco, for example, limit stores to less than six thousand square feet. The intention is to preserve the diversity of businesses operating along each block and to prevent chain retailers from consolidating many small storefronts into block-long superstores, as they have in some areas of New York City. When faced with a size limit, retailers that typically build larger stores will do one of two things: either they won't locate in that city or they will design a smaller store that fits within the cap. Wal-Mart walked away from Ashland, Oregon, with its forty-five-thousand-square-foot limit, but when faced with a cap of one hundred thousand square feet in Tampa, the chain designed a ninety-nine-thousand-square-foot store.[37]

There are three primary reasons cities enact size caps. One derives from a recognition that local consumers have only so much spending power. Not allowing a single store to become so large that it devours much of the pie helps ensure that the town or neighborhood maintains a diversity of competing businesses. The second reason is that smaller stores better fit the scale of many communities, including both small towns and big-city neighborhoods. Vibrant, walkable downtowns and neighborhoods are invariably composed of a mix of many small and midsize uses—rather than a single use that covers ten acres. As the insightful urban observer Jane Jacobs once noted, "A lively city scene is lively largely by virtue of its enormous collection of small elements." A third reason is that, the larger the store, the greater the impacts on its surroundings. The size of the region from which a store pulls customers, and thus the amount of traffic it generates, for example, expands in direct proportion to its scale.[38]

Two planning issues closely related to scale are location and site design. Long before big-box stores, many communities zoned virtually every strip of land along major roadways as far as the eye could see for commercial uses. They were eager to accommodate job-generating development. But in the megastore age, this has helped fuel retail overbuilding and the glut of vacant stores and strip malls as developers leapfrog across the landscape. Some cities are now realizing that a better approach is to designate only areas in and around established business districts for new retail. This keeps fresh investment flowing to these areas, rather than competing against them, and encourages developers to build more-enduring structures. Some cities also require that new retail construction mimic traditional business districts, with multistory buildings erected flush to the sidewalk and parking behind. This type of built environment offers ideal habitat for hatching locally owned businesses, which often lack the resources, name recognition, and advertising clout to succeed in a freestanding location, but can do well clustered with other businesses in a Main Street setting, especially with the added foot traffic generated by second-story offices or apartments.

In addition to defining the appropriate scale and location for stores, a number of cities and towns now are requiring that retail proposals pass an economic- and community-impact analysis to gain approval. These studies put the job and tax claims of developers to the test and give city officials and residents a detailed—and often eye-opening—estimate of the actual effects a project is likely to have. After a study of a proposed Wal-Mart in the town of North Elba, New York, found that the store would derive most of its revenue at the expense of existing businesses and eliminate about as many jobs as it would create, the planning board voted to reject the store, concluding that it would result in chronically "vacant storefronts, a loss of 'critical mass' in the existing downtown areas, and an adverse . . . economic climate." In the past, these studies were undertaken on a case-by-case basis, but cities and towns are now adopting policies that mandate them for all retail proposals over a certain size and establish specific standards that projects must meet in order to be approved.[39]

Proposals for stores over fifteen thousand square feet in the town of Homer, Alaska, for example, must undergo an analysis that looks at the project's impact on jobs and wages, the cost of public services, and the health of the downtown. The city selects an independent consultant to do the study; the developer covers the cost. Mt. Shasta, California, recently enacted similar stipulations, requiring proposals for stores over twenty thousand square feet to undergo an economic-impact review. The process includes a public hearing in which residents may comment on the findings. After its brush with Wal-Mart, Charlevoix Township capped stores at ninety thousand square feet and adopted an ordinance subjecting projects over fifty thousand square feet to additional scrutiny, allowing approval only for those that will "not change the essential character of the area" and will not create "excessive public costs." A number of large cities are also moving to adopt these kinds of policies, although they often apply them only to very large supercenter projects. A Los Angeles law enacted in 2004, for instance, mandates an economic-impact analysis for stores over one hundred thousand square feet that carry groceries.[40]

This approach is not without flaws and potential hazards. Studies done by unqualified or biased consultants (many of whom work primarily for developers) can produce incomplete or, worse, fallacious results. Even when an analysis finds significant negative impacts, city decision-makers may still make a judgment that the benefits outweigh the costs. But nevertheless, implementing these kinds of provisions ensures that at least a framework exists for weighing economic and community impacts, and turning down projects that are harmful. As a woman involved in several big-box campaigns in Oregon explained, "Right now we get stuck fighting these projects on the basis of traffic studies when what really concerns us are the economic and social issues."[41]

A small but growing number of communities are adopting policies that not only address giant stores and shopping centers, but limit the proliferation of other kinds of smaller-format chains. One of the more striking aspects of Arcata, a city of about twenty thousand people along Humboldt Bay in northern California, is the range of goods available from locally owned businesses. Situated around a large grassy plaza, which was used during the gold rush as a staging area for mule caravans headed to the mines, Arcata's town center is home to two locally owned grocery stores, an outdoors outfitter, a computer store, several furniture stores, two video stores, clothing and shoe stores, a pharmacy, two bookstores, a local hotel, and the Minor Theater, the oldest theater built for feature films in the United States. The reason local retailers here have escaped the ruin that has befallen so many town centers is in part a strong popular sentiment in favor of homegrown enterprise. Tom Conlon, Arcata's community development director, traces it to a political shift in the 1970s. Before, he said, "there was always this idea that some big factory was going to fall out of the sky and solve all of our problems." Then a new crop of city councilors started to examine the challenges facing small businesses and to focus on growing the local economy from the ground up. Out of that grew "this community mentality to put your money where your house is."[42]

Supporting local businesses is thus both a local consumer ethic and matter of city policy. Arcata has not allowed sprawling shopping centers and big-box stores. In the late 1990s, the Committee on Democracy and Corporations, which was created by voters to advise the city council on issues related to the influence and impact of corporations, began to examine the potential for Starbucks and other food chains to take over the plaza— a transformation that happened in many similar communities. "We looked at it and realized, we aren't talking about just an aesthetic issue," said Paul Cienfuegos, who has served on the committee since its inception. No one wanted corporate signage spoiling the historic plaza, but the real issue was the structure and mix of businesses citywide. The committee recommended, and the city ultimately adopted, an ordinance that allows no more than nine "formula" restaurants in Arcata at any one time. Formula businesses are legally defined as those that are required by contract or other arrangement to have standardized features and methods of operation that make them similar to businesses elsewhere. Chains can pass muster under such a policy only if they create a unique outlet, different inside and out from all their others; very few are willing to do so. At the time, Arcata had nine formula restaurants, including a Subway and a McDonald's, and the city decided that this was sufficient. Despite some fears that the restriction would impede economic growth, said Ryan Emenaker, chair of the Committee on Democracy and Corporations, demand for storefront space remains vigorous, a new building recently went up downtown, and several new restaurants and stores have opened. Now, the city is considering capping the number of formula retail stores as well.[43]

At least sixteen towns across the country have set limits on formula businesses. The oldest of these ordinances dates to the mid-1980s, but most were enacted since the late 1990s. In 2005, after Hollywood Video announced plans to locate next door to an independent video store, citizens in the coastal paper-mill town of Port Townsend, Washington, successfully petitioned the city to adopt a measure that bars formula businesses over three thousand square feet and limits those smaller than that to one area of town. (As a reference, a typical freestanding Walgreens drugstore is about fifteen thousand square feet.) In a lawsuit challenging one of these laws in Coronado, California, a state appeals court upheld the law, ruling that it did not violate the U.S. Constitution's commerce and equal protection clauses, because its provisions applied to local as well as nonlocal businesses.[44]

Once confined to small towns, these measures are now being taken up in larger cities. San Francisco was the first. Concerned about a common pattern in neighborhood business districts, where local entrepreneurs would bring an ailing area back to life only to be driven out by a cascade of chain stores—San Francisco is home to a staggering seventy-five Starbucks and fifty-five Walgreens outlets—the board of supervisors (equivalent to a city council) adopted a policy that allows neighborhoods to hold hearings and apply additional scrutiny before approving new formula stores or restaurants. Before, said neighborhood activist Ed Bedard, who proposed the policy, the chains would go to elaborate lengths to set up without people knowing. "The scaffolding comes down and suddenly there's a Walgreens," he explained. The law applies only to neighborhood districts; the downtown and touristy Fisherman's Wharf are exempt.[45]

At the request of some neighborhoods, including North Beach and Haight-Ashbury, the city has banned formula businesses entirely from their commercial areas. "Everybody from the merchants organizations to the residents associations loved the individual character of North Beach and wanted to preserve it," said supervisor Aaron Peskin, who represents the district. "It helps sustain local businesses and keeps the money in the community." Asked about market interference, Peskin said neighborhoods have the right to shape commercial development: "In the same way a community can determine they don't want to have casinos or what have you, they can also limit formula businesses." Now, neighborhoods in other cities, including Baltimore and Chicago, are petitioning for similar policies.[46]

This provides a flavor of how some communities are addressing these issues. What works in one place may not fit another. But the essential point is that cities are not at the mercy of developers; they can design land-use policies that foster the kind of retail landscape they want. In addition to land use, cities are also beginning to incorporate a commitment to local businesses in other kinds of decisions and to undo the myriad of advantages that chains have been given over the years. Some cities have made it a matter of policy to give some preference to local businesses for city contracts and purchases, on the grounds that, even if they spend a little bit more, the benefits to the local economy, and ultimately tax revenue, more than make up for it. A growing number of school districts, for example, are buying more food from local farmers, bakers, and dairies. Efforts are also under way to reverse a long trend of moving public buildings—post offices, schools, libraries, city hall—from local business districts to sites out by the big-box stores and strip centers. These public uses are an important part of the mix that makes Main Streets viable; a survey in Iowa found that 80 percent of downtown shoppers planned their visits around a trip to the post office.[47]

Meanwhile, there are several efforts afoot to more fundamentally change the relationship of corporations to local communities. Back in Humboldt County, home of Arcata, a civic group called Democracy Unlimited has gathered signatures for a ballot initiative that would prohibit outside corporations from participating in local elections, including funding campaigns to overturn local laws and zoning decisions. Should it pass, the policy may well end up in the courts, but that's fine, say supporters, who believe it's time for the Supreme Court to reconsider its decision to extend civil rights to corporations. Similarly, two Pennsylvania townships have enacted ordinances maintaining that corporations do not have such rights within their borders. So far, these laws have not been challenged, but another civic group, the Community Environmental Legal Defense Fund, is prepared to defend them, again with an eye to persuading the Supreme Court to rethink its stance.[48]

ACROSS TOWN LINES

Between 1970 and 1990, the year-round population of Cape Cod, Massachusetts, more than doubled to nearly two hundred thousand people. Housing subdivisions and strip shopping centers creeped east from the mainland, threatening to suburbanize the entire peninsula, with dire effects on the Cape's fragile ecosystem. Some thirty-six thousand acres of woodland were lost to development and thousands of acres of shellfish beds were closed due to polluted runoff. Afraid of forever losing the place they loved, the Cape's voters took an extraordinary leap in 1990: they endorsed the formation of a regional planning and regulatory agency, the Cape Cod Commission. Made up of representatives of each of the Cape's fifteen towns, the commission has the authority to review, and reject, development projects that could significantly impact the peninsula's economy and environment. This includes proposals for retail stores larger than ten thousand square feet and housing subdivisions of thirty or more units. The commission does not supplant city planning boards, but rather adds a second layer of review for large projects, in which all of the region's towns are given a say.[49]

In making its decisions, the commission relies on a regional policy plan, which outlines a broad vision for the Cape and includes specific criteria that proposals must meet in order to obtain approval. Updated every few years with input from residents, the plan calls for fostering compact towns and preserving open space. It has detailed standards designed to protect the Cape's economy, environment, character, and quality of life. In terms of retail projects, the economic criteria require the commission to evaluate the store's overall impact on the region's economy, taking into account such factors as jobs created as well as lost, wages, and the costs of public services. The plan advises that "retail sprawl in general is inefficient and unsustainable" and, "in many cases, locally owned businesses should be regarded as more of a benefit to the regional economy than national chains because they tend to keep profits in the area and participate more actively in community life." Applicants bear the burden of proving that a store's benefits outweigh its detriments.[50]

Armed with this charge, the Cape Cod Commission has turned down several big-box stores. Wal-Mart was denied a permit to build in Falmouth in 1993. A Sam's Club proposal met the same fate in Hyannis. In 1994, the commission rejected a proposal for a 120,000-square-foot Costco on undeveloped land along the highway in Sandwich, concluding that it was inconsistent with the region's planning goals and would have an adverse impact on traffic, the environment, and local businesses. Costco filed suit, challenging both the decision and the constitutionality of the commission itself, but eventually dropped the case. In 1997, facing strong opposition from residents and anticipated scrutiny from the commission, Home Depot walked away from plans to build in Yarmouth.[51]

Not all large retail projects have been rejected. In Falmouth, Wal-Mart opened a seventy-three-thousand-square-foot store in an empty Bradlees building, a defunct regional department store chain, while Home Depot was given the green light to take over another Bradlees in Hyannis, opening a store roughly 40 percent smaller than its standard outlet. In one of the commission's most controversial decisions, it voted 7–6 to allow BJ's Wholesale Club to build a seventy-thousand-square-foot store on top of a former gravel pit in Hyannis. Among those who argued against the project was Felicia Penn, director of the grassroots Smart Growth and Planning Coalition, who believes the commission's economic criteria are too weak. They do not, for example, weigh the spin-off economic activity that is lost when local retailers, who patronize other Cape Cod businesses, are displaced by chains like BJ's, which funnel most of their revenue off the peninsula. Retaining these dollars and bolstering local enterprise is crucial to tackling the region's poverty, Penn said. (Although many Americans associate Cape Cod with the Kennedys and affluence, low-wage jobs account for nearly one-third of the Cape's employment and 29 percent of all families do not make enough to cover basic living expenses.)[52]

Nevertheless, the Cape Cod Commission has managed to bring the peninsula's towns together around a shared planning vision. As a result, there are far fewer big-box stores today than there would have been and, with the exception of BJ's, those that have come are smaller than their counterparts elsewhere and are located on sites that were already developed. In addition to its regulatory role, the commission undertakes various long-range regional studies and has an economic-development program focused on high-wage jobs and small-business creation. Despite perennial efforts by developers and others to have it dissolved, the Cape Cod Commission remains popular with residents, as evidenced both by surveys and a ballot initiative in 2000 in which voters supported expanding other aspects of regional government.[53]

Vermont is the only other region of the country that has a similar review process for large-scale development. Enacted in response to the arrival of the state's first interstate highway, which many feared would lead to uncontrolled sprawl, Act 250 requires large development projects to obtain approval both from the local town and from one of several regional commissions. In most cases, retail projects trigger Act 250 review when they are ten or more acres, a threshold substantially higher than Cape Cod's. To pass, projects must meet a variety of environmental and land-use criteria. Act 250 requires that development not create excessive costs for local governments and it strongly favors growth that is contiguous to existing settlements. Some retail projects, including Wal-Mart superstores, have been blocked as a result of Act 250. In other cases, the threat of being denied an Act 250 permit has led retailers to propose opening smaller stores in existing buildings, like Wal-Mart's seventy-thousand-square-foot store in Rutland.[54]

Like any law, Act 250 is only as strong as the public's support for its goals. Wal-Mart has recently proposed building several large supercenters on the outskirts of small towns and villages across Vermont, a move that prompted the National Trust for Historic Preservation to place the entire state on its list of America's Most Endangered Historic Places in 2004. Although local citizens groups and statewide organizations like the Preservation Trust of Vermont are pressing the chain to either stay away or open small downtown stores instead, Wal-Mart has been far more obstinate than in was when it first came to the state in the mid-1990s. The company seems to be betting that a combination of economic hard times in some of these towns and a well-funded public relations campaign can turn public opinion its way and propel it through Act 250 review.[55]

But despite some shortcomings, neither Vermont nor Cape Cod exhibits the destructive rivalry and lack of coordination among neighboring communities that big-box retailers have so easily manipulated elsewhere, spurring excessive overdevelopment and leading towns to accept superstores solely out of a fear that, if they do not, developers will build just over their borders. Yet despite the obvious need for regional cooperation, and the fact that most states explicitly permit and even encourage neighboring towns to enter into joint planning agreements, there are very few places practicing it. Short of regional planning, another approach that could help prevent retail developers from playing cities against one another is tax-base sharing. Under this system, the taxes generated by new development are distributed to all of the cities in a region on the basis of population, so that no individual town has an incentive to welcome a shopping center at its neighbor's expense. So far, tax-base sharing has yet to be fully implemented anywhere, though it has been proposed in California and other states where sales tax competition is fierce.[56]

Meanwhile, with concern about the impact of big-box retailers, especially Wal-Mart, on the rise, a number of state lawmakers have begun to take up the issue. Some states are considering bills that would require that cities undertake economic-impact studies before approving retail development. A bill in New Jersey, for example, calls for cities to study the regional impact of a superstore, including its effect on existing businesses, job quality, and the number of miles residents drive for shopping. A proposal in Vermont—which would apply to projects over seventy-five-thousand square feet, smaller than those covered by Act 250—would require cities to look at several economic issues, including how much of the store's sales would "be retained and redirected into the economy of the community," a provision that would seem to favor local ownership.[57]

States are also debating bills to eliminate subsidies for big-box retailers. Some, including Montana and Maine, have considered taxing big-box stores, both to deter further development and to recoup the added public costs in terms of roads and police services, as well as the expense of workers who rely on Medicaid and other state programs. Two national watchdog campaigns, Wal-Mart Watch and Wake Up Wal-Mart, which are supported by labor unions, are pressing for laws that would improve working conditions for big-box employees. They won a first victory in Maryland in early 2006, with the passage of a law requiring Wal-Mart to spend the equivalent of 8 percent of its payroll costs on providing employee health care. Similar bills have been initiated in thirty states.[58]

This chapter has examined what citizens and local governments are doing to counter the proliferation of mega-retailers and to ensure that local policies adequately account for the economic, community, and environmental costs of these stores and establish appropriate standards and limits. But saying no to the chains is only half of the solution; the other is to strengthen and rebuild locally owned businesses.

NINE

DECLARATION
OF INDEPENDENTS

IN 2004 JULIE SIMPSON OPENED A STORE selling local farm products in
downtown Culpeper, Virginia. A farmer herself, Simpson stocks her own
all-natural pork, chicken, and lamb. She carries grass-fed beef from Hig-
ginbotham Family Farm, milk from Homestead Creamery, and cheeses
from six local cheese-makers. She has bread from a local baker delivered
daily and, on weekends, pastries and pies brought in by local farmers. Not
that long ago, Simpson could not have opened her business, Food for
Thought, in Culpeper. "It was a different place. The building I'm in now
was rundown and all the others nearby were boarded up," she said. "It was
dangerous too." Today the buildings have been restored, half a dozen new
businesses have opened since 2003, and long-standing stores, like the one-
hundred-year-old Clarke Hardware, are reporting a much improved business climate.[1]

The changes seem to have occurred virtually overnight. But they are in
fact the culmination of many small improvements that began in 1998 with
the formation of Culpeper Renaissance, a community organization dedicated to resurrecting the downtown. One of their first initiatives, said Diane Logan, executive director of the group, was organizing a neighborhood
watch to clean up the drug dealing and vandalism that had taken over certain blocks. Then they won a grant to renovate the dilapidated train depot,
worked with the city government to create a low-interest loan fund to encourage property owners to restore their buildings, and began to recruit
entrepreneurs. "I met with Diane and she shared with me the community's
vision. I knew then that it was the right place," said Simpson. With each incremental change, people's perception of downtown Culpeper began to

shift. As their confidence in the district's future grew, so did their willingness to invest their own time and resources.[2]

Three years ago, Gina Schaefer left her corporate job to open a hardware store in the Washington, D.C., Logan Circle neighborhood. "In hindsight it seems kind of crazy. I had no hardware experience and no retail experience," she said. "But business has been amazing. I can't imagine having a boss again." Schaefer had thought about starting a business for some time. She picked hardware because neighborhood residents had listed that as one of their top retail needs in surveys conducted by the Logan Circle Community Association. Schaefer relied on help from a number of sources. The neighborhood group enthusiastically spread the word about the new store. Ace, a buying cooperative owned by independent hardware stores across the country, provided management training and a slew of advice on matters such as what product mix to stock. When banks turned her down, Schaefer was able to secure a $350,000 loan backed by the Small Business Administration. Her only disappointment was the city, which proved more of an obstacle than a source of help. Schaefer had to hire someone to navigate a maze of regulations and permits. Meanwhile, she said, the "big-boxes are getting subsidies all over the place, particularly in the District, because there's such a lack of retail. Target is getting millions. We got nothing and will get nothing."[3]

Logan Hardware occupies a century-old building in a dense neighborhood, which poses certain challenges: the store has no parking and no loading dock, and its five thousand square feet of merchandise spans three levels. But Schaefer says most of her employees and customers do not own a car, so the store fits its context. "I think that America's urban centers are places of opportunity for independent retailers," she said. "People don't think of cities as having communities. But I have the old guy who comes in and talks to all my customers. It's just like a small town." Being nestled together with other local businesses helps, too: "Everyone knows one another and we feed off one another because we're all in a row."

A few months after Logan Hardware opened, Schaefer's husband, Mark, decided to quit his job and join the family business. "He saw how much fun I was having," she said. They opened a second store in another neighborhood and now have a third on the way. They are considering owning as many as five. "Because there is such a dearth of retail here, I have people from all over the District calling to see if I can bring a hardware store to their neighborhood," said Schaefer, who has financed the new stores through an equity matching and lending program Ace set up with the National Cooperative Bank. Schaefer is not especially fearful of competition from big-box stores but, she said, "I do get nervous when I read about [Home Depot and Lowe's] wanting to open fifteen-thousand-square-foot neighborhood stores." The rising cost of real estate in Washington also makes her nervous: rents in Logan Circle have almost doubled since she opened, and property costs are so high now that buying her building is out of the question.

But three years in, things are going well enough that Schaefer has started helping other entrepreneurs. She has been tapped by Ace for an initiative on diversity that aims to make both hardware stores and ownership opportunities more appealing to women, people of color, and young people. Schaefer is also teaching classes at the National Women's Business Center. Unfortunately, she said, only a small fraction of the trainees actually go on to start businesses. "I think the biggest challenge is fear," she said. "There are a lot of sacrifices. You mortgage your house. You may have to eat peanut butter and jelly for a while. For the first three months, I worked twelve-hour days, seven days a week. Not everyone can do that."

Another new independent business on the map is Big Hat Books, which opened in Indianapolis in 2004. "It was something I had always wanted to do," said Liz Houghton Barden, who was born and raised in New York and has spent many hours in the city's legendary bookstores. In 2001 her husband took a job at Butler University and they left New York for Indianapolis. For a while, Barden, who did marketing work, continued to commute to her office in New York, but then she decided it was time to settle in Indianapolis. Although the city has a few specialty bookstores focused on children's books and Christian titles, it did not have a general-interest independent bookstore and hadn't for nearly a decade. "The fact that there wasn't was really good news and it was also really bad news. I thought perhaps no one here reads," said Barden, confessing that she'd never given much thought to the country's heartland before moving here. "But then all the people I had met were huge readers. I knew there had to be more." She started working on a business plan and then spotted a "for rent" sign on a great space in a neighborhood business district. She signed the lease and used her savings and credit cards to buy inventory.[4]

"Business has been great. I met my first-year plan, which is incredible, because I wasn't that conservative," said Barden, adding that the most rewarding part of the store is interacting with the customers. "Every day, you have access to such a spectrum of people." Big Hat Books is small—only twelve hundred square feet—but the space is carefully maximized. All of the bookshelves are on casters so that they can be wheeled out of the way for the many author events and book clubs Barden hosts. Her seven thousand titles are carefully chosen. "People love your edit. I think that's what it boils down to," she said. "We are all bombarded with so much junk and so many choices. A good retailer goes through the morass of sludge to get to the perfect picks." Barden regularly takes her business out into the community by selling books at various lectures and events around town, and she gives a 20 percent discount to her heroes: teachers and librarians. Key to her success has been the advice she has received from bookstore owners around the country and the educational seminars that the American Booksellers Association puts on several times a year. "Everyone in the bookselling community has been unbelievably generous with their time and information and coaching," she said.

In a community thirteen miles northwest of Charleston, West Virginia, there's a new drugstore, Cross Lanes Family Pharmacy. Pharmacist Chad Moles is steadily building his customer base by focusing on personal service and short wait times. Bit by bit, he is also building his ownership stake in the business. Moles graduated from the University of West Virginia's pharmacy school in 2002, worked for chain drugstores for a while, and then was approached by Brac Brown, who owns a pharmacy in a nearby town, about going into business. Brown put up the money and Moles runs the store, funneling part of his earnings into becoming a partner in the business. Ownership, he says, is far superior to working for a chain: "I want to practice pharmacy as I see fit, as opposed to having to have someone at corporate headquarters tell me how to practice pharmacy."[5]

Moles is not alone. Bruce Roberts, a thirty-year pharmacist and executive vice president of the National Community Pharmacists Association (NCPA), has been giving talks about ownership at pharmacy schools for years. He used to be lucky if one or two students approached him afterward. Now he finds he's often swarmed by students eager to go into business for themselves. NCPA has responded with a number of initiatives, including a matching service to connect drugstore buyers and sellers and ownership training. Demand has been so strong that in 2005 the group started offering its ownership workshops twice a year. "We have seen a significant increase in junior partnerships," said NCPA's management and educational affairs director Stacey Swartz, referring to arrangements like Moles's in which a young pharmacist slowly buys out an established owner. In 2002 a remarkable shift occurred: the decline in independent pharmacies that had been under way for more than a decade stopped. From 2002 to 2005 the United States actually experienced a *net increase* in the number of independent pharmacies, enabling independents to maintain their share of the market even as spending on prescriptions soars. The comeback is due partly to the growing interest among phamacists in owning their own businesses and to the fact that many offer superior and much faster service than the chains.[6]

REBUILDING LOCAL RETAIL

If land-use policy is the key to controlling the proliferation of mega-retailers, what's needed to spur the creation of more independent businesses? Four ingredients are especially important. One is having a fertile environment. So many neighborhood and downtown business districts have fallen into states of such lethargic depression that otherwise-viable businesses are unable to take root. To revitalize these districts is to reclaim habitat for local retailers. Doing so requires a long-term, multipronged community effort. The best how-to model—the one used by Culpeper Renaissance—was developed by the National Trust for Historic Preservation. Realizing that the country's historic commercial buildings stood little chance of surviving unless they became economically viable again, the trust set out to help communities rebuild their downtown economies, spinning off a separate division, the National Main Street Center, to carry out the work. It started in small towns, moving into larger cities as the strategy was honed. In the mid-1990s the first Main Street programs were launched in urban neighborhoods in cities like Boston, Washington, and San Diego. "Neighborhood business districts in large cities operate much like downtowns in small towns," explained the center's executive director, Doug Loescher. The Main Street model has now spread to hundreds of towns and neighborhoods nationwide.[7]

Main Street programs are funded and carried out entirely at the local level. The model is not a series of instructions, but rather a framework that helps communities develop and execute their own plan to bring a business district back to life. Most local Main Street programs have one full-time staff person and many citizen volunteers, who serve on committees focused on four aspects of revitalization: organizing broad community support for the plan; improving the downtown's physical structure by rehabilitating buildings and enhancing the pedestrian environment; promoting the district through events; and nurturing business activity. Main Street's core philosophy is that revitalization takes time; making small but consistent advances in all four areas will build a momentum that eventually turns the district around. "Many communities think that there's one big fix that they can do to make it right. The fixes change over time: ballparks, convention centers, hotels, aquariums," noted Kennedy Smith, who directed the National Main Street Center for a dozen years before starting her own consulting practice. "Real long-term success is incremental, not cataclysmic."[8]

Although some communities want them to be, Main Street programs are not a substitute for land-use planning. "Downtown revitalization doesn't just take place downtown; it takes a broader community-planning effort. You can't say you want to have a healthy downtown and still zone all this land for more retail on the outskirts," Smith cautioned. It's a problem beginning to affect Culpeper, where population growth is attracting big-box developers. Downtown revitalization initiatives have the best chance of success if they are backed by a strong land-use plan that limits retail sprawl. While some downtowns can get by serving the whims of tourists and affluent shoppers, truly vibrant community centers need a viable local economic base that meets a substantial and broad array of residents' needs.[9]

Main Street revitalization programs support local retail development partly by improving the physical environment and working to bring more people to the district. Many also provide business-assistance programs and actively recruit new entrepreneurs. As other small towns across Iowa were dying, residents of Corning, a town of just eighteen hundred people in the southwest corner of the state, organized in 1990 to shore up their town center. One of their most effective initiatives, according to director Nancy Carmichael, has been the Business Visitation Program. Every business in town is regularly visited by two volunteers who talk to the owners about their challenges and future plans. Main Street Corning then attempts to solve any problems that surface. It operates like an early-warning system and has averted several store closures. When the owner of the local bakery, Sweet Desires, indicated that he intended to retire from the business, a Main Street committee went looking for a new owner, eventually finding a local woman who had always wanted to be a professional baker and was already selling some of her homemade sweets. Similarly, when the Nebraska chain that owned Corning's single-screen movie theater started to falter, Main Street undertook a special fund-raising effort to repair the roof so that local resident David Brokaw could buy the theater and run it as a viable business. Today, this small town still has a theater showing first-run movies.[10]

Many Main Street programs undertake a market analysis of their district to help guide retail development. (Indeed, any community can do this with the help of free online tools). A market analysis reveals the spending power of local residents and quantifies the demand for goods and services not already well supplied. These gaps are opportunities—both for established local retailers looking to expand, and for new entrepreneurs, who can use the data to help secure a bank loan. The Main Street program in Walla Walla, Washington, which took on the formidable task of resurrecting a downtown that was 30 percent vacant in 1990, having collapsed after shopping malls invaded the region, has used market research to expand several local businesses. A candy shop that did brisk sales over the winter holidays, but struggled in the summer, added ice cream, based on the program's recommendation. It did so well that the owners recently doubled the size of the store. Market research also helped persuade businesses near the mall to relocate downtown. One was an independent bookstore, the Book and Game Company, which moved downtown in 2001 and reported a 35 percent jump in sales the first year.[11]

After shoring up existing retailers, Main Street programs turn to bringing in new businesses. "A good business-development plan should recognize what the local market opportunities might be and then spec out exactly what they'd like to see—these kinds of businesses on the corner, these businesses to function as magnets, these kinds of businesses on this block—so the revitalization organization is thinking like a shopping mall developer would," said Smith. There's an art and science to arranging stores in ways that increase customer traffic. Malls are experts at this, but such coordination is lacking in most downtowns. Left on their own, landlords tend to repeat what has already worked—if restaurants have done well, they lease to more restaurants, which ends up homogenizing the district—or worse, they lease to whomever comes along, turning a prime storefront over to an office user or a retailer who lacks a business plan and is likely to soon fail, contributing to a perception that the downtown is inhospitable. Over time, good Main Street programs earn the trust of property owners and begin to function like retail leasing brokers, maintaining lists of available spaces, advising landlords on what businesses would work best in which locations, reviewing business plans, and recruiting entrepreneurs.[12]

Once a community has identified the kinds of stores it would like to bring to its business district, the temptation is to contact a chain that operates in that category—call Walgreens when you want a pharmacy, for instance. Indeed, some Main Street programs do this, reasoning that the brand will add legitimacy and appeal to their district. Finding independent entrepreneurs takes more patience and persistence, and often a little creativity, but it can be done. When Rite Aid pulled out of Orono, Maine, in 1999, it left the downtown without a key anchor. Rather than trying to attract CVS or Walgreens, the city decided a better option would be a local pharmacy. "We felt it would be more reliable and create a better image for the community," said Gerry Kempen, the town manager at the time. To find one, Kempen sent letters to twelve hundred pharmacists who had received their licenses from the state of Maine. Half a dozen responded and soon the town found its man, Ali Aghamoosa, who had received his license while working for a Maine hospital in 1995 and was then living in Texas. He made the move and soon opened the Orono Pharmacy. "It was certainly more work for the city than bringing in an established company," said Kempen. "But we felt it was well worth the effort."[13]

Another strategy is to look to existing business owners who may want to expand or open second stores. When Safeway pulled out of a Berkeley, California, neighborhood and moved to transfer its site to a chain that sells remainder and off-season goods, the city intervened, making it clear that it would not issue permits for such a business and that what the neighborhood needed was a grocery store. Safeway countered that the site was too small for a modern supermarket. The city turned to Glen and Diane Yasuda, who owned a small food market called the Berkeley Bowl. With the city's support, the couple bought the site, closed their existing store, and reopened the Bowl as a forty-three-thousand-square-foot supermarket that was thriving seven years later. When Grand Rapids, Michigan, decided it needed a bookstore downtown, the Downtown Development Authority appealed to Debra Lambers, owner of the Book Nook & Java Shop in the nearby town of Montague. At first she declined, but after seeing market data and meeting with the mayor, Lambers decided in 2005 to open River Bank Books & Music in a landmark downtown building. "If she can be successful, it will be an inducement for other retailers to come along," said Jay Fowler, the authority's executive director.[14]

After a viable, well-managed environment, a second ingredient needed to spur local business creation is know-how. Mentoring from other local business owners, specialized training, and one-on-one guidance are often cited by new entrepreneurs as crucial to their success—a fact that lends even more urgency to stemming the decline of independent retailers: as they disappear, so too does the nation's collective local-retailing expertise. Trade associations and buying co-ops have stepped up to provide a growing array of programs to assist new entrepreneurs. At the local level and for retailers in categories not represented by a trade group, there's a patchwork of federally created Small Business Development Centers and community-based microenterprise programs that provide some assistance. "He's been a great asset," said Steve Raguski, referring to his adviser at a nearby Small Business Development Center. Raguski left his job as a middle school teacher seven years ago to start Fairhaven Runners, a store that sells gear for walking and running, in Bellingham, Washington. He still meets with the adviser and also participates in a monthly roundtable with a dozen other business owners organized by the center. The store, he said, "has become so much better than even the dreams I had for it."[15]

"We keep our ear to the ground in terms of what our members need," said Greg Walker-Wilson, director of the Mountain Microenterprise Fund, which serves a twelve-county region around Asheville, North Carolina. Since 1990, two thousand people have gone through the fund's business-planning class and half of them have gone on to start businesses. Many are small, home-based enterprises, but a number of larger businesses have been created as well, including a microbrewery, a downtown bodega, and a bookstore. To boost success, the fund has a membership program that gives established business owners access to workshops, discounted accounting and other services, and regular opportunities to connect and share strategies. Unfortunately, there's a good deal of variability from place to place in terms of the availability, robustness, and effectiveness of these business-assistance programs. Although federally created, Small Business Development Centers rely heavily on state grants. Communities should look to beef up these programs, fill in gaps in their offerings, and better publicize their existence.[16]

A third ingredient is affordable space. To nurture start-ups, community groups could create business incubators by buying or leasing one or more large storefronts and dividing the space into many small spaces where new retailers could spend a year or so getting the hang of things and cultivating a customer base before scaling up and moving into a regular storefront. Such an incubator operated in Chicago's Andersonville neighborhood for eighteen years and helped seed a number of the area's most successful retailers. It began in 1987, when Jan Baxter leased a large building on Clark Street, the area's main commercial corridor, and recruited other aspiring entrepreneurs to share the space with her. "We had a unified look throughout the store. It was more like departments, rather than separate shops," she explained. "Everything got rung up on one central cash register." They operated as a co-op, sharing decision-making and splitting the rent based on the number of square feet each business occupied.[17]

Some of the businesses that started in the Landmark, as it was known, did not make it. "There are people out there who think retail is magic; you just fold your arms and wait for people to buy everything," said Baxter. But quite a few did. One was the Ruff N' Stuff pet store. "We both came from corporate backgrounds," said co-owner Kathy Puryear. "This gave us a way to find out if we even wanted to do retail." She and her partner operated their store out of a small space at the Landmark for two years before renting their own space down the block in 1991. In 1997 they expanded into a larger location, still on Clark Street, where they are today, offering three thousand square feet of pet supplies, as well as dog-training classes. Other successful businesses that got their start at the Landmark include a toy store, a photo and framing shop, and a knitting store.[18]

Incubators can also be run by community organizations. While common in other industries, there have been very few devoted to retail. One example is in Watsonville, California. Run by the El Pajaro Community Development Corporation, the incubator was built downtown using redevelopment funds granted to the city following the 1989 earthquake. It opened in 1995, providing small start-up spaces as well as training and other support to help low-income Latino residents establish businesses. Key to the success of any retail incubator is a good location, either along a street that already has lots of customer traffic or a site adjacent to a prominent destination business. El Pajaro's prime location in the heart of the commercial district is one of its strengths, but it's also been something of a challenge: a number of successful businesses that have started in the space, including an ice-cream shop and a restaurant, have been reluctant to leave. "You need to have very clear rules about graduation," said program coordinator Carmen Herrera-Mansir, explaining that El Pajaro failed to put these in place at the beginning and is now drafting a policy to require businesses to transition out once they reach a certain level of financial performance. Among those that have moved on are a computer sales and repair business and a store selling Mexican soccer jerseys and other sports apparel.[19]

Another space-affordability problem arises when a business district becomes so popular that chain stores arrive in droves and rents escalate rapidly, pushing out locally owned businesses and replacing stores that serve local needs with high-end boutiques. "A common pattern is that it's a challenge to get people to locate in your district and then you get those independent businesses to come in and before too long, the property owners start raising the rent and bringing in national tenants," said Alex Padro, director of the Shaw Main Streets program in Washington, D.C. While modest increases in rents are often a good thing—a sign of the health of the district and a source of funds for building maintenance—steep, rapid increases destabilize local businesses, giving them no time to make adjustments. Some communities handle this partly through legislation, adopting ordinances that bar formula businesses and require that new stores be "neighborhood-serving." Berkeley even has a quota system in some of its neighborhoods to ensure that retail stores are not pushed out by restaurants. The other part of the solution is to encourage and help retailers buy their buildings. Some are eligible for the Small Business Administration's 504 loan program, which requires a 10 percent down payment for owner-occupied commercial buildings, as opposed to the standard bank threshold of 30 percent. Gap financing provided by local programs could reduce this to 5 percent. Cities might also consider tax breaks or other incentives to foster owner occupancy for essential neighborhood businesses such as grocers and pharmacies.[20]

Another approach is to set up a community land trust (CLT) to acquire one or more commercial buildings. CLTs were first developed in the 1960s as a means of maintaining affordable housing. In 2005 there were about 125 in operation. They are run by nonprofit corporations and typically get their initial capital through community development block grants, which are available for commercial development as well as housing. CLTs sell homes to low-income families, but retain ownership of the land underneath. The family has most of the rights of home ownership, except that, when they decide to move, they sell the house back to the CLT for an agreed-upon rate of return. This prevents a run-up in the price and makes the house affordable to the next family. So far, CLTs have had limited involvement in commercial real estate. However, the same model could be applied to commercial buildings. Retail spaces could either be sold, like condos, to local businesses under the same sort of agreement, or leased at cost. The space could be reserved only for businesses that are locally owned and provide a needed good or service.[21]

A fourth ingredient is financing. Undercapitalization is a fairly common problem for retailers. Sometimes this is the result of miscalculation and the lack of a solid business plan, but it also flows from a dearth of patient (i.e., long-term) capital for local business development. While entrepreneurs with a good plan, a reasonable credit history, and some training or experience can usually secure the relatively small loans (five thousand to fifty thousand dollars) needed to finance many kinds of stores, for those seeking to open in categories with higher start-up costs (e.g., grocery stores), or to expand an established business with a major investment in inventory or equipment, obtaining a loan is a more formidable task. Bank consolidation has made it harder for small businesses to get loans, according to a 2004 study. "Credit access in markets dominated by big banks tends to be lower for small businesses than in markets with a relatively larger share of small banks," the authors report. But loans are not always an ideal solution: the cost of financing a short-term, seven-year business loan can cripple cash flow at a new or expanding business, and many entrepreneurs cannot stomach putting their house on the line. While the Small Business Administration's 7(a) loan program backs longer-term loans, these are more costly and demand has often outstripped supply.[22]

Another way to finance a business is through equity capital—giving investors a minority-ownership stake in a new store. While an entrepreneur may be able to find friends or family members to invest in his business, there are no funds or other vehicles by which people can invest in capitalizing local businesses generally. Of the $34 trillion in assets that U.S. households possess, only about one in seven dollars is held by banks and credit unions, according to Michael Shuman, author of *The Small-Mart Revolution*. The rest are in stocks, mutual funds, insurance funds, and other vehicles that invest in large corporations and nonlocal development. Even for people who would like to invest part of their savings in a local business fund, no such thing exists. A local merchant can file for state permission to sell stock in her state, which is less costly and complicated than doing so nationally, but none of the mechanisms that support mainstream stock investing exist at this scale. There are no ratings firms, like Standard & Poor's, to provide objective information about the value of such stocks. There are no exchanges for buying and selling. And there are no intermediaries—like mutual funds—that would allow a modest investor to diversify his holdings.[23]

The entities that are perhaps in the best position to overcome these obstacles and funnel more capital into local business development are public pension funds and state governments, which manage sizable portfolios of reserve funds. Meanwhile, one step cities can take is to shift some of their reserve funds into deposits linked to local business lending. In 2005, for example, the city of Santa Cruz, California, began transferring some of the money in its $80 million investment portfolio from corporate and government securities into certificates of deposit held at two locally owned financial institutions, the Bay Area Federal Credit Union and the Santa Cruz County Bank. City Councilor Ryan Coonerty, who proposed the idea, said both institutions will use the funds to expand local business lending.[24]

COMMUNITY-OWNED STORES

"We've been in the black from day one. We're planning on buying the building we're in now and the building next door," said Ken Witzeling, president of the board of the Powell Mercantile, a store owned by 589 local investors in Powell, Wyoming. In 1999 Stage, a chain of small-town department stores, pulled out of Powell, leaving the town's fifty-three hundred residents with no place to buy basic clothing and shoes. The town tried for a while to attract another chain, even phoning Target at one point, but to no avail. Then the chamber of commerce got wind of an enterprising initiative up in Plentywood, Montana, just sixteen miles south of the Canadian border. Faced with a similar retail void, a group of residents sold stock shares for $10,000, raising $190,000 to finance a local department store. "We thought, if a little town of twenty-two hundred could do this, we could too," said Witzeling.[25]

Witzeling, a retired pharmacist, and other community leaders formed a board, incorporated, and filed papers with the state to offer shares in the Powell Mercantile. "We thought we'd have a broader base and sell shares for five hundred dollars," said Witzeling, adding that the corporation's bylaws bar individuals from owning more than twenty shares, to ensure that no one gains a controlling interest. In a matter of months, they sold over eight hundred shares, raising four hundred thousand dollars in capital. "We told them right straight out that this was not a moneymaking deal. You are investing in Powell," said Witzeling. To succeed, the board knew that it would need a buyer with strong credentials and industry contacts. Early on, Witzeling had approached Mike Reile, a former district manager for Stage who had taken early retirement in Powell when the chain downsized. "I went to him and asked, do you think it will work? He said, no I don't think it will; you need to be part of a buying group," said Witzeling. "But when he saw the stock sales take off, he got real enthused and he said, if you are really serious, I'll be your buyer."

The Merc, as it is known locally, opened in 2002, selling affordable, name-brand clothing and shoes for the entire family out of the seven-thousand-square-foot downtown storefront space once occupied by Stage. Even with Reile's contacts, suppliers at first had a tough time believing that a community-owned corporation was a viable account. But after six months, Witzeling said, "salesmen started calling on us." The Merc has exceeded its revenue projections from the start, taking in $500,000 the first year, $560,000 the next, and $625,000 in 2005. Good buying and customer service have been key, said store manager Paul Ramos. Some had predicted that the Merc would not be able to survive with a Wal-Mart twenty-five miles away in Cody, but the store has managed to hold its own. Having no debt to service and no investors clamoring for a certain rate of return helps keeps prices down. "We're probably not quite as low as Wal-Mart," said Ramos, "but we're close and we usually do better than the mall up in Billings."[26]

Not only has the store done well itself, but it has boosted sales at other downtown businesses, including a local hardware store, pharmacy, movie theater, fabric store, and several restaurants. "Since the store opened, the street is parked full all the time," said Witzeling. Perhaps the greatest reason for the store's success is the community's sense of controlling its own destiny. "They all refer to it as 'our store.' Not 'the store,' or 'that store.' It's 'our store,'" he said. "It's pride of ownership."

The Merc has turned a profit every year since its opening. The company has not issued a dividend yet, opting instead—with the enthusiastic support of shareholders who assemble and vote at its annual meeting—to plow the profits into expanding the business. The first year, the Merc leased a second, three-thousand-square-foot space a few doors down for its teenager and baby departments. Now, the Merc is planning to acquire the building that houses its main store and has put up another $65,000 in cash to buy a vacant building next door. To secure the rest of the funding needed to purchase the second building, the Merc has asked the Powell City Council to sponsor a request for a $185,000 community development block grant from the state. If the deal goes through, the Merc will combine the adjacent storefronts, merging all of its merchandise into one fourteen-thousand-square-foot space.[27]

As word of the venture spread, Witzeling and others involved in the Powell Mercantile started getting calls from people across the country wanting to know what it would take to start their own community-owned stores. They have happily shared their knowledge, providing copies of their bylaws, warning about mistakes and pitfalls, and giving tour after tour of the store to visiting delegations from far and wide. One such delegation came from Ely, Nevada, an isolated mountain town of about four thousand people that lies 280 miles north of Las Vegas and about the same distance southwest of Salt Lake City. In 2003 JC Penney announced it would close its Ely store, leaving residents with a 190-mile trip just to buy socks and T-shirts. Worse, local businesses feared, if people left to buy socks, they'd inevitably start buying other things out of town too. "You have to give people variety. Without a full clothing store, people would just go out of town," said Tom Bath, whose grandfather came to Ely in 1904, when it was a copper-mining boomtown, and opened a saloon. The Baths have been in business ever since, starting Bath Hardware in 1948, which Tom Bath runs today, along with a local sporting goods store. His wife has a drugstore in town.[28]

Bath and other Ely residents began looking for a solution. They heard about the Powell Mercantile, flew up to see the store for themselves, and decided that there was no reason they couldn't do the same thing. A local attorney helped them with the paperwork. At first, stock sales were brisk, said Jack Smith, who serves on the Ely City Council and the board of what is now known as the Garnet Mercantile. But after raising about $200,000, in increments of $500 a share, things hit a lull, and the group of eight directors—the only ones allowed to sell the stock—had to redouble their efforts. They started spending evenings phone-banking down at the local lumberyard, which had offered up its eight phone lines for the cause, and set up a sidewalk booth during Ely's big July Fourth celebration. Shares started to move again and, in the end, they surpassed their goal, selling 985 shares and capitalizing the new business with $492,500. It took six months to get the store ready, with everyone from high school students to seniors pitching in to remodel the interior. A local arts group restored the building's 1930s-style facade with period signage and a hand-painted fashion mural.[29]

"Instead of this town folding up, we pulled ourselves up by the boot-straps," said Dan Leoni, the Garnet Mercantile's general manager. Leoni managed JC Penney stores across rural America for thirty-seven years before retiring when his last store, in Ely, closed. "I took a two-month retirement," he said with a light chuckle. The store's offerings—clothing, shoes, and "soft" home goods like towels and sheets—are roughly comparable to what Penney's carried, both in terms of mix and price. There have been some surprises: men's jeans have not done as well as expected, while the store has been a hit with teenage girls. At the end of the first year, the Merc had cleared $540,000 in sales, a bit higher than the board's goal.[30]

Ely is not the only town to follow Powell's lead. Half a dozen community-owned department stores are now operating across Rocky Mountain towns. Four of them—those in Ely and Powell, along with Washakie Wear in Worland, Wyoming, and Our Clothing Store in Torrington, Wyoming—have formed a buying group run by the Powell Mercantile's buyer, Mike Reile. It enables them to get volume discounts and minimize excess inventory by splitting cases among themselves. A fifth, the Carbon Mercantile in Rawlins, Wyoming, was the latest to join, in 2006.[31]

By 2006, the idea of community-owned corporations had begun to spread beyond the Rockies. A group of residents in Greenfield, Massachusetts—the town that rejected Wal-Mart in 1993—spent more than a year drafting a detailed business plan and a fifty-page stock prospectus for the Greenfield Mercantile, a store that will sell low-priced clothing, jewelry, housewares, and small appliances. They started selling stock in the spring of 2006 with the aim of raising $565,000 and opening downtown in 2007. Their board includes the chief operating officer of the Greenfield Savings Bank, the director of the local community-development corporation, a member of the city council, and several local business owners. "Even if we raise the money, we won't go forward unless we find the right location, manager, and buyer," said board member and documentary filmmaker Steve Alves.[32]

Greenfield residents already have experience with community ownership through the Green Fields Market, a thriving food store that has been downtown since the early 1990s and did more than $5 million in sales in

2005. The market operates as a membership cooperative; its thousands of members own and democratically control the store, with surplus revenue rebated to them at the end of the year. Food co-ops, which first began to proliferate in the 1960s and 1970s, have been remarkably successful. In 2005 there were over three hundred and growing. (Indeed, a new initiative, the Food Co-op 500, plans to expand the number to five hundred by 2015.) They generate $33 billion in annual sales, accounting for 4 percent of the grocery market. Some are small, casual outfits; others, like the Wedge in Minneapolis, rank among the nation's most sophisticated grocers. Together, they paint a potential bright future for community-owned department stores. Because the mercantiles, unlike most stock corporations, limit how much stock any one person can own—Greenfield limits shareholders to no more than one hundred shares or 3 percent of all shares—they have a democratic structure fairly similar to co-ops.[33]

Alves said that the Greenfield Mercantile considered a cooperative structure, but opted against it, because they think they can raise more capital by offering stock, which they plan to sell for one hundred dollars a share in five-share bundles. Alves hopes, however, that the Merc will replicate other aspects of the Green Fields Market. "The co-op is much more than a store," he said, describing it as a hub of information exchange and community interaction. "When you are there shopping, you are taking care of your personal needs while taking care of your community. That's what we want for the department store."

Like the mercantiles in the West, the Greenfield Mercantile was hatched partly in response to the bankruptcy of a regional chain of discount stores called Ames, which left Greenfield and other towns in New England without a place to buy inexpensive clothing and housewares. Greenfield does have a midpriced department store, the venerable family-owned Wilson's, which has been around since 1882. The goal of the mercantile, which has the support of Wilson's, is to expand the range of low-priced goods available without having to resort to a big box. But while the motivations are similar to those in Ely and Powell, the competitive context is very different. Greenfield is hardly isolated; it has four Wal-Mart stores less than twenty miles away. So the mercantile's success will rest less on convenience and more on the community's determination to forge a viable alternative for meeting local needs. Several New England towns that also lost Ames but do not want Wal-Mart, like Middlebury, Vermont, are eagerly watching Greenfield, with an eye toward launching their own hometown stores.[34]

DEVELOPING WITH LOCALS

As we have seen, independent retailers are systematically excluded from most new development and major redevelopment projects. Unlike the town founders of old, who erected enduring structures specially designed to fit their surroundings, much of today's real estate development industry is formulaic and builds only for the short-term. The conventional approach is to take a standard, off-the-shelf "product"—say a power center with two big boxes, three midsize boxes, and a restaurant pad—and drop it into a nonspecific location, like a major intersection or highway interchange. Financing such an endeavor requires a roster of familiar, credit-worthy tenants and, because banks and equity investors have extremely short time horizons for returns on real estate, the project must have strong cash flow in the first few years. To satisfy these demands, developers often use low-quality materials and turn to retail leasing brokers, who lease the project to an array of big-name chains that open almost overnight. Even developers who want to create something better find themselves trapped by the system.[35]

"These are the forces that lead to the 'could be anywhere' nature of America's built environment and that encourage developers generally to build and flip projects within a few years of construction," explained Christopher Leinberger, a real estate developer and fellow at the Brookings Institution. Because they are usually out within five to seven years, developers have no stake in the long-term costs or benefits of their projects. How well the buildings will age, whether the tenants are likely to abandon the location, whether the structures can easily be converted to other uses, or whether the project contributes to the health and vitality of the community makes little difference. One consequence is that, while vibrant Main Streets tend to add value to nearby homes, conventional shopping centers often have the opposite effect: they reduce adjacent property values.[36]

Leinberger argues for completely restructuring the way development is financed by dividing the capital into three separate investment pools with different time horizons. Short-term investors (one to five years) would have first access to the income stream and, in exchange for this preferred position, would accept a lower rate of return than conventional financing. A second pool of medium-term investors (beyond five years) would include the landowner, developer, and others who stand to benefit from the rising income generated by a well-built project. The long-term pool (beyond twelve years) could be provided by the city. Rather than subsidizing projects, Leinberger argues, cities should become patient equity investors. This would enable them to shape development to maximize the community benefits (by, for example, stipulating that the businesses be locally owned) and also, eventually, receive a direct return on their investment.[37]

Having a public-ownership stake can make all the difference. In 2004 Austin, Texas, moved to have five city-owned blocks near City Hall redeveloped with a mix of housing, offices, and retail. In its deal with the developer, the city set a goal of having at least 30 percent of the retail space go to locally owned businesses. The developer worked with a local broker, Frank Seely, who knew the community and was able to secure agreements with both start-up businesses and merchants looking to open second locations. So far, the Second Street District, which is only partially completed, has exceeded the city's goal. Of the twenty-four spaces leased by the end of 2005, seventeen were occupied by local businesses, like The Home Retreat and Eliza Page jewelers. Their leases were structured to gradually increase the rent to market rate, giving the merchants an opportunity to establish a customer base downtown, which has been something of a retail dead-zone for years. Seely said that leasing to locals has been good for the viability of the project: "People are not going to drive past a Chili's or a Gap to come downtown and shop at a Chili's or a Gap."[38]

The city's desire to bring local businesses downtown was ignited in part by the advocacy of the Austin Independent Business Alliance (AIBA). This coalition of 350 locally owned businesses, formed in 2002, has been waging a creative and attention-grabbing marketing campaign aimed at encouraging Austinites to support independent businesses. AIBA has had a remarkable impact on the thinking (and shopping habits) of residents, city officials, and, most recently, developers. In resident surveys, developers have tracked a growing desire for locally owned retailers. Frustrated with their inability to satisfy this demand, several developers approached AIBA to see whether the group could help them fill the gap. In the fall of 2004, AIBA organized a meeting of five developers, five independent businesses, a few lenders, and someone from the city's Small Business Development Program.[39]

"It was a very interesting conversation," said AIBA director Melissa Miller. "The net of the whole thing was that all parties wanted to grow and to work together, but that there was a lack of trust." Local businesses complained that they had been shut out, while developers courted and accommodated their chain competitors. Developers complained that local entrepreneurs were often reluctant to share their financials, without which securing financing for a project is impossible. Plus, they said, local merchants are not on the radar screen of most leasing brokers, who play a key intermediary role and have intimate knowledge of the expansion plans and location requirements of national chains.[40]

As an initial step to bridging the divide, AIBA hosted a trade show modeled on the annual convention of the International Council of Shopping Centers (ICSC). Held in Las Vegas each spring, the ICSC trade show functions as a matchmaking venue for developers and chains, with a liberal sprinkling of city officials peddling potential development sites and subsidy deals to both parties. AIBA's local variation was held the week before the ICSC show in May 2006 and gave existing and aspiring local business owners a chance to meet with Austin developers and see their plans. The CLIC trade show—the acronym stands for Connecting and Linking Independents with Commercial Developments—also featured workshops for merchants on such topics as business planning, lease negotiations, and marketing.[41]

Neil Takemoto is working to catalyze similar confluences of investors, developers, city officials, and local entrepreneurs in other cities. The director of CoolTown Studios and cofounder of the National Town Builders Association, a trade group of new urbanism developers, Takemoto points with frustration to the many heavily subsidized downtown redevelopment projects, such as Louisville's Fourth Street Live and Kansas City's Power & Light District, that are filled with chains. He believes the returns, both to cities and developers, would be greater if these projects featured unique, local businesses, because they would increase the value of nearby housing and attract "creative economy" enterprises. CoolTown Studios is working to find and link like-minded developers with investors and to establish a mechanism for brokering space to local retailers.[42]

There are a few examples of redevelopment projects that have primarily featured locally owned businesses. One is Berkeley's Fourth Street, which was redeveloped in the late 1990s. Another is Shaker Square, a seventy-five-year-old, octagonal shopping center originally built around a streetcar line at the entrance to Shaker Heights, an early Cleveland suburb. The square was redeveloped in 2000 and leased to a number of national chains, including Wild Oats and The Gap. But the chains did not fare well and began closing a couple of years later after plans for a nearby lifestyle center were announced. Local developer Peter Rubin, of the Coral Company, which has done several standard chain retail projects, bought Shaker Square when it was about half empty. Rubin has opted to redevelop it with locally owned businesses. "There's a higher success probability with them," he said. Rather than trying to attract regional shoppers, as the previous developer did, Rubin is aiming to serve the immediate neighborhood. By day, Shaker Square provides groceries and other basic needs, and at night it becomes an entertainment venue, with local restaurants and a restored 1937 movie theater.[43]

About 40 percent of the merchants are single-location independents, like Dewey's Fair Trade Coffee House. Another 40 percent are local businesses with more than one location, like Dave's Supermarket, which located its seventh Cleveland store at the square. Rubin also recruited local restaurateur Sergio Abramoff to open a second restaurant, and brought in Playmatters Toys, which now has four stores in the city. The last 20 percent are national chains. "It's a tougher way to go," said Rubin, who assembled a patchwork of new-market and historic-rehabilitation tax credits, which are available for certain kinds of investment in historic and economically distressed neighborhoods, to make the financing work. National retailers, he noted, have entire divisions devoted to handling the many details involved in opening new stores. Local retailers often need more help. "There's a plus side to that, though. The national retailers have no flexibility. With the local stores, we were able to influence how they looked, their signage, and their window decor." The new Shaker Square has been praised by neighborhood groups, but it is too early to tell whether it will succeed.

STRENGTH IN NUMBERS

"I am on the radar of all the record labels now. Being part of [an alliance] legitimated us in a way. If I were on my own, I wouldn't get nearly the love and attention that I do," said Doyle Davis, owner of Grimey's New & Preloved Music in Nashville. Davis, whose two childhood dreams were owning a record store and creating a record label, bought Grimey's in 2003. At the time, it was a tiny outfit selling used CDs out of an old house. He moved it to a new space on Eighth Avenue, tripled its size, and started offering new albums as well as used. He also joined the Alliance of Independent Media

Stores (AIMS), which he counts as "one of the smartest things I ever did in running this business" and credits with helping him post double-digit revenue growth in 2005.[44]

AIMS is a coalition of thirty-one independent music stores that negotiate collectively with record labels to promote artists. A label looking to introduce a new band might approach AIMS about featuring the album in all of its member stores with a special sale price, posters, and live in-store events with the band. Or a label might submit an album for inclusion on in-store listening posts that feature a rotating selection of thirty albums chosen by AIMS members. Working in concert, the stores are able to get more attention from the labels and obtain some of the same rebates and promotional fees flowing to the chains. Not only does AIMS give local owners more clout, it frees up their time. "I spend time on the phone with the labels, so they can spend time working on their stores," said AIMS director Eric Levin, who owns Criminal Records in Atlanta.[45]

AIMS is one of several music-store coalitions that have formed since the mid-1990s. Each has kept its membership relatively small, in part because they need to be able to guarantee that members will follow through on deals with the labels. Some also specialize in certain genres (hip-hop, alternative, etc.) or work with independent record labels that can afford to run promotions in only a few dozen stores. The oldest, the Coalition of Independent Music Stores (CIMS), pioneered the alliance concept in 1995 and counts seventy stores as members. "Originally the game plan was to provide a one-stop marketing vehicle for the record labels and distribution companies—in the same way they could just call once for Target stores. United, it gave us a bigger voice in the industry," said Waterloo Records owner and CIMS cofounder John Kunz. "But the biggest bonus has been the ability to bounce ideas off fellow store owners and share problems."[46]

Like Kunz, many music store owners report that more valuable than the added clout, or even than the financial benefits, has been the camaraderie that these coalitions have fostered. "It enables me to take advantage of the collective wisdom and knowledge of all these record store owners," said Davis, who regularly connects with fellow AIMS members at various gatherings and by phone and e-mail. "I was brand-new at running a record store. It's been invaluable having these guys teach me how to do this." Levin confirms that what was initially a secondary benefit of the coalition has become perhaps its most significant achievement: "It's hard to quantify, but it's really powerful. We share those experiences and take from one another those good ideas." Next on the horizon, CIMS, AIMS, and other coalitions are pooling their resources to build a system that will enable their members to sell music downloads on their own Web sites and at in-store kiosks. "I don't know how much business it will do," said Davis, "but it's important in the eyes of my customers, who will say, wow, they are really keeping up with the times."

Cooperation is becoming increasingly essential to the survival of independent businesses, many of which are now banding together to share strategies, secure better deals from suppliers, and undertake endeavors that would be impossible for an individual store to do on its own. "We've seen an explosion of retailer-owned purchasing cooperatives," said Paul Hazen, executive director of the National Cooperative Business Association, which reports that the number of purchasing co-ops has doubled since 1995 to more than three hundred. They have an estimated fifty thousand independent business members. These buying groups are owned and controlled by their members, with any profits returned as rebate checks. Like chains, most obtain volume discounts and scale efficiencies by negotiating directly with manufacturers and managing their own distribution centers. Many also provide other services. "The best look at how they can make their members more successful businesses," said Hazen, which may entail anything from training programs to specialized market research.[47]

The first thing Jim Stevens did when he bought a sixty-year-old hardware store in Wilmington, North Carolina, was join Do It Best, a purchasing co-op owned by about forty-two hundred independent hardware stores. "It's the buying power. It allows independent merchants to compete with just about anybody," he said. Once the smallest hardware store in the area, Stevens has since moved to a larger building, relying on the co-op's extensive market and demographic research to figure out which product categories to expand. "That's a pretty sophisticated science these days," he said. One department Stevens Hardware added was carpet and flooring. "Because of Do It Best, we didn't have to apply for an account with each vendor. It's done automatically and we get the national pricing," he said.[48]

Hardware co-ops are among the earliest purchasing co-ops; they date back to the first half of the twentieth century. Although a few stores, like the fiercely independent and wildly popular McGuckin's in Boulder, Colorado, have opted not to join a co-op and to handle their own purchasing, the vast majority of the nation's twenty thousand local hardware stores belong to one. The largest three are Ace, Do It Best, and True Value, which together have about fourteen thousand members and account for roughly $33 billion in consumer spending. (Lowe's did $36 billion in sales in 2005, while Home Depot took in $73 billion.) Because each store carries a different product mix—some have extensive flooring sections, others stock housewares—the co-ops cannot completely match the distribution efficiencies of the chains. But they come fairly close, which is what enables skilled hardware-store owners to routinely meet or even beat big-box pricing. Beyond purchasing, the co-ops offer help with expansion, financing, employee training, inventory management, market research, and advertising.[49]

An ongoing challenge for retailer-owned co-ops is figuring out how best to balance the advantages of local ownership—individual entrepreneurs working to meet the unique needs of a local market—with the benefits that accrue from a shared brand-name and well-honed national strategy. Each of the hardware co-ops has struck a different balance. Do It Best has leaned more toward emphasizing the local. "We ought to focus on helping members accent ties to their communities," CEO Bob Taylor has told reporters. The co-op does no national advertising and, while many of its members display the Do It Best logo, it's often subordinate to the name of the local store. "We have the logo on our building, which helps when people move here. They know the Do It Best name," said Stevens. "But still our strongest point is our own name, Stevens Hardware. That's their policy, you grow your own name." Do It Best offers many of its services on an à la carte basis, giving members flexibility in how much of the co-op's formula they adopt and enabling each to invest in only those programs they find worthwhile.[50]

Ace members have opted for a more unified strategy. The co-op has invested heavily in advertising the Ace brand, which some of its forty-nine hundred members display more prominently than their own store names. In 2003, after conducting research on the characteristics of the strongest hardware stores and concluding that some of its members did not adequately represent the brand, Ace launched Vision 21, a set of standards—covering merchandise mix, store layout, employee training, and more —that it asked its members to meet. So far, about twenty-two hundred have done so, bringing a more uniform look and operation to their stores. Another six hundred have opted out and have removed the Ace brand from their signage, although they continue to participate in the buying program. The remaining twenty-one hundred stores are at some stage in the process. Some local owners have grumbled about the incursion on their autonomy and a franchise mentality. But Ace points to the stronger financial per-formance of those who do make the upgrades. "While that entrepreneur-ship is our most significant advantage, it's also challenging," said Ken Nichols, vice president of retail operations. "We can't drive change by man-date. We have to earn their trust and deliver proof that something will work economically."[51]

Ace has also been working aggressively to help existing members open more outlets and assist new owners, like Gina Schaefer, in getting started. The co-op has set an ambitious goal of seeding eleven hundred new hard-ware stores by 2010. "We think there are great opportunities to put stores in intercept locations between homes and big boxes," said Nichols. The co-op offers generous incentives to members who want to expand their stores or open additional ones—funded, of course, by the entire member-ship—and an equity-matching program that leverages the co-op's ability to borrow at low rates to assist new owners. While the number of inde-pendent hardware stores overall continues to decline, in 2005 Ace came close to breaking even. It had 127 members go out of business, but added 117 new stores (not counting conversions from other co-ops). Most were branch outlets opened by established owners, but 30 were started by new owners. Because many of the new stores were larger, overall square footage increased.[52]

Now the cooperative model pioneered by hardware stores—and also by grocery stores, thousands of which belong to co-ops, like Unified Western Grocers and Associated Grocers of New England, which formed in the 1930s to counter A&P's market power—is being adopted in a growing number of retail categories as independents of all kinds seek more leverage. The rea-son that *Consumer Reports* found that local appliance dealers offer compa-rable or better prices than the big boxes is in part that most belong to purchasing co-ops, like Intercounty Appliance, that buy in volume and run their own warehouses. Local pharmacies, too, are now served by several buying groups. Food co-ops purchase through the National Cooperative Grocers Association. Local remodeling contractors, who are increasingly squeezed by the installation services offered by Home Depot and Lowe's, have formed a buying group called Max Equity.[53]

One of the more successful endeavors in this arena is CCA Global. In the 1980s Howard Brodsky and Alan Greenberg created a purchasing co-op for carpet stores under the banner Carpet One. It did so well that in 2000, they began spinning out new co-ops for independent lighting stores, bicycle dealers, and formal-wear shops—all under the CCA Global umbrella. Each co-op offers a mix of services based on the needs of those particular stores, but they are able to leverage the combined size of all the co-ops to negoti-ate even better deals on common services, like liability insurance and credit card rates.

"It has saved us an enormous amount of money," said Marilyn Shulman, who owns Bay Shore Lighting, a sixty-one-year-old Long Island lighting store founded by her father. Lighting One, which has about 130 members nationally, has cut her credit card rates, organized online training for her employees, and provided high-quality radio and newspaper ads. "Some of the things we could probably do on our own, but only with difficulty and great expense," she said. Other co-op benefits, such as the store's own private-label credit card that enables Bay Shore to offer extended payment terms like the chains do ("no interest for six months"), would have been totally out of reach. "We could never negotiate that on our own," Shulman said. In 2006, thanks to a deal the co-op worked with manufacturers, co-op members were carrying a line of lighting fixtures specially designed for them and not available at chains.[54]

Some co-ops and trade associations are also helping their members de-velop sophisticated e-commerce capabilities. When the Web first emerged, some speculated that major chains would find themselves mired in their own extensive physical infrastructure and toppled by more-nimble on-line retailers. Some also said that online retailing would be the salvation of small businesses by giving them access to a global market. Neither predic-tion has been borne out. With the exception of Amazon.com, online re-tailing has been the domain of major chains. A list of the top Internet retailers includes a familiar roster of chains like Target, Wal-Mart, The Gap, Best Buy, and Office Depot. As the dot-com boom and bust illustrated, it takes a huge pile of cash to build a viable brand from scratch. Most of the Web-only retailers that tried, failed. Amazon.com managed to pull it off, but only because Wall Street allowed the company to lose a total of $2.4 bil-lion from 1995 to 2005. (Many former bookstore owners grimly point out that they'd still be in business if granted the same reprieve from having to operate in the black.)[55]

While retailers that offer specialized products can build a global market through the Web, for more mundane goods, people are generally inclined to shop online at companies they are already familiar with. This is where the real opportunity lies for many independent retailers: using the Web to expand services and sales to local customers, not trying to reach a global market. Rather than letting their own customers become chain store patrons when they go online—which people are doing more of each year— independents should make it possible for them to shop locally on the Web.

Both Do It Best and Ace have developed e-commerce sites that offer more than fifty thousand items and all the convenience of online shopping, but credit the proceeds of each sale to the customer's own local hardware store. One can buy a hammer at three o'clock in the morning or order a giant riding lawn mower that the local store does not have room to stock. The item can either be shipped home or, at no freight cost, picked up at the local store. In 2005 Ace took in about $6 million in sales online, or about $1,300 per member—not big business, but the co-op says the site drives sales at stores by providing product information and how-to advice. To boost online orders, local hardware stores may need to do more to let their customers know that these Web sites exist—through fliers stuffed in every shopping bag, local advertising, or in-store computer kiosks. Otherwise, what are normally loyal customers may end up making their online buys at Home Depot, Lowe's, or Sears.[56]

Independent bookstores have developed similar initiatives. About three hundred now have e-commerce sites that allow customers to search and order from a vast database of titles—with those in stock shipped by the local store and others drop-shipped by a wholesaler. These sites are powered by either BookSite, a shared platform developed in 1996 by Dick Harte, owner of Rutherford's Book Shoppe in Delaware, Ohio, or BookSense.com, created by the American Booksellers Association. These competing technologies enable local bookstores to have their own unique Web sites, with their own look and feel, list of author events, and book reviews. It's only the invisible backend functions (the database, the shopping cart, and so on) that are shared. So, for example, both Schuler Books and the Harvard Book Store utilize BookSite, but their Web sites are very different.

Some stores do more than others to advertise their Web sites to customers. St. Helen's Book Shop in St. Helens, Oregon, includes the message "Shop our 24-hour store where everything is 15 percent off" on everything from newspaper ads to store receipts. Village Books in Bellingham, Washington, features store banners and bookmarks that say "Shop 24/7." Although the store does relatively modest business online, according to owner Chuck Robinson, the site drives in-store sales by boosting turnout at author events and lowers costs by enabling customers to see whether a title is in stock without having to phone the staff. It also enables Village Books to have affiliates—Web sites of local organizations and authors who link to the store's site and receive a referral fee for any resulting sales (as many now do with Amazon.com).[57]

SHOP LOCALLY OWNED

Spend a little time in Austin, Texas, and it's not long before you notice the messages. Bumper stickers advise, "Think independently. Shop locally owned." Banners hanging on storefronts read, "Local Spoken Here." T-shirts urge, "Keep Austin Weird." Circular yellow decals on the entrances of local businesses feature a blue armadillo in sunglasses and the words, "Austin Independent Business Alliance." Indeed, the armadillo is everywhere—in newspaper ads, on the cover of a free guide to locally owned independent businesses, on posters reminding people to "Break the Chain Habit." All of these messages are part of an ongoing effort by the Austin Independent Business Alliance (AIBA) to build support for locally owned businesses. AIBA came together in 2002 amid mounting concerns about the number of chains moving into the city. Steve Bercu, owner of BookPeople, called a meeting of a few dozen local businesses and proposed that they form an alliance to counter the chain store trend. Those in attendance included the owners of some of the city's most prominent local businesses: Waterloo Records & Video, *The Good Life Magazine,* the outfitter Whole Earth Provision, Wheatsville Co-op, the public television station KLRU, and the Austin Motel. "Almost everyone thought it was a great idea," Bercu recalled.[58]

Not long after that initial meeting, Borders announced plans to open a superstore at the same intersection occupied by BookPeople and Waterloo Records. Suddenly the generalized concerned that had prompted AIBA became particular and immediate. BookPeople and Waterloo fought back, commissioning the study discussed in Chapter 2 that found that the chain would drain dollars from Austin's economy. The ensuing controversy triggered a flood of new members for AIBA and made the chain store issue front-page news. "If we hadn't had that fight and gotten in the newspaper every day for eight months, I doubt we would have gotten the membership we did," said Bercu. "It was even good when the paper would carry an editorial against us. The guy would say we were a bunch of whiners and before

I could finish reading the article, we would have all these people in the store. Everyone rallied around us." Borders backed out.

Today AIBA has 350 member businesses, from banks and credit unions to coffeehouses and bakeries, hardware and home-furnishings stores. Dues are $175 a year and day-to-day operations are managed by the board and an executive director, Melissa Miller. AIBA's mission is to promote and support locally owned businesses, which it does through its ongoing public-awareness campaign and periodic events that focus media attention on the issue. One is Austin Unchained, which started in 2003 and was such a hit that it has since become an annual affair. Held on a Saturday in November, Austin Unchained is a call to all residents to shop only at locally owned businesses for the day. Posters feature the blue armadillo breaking out of metal chains. Referencing a study by the firm Civic Economics that found that just one day of shunning the chains for local stores would add $14 million to Austin's economy—because the local stores spend more of their revenue with other local businesses—the posters advise, "Before you spend your next dollar, just think what $14 million a day would do for Austin."

"It's a big media event every year," said Bercu. "You have people in the media asking, What's this all about? That's an opportunity to talk about the value of independent business, about the economic benefits and the cultural diversity and what makes Austin unique." Each year, Austin Unchained is covered by the city's television and radio stations and its major print media, offering numerous opportunities for AIBA to get its message out. But Bercu says the key to a more enduring shift in consciousness and shopping habits is to keep the conversation going. "Just because people are talking about you a lot, that doesn't mean they will be in three or six months," he said. To that end, AIBA tries to find as many opportunities as it can to draw attention to locally owned businesses and to galvanize public discussion. It annually publishes a free and widely available directory of the city's local businesses, organized by category. The guide not only helps people identify alternatives to the chains, but it is loaded with facts about the economic and community contributions of locally owned businesses.

AIBA hopes that "locally owned" will eventually become a powerful and sought-after selling point. "My personal goal is to have people feel uneasy about not shopping at a locally owned business," said Bercu. "So when you walk into that chain, you feel like you are letting your city down. Just like you feel you are letting yourself down when you order the triple-meat cheeseburger." While Bercu believes that AIBA is having an effect on people's choices, he admits that the group has not yet found a way to measure this empirically. "So far the biggest evidence of effectiveness is the receptive attitude we have at the city council. The city council is now paying attention to us in a substantial way," he said. The council regularly solicits input from AIBA, which learned early on how to talk the city's language. "Our members collectively employ six thousand people. That makes us one of the top five employers in the city," said Rebecca Melancon, publisher of *The Good Life,* a local monthly magazine, and vice president of AIBA. "When I'm sitting across from a city council member, I say, how much would the city pay to bring a company here with 350 jobs? A million dollars? If we put fifty thousand dollars into some of these programs that would help each of our members expand and hire one person, we could create those jobs for a whole lot less than a million dollars."[59]

One program that AIBA pioneered and pitched to enthusiastic city officials is IBIZ—Independent Business Investment Zones. The goal is to identify and organize clusters of businesses that exist in neighborhoods across the city—some as small as a block or two. Each IBIZ district—there is one so far—sets its own goals, based on whatever problems local businesses face, and works with neighborhood organizations and the city to solve them. The city's role may be as simple as making modest street improvements, posting signs that cultivate the district's identity, or promoting a monthly event. The first IBIZ, the Guadalupe District, for example, now celebrates Third Thursday every month with live music, street performers, and businesses that stay open until 10 PM. Or the city's role might be as involved as making distressed districts eligible for special tax breaks and public investment, or helping business owners in gentrifying districts to buy their buildings, to avoid being squeezed out by rising rents. Some have proposed that IBIZ districts receive special designation in the city's zoning code, helping neighborhoods preserve their scale and local character.

City officials say that AIBA has helped them be much more in touch with the needs and issues facing the city's locally owned businesses, which has influenced their actions and in turn improved the city's image in the eyes of many merchants. "The main contact most people have had with the city is when they come out to tear the road up in front of your business. That dynamic is changing," said Bercu. AIBA has also improved the relationship between business owners and neighborhood groups, which Melancon said used to be more antagonistic. Now neighborhood groups see local retailers as allies on quality-of-life issues. Both are banding together, for example, to back a city measure to impose limits and standards on new retail development. Some neighborhoods are also pushing to ban formula businesses. The Austin Neighborhood Council recently approach AIBA about partnering to implement IBIZ. Meanwhile, AIBA is moving forward on the CLIC initiative with developers. "If we can link neighborhoods and business owners and developers all together, then we can do big things," said Melancon.

The best thing about AIBA is that it's not the only one of its kind. Similar Independent Business Alliances have sprung up in more than three dozen communities since 1998. The very first one—the one that inspired Steve Bercu to call that initial meeting—was the Boulder Independent Business Alliance (BIBA). It was founded by another bookseller, David Bolduc, who owns the Boulder Bookstore, and Jeff Milchen, a community organizer. "Many communities around the country were rapidly being paved over by big-box stores. I realized that without conscious planning and organizing, Boulder was going to follow that same path," said Milchen. He and Bolduc recruited ten local business owners and together they launched BIBA in 1998. It quickly grew to over 150 members and started covering the city with messages about the value of local businesses. Window decals identified businesses as locally owned. Bumper stickers urged, "Put Your Money Where Your House Is." Paper cups at all the local cafés offered customers a word of thanks: "By buying this beverage from a local independent business, you've just helped keep Boulder the great town we all love." Bookmarks given out at local book, music, and video stores offered five reasons to buy local. Number 4: "Do you really want Wal-Mart deciding what gets recorded?"[60]

Soon word of BIBA's activities spread and Milchen started getting calls from business owners across the country. In 2001 he and Jennifer Rockne, who had been working as BIBA's outreach director, founded the American Independent Business Alliance (AMIBA) to help seed similar initiatives across the country. Today, there are nineteen local business alliances in their network and more in the formative stages. They include groups in small towns like Warwick, New York, and in big cities, like Minneapolis–St. Paul, where the Metro Independent Business Alliance is building its membership and visibility neighborhood by neighborhood. "Last year was the biggest jump and the number of inquiries is growing rapidly," said Rockne, noting that the idea's appeal is so strong that almost every time she travels to do a workshop for business owners, they form an alliance. Among the new ones are Homegrown El Paso, with more than eighty members, and the Raleigh Independent Business Alliance, which debuted by offering a Citizen Unchained card that sells for twenty-five dollars and provides a year's worth of discounts at locally owned businesses. Mayor Charles Meeker was the first to buy one. "I want to make this an issue in all of our political campaigns," said executive director Linda Watson. "Our message is that, rather than raising taxes or lowering services, you can make the pie bigger by keeping the money here. We're not focusing on being anti-Wal-Mart or anti-chain. But we are saying there's a cost and here's the other path."[61]

AMIBA sees its role both as providing technical assistance to newly forming alliances and bolstering existing ones by disseminating how-to kits and facilitating an exchange of strategies among them through its Web site, regular conference calls, and personal advising. In 2002 the Tampa Independent Business Alliance came up with the idea of Independents Week, seven days of events coinciding with July Fourth. "As we celebrate our nation's independence, we invite you to join us in celebrating our great local independents," posters read. It was a huge success, with coverage in the *Tampa Tribune* and on a television station that broadcast its morning news program from a different local business each day that week. AMIBA soon took Independents Week national, providing how-to kits to other alliances. It also expanded on Austin's initiative with America Unchained, a special buy-local day and media event in November. Not only do local alliances participate, but AMIBA provides how-to assistance to Main Street groups and other local organizations that want to take part.

One great idea that is bound to spread is the Santa Fe Shares card, an electronic loyalty card that enables people to rack up and redeem rebates by shopping at locally owned businesses in Santa Fe, New Mexico. The card is the creation of another AMIBA affiliate, the Santa Fe Alliance (SFA), which, with a membership of 675 independent businesses, is one of the largest in the country. Its slogan, "Keep Our Independents," appears on window decals, bookmarks, and ads around town. The goal of the new Santa Fe Shares card, said SFA cofounder David Kaseman, is to encourage people to make local businesses their first choice. With a magnetic strip that records activity, the card looks much like the loyalty and gift cards that major chains offer—except that it works at dozens of local businesses, each of which offers cardholders a percentage rebate on their purchases.[62]

After deduction of a fee to fund the program, half of the rebate goes to support a school, church, or nonprofit chosen by the cardholder. The other half accumulates on the card and can be spent at any participating local business. It's fairly easy for businesses to participate: the cards can be swiped in the same terminals used for credit card purchases. Networked software records the transactions and settles the accounts among the businesses. A local bank, Los Alamos National Bank, is making all of its new credit cards also function as Santa Fe Shares cards. "They are going to market this with us and be the bank that cares about locally owned businesses," said Kaseman. The card is not without precedent. In 2000 a dozen local merchants on the Hawaiian island of Maui started a joint Ohana Savers card.[63]

AMIBA is not the only initiative of its kind. In 2001 the Business Alliance for Local Living Economies, or BALLE, was started by Judy Wicks, who owns the White Dog Café in Philadelphia, and Laury Hammel, owner of Longfellow Sports Clubs in Wayland, Massachusetts. Both had previously been involved in efforts to encourage corporations to be more environmentally and socially responsible. But in 1999—a year that saw Ben & Jerry's, a beacon of corporate responsibility, taken over by the global food giant Unilever, and thousands gather in Seattle to protest the World Trade Organization and the growing power of transnational corporations— Hammel and Wicks began to rethink their approach. The real solution, they decided, was to rebuild local enterprises that were firmly rooted in, and accountable to, their communities. They linked up with others who shared this view, including Michael Shuman and David Korten, author of *When Corporations Rule the World,* and created BALLE, a national network that by 2006 had more than two dozen local affiliates.[64]

One of the most successful is Sustainable Connections, a coalition of nearly five hundred independent businesses in a region of northwest Washington centered on the city of Bellingham. "Our focus is multipronged: how can we build an economy that sustains itself, our community, and the environment for the long-term?" said executive director Michelle Long. Part of the group's mission is to help local businesses make their operations more environmentally sustainable through initiatives on such things as switching to renewable power and installing bike racks. It also aims to shift more spending to locally owned businesses through a campaign called Think Local First. "The goal is to make people aware of local businesses and to think of them first. It's about giving that opportunity to your neighbors before choosing the typical [chain store] option," said Fairhaven Runners owner Steve Raguski.[65]

Today, the Think Local First logo—which depicts nearby Mount Baker and the words, "Think Local, Be Local, Buy Local"—appears on hundreds of storefronts, posters, T-shirts, bumper stickers, fliers, and newspaper advertisements. Special events occur throughout the year. There's Buy Local Week in December, which features various contests in which people who shop at local businesses can win prizes, like an iPod loaded with local music or a month's worth of free meals at thirty different local restaurants. They join in Independents Week in July, when residents are encouraged to finish the sentence, "I shop local because . . ." on red, white, and blue sticky-notes that business owners post on their storefronts in a fluttering display of local patriotism. September brings Eat Local Week, which focuses on local farms, grocers, and restaurants. Each year, Sustainable Connections publishes a *Where the Locals Go* coupon book, which was the best-selling book in Whatcom County in 2005; it even beat the latest *Harry Potter* and *The Da Vinci Code*. The group regularly prints newspaper inserts that highlight local businesses. In 2005 it published *A Guide to Where the Locals Go* to help tourists find alternatives to familiar brands like Starbucks: "Please support our independents while you're in town and we'll do the same when we visit your hometown."[66]

Before Think Local First started in 2003, business owners rarely had customers raise the issue. Now many say they get calls every week from people who want to know whether they are locally owned before they come in. "I heard it dozens of times during the holidays. Customers would say they came here because we are independent and they had chosen not to shop on the other side of the freeway—that's where the boxes and the chains are," said Rebecca Wiswell, owner of Rebecca's Flower Shoppe. More than any one event, said Chuck Robinson of Village Books, it's the intensity and repetition of the message that is making a difference in people's choices. "We hear more customers talking about their devotion to buying locally," he said. "The facts speak so clearly," added Ken Bothman, who owns La Fiamma Wood Fire Pizza and is opening a new burger joint in town. "Everything we put out includes facts about the local economy. Those start to stick after a while. People start to realize this isn't just a small idea; it's a really big idea." The coalition's latest endeavor is a striking series of posters, each a black-and-white photograph of a local business owner in front of his or her enterprise, along with a quote from the owner about the business and its place in the community.[67]

Business owners say the campaign has also led them to source more goods and services locally. "We thought we were pretty committed already to buying locally, but once the campaign got under way and it was in our consciousness all the time, we started rethinking some of our own purchases," said Robinson. Requests started pouring in to the Sustainable Connections office from grocers and chefs who wanted to know how they could include more locally grown food, said Long. That led the group to start a program to rebuild the shattered distribution web that once connected local farmers with local businesses. They began by surveying and mapping local farm products. Now Sustainable Connections hosts regular trade meetings that introduce farmers to local buyers. To generate media attention for the initiative, they entered a team of people dressed up like vegetables in the annual Ski to Sea marathon. "We had a tomato do the bicycle leg," said Long. The veggies didn't win, but they did end up on the local news.[68]

Similar Local First campaigns are under way in a dozen other cities where BALLE has local affiliates, including places as diverse as Philadelphia and Grand Rapids, Salt Lake City and San Francisco. "People have seen the destruction wrought by chains, and they're realizing that their communities are in danger," said Betsy Burton of The King's English bookstore in Salt Lake City, regarding the enthusiastic response she and three hundred other local business owners received when they launched Buy Local First Utah in the fall of 2005. "You cast a vote every time you spend a dollar. And every vote you cast helps to shape your community."[69]

It's too early to tell how effective these efforts will be in reversing the decline of independent businesses. But there are some intriguing indications of their influence on the public consciousness. "I think one measure is the fervor with which the national chains are trying to make themselves seem local. Their PR and advertising is working so hard to convince people that these stores are part of the community," said Chuck Robinson. Franchises and chains in Bellingham, Boulder, and Bozeman, Montana—another city with an Independent Business Alliance—have either tried to join these campaigns or gone to lengths to project an image of localness and community involvement. "When the opposition tries to co-opt your message, that's a sign that you are having an impact," said AMIBA's Milchen.[70]

Long term, both BALLE and AMIBA, which regularly communicate and collaborate, envision developing a political counterweight to groups like the U.S. Chamber of Commerce, which espouses the virtues of small business but pushes a policy agenda that strongly favors large corporations. For years, local businesses have largely aligned themselves with this agenda, endorsing the idea of a single, unified pro-business politics. But that alignment is beginning to break apart, as more local business owners see little future for themselves in a world of race-to-the-bottom labor and environmental standards that reward footloose global mobility and penalize community roots. "We want to see hundreds of Independent Business Alliances across the country," said Milchen. "Ultimately, the goal is to create a national shift in the culture and a challenge to the assertion that what's good for transnational corporations is good for America."

There is nothing inevitable about the decline of locally owned businesses. Public policy decisions and our own, often shortsighted, shopping choices have undermined their survival and propelled the proliferation of mega-retailers. But trends are not destiny. The future is open. As public awareness builds of the hidden costs of this shift, a growing number of communities are charting a different course, adopting policies and economic-development strategies that actively nurture and rebuild local enterprises. Independent businesses are banding together to gain efficiencies through purchasing cooperatives and a stronger public presence through local business alliances and "buy local" campaigns. Implemented more broadly, these initiatives could usher in a future America that is not dominated by a handful of global corporate giants and is instead a place of thriving, entrepreneurial local economies and vibrant, self-reliant communities.

ACKNOWLEDGMENTS

THIS BOOK IS A PRODUCT OF the Institute for Local Self-Reliance (ILSR), an extension of ILSR's many years of research, analysis, and on-the-ground work on how to build strong, sustainable, self-reliant communities. I have been very fortunate to have found a working home at ILSR, which provided the material support without which this book would not have been written.

I owe a special debt to David Morris, whose wise counsel and keen insights about the world have long been invaluable, and who carefully read and thoughtfully commented on drafts of this manuscript. Whatever shortcomings and flaws that remain are my own. My colleagues at ILSR are a terrific bunch who do inspiring work and from whom I have learned a great deal.

I am grateful to all of the people who agreed to be interviewed for this book and generously gave of their time and expertise. Chuck D'Aprix contributed valuable research to the final chapter.

Like all books, this one is built on the work of many other writers, including Joanna Blythman, Barbara Ehrenreich, Liza Featherstone, Thom Hartmann, Jane Jacobs, Marjorie Kelly, David Korten, James Howard Kunstler, Greg LeRoy, David Morris, Al Norman, Ray Oldenburg, Eric Schlosser, E. F. Schumacher, and Michael Shuman.

I want to thank David Korten, who first suggested I write this book. My agent, Anna Ghosh, was wonderfully enthusiastic about this project and found a great home for it in Beacon Press, which has been independently publishing books for more than 150 years. I am also indebted to Gayatri Patnaik, for her wise editing and guidance, and Melissa Dobson, whose fine-tuning of the text much improved the final product.

I am grateful to all of my friends and family, who patiently endured my long working hours and general preoccupation during the months of writing, and especially for Jacob, who cheerfully allowed this book to occupy his life as well as mine.

NOTES

INTRODUCTION

1. There is no commonly agreed upon definition, but in this book, a locally owned, independent business is majority owned by one or more people who live in the community, who have full decision-making power over the business, and who operate few enough outlets that they remain personally connected to their employees and customers. This excludes most franchise outlets, like McDonald's and Subway, which are ostensibly owned by a local entrepreneur who invests time and money in the business, but who does not have full decision-making power. Franchise owners must follow rules handed down by the franchise corporation, which also takes a share of the profit. There is no hard and fast rule about the number of outlets an independent business can operate before it begins to function more like a chain, but the regular presence of the owner working at the stores is a good indicator. Businesses with two to three outlets usually pass the test, and those with more than a dozen rarely do. Those in between might fall on either side.

2. For an account of this well-known event, which highlights the economic power of and animosity toward the East India Company, see Thom Hartmann, *Unequal Protection: The Rise of Corporate Dominance and the Theft of Human Rights* (Emmaus, Pa.: Rodale, 2002).

ONE: CHAIN STORE WORLD

1. Godfrey M. Lebhar, *Chain Stores in America, 1859–1962* (New York: Chain Store Age Books, 1971), 24–51; Ann Satterthwaite, *Going Shopping: Consumer Choices and Community Consequences* (New Haven, Conn.: Yale University Press, 2001), 39–40.

2. See the U.S. Census Bureau's *Census of Distribution* in 1929 and *Census of Business* in subsequent years for statistics on the market share of chain stores. Charles Daughters, *Wells of Discontent* (New York: Newson, 1937).

3. Michael Sandel, *Democracy's Discontent: America in Search of a Public Philosophy* (Cambridge, Mass.: Harvard University Press, 1996), 227–31; Thomas W. Ross,

"Store Wars: The Chain Tax Movement," *Journal of Law and Economics* 29 (Apr. 1986): 127; Lizabeth Cohen, *A Consumers' Republic: The Politics of Consumption in Postwar America* (New York: Knopf, 2003), 112–65.

4. Cohen, *A Consumers' Republic,* 257–89; Satterthwaite, *Going Shopping,* 46–51; Bob Ortega, *In Sam We Trust: The Untold Story of Sam Walton and Wal-Mart, the World's Most Powerful Retailer* (New York: Three Rivers Press, 2000), 33–49; International Council of Shopping Centers, "A Brief History of Shopping Centers," June 2000, available at www.icsc.org; James Lowry, "The Fight for Survival by Independent Retailers," *USA Today Magazine,* July 1, 2000, 22; Tom Hanchett, "Talking Shopping Center: Federal Tax Policy, Commercial Sprawl, and the Decline of Community," *Long Term View* 4, no. 2 (1998): 46–50; James J. Farrell, *One Nation under Goods: Malls and the Seductions of American Shopping* (Washington, D.C.: Smithsonian, 2003), 28.

5. Cohen, *A Consumers' Republic,* 257–89; Lebhar, *Chain Stores in America,* statistical supplement, 22.

6. Kenneth T. Jackson, "All the World's a Mall: Reflections on the Social and Economic Consequences of the American Shopping Center," *American Historical Review* 101, no. 4 (Oct. 1996): 1116; Farrell, *One Nation under Goods,* 7; Cohen, *A Consumers' Republic,* 257–89.

7. Thomas W. Hanchett, "U.S. Tax Policy and the Shopping Center Boom of the 1950s and 1960s," *American Historical Review* 101, no. 4 (Oct. 1996): 1082–1110; Malcolm Gladwell, "The Terrazzo Jungle: Fifty Years Ago, the Mall Was Born. America Would Never Be the Same," *New Yorker,* Mar. 15, 2004; Satterthwaite, *Going Shopping,* 52.

8. Hanchett, "Talking Shopping Center," 46 50.

9. Ortega, *In Sam We Trust,* 57–59; Karen Olsson, "Up against Wal-Mart," *Mother Jones,* Mar./Apr. 2003; "A Willingness to Experiment," *MMR,* Dec. 9, 2002, 78.

10. Ortega, *In Sam We Trust,* 57–60.

11. "30 Years of K-Mart," *Discount Store News,* Feb. 17, 1992; "Dayton's Dream Is On Target: 30-Year History of Dayton Hudson Corp.," *Discount Store News,* Apr. 20, 1992; "30 Years of Discounting," *Discount Store News,* Sept. 21, 1992.

12. Stacy Botwinick, "Thinking outside the Toy Box: Charles Lazarus Raises TRU to Be a 'Natural Born Category killer,'" *Playthings,* July 1, 2003, 24; "Toys 'R' Us Holds a Pioneering Position in the Annals of 20th Century American Retailing," *Discount Store News,* Apr. 17, 2000; Roger Thompson, "There's No Place Like Home Depot," *Nation's Business,* Feb. 1992; Circuit City stores, company timeline, http://investor.circuitcity.com/history.cfm.

13. Dee Wedemeyer, "Those Low-Priced Price Clubs," *New York Times,* May 18, 1986; John Helyar, "The Only Company Wal-Mart Fears: Nobody Runs Warehouse Clubs Better than Costco, Where Shoppers Can't Resist Luxury Products at Bargain Prices," *Fortune,* Nov. 24, 2003; "Twenty Years Young and Building for the Future: Sam's Club," *DSN Retailing Today,* Apr. 1, 2003.

14. National Retail Federation, "Top 100 Retailers (1996)" and "Top 100 Retailers (2005)," available at www.stores.org.

15. National Retail Federation, "Top 100 Retailers (1998)" and "Top 100 Retailers (2005)"; "Dayton's Dream Is On Target"; Julie Schlosser, "How Target Does It," *Fortune,* Oct. 18, 2004, 100; "2005 Annual Report," *Do-It-Yourself Retailing,* Dec. 2005, 29; Carol Emert, "Staying Alive amid Office Superstores," *San Francisco Chronicle,* June 20, 1998, E1; "The Top 100 Consumer Electronics Retailers," *Twice,* May 3, 2004.

16. Joseph Tarnowski and Walter Heller, "The Super 50," *Progressive Grocer,* May 1, 2004, 59–64; William H. Borghesani, Peter L. de la Cruz, and David B. Berry, "Controlling the Chain: Buyer Power, Distributive Control, and New Dynamics in Retailing," *Business Horizons,* July/Aug. 1997; "Rural Poor Struggle to Find Healthy Food," Associated Press, July 5, 2004; Alex Daniels, "Retailing 'All about Distribution,'" *Arkansas Democrat-Gazette,* Oct. 13, 2002, 67.

17. National Retail Federation, "Top 100 Retailers (1998)" and "Top 100 Retailers (2005)"; Kris Hundley, "An Overdose of Corner Drugstores?" *St. Petersburg Times,* Feb. 27, 2004, D1; Marc Levy, "Rite Aid Girding for First Expansion since Near-Collapse," Associated Press, July 27, 2004.

18. David Kirkpatrick, "Book Buyers Stay Busy but Forsake Bookstores," *New York Times,* June 30, 2003, C1; John Mutter, "Book Sense Turns Five: Independents Celebrate Unity and Growth in Market Share," *Publishers Weekly,* May 31, 2004, 26; Richard Howorth, "Independent Bookselling & True Market Expansion," report presented at the American Booksellers Association annual membership meeting, May 1, 1999; "Independent Bookstore Sales Continue Upward Trend," *Bookselling This Week,* May 19, 2005; Melinda Saccone, "Big Rentailers Gobbling Up More of the Market: Top Five Rentailers' Video Rental Market Share Grew to 60 Percent at Midyear, VSM Survey Finds," *Video Store,* Oct. 5, 2003, 30; "Sacramento's Independent Music Stores Distinguish Themselves from the Chains," *Knight Ridder Tribune Business News,* Jan. 3, 2003, 1.

19. Rick Anderson, "Starbucks: Just Getting Started," *Seattle Weekly,* Apr. 30, 2003, 11; Michael Sasso, "Chinese Chains Try to Take Out Independents," *Tampa Tribune,* Nov. 17, 2004, 1; Jack Robertiello, "Saving Private Restaurants: Some Independent Restaurateurs Are Working Together to Stay Alive," *Cheers,* July 1, 2004, 35.

20. Even eBay, which provides an outlet for thousands of part- and full-time entrepreneurs, derives an increasing share of its total sales from big chains, like Best Buy, that have set up their own branded stores within the larger site. EBay had $17.5 billion in nonautomotive sales in 2003, some portion of which might be better classified as garage sale, rather than retail, merchandise. Glynn Davis, "The Web's Wal-Mart: As EBay Widens Its Brief to Attract the Corporate Dollar, a Bruising Battle for Online Supremacy Is in the Cards," *Guardian,* Aug. 5, 2004, 24; Love quote taken from his introduction to *Internet Retailer, Top 300 Guide: Profiles and Statis-*

tics of America's 300 Largest Retail Web Sites Ranked by Annual Sales, 2004 edition; Amazon.com annual reports, 1995–2003.

21. U.S. Central Intelligence Agency, *The World Factbook 2005,* Jan. 1, 2005; "Wal-Mart: How Big Can It Grow?" *Economist,* Apr. 15, 2004; Anthony Effinger, "Wal-Mart Spares No Effort to Defeat Unionization Bid," *Los Angeles Business Journal,* Feb. 9, 2004; "In the Shadow of a Giant," *Investors Chronicle,* Oct. 3, 2003; Andrew Browne, "As Congress Blusters about Trade with China, U.S. Companies Play Coy over Profits," *Wall Street Journal,* Feb. 13, 2006.

22. Steve Lohr, "Discount Nation: Is Wal-Mart Good for America?" *New York Times,* Dec. 7, 2003; Kris Hudson, "Wal-Mart Upsets Apple Cart in Dallas–Fort Worth Market," *Wall Street Journal,* Feb. 14, 2006; *Wal-Mart Apparel: Beyond Basics* (Columbus, Ohio: Retail Forward, Sept. 2003); Mike Troy, "A Force Even Category Killers Can't Catch," *DSN Retailing Today,* June 9, 2003; Michael Barbaro, "Wal-Mart Triggers Tumult in Toyland: Independent Stores Can't Match Chain's Buying Power," *Washington Post,* May 31, 2004, E1; Dan Baum, "God and Satan in Bentonville," *Playboy,* Nov. 1, 2003, 64; Kurt Indvik, "Three Channels, Three Results," *Video Store,* Apr. 25, 2004, 20; "The Top 100 Consumer Electronics Retailers," *Twice,* May 3, 2004.

23. *Wal-Mart Food: Big, and Getting Bigger* (Columbus, Ohio: Retail Forward, Sept. 2003); Charles Fishman, *The Wal-Mart Effect* (New York: Penguin, 2006), 160; Barbaro, "Wal-Mart Triggers Tumult in Toyland"; "The Behemoth from Bentonville," *Economist,* Feb. 23, 2006.

24. Mike Troy, "Where Will Wal-Mart Expand To Next?" *DSN Retailing Today,* June 9, 2003; Amy Feldman, "How Big Can It Get?" *Money,* Dec. 1999, 158; "Wal-Mart: How Big Can It Grow?" *Economist*; Mike Troy, "Wal-Mart Is Still Bullish on Supercenter Growth," *Drug Store News,* Oct. 20, 2003.

25. Some retailers report even smaller ratios. Bed Bath & Beyond derived only 28 percent of its revenue growth in 2003 from what investors call "same-store" sales. Bed Bath & Beyond, 2003 annual report; Lowe's, 2003 annual report; Wal-Mart, 2004 annual report; Tim Craig, "When the Talk Is Downtown, Expect More from Target," *DSN Retailing Today,* June 7, 2004, 6.

26. Craig, "When the Talk Is Downtown"; Meyers quoted in Debbie Howell, "Retail Experiments in Cities Starting to Pay Off," *DSN Retailing Today,* Aug. 2, 2004, 17; James Goodno, "Rethinking Retail: Big Box Stores Are Getting a Mixed Reception in Large Cities," *Planning,* Nov. 1, 2004, 10; Inga Saffron, "Address Alone Does Not Make Philadelphia's Ikea 'Urban,' " *Philadelphia Inquirer,* Aug. 27, 2004, E1; Brod Bagert Jr., "Hope VI and St. Thomas: Smoke, Mirrors and Urban Mercantilism" (master's thesis, London School of Economics, Sept. 2002); Theresa Howard, "Big-Box Stores Squeeze into Big Apple," *USA Today,* Oct. 18, 2004; Karen Bellantoni, "Big-Box Retailers Target Manhattan," *Real Estate Weekly,* Jan. 28, 2004; Lauren Weber, "Big-Box Retailers Increasingly Set Sights on New York City Market," *Knight Ridder Tribune Business News,* Feb. 9, 2004, 1.

27. Glass quoted in Lorrie Grant, "An Unstoppable Marketing Force: Wal-Mart Aims for Domination of the Retail Industry—Worldwide," *USA Today,* Nov. 6, 1998, B1; Menzer quoted in Andy Rowell, "Welcome to Wal-World: Wal-Mart's Inexhaustible March to Conquer the Globe," *Multinational Monitor,* Oct. 1, 2003, 13; Harry R. Weber, "Nardelli Says to Expect 'Unlimited Growth' at Home Depot, Possible International Expansion," Associated Press, Nov. 18, 2003; Costco, 2003 annual report.

28. T. Hernandez, K. Jones, and A. Maze, *US Retail Chains in Canada* (Toronto: Centre for the Study of Commercial Activity, Nov. 2003); Jones quoted in Dick Loek, "Suburban Big Boxes Hurt Downtowns," *Toronto Star,* Nov. 28, 2002; Peter Shawn Taylor, "Home Fires Burning," *Canadian Business,* Oct. 11, 2004, 76.

29. Greg Masters, "Wal-Mart's Global Challenge," *Retail Merchandiser,* May 1, 2004; Tim Weiner, "Wal-Mart Invades, and Mexico Gladly Surrenders," *New York Times,* Dec. 6, 2003, A1; Ricardo Sandoval, "A Force to Be Reckoned With: Mexican Firms Link to Fight Wal-Mart," *Dallas Morning News,* Mar. 31, 2004, D1.

30. Flora Guerrero Goff, e-mail communications, Nov. 2002 and Feb. 2003; Fred Rosen and Irene Ortiz, "Mega-Stores Destroy Historic Site," *NACLA Report on the Americas,* Jan. 1, 2004, 11; and Civic Front for the Defense of Casino de la Selva Web site.

31. Sinegal was quoted in Jim Erickson et al., "Attack of the Superstore: Local Retailers Are Threatened, Governments Are Worried, but Foreign Chains Are Taking Over Asia," *Time International,* Apr. 29, 2002, 20; Michael Zielenziger, "Costco Opens in the Land of Miniature, but Will Japan Buy Buying in Bulk?" *San Jose Mercury News,* Jan. 2, 2001; "Costco Supermarket Aims to Open 50–70 Outlets in Japan," Jiji Press Ticker Service, Nov. 15, 2001; James Brooke, "Japanese Shoppers Get Taste of Wal-Mart; Verdict Mixed on Spacious Supercenter," *International Herald Tribune,* May 12, 2004; Ian Rowley, "Wal-Mart's Waiting Game in Japan," *Business Week,* Dec. 21, 2005.

32. "2004 Global Powers of Retailing," *Stores,* Jan. 2004; Julian Oram, Molly Conisbee, and Andrew Simms, *Ghost Town Britain II: Death on the High Street* (London: New Economics Foundation, Dec. 2003); Molly Conisbee et al., *Clone Town Britain: The Loss of Local Identity on the Nation's High Streets* (London: New Economics Foundation, Aug. 2004); Simms was quoted in New Economics Foundation, "Ghost Town Britain Crisis Hidden in Christmas Glitz," press release, Dec. 15, 2003.

33. Joanna Blythman, *Shopped: The Shocking Power of British Supermarkets* (London: Fourth Estate, 2004), 226–33; Peter Gumbel, "Welcome to the New Frontier; E.U. Accession Will Boost the Economies of Central and Eastern Europe. But in the Short Term, the New Members Will Face Tougher Competition. Can They Cope?" *Time International,* Apr. 12, 2004, 38.

34. Blythman, *Shopped,* 234–35; Wal-Mart, 2004 annual report; Mark O'Neill,

"Retailers under Siege with 'Wolves' at the Door," *South China Morning Post,* Nov. 24, 2004, 12.

35. Jack Neff, "Wal-Marketing: How to Benefit in Bentonville," *Advertising Age,* Oct. 6, 2003, 1; Anne D'Innocenzio, "Wal-Mart Suppliers Flocking to Arkansas," Associated Press, Sept. 21, 2003; Fishman, *The Wal-Mart Effect.*

36. Mary Brandel, "RFID: Smart Tags, High Costs," *Computerworld,* Dec. 15, 2003; Christine Spivey Overby, *RFID At What Cost?* (Cambridge, Mass.: Forrester Research, Mar. 1, 2004).

37. Marc Greenberger and Randi Lass, "A Fundamental Change in Retail: Scan-Based Trading, No Inventory Costs for Retailers," *Chain Drug Review,* May 19, 2003, 3; Marc Greenberger, "SBT: From Theory to Practice," *Chain Drug Review,* June 30, 2003, 3.

38. Anne Zieger, "Retailer Chargebacks: Is There an Upside?" *Frontline Solutions,* Oct. 1, 2003; John Caulfield, "Large Dealers Enforce Their Policies with Fines, Debits," *National Home Center News,* Aug. 6, 2001, 1; Mary Ethridge, "Muscling the Market: Powerful Superstores Are Squeezing Creative Products and Independent Merchants out of the Retail Industry, Insiders Say," *Detroit Free Press,* Aug. 17, 2000, C1.

39. Caulfield, "Large Dealers."

40. Charles Fishman, "The Wal-Mart You Don't Know," *Fast Company,* Dec. 2003, 68; Mary Ethridge, "Rubbermaid Suffers in Battling Wal-Mart: Wooster Firm's Fall Results in Part from Retailer's Move to Drop Its Products," *Akron Beacon Journal,* July 16, 2000, A11.

41. Neff, "Wal-Marketing"; Jerry Useem, "One Nation under Wal-Mart: How Retailing's Superpower—and Our Biggest Most Admired Company— Is Changing the Rules for Corporate America," *Fortune,* Feb. 25, 2003.

42. Brae Canlen, "Shut Out: Shutter Vendor Sues for Lost Business; When Small Business Meets Big Box, Caution Is Key," *Home Channel News,* July 14, 2003, 3; "Dependent on Home Depot," *Atlanta Business Chronicle,* June 11, 2004.

43. Jack Neff, "Bentonville or Bust: As Wal-Mart's Presence in Food Grows, Will All Career Paths Lead to Arkansas?" *Food Processing,* Mar. 1, 2003, 30.

44. Dina ElBoghdady, "Knockoffs for the Toy Box?" *Washington Post,* Nov. 23, 2003, F1; Useem, "One Nation under Wal-Mart"; D'Innocenzio, "Wal-Mart Suppliers Flocking to Arkansas"; Jennifer Waters, "Wal-Mart Expands ILO Electronics Brand," MarketWatch.com, Oct. 12, 2004; Ellen Gabler, "Best Buy Rolls Out Low-Cost Line of TVs, DVD Players, PCs," *Minneapolis–St. Paul Business Journal,* Oct. 8, 2004; 5; Ethridge, "Muscling the Market."

45. Useem, "One Nation under Wal-Mart"; Neff, "Wal-Marketing."

46. Bruce Upbin, "Wal-Mart Rolls Back the Middleman," *Forbes,* Apr. 2, 2004.

47. Sandra Stringer Vance, *Wal-Mart: A History of Sam Walton's Retail Phenomenon* (New York: Twayne, 1994).

48. For another account of the state of independent retailing in Bentonville, see Andrew A. Green, "Under the Giant's Shadow: Another Side of Sam Walton's Huge Success Is Revealed in the Arkansas Town Where He First Got the Idea That Revolutionized Retailing," *Baltimore Sun,* Apr. 16, 2002, A2.

49. Ann Christopherson, interview, Aug. 11, 2004.

50. Oren Teicher, interview, June 15, 2004; "Depot Comps Up Despite Cannibalization," *Home Channel News Newsfax,* May 31, 2004, 1; and Lisa R. Schoolcraft, "Cannibalization Feeds HD growth," *Atlanta Business Chronicle,* May 9, 2003, A1.

51. Scott Lockwood, interview, Aug. 20, 2004.

52. Ibid.

53. Ibid.

54. Tom Tracy, interview, Aug. 23, 2004.

55. Don VanCleave, interview, Aug. 13, 2004; Ian Austin, "Big Stores Make Exclusive Deals to Bring In Music Buyers," *New York Times,* Dec. 29, 2003, C1.

56. Flickinger was quoted in D'Innocenzio, "Wal-Mart Suppliers Flocking to Arkansas"; Barbaro, "Wal-Mart Triggers Tumult in Toyland."

57. Bob Allen, interview, June 17, 2004.

58. Peter Rubin, interview, Nov. 2004; Gayle Shanks, interview, Aug. 12, 2004.

59. Laurie Roberts, "Shopping Center More Important than Landowners," *Arizona Republic,* June 23, 2004, B12; Ginger D. Richardson, "Gordon to Cities: Tax Lures Must End," *Arizona Republic,* May 19, 2004, A1.

TWO: FADING PROSPERITY

1. Mike Castles, interview, July 19, 2005.

2. Ibid.

3. Ibid.

4. Jaclyn Giovis, "Target Set for Sugarcreek," *Dayton Daily News,* Sept. 2, 2004; James B. Arndorfer, "Fighting the Wal-Mart Tide," *Crain's Chicago Business,* Aug. 18, 2003; "Home Depot Plans Salem Store," *Statesman Journal,* Mar. 22, 2005.

5. Bob Sowers, interview, July 25, 2005; Phil Ewing, " 'Always Low Prices' Undermining Athens," University Wire, Sept. 9, 2004.

6. Chris Boring, interview, Mar. 28, 2005.

7. Gretchen Morgenson, "Stocks, Pay and Videotapes: The Sequel," *New York Times,* Nov. 28, 2004, B3.

8. Kenneth E. Stone, "Competing with the Discount Mass Merchandisers" (Department of Economics, Iowa State University, 1995).

9. David Neumark, Junfu Zhang, and Stephen Ciccarella, "The Effects of Wal-Mart on Local Labor Markets" (working paper, Public Policy Institute of California, San Francisco, Apr. 2006).

10. U.S. Department of Labor, Bureau of Labor Statistics, "Employees on Nonfarm Payrolls by Industry Sector and Selected Industry Detail," multiple years; Sam Porter and Paul Raistrick, "The Impact of Out-of-Centre Food Superstores on Lo-

cal Retail Employment" (occasional paper, National Retail Planning Forum, London, 1998).

11. Wal-Mart's public relations site, www.walmartfacts.com; Simeon Teqcl, "Every Day Higher Sales: Wal-Mart Wunderkind Walmex Shows Them How It's Done in a Down Economy," *Latin Trade,* Aug. 2003; "Home Depot, Lowe's Squeeze Independent Contractors," *Hometown Advantage Bulletin,* July 26, 2005. The Rutland survey was undertaken by DANTH, Inc., in 1998.

12. Stone, "Competing with the Discount Mass Merchandisers"; Brenden Sager, "Too Close for Comfort? Some Say Super Wal-Marts Three Miles Apart Is Overdoing It," *Atlanta Journal Constitution,* July 6, 2005, B1.

13. Frank Deaner, interview, July 19, 2005.

14. Lisa Ludovici, interview, July 19, 2005.

15. Mike Buffington, interview, Jan. 31, 2005; Elise Burroughs, "This Year's Retail," *Presstime,* Mar. 2001; Mark Fitzgerald, "Monster in a Box: Small-Town Papers Know All the Ways Wal-Mart Supercenters Can Kill Their Best Retail Advertisers; Big-City Papers Are About to Learn," *Editor and Publisher,* May 27, 2002; Paul Ginocchio et al., "Wal-Mart Takes a Bite out of Local," Deutsche Bank Securities, New York, Sept. 20, 2004.

16. Ron Ence, interview, July 25, 2005; Doug Krukowski, interview, July 18, 2005.

17. Matt Cunningham, interview, July 15, 2005.

18. Dan Houston, interview, Feb. 2003; *Economic Impact Analysis: A Case Study of Local Merchants vs. Chain Retailers* (Austin, Tex., and Chicago: Civic Economics, December 2002).

19. Houston interview; *Economic Impact Analysis: A Case Study of Local Merchants vs. Chain Retailers.*

20. *Economic Impact Analysis: A Case Study of Local Merchants vs. Chain Retailers.*

21. *The Andersonville Study of Retail Economics* (Austin, Tex., and Chicago: Civic Economics, October 2004).

22. Ibid.

23. Institute for Local Self-Reliance and Friends of Midcoast Maine, *The Economic Impact of Locally Owned Businesses vs. Chains: A Case Study in Midcoast Maine,* September 2003, www.newrules.org/retail/midcoaststudy.pdf.

24. Cunningham interview.

25. Larisa Brass, "Dairy Farmers Feeling Squeeze; Big Conglomerates Make It Hard for Small Milk Producers to Compete," *Knoxville News-Sentinel,* Aug. 1, 2004, C1; Mary Hendrickson et al., "Consolidation in Food Retailing and Dairy: Implications for Farmers and Consumers in a Global Food System" *British Food Journal* 103, no. 10 (Nov. 2001): 715–28; Mary Hendrickson, interview, July 12, 2005.

26. Russ Kramer, interview, July 14, 2005; Hendrickson et al., "Consolidation in Food Retailing and Dairy."

27. Kramer interview; Wal-Mart, 2005 annual report, 53.

28. Friends of the Earth, "Media Briefing: Home Grown Apples in Short Supply in Big Supermarkets," Nov. 18, 2003, www.foe.co.uk; Celia W. Dugger, "Supermarket Giants Crush Central American Farmers," *New York Times,* Dec. 28, 2004; Sarah Cox, "Outside the Big Box," *Vancouver Georgia Straight,* June 30, 2005.

29. Paul Buxman, interview, July 18, 2005.

30. Michael Catalano, interview, July 29, 2005; Sanford Nax, "Small Stores Struggle Facing Stiff Competition from Larger Chains," *Fresno Bee,* Aug. 12, 2001, C1.

31. Buxman interview.

32. Karin Rives, "Black & Decker to Close Fayetteville, N.C., Factory by December 2006," *News & Observer,* Apr. 14, 2005; "Black & Decker Closure Leaves Easton with Holes to Fill," Associated Press, Nov. 20, 2002; Terry C. Evans, "Pricing Pressures Force Black & Decker to Restructure," *Home Channel News,* Mar. 4, 2002; Martha McNeil Hamilton, "Black & Decker to Shut Plants," *Washington Post,* Jan. 30, 2002.

33. L. A. Lorek, "End of a U.S. Manufacturing Era," *San Antonio Express-News,* Dec. 14, 2003, 1L; Mary Anne Ostrom, "Levi's Struggles to Find Its Fit in a World Market," *Contra Costa Times,* Sept. 7, 2004; Mike Sangiacomo, "Etch A Sketch Heads East: Toy's Made-in-Ohio Era Draws to a Close," *Cleveland Plain Dealer,* Dec. 23, 2000, B1; David Moberg, "Maytag Moves to Mexico," *In These Times,* Jan. 17, 2005, 22; Jeffrey Sparshott, "U.S. Textile Industry Unraveling," *World and I,* Feb. 1, 2005.

34. "Best Buy Fights Mass Merchant Price Pressure," *HFN,* July 4, 2005; "Home Depot Looks Abroad for Bargains," *Atlanta Business Chronicle,* Apr. 23, 2004; "Wal-Mart to Convene Board Meeting in China," Xinhua News Agency, Mar. 5, 2004.

35. Fred Tedesco, interview, Aug. 31, 2003.

36. Lori G. Keitzer, *Job Loss from Imports: Measuring the Costs* (Washington, D.C.: Institute for International Economics, 2001), 4.

37. Senator Byron Dorgan, "Jobs in America," speech delivered on the Senate floor on Nov. 4, 2003; Greg Barrett, "Forces of Global Economy Usher In Uneasy Change for Low-Skilled Workers," Gannett News Service, Dec. 3, 2002.

38. "American Bargain Shopping Holds Down Wages of Foreign Workers," NBC News Transcripts, *Dateline NBC,* June 17, 2005; "How Can Wal-Mart Sell a Denim Shirt for $11.67?" New York: National Labor Committee, June 20, 2005, available at nlcnet.org; Testimony of Masuma, factory worker from Bangladesh, National Labor Committee, available at www.nlcnet.org, www.nlcnet.org/campaigns/bangtour/maksuda.shtml.

39. *Yu Jin Nicaragua S.A.* (New York: National Labor Committee, 2003); Doris Hajewski, "The Unsettling Price of Low-Cost Clothes," *Milwaukee Journal Sentinel,* Dec. 31, 2000, A1; John Raymond, "No Fun or Games: Chinese Sweatshops Churn Out Toys for the United States," *In These Times,* Apr. 15, 2002, 4; Peter S. Goodman and Philip P. Pan, "Chinese Workers Pay for Wal-Mart's Low Prices," *Washington Post,* Feb. 8, 2004, A1.

40. Sabrina Eaton, "It's China's Gain and Cleveland's Pain: Low Wages Lure Mr. Coffee to Mexico, Far East," *Cleveland Plain Dealer,* Nov. 15, 2004, A1; Ginger Thomson, "El Salvador: Fraying the Textile Industry," *New York Times,* Mar. 25, 2005; "Wal-Mart, Gap Look to India as China's Yuan May Rise," *Bloomberg News,* July 11, 2005.

41. *Toys of Misery 2004* (New York: National Labor Committee and China Labor Watch, February 2004), www.nlcnet.org/campaigns/he-yi/he-yi.shtml; Peter S. Goodman and Philip P. Pan, "Chinese Workers Pay for Wal-Mart's Low Prices," *Washington Post,* Feb. 8, 2004, A1.

42. Charles Kernaghan, *Wal-Mart Whistleblower Speaks Out: Working for Wal-Mart as a Monitor* (New York: National Labor Committee, June 2005), www.nlcnet.org/news/james_lynn.shtml; Stephen Greenhouse, "Fired Officer Is Suing Wal-Mart," *New York Times,* July 1, 2005.

43. Interviews with Jon Lehman, conducted by the PBS show *Frontline,* June 4 and Oct. 7, 2004 (transcript available at www.pbs.org); "How Can Wal-Mart Sell a Denim Shirt for $11.67?"

44. "Penofin Pulls Out of Big Box Stores," *BuildingOnline.com,* May 18, 2005.

45. Jamie Kreisman, interview, Aug. 29, 2005.

46. "John Turner" is not his real name. Interview, Aug. 6, 2005.

47. Jim Hopkins, "Wal-Mart's Influence Grows," *USA Today,* Jan. 29, 2003; Annette Bernhardt, "The Wal-Mart Trap," *Dollars & Sense,* Sept./Oct. 2000.

48. Richard Drogin, *Statistical Analysis of Gender Patterns in Wal-Mart Workforce* (Berkeley, Calif.: Drogin, Kakigi & Associates, Feb. 2003); "Reviewing and Revising Wal-Mart's Benefits Strategy," memorandum to the Wal-Mart board of directors from Susan Chambers, undated document given to the *New York Times* in October 2005; Chris Serres, "Teflon Target," *Minneapolis Star Tribune,* May 22, 2005; Bernie Hesse, organizing director, United Food and Commercial Workers Local 789, interview, July 14, 2005. Retail workers share information with one another on wage rates at a number of online forums, including www.retailworker.com; www.targetunion.com; and www.bordersunion.com.

49. Economic Policy Institute, "Basic Family Budget Calculator," available at www.epi.org; Ann Zimmerman and Joe Flint, "TV Shows Discover New Setting: Wal-Mart," *Wall Street Journal,* Nov. 22, 2004, B1.

50. Lisa Girard, "Big-Box Lawsuits Keep Piling Up: Legal Woes Haunt Warehouse Dealers," *Home Channel News,* May 20, 2002; "Home Depot Accused of Bias Again," *Social Issues Reporter,* Oct. 2001; Amy Tsao, "Ganging Up on Mega-Retailers: Giant Class Actions Hit Wal-Mart First and Now Costco," *Business Week Online,* Aug. 19, 2004; Norm Alster, "When Gray Heads Roll, Is Age Bias at Work?" *New York Times,* Jan. 30, 2005; Denise Mott's deposition and others are available at www.walmartclass.com.

51. Serres, "Teflon Target"; Hesse interview; Greg Schneider and Dina El Boghdady, "Stores Follow Wal-Mart's Lead in Labor: Competitors Struggle to Match

Savings from Non-Union Workforce," *Washington Post,* Nov. 6, 2003, A1; Bernard Wysocki Jr. and Ann Zimmerman, "Wal-Mart Cost-Cutting Finds Big Target in Health Benefits," *Wall Street Journal,* Sept. 30, 2003; AFL-CIO, "Wal-Mart: An Example of Why Workers Remain Uninsured and Underinsured," Oct. 2003.

52. Bob Ortega, *In Sam We Trust: The Untold Story of Sam Walton and Wal-Mart, the World's Most Powerful Retailer* (New York: Three Rivers Press, 2000), 142–43; Ann Zimmerman, "Costco's Dilemma: Be Kind to Its Workers, or Wall Street?" *Wall Street Journal,* Mar. 26, 2004, B1; Christine Frey, "Costco's Love of Labor," *Seattle Post-Intelligencer,* Mar. 29, 2004, C1; Steven Greenhouse, "How Costco Became the Anti-Wal-Mart," *New York Times,* July 17, 2005; Marjorie Kelly, *The Divine Right of Capital* (San Francisco: Berrett-Koehler, 2001).

53. Hesse interview; Ruth Milkman, "Supermarket Workers' Union Fails in California," TomPaine.com, Mar. 8, 2004.

54. "Suit Claims Home Depot Cheated Workers," *Bloomberg News,* July 22, 2005; Steven Greenhouse, "Altering of Worker Time Cards Spurs Growing Number of Suits," *New York Times,* Apr. 4, 2004; "Off the Clock: Unpaid Overtime Practices Bite Back," *Chain Store Age,* Feb. 2003; Amy Joyce, "California Jury Backs Wal-Mart Workers," *Washington Post,* Dec. 23, 2005, D1; H. J. Cummins, "The Great American Pushback: Wage-and-Hour Lawsuits Have Become the Most Common Form of Workplace Cases in Federal Courts," *Minneapolis Star Tribune,* Mar. 22, 2004, D1; "Former Workers Sue Wal-Mart, Seek Class-Action Status in Minnesota," *Knight Ridder Tribune Business News,* Sept. 11, 2003; Alison Boggs, "Off the Clock; Lawsuits Accuse Wal-Mart of Shorting Workers' Wages," *Spokesman Review,* Jan. 26, 2003, D1; Shirleen Holt, "Wal-Mart Workers' Suit Wins Class-Action Status," *Seattle Times,* Oct. 9, 2004, E1.

55. Cathy Ruckelshaus, interview, Aug. 9, 2005; Ross Eisenbrey, Economic Policy Institute, interview, Aug. 9, 2005; Steven Greenhouse, "In-House Audit Says Wal-Mart Violated Labor Laws," *New York Times,* Jan. 13, 2004.

56. "Too Valuable to Be Kept: Employees Find That Success Leads to Higher Pay—and Vulnerability When Companies Look to Cut Costs," *Wall Street Journal,* June 23, 2003, 1D; Christie Toth, "The NOC on Wal-Mart: Maine's Second-Largest Employer Is under Review for Contesting an Unreasonable Number of Workers' Comp Claims," *Portland Phoenix,* June 3, 2005; Annette Bernhardt, Anmol Chaddha, and Siobhán McGrath, *What Do We Know about Wal-Mart?* (New York: Brennan Center for Justice, Aug. 2005).

57. Tenisha Mercer, "Home Depot Union Vote Set," *Detroit News,* July 27, 2004; Simon Head, "Inside the Leviathan," *New York Review of Books,* Dec. 16, 2004; Michael Forman, UFCW Canada spokesman, interview, Dec. 4, 2004; Donald Mckenzie, "Company Shutters Quebec Store Rather Than Allow Union," *Canadian Press,* Feb. 9, 2005.

58. Nadia Gergis, "Minimum Wage Amendment Divides Region's Businesses," *Stuart (Fla.) News,* Oct. 28, 2004, D1; Joni James, "Wage Law Opponents Spend

$1-Million," *St. Petersburg Times,* Oct. 19, 2004, D1; David Yudkin, co-owner of Hot Lips Pizza, interview, July 19, 2005; Karen Kraut, Scott Klinger, and Chuck Collins, *Choosing the High Road: Businesses That Pay a Living Wage and Prosper* (Washington, D.C.: United for a Fair Economy, 2000).

59. Massachusetts Executive Office of Health and Human Services, "Employers Who Have 50 or More Employees Using Public Health Assistance," Feb. 1, 2006; Howard Fischer, "Wal-Mart 1st in State Aid Enrollees," *Arizona Daily Star,* July 30, 2005; Brian Baskin, "Top 9 Employers in State Have 9,698 Getting Public Aid; 3,971 of Them Work at Wal-Mart," *Arkansas Democrat-Gazette,* Mar. 17, 2005.

60. "Is the proposed Ikea in New Rochelle Worth It?" *Journal News,* Oct. 31, 2000 (citing an analysis of the effect of a big-box store on nearby home values done by Elliot Sclar, an urban planning professor at Columbia University); Thomas Muller and Elizabeth Humstone, *What Happened When Wal-Mart Came to Town? A Report on Three Iowa Communities with a Statistical Analysis of Seven Iowa Counties* (Washington, D.C.: National Trust For Historic Preservation, 1996).

61. Steven Falk, "Goodbye, Fees; Hello, Costco," *Los Angeles Times,* Jan. 18, 2003; Public Policy Institute of California, "City Competition for Sales Taxes: Symptom of a Larger Problem?" research brief, July 1999; *Supercenters and the Transformation of the Bay Area Grocery Industry: Issues, Trends, and Impacts* (San Francisco: Bay Area Economic Forum, 2004), 74–81; Paul G. Lewis, "Retail Politics: Local Sales Taxes and the Fiscalization of Land Use," *Economic Development Quarterly* 15, no. 1 (2001): 21–35.

62. Maine State Planning Office, "The Cost of Sprawl," May 1997; Mark Muro and Robert Puentes, *Investing in a Better Future: A Review of the Fiscal and Competitive Advantages of Smarter Growth Development Patterns* (Washington, D.C.: Brookings Institution Center on Urban and Metropolitan Policy, Mar. 2004); *The Fiscal Cost of Sprawl: How Sprawl Contributes to Local Governments' Budget Woes* (Denver: Environment Colorado Research and Policy Center, Dec. 2003); Robert W. Burchell et al., *The Cost of Sprawl—2000* (Washington, D.C.: Transportation Research Board, 2002).

63. TischlerBise was then called Tischler & Associates. Tischler & Associates, "Fiscal Impact Analysis of Residential and Nonresidential Land Use Prototypes," prepared for the Town of Barnstable, July 1, 2002.

64. Chellman study quoted in Andres Duany, Elizabeth Plater-Zyberk, and Jeff Speck, *Suburban Nation: The Rise of Sprawl and the Decline of the American Dream* (New York: North Point Press, 2001), 22.

65. Josh Hafenbrack, "State Road 7 Business Boom Brings Problems for Police," *Fort Lauderdale Sun-Sentinel,* Feb. 21, 2005; Alexandra Sage, "Crime Linked to Wal-Mart Supercenter Overwhelms Small-Town Cops," Associated Press, May 7, 2004; Ryan Robinson, "Would Target Drive Up Crime, Taxes in E. Lampeter?" *Lancaster New Era,* Mar. 25, 2003; Earnest Winston, "Town No Longer Sold on Retail Development," *Charlotte Observer,* May 26, 2003.

66. Tischler & Associates, "Fiscal Impact Analysis of Residential and Nonresidential Land Use Prototypes"; Christopher Cullinan, interview, Jan. 2003.

67. Paul Tischler, president of TischlerBise, interview, Aug. 22, 2005; Randall Gross, principle at Development Economics, interview, Aug. 18, 2005; City of Dublin, Ohio, *1997 Community Plan,* 193–95; City of Delaware, Ohio, *Comprehensive Plan: Growth Management Element,* Feb. 9, 2004, 2.12–2.14; *Northeast Ohio Regional Retail Analysis,* prepared by the Cuyahoga County Planning Commission for the Northeast Ohio Areawide Coordinating Agency, Aug. 2000, 152–53, 172.

68. Economic Policy Institute, "Share of Aggregate Family Income Received by Quintile and Top 5% of Families, 1947–2003"; Economic Policy Institute, "Annual Work Hours for Middle-Income Husbands and Wives with Children, Age 25–54, 1979–2002"; Peter G. Gosselin, "If America Is Richer, Why Are Its Families So Much Less Secure?" *Los Angeles Times,* Oct. 10, 2004; Griff Witte, "As Income Gap Widens, Uncertainty Spreads," *Washington Post,* Sept. 20, 2004, A1.

69. Economic Policy Institute, "Share of Aggregate Family Income"; Nicholas Stein, "Exploding Myths about the Poor," *Fortune,* Sept. 16, 2003; Economic Policy Institute, "Jobs Shift from Higher-Paying to Lower-Paying Industries," *Economic Snapshots,* Jan. 21, 2004; "Faltering Meritocracy in America," *Economist,* Jan. 1, 2005.

70. Stephan Goetz and Hema Swaminathan, "Wal-Mart and County-Wide Poverty" (Department of Agricultural Economics and Rural Sociology, staff paper no. 371, Penn State University, Oct. 2004).

71. Mike Ivey, "Arrogant Wal-Mart Just Bides Its Time," *Madison (Wis.) Capital Times,* Mar. 26, 2002, C8; Bill Schanen, interview, Aug. 31, 2005.

72. Hector Gutierrez, "Lafayette OKs Efforts to Entice Wal-Mart," *Rocky Mountain News,* Jan. 1, 2005.

73. Morris Newman, "Lancaster Buys a Costco Store," *California Planning & Development Report,* Mar. 2002.

74. Fitzgerald, "Monster in a Box"; Joe Mullich, "When Wal-Mart Is Gone," *My Business,* Dec./Jan. 2005.

75. Ibid.; Richard Lipsky, interview, Feb. 14, 2005.

76. Karl F. Seidman, "Smart Growth and Economic Development: Evidence and Lessons for the Future of Massachusetts," report to the Boston Society of Architects' Civic Initiative for Smart Growth, 2004, 17–19; David Salvesen and Henry Renski, "The Importance of Quality of Life in the Location Decisions of New Economy Firms" (University of North Carolina Center for Urban and Regional Studies, January 2003); Collaborative Economics, "Linking the New Economy to the Livable Community" (white paper sponsored by the James Irvine Foundation, 1998); John L. Crompton and Lisa L. Love, "The Role of Quality of Life in Business (Re)location Decisions," *Journal of Business Research* (Mar. 1999); Local Government Commission, "The Economic Benefits of Walkable Communities" (undated report); *Growth in the Heartland: Challenges and Opportunities* (Washington, D.C.: Brookings Institution, Dec. 6, 2002), 50–51; David Bollier, *How Smart Growth Can Stop*

Sprawl (Washington, D.C.: Essential Books, 1998); John Crompton, *Parks and Economic Development* (Chicago: APA Planning Advisory Service, 2001); Angus King, speech given at the Smart Growth Summit in Augusta, Maine, Dec. 10, 2004.

THREE: COMMUNITY LIFE

1. The study was originally published in 1946 by the U.S. Senate's Special Committee to Study the Problems of American Small Business, and reprinted in Walter Goldschmidt, *As You Sow: Three Studies in the Social Consequences of Agribusiness* (Montclair, N.J.: Allanheld, Osmun, 1978).

2. At the time, Mills and Ulmer did not reveal the actual cities in their study. Subsequent research determined that the matched pairs were Grand Rapids and Flint, Michigan; Kalamazoo and Dearborn, Michigan; and Rome, New York, and Nashua, New Hampshire. C. Wright Mills and Melville J. Ulmer, "Small Business and Civic Welfare," originally published in 1946 by the U.S. Senate's Special Committee to Study the Problems of American Small Business, and reprinted in Michael Aiken and Paul F. Mott, eds., *The Structure of Community Power* (New York: Random House, 1970).

3. Thomas A. Lyson, "Big Business and Community Welfare: Revisiting a Classic Sociological Study" (unpublished paper, Ithaca, N.Y.: Cornell University, n.d); Thomas Lyson, interview, Sept. 14, 2005.

4. Goldschmidt recounts these events in *As You Sow*.

5. Lyson, "Big Business and Community Welfare." In another study, Lyson looked at more than four hundred agricultural counties and likewise found that those with many small farms had a larger independent middle class and less crime, poverty, unemployment, and low-birth-weight babies. T. A. Lyson, R. J. Torres, and R. Welsh, "Scale of Agricultural Production, Civic Engagement, and Community Welfare," *Social Forces* 80, no. 1 (2001): 311–27.

6. Indeed, rootedness and local business vitality are self-reinforcing: long-term residents are more likely to support local merchants than are recent arrivals. Michael D. Irwin et al., "A Multilevel Model of the Effects of Civic and Economic Structure on Individual Nonmigration," *Population* 59, no. 5 (2004): 567–92.

7. Tolbert measured the level of local versus chain retail in each state using both the percentage of the state's retail workforce employed by locally owned stores and the percentage of retail wages paid to employees of locally owned businesses. Charles M. Tolbert, "Minding Our Own Business: Local Retail Establishments and the Future of Southern Civic Community," *Social Forces* 83, no. 4 (June 2005): 1309–28; Robert D. Putnam, *Bowling Alone: The Collapse and Revival of American Community* (New York: Simon & Schuster, 2000).

8. Charles Tolbert, interview, Sept. 26, 2005.

9. Lyson interview.

10. Jane Jacobs, *The Death and Life of Great American Cities* (New York: Random House, 1961), 61.

11. Ibid., 56.

12. Tolbert interview.

13. Ibid.

14. Neal Coonerty, interview, Sept 22, 2005, and Oct. 7, 2005; Christina Waters, "The Key to the City," *Metro Santa Cruz*, Nov. 7–13, 1996; Robin Musitelli, "Community Gets Behind the Books," *Santa Cruz Sentinel*, Oct. 18, 1994, 1.

15. Burt Saltzman, interview, Jan. 2005.

16. Callahan made his comments on his blog, Callahan's Cleveland Diary, on Feb. 28, 2005, http://cleveland_diary.blogspot.com; Saltzman interview.

17. Mary Allen Lindemann, interview, Sept. 15, 2005.

18. Ibid.

19. Judy Wicks, interview, Sept. 21, 2005.

20. "Feds Subpoena Home Depot Records in Hazardous Waste Probe," Associated Press, July 29, 2005; Lisa Eckelbecker, "Wal-Mart Fined for Oil Violations," *(Mass.) Telegram & Gazette*, Oct. 21, 2005, E1; "Big Box Stores in Western Massachusetts Pay Penalties for Air Quality and Hazardous Waste Violations," States News Service, Aug. 11, 2005; "State Sues Wal-Mart for Environmental Violations," Connecticut Attorney General's Office press release, May 2, 2000. Noise violations have been detailed in numerous press accounts. See, for example, Freddie Yap, "Atascadero, Calif., Neighbors Concerned about Home Depot Noise Ruling," *Tribune*, July 19, 2002; Stephanie Erickson, "Home Depot Truck Noise Rattles Family," *Orlando Sentinel*, Mar. 21, 2001, 1; Thomas Frank, "A Big, Noisy Neighbor: Home Depot Din Riles Residents," *Newsday*, Sept. 23, 1998, A7; Scott M. Larson, "Wal-Mart Noise Disturbs Residents," *Hattiesburg American*, June 18, 2002, A1; Jack Komperda, "How Loud Is Lowe's?" *Chicago Daily Herald*, May 17, 2005, 4; Susan Voyles, "Reno City Council Seeks Closure of Home Depot Location," *Reno Gazette-Journal*, Nov. 18, 2005.

21. David Barboza, "Keeping Walgreens on Main St.," *New York Times*, Dec. 6, 1998, 2.

22. Steve Kapitan, interview, Sept. 21, 2005; description of the post office provided by the Taming the Wild Prairie project at http://dig.lib.niu.edu/dekalb; National Trust for Historic Preservation memo, "Demolished Historic Building: Lancaster, Pennsylvania," undated; Carl Rotenberg, "Audubon Inn Ordinance Source of Ire," *Norristown (Pa.) Times Herald*, Nov. 7, 2003.

23. National Trust for Historic Preservation memo, "Demolished Historic Building: Leroy Theater, Pawtucket, Rhode Island," undated; Hartford Preservation Alliance newsletter, autumn 2002; Tom Condon, "Reassess Plans for Pharmacy," *Hartford Courant*, Dec. 20, 2001, B1; Greg Sekula, interview, Sept. 21, 2005.

24. Erica Taylor, interview, Oct. 4, 2005; Margaret Foster, "Bank Survives Dillinger and Walgreens," *Preservation Magazine*, June 24, 2003.

25. Margaret Foster, "Historic House Demolished for Target Parking Lot,"

Preservation Magazine, Nov. 12, 2002; Kay Demlow, Hillsboro Historical Society, interview, Sept. 21, 2005.

26. Jack Gold, interview, Oct. 4, 2005; John McGettrick, cochair of the Red Hook Civic Association, interview, Sept. 18, 2005; Margaret Foster, "To Clear Site for Home Depot, Owner Illegally Demolishes Nashville House," *Preservation Magazine,* Oct. 5, 2005.

27. Store counts from Starbucks.com; Brad Wong, "Great Wall Breached: Starbucks Sets Up Shop," *Seattle Post-Intelligencer,* Sept. 22, 2005.

28. Ray Oldenburg, *The Great Good Place: Cafes, Coffee Shops, Bookstores, Bars, Hair Salons, and Other Hangouts at the Heart of Community,* 2nd ed. (New York: Marlowe & Company, 1999).

29. Ibid., 21–85; 70.

30. Hollie Lund, "Testing the Claims of New Urbanism: Local Access, Pedestrian Travel, and Neighboring Behaviors," *Journal of the American Planning Association,* Sept. 22, 2003), 414–29.

31. Putnam, *Bowling Alone,* 213–14.

32. Karl Knudson, interview, Mar. 4, 2005.

33. Virginie-Alvine Perrette, interview, Sept. 18, 2005; David Bolduc, interview, Oct. 5, 2005.

34. A Wal-Mart representative made the comment about being "the gathering place of the community" in Brian Grow, Steve Hamm, and Louise Lee, "Some Companies Are Taking a More Strategic Tack on Social Responsibility. Should They?" *Business Week,* Aug. 15, 2005, 76.

35. Michelle J. Lee, "New Look Planned for Proposed Store," *Poughkeepsie Journal,* Jan. 31, 2005, B3.

36. Lori Buttars, "Centerville Wal-Mart Plan: 'Nicest One in Utah?'" *Salt Lake Tribune,* Oct. 7, 2005, B5; Dan Burden, interview, Sept. 12, 2005.

37. "Donations to Nonprofits Mark Wal-Mart Opening," *Dallas Morning News,* Aug. 24, 2000, C1; Marianne Wilson, "More than Just Causes," *Chain Store Age,* Aug. 1, 2000, 37.

38. Katherine Echols, "Nonprofits Recipients of Donations from Target," *Houston Chronicle,* Oct. 24, 2002, 7; Randall Gross, interview, Aug. 18, 2005.

39. Cone Inc., www.coneinc.com; Peter J. Gallanis, "Community Support Is a Powerful Tool," *DSN Retailing Today,* July 24, 2000.

40. Steve Coffin, "This Isn't Charity," *National Post,* Dec. 22, 2004, A21; Kevin Lane Keller, "Branding Shortcuts: Choosing the Right Brand Elements and Leveraging Secondary Associations Will Help Marketers Build Brand Equity," *Marketing Management,* Sept. 2005, 18.

41. Paul G. Schervish and John J. Havens, "Wealth and the Commonwealth: New Findings on Wherewithal and Philanthropy," *Nonprofit and Voluntary Sector Quarterly,* Mar. 2001; Institute for Local Self-Reliance and Friends of Midcoast

Maine, *The Economic Impact of Locally Owned Businesses vs. Chains: A Case Study in Midcoast Maine,* Sept. 2003, www.newrules.org/retail/midcoaststudy.pdf.

42. Patricia Frishkoff, *Business Contributions to Community Service* (Washington, D.C.: Small Business Administration, 1991); Patricia Frishkoff, interview, Dec. 2001.

43. Alexis de Tocqueville, *Democracy in America,* translated by G. Lawrence, edited by J. P. Mayer (London: Fontana Press, 1994), 62–63.

FOUR: BLIGHTED LANDSCAPE

1. Janet H. Cho, "A Legacy in the Making," *Cleveland Plain Dealer,* Oct. 25, 2004.

2. Wendy Sattin, director of Restore Cleveland, a program of the Cleveland Neighborhood Development Coalition, interview, Feb. 15, 2005; Steve Presser, owner of Big Fun, interview, Mar. 8, 2005.

3. Presser interview; Tommy Fello, interview, Mar. 9, 2005.

4. Jim Kastelic, former deputy director of the Cuyahoga County Planning Commission, interview, Feb. 9, 2005; Lou Tisler, executive director, First Suburbs Consortium Development Council, interview, Mar. 2, 2005. Christopher Montgomery, "As New Shopping Centers Rise in Suburbs, Area's Older Communities Are Left Behind," *Cleveland Plain Dealer,* Oct. 24, 2004.

5. Kastelic interview; *Northeast Ohio Regional Retail Analysis,* prepared by the Cuyahoga County Planning Commission for the Northeast Ohio Areawide Coordinating Agency, Aug. 2000.

6. C. B. Richard Ellis, "Greater Cleveland 2004 Retail Market Report," Jan. 2005; *Northeast Ohio Regional Retail Analysis.*

7. Kastelic interview; Julie Langan, interview, Sept. 22, 2004.

8. David Beach, interview, Feb. 8, 2005.

9. Presser interview.

10. *Northeast Ohio Regional Retail Analysis;* Cuyahoga County Regional Planning Commission, "Land Use Impact Analysis for the ODOT District 12 I-71 Major Investment Study," April 1998; Case Western Reserve University Center for the Environment, "The Regional Environmental Priorities Project," published in Ohio Environmental Protection Agency, *Ohio State of the Environmental Report,* Dec. 1995.

11. *Northeast Ohio Regional Retail Analysis.*

12. Jim White, interview, Mar. 1, 2005.

13. Kennedy Smith, principal, The Clue Group, interview, Mar. 15, 2005.

14. Smith interview; Ed McMahon, interview, Mar. 2, 2005.

15. Meredith Goad, "On Marsh, a Great Divide: A Bangor Wetland Is the Subject of a Dispute between Builders and Birdwatchers," *Portland Press Herald,* Feb. 23, 2003; Paul Bartels, "Board OKs Zoning for Mall; Target Store Planned on Acres of Wetlands," *Times-Picayune,* Aug. 8, 2001; Sarah Coppola, "City Settles Lowe's Lawsuit," *Austin American-Statesman,* Mar. 4, 2005.

16. William J. Reilly, *The Law of Retail Gravitation* (New York: Knickerbocker, 1931); Michael D. Beyard and W. Paul O'Mara, *Shopping Center Development Handbook*, 3rd ed. (Washington, D.C.: Urban Land Institute, 1999); Seth Harry, Seth Harry & Associates, interview, Mar. 29, 2005.

17. Harry interview; Congress for the New Urbanism, *Council Report VI on Retail*, published by The Town Paper and the Knight Program in Community Building, Feb. 2004; *New Urban Post VIII: A Compilation of Online Discussions about the New Urbanism*, published by the Knight Program in Community Building, Feb. 2004.

18. Harry interview; *Council Report VI on Retail; New Urban Post VIII.*

19. Harry interview; Richard Knitter, interview, Mar. 31, 2005; Robert Strauss, "Wal-Mart Zeros In on a South Jersey Township," *New York Times,* Mar. 20, 2005.

20. "About one in three of the trips Americans take each day is related to shopping": This ratio is derived by excluding return trips home, which are counted as separate trips in the data compiled by the U.S. Department of Transportation's *2001 National Household Travel Survey*, available at http://nhts.ornl.gov/2001.

21. Kiffi Summa, interview, Oct. 9, 2003.

22. Pat S. Hu and Timothy R. Reuscher, *Summary of Travel Trends: 2001 National Household Travel Survey* (Washington, D.C.: U.S. Department of Transportation, December 2004), 16.

23. Robert Cervero and Carolyn Radisch, "Pedestrian versus Travel Choices in Automobile Oriented Neighborhoods" (working paper, Institute of Urban and Regional Development, University of California at Berkeley, July 1995).

24. That residents of car-dependent suburbs like Lafayette would walk more if walking were a viable option was demonstrated by a recent study in Seattle that tracked families moving from the suburbs to more traditional neighborhoods and found that their driving patterns changed immediately. As soon as driving was no longer a necessity, they took more trips on foot. Kevin J. Krizek, "Residential Relocation and Changes in Urban Travel: Does Neighborhood-Scale Urban Form Matter?" *Journal of the American Planning Association,* June 22, 2003, 265.

25. Ruth Steiner, *Traditional Neighborhood Shopping Districts: Patterns of Use and Modes of Access* (monograph 54, Institute of Urban and Regional Development, University of California at Berkeley, 1997).

26. Hu and Reuscher, *Summary of Travel Trends: 2001,* 16; Andres Duany, Elizabeth Plater-Zyberk, and Jeff Speck, *Suburban Nation: The Rise of Sprawl and the Decline of the American Dream* (New York: North Point Press, 2001), 115.

27. Scott Bernstein et al., *Driven to Spend: Pumping Dollars out of Our Households and Communities* (Washington, D.C.: Surface Transportation Policy Project; Chicago: Center for Neighborhood Technology, June 2005); Brian Ketcham, P.E., "Making Transportation Choices Based on Real Costs," paper presented at the Transportation 2000 Conference, Snowmass, Colo., Oct. 6, 1991; Brian Ketcham, personal communication, May 22, 2006.

28. Cuyahoga County Planning Commission, *Northeast Ohio Regional Retail Analysis,* 162, 271.

29. Deborah Schoch, "Ships Are Single Largest Polluter of Air at Port of LA, Study Finds," *Los Angeles Times,* July 8, 2004; George Raine, "Ports Just Keep Getting Busier," *San Francisco Chronicle,* Mar. 6, 2005; "Is Wal-Mart Good for America?" American Radioworks, November 2004; Los Angeles Sierra Club's Harbor Vision Task Force, www.angeles.sierraclub.org.

30. U.S. Bureau of Transportation Statistics, *Freight Shipments in America,* April 2004; David L. Greene and Andreas Schafer, *Reducing Greenhouse Gas Emissions from U.S. Transportation* (Arlington, Va.: Pew Center on Global Climate Change, May 2003).

31. Brain Halweil, *Eat Here: Reclaiming Homegrown Pleasures in a Global Supermarket* (New York: Norton, 2004), 30.

32. C. L. Arnold and J. C. Gibbons, "Impervious Surface Coverage: The Emergence of a Key Environmental Indicator," *Journal of the American Planning Association* 62, no. 2 (1996): 243–59; Melanie Stein, "Sprawl and Water Pollution," *Conservation Matters,* autumn 2004.

33. Thomas Schueler, "The Importance of Imperviousness," *Watershed Protection Techniques* 1, no. 3 (1994): 100–111.

34. Ibid.; Arnold and Gibbons, "Impervious Surface Coverage"; Mark Clayton, "A Parking Lot Effect," *Christian Science Monitor,* Feb. 5, 2004.

35. EPA press releases dated Feb. 13, 2003, and May 12, 2004.

36. See, for example, www.deadmalls.com.

37. Pricewaterhouse Coopers and Lend Lease Real Estate Investments, "Emerging Trends in Real Estate," 2002 and 2003; Pricewaterhouse Coopers and Urban Land Institute, "Emerging Trends in Real Estate," 2004.

38. Congress for the New Urbanism and Pricewaterhouse Coopers, "Greyfield Regional Mall Study," January 2001; Robert Antall, interview, Feb. 8, 2005.

39. Chris Kenton, "To Save a Town, Why Did They Destroy It?" *Business Week Online,* Sept. 1, 2004.

40. "Seeking Solutions to Reduce Big Box Blight," report of the Planning Commission's Big Box Committee on Why Retail Windows Go Dark, presented to the Charlotte City Council, May 21, 2001; Chris Boring, retail consultant and president of Boulevard Strategies, interview, Mar. 28, 2005; R. H. Johnson Company, *2003 Kansas City Metropolitan Shopping Center Report;* Knitter interview; Lisa Tanner, "Good as New," *Dallas Business Journal,* Aug. 6, 2004, 4; Andy Ostmeyer, columnist with the *Joplin Globe,* interview, Nov. 23, 2004.

41. Geoff Dougherty, "Kmart Vacancies May Put It in Box," *Chicago Tribune,* Jan. 9. 2005; Eric M. Weiss, " 'Big-Box' Stores Leave More than a Void," *Washington Post,* Jan. 20, 2004, B1; Lee Shearer, "Group Hunts Down Vacant 'Big Box' Stores in Athens, Ga., Area," *Athens Banner-Herald,* June 16, 2004.

42. A list of currently available Wal-Mart stores can be found on the company's realty division's Web site at www.wal-martrealty.com.

43. Melanie Payne, "Wal-Mart Targeted by Official," *Sacramento Bee,* Mar. 6, 2004; Janet Johnston, Bardstown County Planner, interview, Apr. 1, 2005; Wal-Mart, 2004 annual report.

44. Knitter interview.

45. Boring interview.

46. Mary Hopper, former member of the Charlotte-Mecklenburg Planning Commission, interview, Mar. 25, 2005; Tom Flynn, Charlotte economic development director, interview, Mar. 28, 2005; Deborah Currier, realtor with Currier Properties, interview, Mar. 31, 2005.

47. Weiss, " 'Big-Box' Stores Leave More than a Void."

FIVE: SOMETIMES LOW PRICES

1. The survey of video store prices was conducted in November 2005 by phone and included Blockbuster outlets and nearby independent competitors in Boulder, Colo.; Chicago, Ill.; Portland, Maine; Saint Paul, Minn.; and Syracuse, N.Y.

2. Eric Anderson and Duncan Simester, "Mind Your Pricing Cues," *Harvard Business Review* 81, no. 9 (Sept. 2003): 96; Barry J. Babin, David M. Hardesty, and Tracy A. Suter, "Color and Shopping Intentions: The Intervening Effect of Price Fairness and Perceived Affect," *Journal of Business Research* 56, no. 7 (July 2003).

3. Anderson and Simester, "Mind Your Pricing Cues," 96; Robert Koci, "The Perfect Price," *Hardware Merchandising,* Feb. 2001, 52; Donald Lichtenstein, marketing professor at the University of Colorado, interview, Nov. 10, 2005; Kenneth Stone, economics professor at Iowa State University, interview, Nov. 16, 2005.

4. Bill Lee, interview, Nov. 16, 2005.

5. Anderson and Simester, "Mind Your Pricing Cues," 96.

6. Clifford S. Barber and Brian C. Tietje, "A Distribution Services Approach for Developing Effective Competitive Strategies against 'Big Box' Retailers," *Journal of Retailing and Consumer Services* 11 (2004): 95–107; Paul Menser, "Hardware Hardball," *Idaho Falls Post Register,* June 6, 2005, A1; Scott Wright, spokesman for the National Retail Hardware Association, interview, Nov. 14, 2005; Catherine Trevison, "Nuts and Bolts Keep Changing," *Oregonian,* June 10, 1999, 1; Lee interview.

7. Steven Tanner, interview, Nov. 14, 2005.

8. Kenneth Stone, interview, Nov. 16, 2005; Alex Daniels, "Wal-Mart Fights Laws on Below-Cost Gas Sales," *Arkansas Democrat-Gazette,* July 4, 2004.

9. Interviews with Jon Lehman, conducted by the PBS show *Frontline,* June 4 and Oct. 7, 2004, transcript available at www.pbs.org.

10. Race Cowgill, interview, Jan. 16, 2006; George Anderson, "Taking Shoppers Back from Wal-Mart," Retail Wire, www.retailwire.com, Jan. 10, 2006.

11. Loyalty cards are one tactic that some retailers use to discourage cherry-

picking. See Sharon L. Crenson, "Retail Research Takes Off," *Wharton Alumni Magazine* (spring 2005); Donald Lichtenstein, interview, Nov. 10, 2005.

12. Indeed, in 1994, the National Advertising Review Board, established by advertisers to police the industry, ruled that Wal-Mart should change its slogan, which at the time was, "Always the low price. Always." The NARB said that this was a colloquial way of saying, "Always the lowest price," and that Wal-Mart could not prove such a claim and therefore its slogan failed to meet truth-in-advertising standards. Wal-Mart subsequently dropped the word "the" from its slogan. See Frances Cerra Whittelsey, "Fostering Truth in Advertising," *Nation's Business,* July 1998, 66. "Where to Buy Appliances: Big Stores Aren't Necessarily the Best," *Consumer Reports,* Sept. 2005, 32.

13. Stone interview.

14. John Reny, interview, Dec. 9, 2005.

15. Rick Karp, interview, Nov. 15, 2005; data from *Appliance Magazine,* as compiled by ReclaimDemocracy.org; Juliet Schor, "Clothes Encounters," *Orion,* Oct. 2004; Heather Rogers, *Gone Tomorrow: The Hidden Life of Garbage* (New York: New Press, 2005), 2.

16. This practice has taken on a new dimension on the Web as retailers can and do charge individual customers variable prices depending on personal characteristics and shopping patterns. See Joseph Turow, Lauren Feldman, and Kimberly Meltzer, *Open to Exploitation: American Shoppers Online and Offline* (Philadelphia: Annenberg Public Policy Center of the University of Pennsylvania, June 2005); *Supermarkets: A Report on the Supply of Groceries from Multiple Stores in the United Kingdom* (London: Competition Commission: 2000), 125–26, 131–32; Portsia Smith, "Competition Drives Prices at Area Grocery Stores," *Freelance-Star,* Mar. 10, 2005; Neil Downing, "Prices Can Vary from Store to Store," *Providence Journal,* Oct. 13, 2003; Dan Scheraga, "One Price Doesn't Fit All: Variable Pricing among Stores," *Chain Store Age,* Mar. 1, 2001, 104.

17. Hometown Merchants Association of Nebraska and Kacie Clarke, "Impact of Supercenters on Nebraska Economy," April 2004.

18. Maine Department of Human Services, "Fall 2003 Drug Pricing Survey," October 2003; Consumers' Checkbook, "Prescription Drugs: Smart Shopping Yields Big Savings," 2004, www.checkbook.org; Sutherland Institute, "Comparing Apples to Apples: Prescription Pricing in Utah," news release, June 25, 2004.

19. Barnes & Noble does offer a membership card for twenty-five dollars a year that gives customers a 10 percent discount. For someone who spends four hundred dollars a year on books, that works out to a discount of just under 4 percent (after accounting for the membership fee). Many independent bookstores offer their own frequent-buyer programs. David D. Kirkpatrick, "Quietly, Booksellers Are Putting an End to the Discount Era," *New York Times,* Oct. 9, 2000, A1; Suzanne Sataline, "Books Cost Too Much," *Washingtonian,* Feb. 2003, 91; Oren Teicher, interview, Nov. 11, 2005.

20. Supreme Court of Arkansas, *Wal-Mart Stores v. American Drugs,* 1995.

21. Jerry Hausman and Ephraim Leibtag, "Consumer Benefits from Increased Competition in Shopping Outlets: Measuring the Effect of Wal-Mart" (Cambridge, Mass.: National Bureau of Economic Research, working paper 11809, Dec. 2005).

22. Hausman and Leibtag, "Consumer Benefits from Increased Competition in Shopping Outlets"; Patricia Callahan and Ann Zimmerman, "Wal-Mart Tops Grocery List with Its Supercenter Format," *Wall Street Journal,* May 27, 2003; Carol Radice, "America's Top Metros: 2005 State of the Industry," *Grocery Headquarters,* Apr. 1, 2005.

SIX: MONOPOLIZED CONSUMERS

1. Crystal Cody, "With Sizzling Sales, Wal-Mart Wants Say in Meat Production," *Arkansas Democrat-Gazette,* June 26, 2005.

2. David D. Kirkpatrick, "Report to the Authors Guild Midlist Books Study Committee," 2000.

3. Kirkpatrick, "Report to the Authors Guild Midlist Books Study Committee."

4. Randy Kennedy, "Cash Up Front," *New York Times,* June 5, 2005, 14; Kirkpatrick, "Report to the Authors Guild Midlist Books Study Committee."

5. Betsy Burton, interview, Nov. 11, 2005.

6. Oren Teicher, interview, Nov. 11, 2005; Burton interview; Kennedy, "Cash Up Front"; Kirkpatrick, "Report to the Authors Guild Midlist Books Study Committee."

7. Barbara Kingsolver, interview, Dec. 6, 2005.

8. Richard Howorth, interview, Nov. 10, 2005.

9. Karen Torres, interview, Mar. 24, 2006; Craig Popelars, interview, Nov. 28, 2005.

10. Popelars interview.

11. Paul Aiken, interview, Nov. 10, 2005; executive with a major publishing house, name withheld, interview, Nov. 22, 2005.

12. Kirkpatrick, "Report to the Authors Guild Midlist Books Study Committee"; Edward Guthmann, "Before 'The Kite Runner,' Khaled Hosseini Had Never Written a Novel," *San Francisco Chronicle,* Mar. 14, 2005, C1.

13. Chuck Robinson, interview, Nov. 28, 2005; Howorth interview.

14. Neal Coonerty, interview, Sept. 22, 2005, and Oct. 7, 2005.

15. David Kirkpatrick, interview, Nov. 28, 2005; Coonerty interview; "Chains Increasingly Determine What Books Are Published," *San Jose Mercury News,* Nov. 3, 1997, C4.

16. Popelars interview.

17. John Kunz, interview, Nov. 15, 2005.

18. Ibid.

19. Figures provided by the Almighty Institute of Music Retail and *Billboard* in Nov. 2005.

20. Kunz interview; Don VanCleave, interview, Nov. 30, 2005.

21. Mark A. Fox, "Market Power in Music Retailing: The Case of Wal-Mart," *Popular Music and Society,* Oct. 1, 2005, 501; Amy Schiller, "The Wal-Mart Thought Police," *Campus Progress,* Aug. 16, 2005; Roger Ebert, "Blockbuster Not a Friend to Film Buffs: Video Chain's Slice- and-Dice Approach Ruins Artists' Intent," *National Post,* Dec. 13, 2002.

22. Ed Christman, "Big-Box Chains Slash Music Prices," *Billboard,* Nov. 28, 2004; Kunz interview.

23. Steve Morse, "Competition Has Retailers Singing a New Tune: Exclusive CD Deals," *Boston Globe,* Nov. 7, 2005, B7; Chris Serres, "Chained Melodies: National Retailers Are Getting Exclusive Deals to Sell Music CDs," *Minneapolis Star Tribune,* Aug. 13, 2005, D1; Ed Christman, "Retail Groups Warn Labels Against Exclusives," *Billboard,* Oct. 2, 2004; Ed Christman, "Indie Retailers Find 'Superior' Not So Super," *Billboard,* Sept. 4, 2004

24. Ed Christman, interview, Dec. 3, 2005; Kunz interview.

25. Teicher interview.

26. Tod Herskovitz, interview, Nov. 8, 2005.

27. Herskovitz interview; Blockbuster CFO Larry Zine provided the figure on titles during a conference call with investors on Feb. 17, 2005, as transcribed by Events Transcripts.

28. Herskovitz interview.

29. Chris Anderson, "The Long Tail," *Wired,* Oct. 2004, www.wired.com/wired/archive/12.10/tail.html.

30. Anderson, "The Long Tail"; Blockbuster CFO Larry Zine provided the figure on titles during a conference call with investors on Feb. 17, 2005, as transcribed by Events Transcripts.

31. Sheri LaPres, interview, Nov. 29, 2005; Paul Bond, "Amazon's New Lease on Shelf Life," Reuters, July 26, 2005; Chris Anderson, e-mail communication, Nov. 15, 2005.

32. Anderson's *Wired* article reported that half of Amazon.com's book sales came from outside its top 130,000 titles, which he described as the typical inventory of a Barnes & Noble superstore. He subsequently corrected the figure on his blog, estimating that 20 to 30 percent of Amazon.com's sales come from beyond the top 100,000 titles, a more-accurate count of a superstore's inventory. Anderson e-mail communication; Kirkpatrick interview.

33. Kingsolver interview.

34. David Rochefort, interview, Nov. 11, 2005.

35. "Time to Switch Drugstores?" *Consumer Reports,* Oct. 2003, 30.

36. James Frederick, "Beset by Challenges, Pharmacy Faces Better Times," *Drug Store News,* Aug. 22, 2005, 27; Tony Adams, "Prescribing Customer Satisfaction: Independent Pharmacies Threatened More by Mail in Prescriptions than Chain Stores," *Columbus Ledger-Enquirer,* Oct. 24, 2004, Q4; Sheannon Mortland, "Small,

Local Pharmacies Seeking Rx for Survival," *Crain's Cleveland Business,* Oct. 31, 2005, 1; Mike Duff, "Mandatory Mail Order Threatens Motor City Business," *Drug Store News,* June 6, 2005, 100.

37. James Langenfeld and Robert Maness, "The Cost of PBM Self-Dealing under a Medicare Prescription Drug Benefit," Sept. 9, 2003, www.ncpanet.org/pdf/pbm-selfdealing090903.pdf; Frederick, "Beset by Challenges, Pharmacy Faces Better Times."

38. Rich Youngers, interview, Nov. 28, 2005; Henry Miller, "The Box May Be Big, but Fish Tales Not Included," *Statesman Journal,* Sept. 1, 2005.

39. Bill Murray, interview, Nov. 21, 2005.

40. Ibid.

41. Mike McGettigan, interview, Nov. 21, 2005; Jim Doyle, "Bikes Had Defective Design, Expert Says," *San Francisco Chronicle,* Dec. 10, 2005; National Bicycle Dealers Association, "Industry Overview 2005," www.nbda.com.

42. Harold Ellis, interview, July 18, 2005.

43. Jeff Franklin, interview, Nov. 18, 2005.

44. Maria Weiskott, interview, Nov. 18, 2005; Dina ElBoghdady, "Knockoffs for the Toy Box?" *Washington Post,* Nov. 23, 2003, F1.

45. Tom Murdough, interview, Nov. 22, 2005; Weiskott interview; Franklin interview.

SEVEN: UNCLE SAM'S INVISIBLE HAND

1. Kevin Ohm, interview, Jan. 3, 2006; Kevin Nyburg, interview, July 26, 2005.

2. "Vote Set on Lowe's Project in Brookings," Associated Press State & Local Wire, Aug. 24, 2005; "The Top Ten Reasons Why the City of Brookings Should Not Incentivize Retail Development," Citizens Against Retail Subsidies, fact sheet; Ohm interview; Nyburg interview.

3. Ohm interview; election figures provided by the City of Brookings.

4. Anna M. Tinsley, "Tax Breaks May Be in Line for SuperTarget and LG," *Fort Worth Star-Telegram,* Aug. 24, 2005; Amy Martinez, "Dismissal Sought for Incentives Lawsuit: Suit Challenges Money for Target," *News & Observer,* Apr. 6, 2005, D1; Pat Harper, "Home Depot Gets $2 Million Tax Incentive for Mokena Site; Opponents Call Rebate Deal Too Costly," *Chicago Tribune,* Sept. 10, 2003; Kathy Sutin, "Maplewood Approves Plan for Lowe's," *St. Louis Post-Dispatch,* Dec. 1, 2003; Philip Mattera and Anna Purinton, *Shopping for Subsidies: How Wal-Mart Uses Taxpayer Money to Finance Its Never-Ending Growth* (Washington, D.C.: Good Jobs First, May 2004).

5. Scott Ray, "Lake in the Hills Working on Sales Tax Deal to Entice Costco," *Chicago Daily Herald,* Sept. 11, 2003; J. E. Espino, "Village Store Project Gets OK," *Post-Crescent,* Dec. 23, 2004; Frank Green, "Six San Diego Redevelopment Projects Awarded Federal Tax Credits," Knight Ridder, Dec. 19, 2002.

6. The fevered pursuit of Nordstrom seems to have ebbed recently, after the city

of Spokane disclosed that it was having trouble paying back the U.S. Department of Housing and Urban Development loans it had taken to finance a store that has failed to generate as much tax revenue as expected. Good Jobs First, "Case Study of Nordstrom Inc.," www.goodjobsfirst.org/corporate_subsidy/nordstrom.cfm; Good Jobs First, "Case Study of Cabela's, Inc.," www.goodjobsfirst.org/corporate_subsidy/cabela.cfm; Jim Hightower, "Free Enterprise Socialism," *Austin Chronicle,* June 17, 2005; "Cabela's Business Park to Get 10 New Companies," *Charleston Daily Mail,* Mar. 2, 2005, A1.

7. Jerousek Madelaine, "Suit against W.D.M. Mall Thrown Out," *Des Moines Register,* Feb. 28, 2002, A1; Bill Lodge, "Garland Gets Its Mall: After Years of Planning and Negotiation, Firewheel to Open," *Dallas Morning News,* Oct. 6, 2005, B1.

8. David Clucas, "Sales Tax Incentives Helped Lafayette Hang onto Wal-Mart," *Boulder County Business Report,* Apr. 1, 2005; Elizabeth Gudrais, "Target Paid $4 million for Land at Mall Site," *Providence Journal,* Dec. 13, 2004; Greg LeRoy, *The Great American Jobs Scam: Corporate Tax Dodging and the Myth of Job Creation* (San Francisco: Berrett-Koehler, 2005).

9. Chris Michlewicz, "Parker Gives Target 6 Million Reasons to Stay," *Douglas County News-Press,* June 23, 2005; "Belleville Wal-Mart Project to Add 300 Jobs, Mayor Says," *St. Louis Post-Dispatch,* Mar. 27, 1993; Lisa P. White, "Council OKs Wal-Mart Incentives," *Belleville News-Democrat,* Jan. 12, 2006.

10. Herb Booth, "City Pins Hopes on Costco after Big-Box Exodus," *Dallas Morning News,* Dec. 12, 2005; Joseph Bryant, "Montgomery Says Mission Is to Halt Bad Spending," *Birmingham News,* Oct. 21, 2005, B1; David Koch, "Desperate Towns," *Retail Traffic,* Apr. 1, 2005, 26; John Archibald, "Wal-Mart's Move Leaves Retail Crater," *Birmingham News,* May 5, 2005, C1.

11. Not every state uses the term "TIF"; Utah's RDA districts are essentially TIF districts. Some states allow not just property taxes, but also sales taxes, to be diverted through TIF to developers, which creates "a super-subsidy for sprawling retail," according to Greg LeRoy. An excellent examination of corporate subsidies generally and TIF in particular can be found in LeRoy, *The Great American Jobs Scam.* Other sources include: Alyssa Talanker and Kate Davis, *Straying from Good Intentions: How States Are Weakening Enterprise Zone and Tax Increment Financing Programs* (Washington, D.C.: Good Jobs First, 2003); *Who Pays for the Only Game in Town?* (Chicago: Neighborhood Capital Budget Group, 2002); Daniel McGraw, "Giving away the Store to Get a Store: Tax Increment Financing Is No Bargain for Taxpayers," *Reason,* Jan. 1, 2006, 34.

12. *Wisconsin's Tax Incremental Finance Law: Lending a Hand to Blighted Areas or Turning Cornfields into Parking Lots?* (Madison: 1000 Friends of Wisconsin, Oct. 1999); Brad Stephenson, "Mt. Nebo Pointe Groundbreaking Scheduled Despite Opposition," *Pittsburgh Post-Gazette,* Oct. 29, 2003; Mike Ivey, "TIF, Other Development Abuses Cited," *Capital Times,* Aug. 13, 2003.

13. Thomas Luce, *Reclaiming the Intent: Tax Increment Financing in the Kansas*

City and St. Louis Metropolitan Areas (Washington, D.C.: Brookings Institution, April 2003); Tim Bryant, "Decision Upholds Broad Use of Tax Breaks for Developers," *St. Louis Post-Dispatch*, Jan. 27, 2005; Nancy Cambria, "Jennings OKs TIF to Help Northlands Shopping Center," *St. Louis Post-Dispatch*, Mar. 3, 2005; Elisa Crouch, "TIF Districts in St. Charles County," *St. Louis Post-Dispatch*, June 3, 2003.

14. Neighborhood Capital Budget Group, www.ncbg.org/tifs.

15. Lesley Wright, "Developer Subsidies under Fire," *Arizona Republic*, Feb. 29, 2004, A1; Mike Sunnucks, "Development Subsidies Flourishing Despite 'No Incentive' Zones," *Business Journal of Phoenix*, Nov. 4, 2005; Kimber Lanning, interview, Mar. 4, 2005.

16. Rick Cole's remarks were made as part of a debate on the issue presented in *Metro Investment Report*, Mar. 2002; Paul G. Lewis and Elisa Barbour, *California Cities and the Local Sale Tax* (San Francisco: Public Policy Institute of California, 1999).

17. Mattera and Purinton, *Shopping for Subsidies*; William Moyer, "Leaders Urge Best Buy to Employ Local Builders," *Press & Sun-Bulletin*, May 13, 2002; Heath Hixson, "Target, DeKalb Seal $110M deal," *Rockford Register Star*, Nov. 9, 2004; Paul Chesser, "On Milking a State's 'Cash Cow': Ernst & Young Advises Businesses on How to Maximize Subsidies from State Governments," *Carolina Journal*, May 20, 2004.

18. Mattera and Purinton, *Shopping for Subsidies*.

19. Peter Mills, interview, May 2004; Erin Stewart, "Recruiting of Retailers Debated at Utah Taxpayers Conference," *Deseret Morning News*, Apr. 27, 2005.

20. See the New Rules Project at www.newrules.org/retail/veto.html for more details on legislative efforts to curb welfare for big-box retailers. Harper was quoted in Laurie Roberts, "Great Bill on City Waste Voted Down, of Course," *Arizona Republic*, Mar. 10, 2004, B2.

21. Other examples include a seventy-five-year-old woodworking business in Harlem seized for Home Depot and Costco; a neighborhood in Alabaster, Alabama, seized for Wal-Mart; and forty-five homes in Arnold, Missouri, turned over to Lowe's. Citizens have succeeded in thwarting some condemnations, including plans by New Rochelle, New York, to level a neighborhood for a three-hundred-thousand-square-foot Ikea furniture store and an attempt by Pittsburgh mayor Tom Murphy to raze sixty buildings and remove 125 businesses—most locally owned—for a massive chain retail complex. Dean Starkman, "Cities Use Eminent Domain to Clear Lots for Big-Box Stores," *Wall St. Journal*, Dec. 8, 2004; Elsa Brenner, "Homes Taken, Lives Rebuilt," *New York Times*, July 31, 2005; Dana Berliner, *Public Power, Private Gain* (Washington, D.C.: Institute for Justice, April 2003); Nicole Warburton, "Blighted or Oppressed?" *Deseret Morning News*, Dec. 12, 2005.

22. Michael Mazerov at the Center on Budget and Policy Priorities has produced several excellent reports on state corporate income tax issues, including the Geoffrey Loophole, that are available at www.cbpp.org. See, for example, "Closing

Three Common Corporate Income Tax Loopholes Could Raise Additional Revenue for Many States," May 23, 2003. An excellent piece of investigative reporting on the issue is Glenn R. Simpson, "Diminishing Returns: A Tax Maneuver in Delaware Puts Squeeze on States," *Wall Street Journal*, Aug. 9, 2002, A1.

23. Simpson, "Diminishing Returns"; Barry Massey, "New Mexico Wins Far-Reaching Court Ruling in Tax Case," Associated Press, Nov. 28, 2001.

24. Michael Mazerov, interview, Dec. 19, 2005; *Corporate Tax Sheltering and the Impact on State Corporate Income Tax Revenue Collections* (Washington, D.C.: Multistate Tax Commission, July 15, 2003).

25. Mazerov interview; Michael Mazerov, "Combined Reporting: The Key to a Robust and Fair State Corporate Income Tax in Arkansas," presentation before the Arkansas General Assembly, Joint Meeting of the House and Senate Committees on Revenue and Taxation, Little Rock, Jan. 14, 2003; Simpson, "Diminishing Returns."

26. Richard D. Pomp, *Taxing Smarter and Fairer: Proposals for Increased Accountability and Transparency in the Connecticut Tax Structure* (Hartford: Connecticut Common Cause, Mar. 21, 2005); Charles Thompson, "Rendell Regrets Inaction on Taxes," *Patriot-News*, July 12, 2005.

27. After multistate companies combine their income from various subsidiaries, they then have to determine what portion of their earnings are taxable in each state in which they operate. States require companies to apportion their income based on formulas that typically consider what percentage of their sales, property, and payroll is located in each state. The states that have adopted combined reporting are Alaska, Arizona, California, Colorado, Hawaii, Idaho, Illinois, Kansas, Maine, Minnesota, Montana, Nebraska, New Hampshire, North Dakota, Oregon, Utah, and Vermont. Some states have also attempted to recover revenue from companies engaged in this scheme through the courts, but that approach is costly and has yielded mixed results, with some courts ruling in favor of the states and others siding with the companies. Mazerov interview.

28. The argument offered publicly about why combined reporting should not be adopted is that it would cause companies to flee to other states, taking jobs with them. That's certainly not true with regard to retailers, who need to be near their customers, and there is no evidence that it's true of manufacturers, either. In fact, seven of the ten states that have had the strongest manufacturing job growth since the 1980s are also states with combined reporting, according to Mazerov. Peter Wirth, "Commentary: Let's Level the Playing Field for Businesses," *Santa Fe New Mexican*, Aug. 13, 2005, A7; Dan Levine, "Going After the Small Businessman," *Connecticut Law Tribune*, Apr. 18, 2005, 10.

29. Governor Jim Douglas's State of the State address was delivered on Jan. 6, 2004, in the Vermont House of Representatives. "Vermont Closes Chain Store Tax Loophole," *Hometown Advantage Bulletin*, Aug. 9, 2004.

30. Mazerov interview.

31. Bill Petrocelli, interview, Jan. 6, 2006.

32. *National Bellas Hess, Inc., v. Department of Revenue of the State of Illinois*, 386 US 753, 1967; *Quill Corporation v. North Dakota*, 504 US 298, 1992.

33. The other states reserved the right to go after these companies for unpaid taxes. Donald Bruce and William F. Fox, "State and Local Sales Tax Revenue Losses from E-Commerce: Updated Estimates" (Center for Business and Economic Research, University of Tennessee, Sept. 2001); Michael Mazerov, e-mail communication, Jan. 10, 2006.

34. Information on the Streamlined Sales Tax Project can be found at streamlinedsalestax.org; Gary Rivlin, "A Retail Revolution Turns Ten," *New York Times*, July 10, 2005; Petrocelli interview.

35. Although much of the policy rhetoric of this period embodied this belief in the democratic virtues of small-scale enterprise, it should be noted that actual legislation and court decisions pulled in different directions. In the 1930s, for example, states both adopted antitrust laws to support small businesses and made it easier for large conglomerates to form holding companies. For a detailed and nuanced treatment, see Richard C. Schragger, "The Anti–Chain Store Movement, Localist Ideology, and the Remnants of the Progressive Constitution, 1920–1940," *Iowa Law Review* 90 (2005): 101–84. Also see Michael Sandel, *Democracy's Discontent: America in Search of a Public Philosophy* (Cambridge, Mass.: Harvard University Press, 1996), 231–49. Sherman quote from *Congressional Record* 21, 2457. Franklin D. Roosevelt, "Appendix A: Message from the President of the United States Transmitting Recommendations Relative to the Strengthening and Enforcement of Anti-Trust Laws," *American Economic Review* 32, no. 2 (June 1942): 119–28.

36. Today, the debate over the proper goals of antitrust policy has moved even further from its populist roots. A small but growing contingent of scholars argue that the focus should not be on lowering prices, but rather on increasing the aggregate wealth of society. In this view, a merger between two companies should be allowed if it will produce greater efficiencies, even if the combined entity has sufficient market power to charge higher prices. That is, antitrust policy should support increased efficiencies, even if the resulting wealth is passed not to consumers, but to investors in the form of greater profits. Albert A. Foer and Robert H. Lande, "The Evolution of United States Antitrust Law: The Past, Present, and (Possible) Future," *Nihon University Comparative Law* (1999): 149–72; Albert Foer, "The Goals of Antitrust: Thoughts on Consumer Welfare in the U.S." (working paper, American Antitrust Institute, Washington, D.C., Aug. 31, 2005).

37. Patrick Bolton, Joseph F. Brodley, and Michael H. Riordan, "Predatory Pricing: Strategic Theory and Legal Policy," *Georgetown Law Journal* 88 (2000): 2239–2330; Robert H. Lande, "Beyond Chicago: Will Activist Antitrust Arise Again?" *Antitrust Bulletin*, spring 1994; Albert A. Foer, "Small Business and Antitrust: Why the Little Guys Left the Fold and Why They Should Return," paper presented at Small Business Administration conference, Washington, D.C., Jan. 21, 2000.

38. *Matsushita Elec. Industrial Co. v. Zenith Radio*, 475 US 574, 1986; *Brooke Group Ltd. v. Brown & Williamson Tobacco Corp.*, 509 US 209, 1993; Gregory T. Gundlach, "Price Predation: Legal Limits and Antitrust Considerations," *Journal of Public Policy and Marketing* 14, no. 2 (fall 1995): 278; Kenneth Glazer, "Predatory Pricing and Beyond: Life after Brooke Group," *Antitrust Law Journal*, Mar. 22, 1994, 605; Albert Foer, interview, Dec. 21, 2005; Bolton, Brodley, and Riordan, "Predatory Pricing."

39. This brief explanation offers only a rough and incomplete summary of the current scholarship. Those seeking a detailed discussion should see Foer, "Small Business and Antitrust," and Bolton, Brodley, and Riordan, "Predatory Pricing."

40. Ibid.

41. Norman W. Hawker, "Wal-Mart and the Divergence of State and Federal Predatory Pricing Law," *Journal of Public Policy and Marketing* 15, no. 1 (spring 1996); David L. Kurtz et al., "Wal-Mart Fights the Battle of Conway, Arkansas, Predatory Pricing Suit," *Business Horizons*, Sept. 1996.

42. Supreme Court of Arkansas, *Wal-Mart Stores, Inc., v. American Drugs, Inc.*, Jan. 9, 1995.

43. Hawker, "Wal-Mart and the Divergence of State and Federal Predatory Pricing Law"; Foer interview.

44. Tom Daykin, "Wal-Mart Faces State Charges of Illegally Cutting Prices to Ward Off Competitors," *Milwaukee Journal-Sentinel*, Sept. 26, 2000; Bill Oemichen, interview, Jan. 3, 2006.

45. Oemichen interview; Mike Ivey, "Wal-Mart Settles Price Complaint," *Capital Times*, Aug. 13, 2001.

46. For a sampling of this debate in three states, see Will Rodgers, "Legislator Seeking to Repeal Gas Law," *Tampa Tribune*, Dec. 3, 2005; Steven Oberbeck, "Should Gas-Price Laws Expire?" *Salt Lake Tribune*, Oct. 20, 2005; and Pat Doyle, "Drive to Repeal Gas Price Law Picks Up Speed," *Minneapolis Star Tribune*, Sept. 29, 2005.

47. Mark Skidmore, James Peltier, and James Alm, "Do State Motor Fuel Sales-below-Cost Laws Lower Prices?" *Journal of Urban Economics* 57, no. 1 (2005): 189–211.

48. "Court: Wal-Mart Hurts Competition," Associated Press, Nov. 12, 2002; Greg Masters, "Wal-Mart's Global Challenge," *Retail Merchandiser*, May 1, 2004; Carol Matlack, "Wal-Mart's Overseas Stumbles: The Discounter Has Been Facing an Uphill Battle in Britain and Germany," *Business Week*, July 27, 2005; "Wal-Mart Closes More German Stores, Lowest German Presence since Market Entry," AFX News Limited, Feb. 21, 2006.

49. Godfrey M. Lebhar, *Chain Stores in America, 1859–1962* (New York: Chain Store Age Books, 1971); Schragger, "The Anti–Chain Store Movement"; Patman quoted in Jonathan J. Bean, *Beyond the Broker State: Federal Policies toward Small Business, 1936–1961* (Chapel Hill: University of North Carolina Press, 1996).

50. Lebhar, *Chain Stores in America*.

51. Terry Calvani and Gilde Breidenbach, "Living with the Robinson-Patman Act: An Introduction to the Robinson-Patman Act and Its Enforcement by the Government," *Antitrust Law Journal* 59 (1990–1991); the committee report was quoted in a statement given by J. H. Campbell Jr. of the National Grocers Association before the Antitrust Modernization Commission on July 28, 2005; Mikva was quoted in David Balto, "In Defense of Robinson-Patman: In Defense of Small Business," *Legal Times*, Oct. 13, 1997, 23.

52. The courts have opted to subject certain kinds of Robinson-Patman Act cases, known as primary-line cases, to the standards of *Brooke Group*. Primary-line cases involve price discrimination that injures other sellers, as opposed to secondary-line cases, in which the ones injured are competing buyers. Because injury to small buyers (local retailers) is the issue here, secondary-line cases are the focus of this discussion. Foer, "Small Business and Antitrust"; William H. Borghesani, Peter L. de la Cruz, and David B. Berry, "Controlling the Chain: Buyer Power, Distributive Control, and New Dynamics in Retailing," *Business Horizons*, July 17, 1997; Bruce Spiva, interview, Jan. 3, 2006.

53. Complete transcripts of the trial are available at www.bookweb.org.

54. Bruce Spiva, "Comments of the American Booksellers Association to the Antitrust Modernization Commission Robinson-Patman Act Panel," July 28, 2005; Donald S. Clark, secretary of the FTC, "The Robinson-Patman Act: Annual Update," speech before the Robinson-Patman Act Committee Section of Antitrust Law, delivered in Washington, D.C., Apr. 2, 1998; John Kirkwood, interview, Jan. 5, 2006.

55. Spiva, "Comments of the American Booksellers Association"; Clark, "The Robinson-Patman Act", Domnitz was quoted in "Independent Booksellers Confident on Eve of Trial," *Bookselling This Week*, Apr. 5, 2001.

56. Carla Jimenez, interview, Aug. 23, 2004.

57. David D. Kirkpatrick, "Smaller Bookstores Find Court Struggle against Two Chains," *New York Times*, Apr. 20, 2001; "Court Rules on Summary Judgment," *Bookselling This Week*, Mar. 21, 2001; American Booksellers Association, "ABA Litigation Update: The Case Settles," Apr. 19, 2001.

58. Kirkpatrick, "Smaller Bookstores End Court Struggle"; Jimenez interview.

59. David Balto, interview, June 28, 2005; "Independent Theaters Fight Chains for Access to Hit Movies," *Hometown Advantage Bulletin*, May 4, 2004.

60. *Supermarkets: A Report on the Supply of Groceries from Multiple Stores in the United Kingdom* (London: Competition Commission, 2000); Breaking the Armlock, www.breakingthearmlock.com; Charlotte Denny and Charlotte Moore, "OFT Sends in Auditors as New Code Fails to Break Supermarkets' Armlock," *Guardian*, Feb. 21, 2004; Richard Fletcher, "The Supermarkets' Code of Malpractice: The Competition Commission Probe into the Future of Safeway Revealed How the Big Chains Exploit Suppliers," *Sunday Telegraph*, Sept. 28, 2003; Sean Poulter, "Suppliers Paid Millions to 'Bullying' Supermarkets," *Daily Mail*, Mar. 23, 2005. A similar

code governing supplier relations has been imposed on Wal-Mart by the Mexican government, which found that the retailer had violated antitrust laws. Wal-Mart controls half of all grocery sales in Mexico. "Mexico Antitrust Agency Ends Wal-Mart Probe, with Conditions," Associated Press, Mar. 13, 2003.

61. Transcript of a public hearing of the Antitrust Modernization Commission (AMC) held on July 28, 2005; testimony of the Business Roundtable, submitted to the AMC on Nov. 4, 2005; Albert A. Foer, *Half-Time at the Antitrust Modernization Commission* (Washington, D.C.: American Antitrust Institute, Dec. 1, 2005); Foer interview.

62. "Interchange Rate Future in U.S. Is Up for Grabs," *Electronic Payments Week*, Mar. 29, 2005.

63. John B. Kirkwood, "Buyer Power and Exclusionary Conduct: Should *Brooke Group* Set the Standards for Buyer-Induced Price Discrimination and Predatory Bidding?" *Antitrust Law Journal* 72, no. 2 (2005); John Kirkwood, interview, Jan. 5, 2006; "The Robinson-Patman Act Should Be Reformed, Not Repealed," testimony submitted to the AMC by the American Antitrust Institute Working Group on the Robinson-Patman Act, July 1, 2005.

64. "Independent Pharmacists Fight Discriminatory Health Plans," *Hometown Advantage Bulletin*, Nov. 1, 2003; "New York Plan to Replace Old Sidewalk Newsstands Will Unseat Longtime Vendors," Associated Press, Sept. 19, 2004; Robert Bookman, interview, Dec. 16, 2005; Rachel Lianna Davis, "Eighth Street: Wal-Mart's Driveway," *Benton County Daily Record*, Aug. 21, 2005.

65. Ritu Kalra, "Report Slams Wal-Mart Deal," *Hartford Courant*, Nov. 1, 2005; "Inspection Pact Ends for Wal-Mart Stores," *New York Times*, Jan. 19, 2006.

EIGHT: COMMUNITIES UNCHAINED

1. Eleanor Kinney, interview, Jan. 4, 2005; Jenny Mayher, interview, Jan. 16, 2006.

2. John M. Broder, "Voters in Los Angeles Suburb Say No to a Big Wal-Mart," *New York Times*, Apr. 8, 2004.

3. "Not in My Backyard: An Analysis of Community Opposition to U.S. Big Box Retail," *Bernstein Research Call*, Apr. 25, 2005; Walton wrote this in his autobiography, *Made in America: My Story* (New York: Bantam, 1993); Jeff Doss quoted in David Meekel, "Wal-Mart Flacks Detail Plan—Again," *Lebanon (Pa.) Daily News*, July 13, 2005.

4. Examples of cities that have included in their plans an intention to support locally owned businesses and downtown vitality include Corvallis, Oregon, which calls for building an economy with a "predominance of small, locally-owned businesses." The plan in Skaneateles, New York, reads, "Rather than establishing competing shopping centers in the Town to provide basic goods and services, the Village commercial center... should remain the center for shopping in the community."

5. For a detailed account of the Hailey case, see Constance Beaumont, *Smart*

States, Better Communities (Washington, D.C.: National Trust for Historic Preservation, 1996). The Vermont case is *In re Wal-Mart Stores, Inc.*, 702 A.2d 397, 1997. It is also discussed in Daniel J. Curtin Jr., "Regulating Big Box Stores: The Proper Use of the City or County's Police Power and Its Comprehensive Plan," *Vermont Journal of Environmental Law* 6 (2005). The Lawrence case is *Jacobs v. City of Lawrence* before the District Court of Douglas County, Kansas, in 1989, and the U.S. 10th Circuit Court of Appeals in 1991.

6. Bob Hoffman, interview, Jan. 18, 2006; Marell Staffel, interview, Jan. 19, 2006.

7. Ibid.

8. Ibid.

9. Ibid.

10. Ibid.; Rob Wooley, "Charlevoix Big-Box Battle: Part Two," Michigan Land Use Institute, www.mlui.org, Nov. 5, 2005.

11. Norman provides a detailed description of this four-point approach in his book, *Slam-Dunking Wal-Mart* (Atlantic City, N.J.: Raphel Marketing, 1999). Also see his Web site, www.sprawl-busters.com.

12. See Norman, *Slam-Dunking Wal-Mart,* for an account of the Greenfield fight. "Hood River Residents Link Arms around Our Town," *Hometown Advantage Bulletin,* Aug. 1, 2002.

13. Karl Knudson, attorney for Decorah Citizens for Responsible Development, interview, Mar. 3, 2005; Joel Palmer, "Iowa Court Decision Leaves Decorah Wal-Mart Supercenter in Limbo," Knight Ridder Tribune Business News, Apr. 3, 2003; "Parties Settle Lengthy Legal Battle over Wal-Mart Store," Associated Press, Aug. 24, 2003; "Wal-Mart Buys Land Despite City Rejection of Plans," Associated Press, June 11, 2005.

14. Terri Hardy, "Sacramento Officials Approve Big-Box Ordinance," *Lodi (Calif.) News Sentinel,* Jan. 5, 2006.

15. "Supercenter Opposition Turns In List of Supporters," *Aberdeen American News,* June 4, 2005; Scott Waltman, "City Awaits Fiscal Report," *Aberdeen American News,* June 3, 2005; Scott Waltman, "Retailer Accused of Vote Buying," *Aberdeen American News,* May 7, 2005.

16. "Home Depot Campaign Bucks," *Sprawl-Busters Newsflash,* Feb. 4, 2000; Dan McGillvray, "$174,000 Helped Augusta Crossing Win," *Kennebec Journal,* July 15, 2005; Rachel Peterson, "Wal-Mart Spent Triple Its Prop. 100 Foes," *Arizona Daily Sun,* June 19, 2005; Mark Shaffer, "Wal-Mart Backers Win a Squeaker in Flagstaff," *Arizona Republic,* May 18, 2005.

17. See Liza Featherstone's insightful article on Wal-Mart's racial politics, "Race to the Bottom," *Nation,* Mar. 28, 2005. John McGettrick, interview, Sept. 18, 2005. For more on Ikea in Red Hook, see longtime urban advocate Mary Campbell Gallagher's excellent blog at www.bigcitiesbigboxes.com. Mark N. Ramirez, " 'Big-Box' Stores: A Matter of Class?" *Bennington Banner,* Mar. 30, 2005; Meg Campbell, member of Citizens for a Greater Bennington, interview, Apr. 7, 2005.

18. "Council Gives In to Wal-Mart," *Grand Island Independent*, Jan. 30, 2004; Michael Melio, interview, Jan. 24, 2006; Peggy McGehee, attorney for Westbrook Our Home, e-mail communication, June 26, 2005.

19. Interview with members of the coalition, including Emily Simon and M'Lou Christ, Sept. 28, 2005; Amy Hsuan, "Burnside Activists Mark Victory over Big-Box Plan," *Oregonian*, Jan. 21, 2005.

20. Interview with members of the coalition; Hsuan, "Burnside Activists Mark Victory over Big-Box Plan."

21. George Sherman, Sydney Yuan, and Don Sather, group interview, Jan. 11, 2006; "Frisco, Colorado, Defeats Home Depot," *Hometown Advantage Bulletin*, Dec. 14, 2005.

22. Sherman, Yuan, and Sather, group interview.

23. An excellent book on the rise of the consumer is Lizabeth Cohen's *A Consumers' Republic: The Politics of Consumption in Postwar America* (New York: Knopf, 2003).

24. Godfrey M. Lebhar, *Chain Stores in America, 1859–1962* (New York: Chain Store Age Books, 1971).

25. Richard C. Schragger, "The Anti–Chain Store Movement, Localist Ideology, and the Remnants of the Progressive Constitution, 1920–1940," *Iowa Law Review* (2005): 101–184; Paul Ingram and Hayagreeva Rao, "Store Wars: The Enactment and Repeal of Anti-Chain-Store Legislation in America," *American Journal of Sociology*, Sept. 2004, 446–487; Edward G. Ernst and Emil M. Hartl, "Chains versus Independents: The Fighting Independents," *Nation*, Dec. 3, 1930, 606–8; Louisiana Public Broadcasting, transcript of video program, "Making Waves: Louisiana's Radio Story," Aug. 9, 2005; Legacy Recordings recently released the chain store sermon on an album titled, *The Best of Reverend J. M. Gates.*

26. Michael Sandel, *Democracy's Discontent: America in Search of a Public Philosophy* (Cambridge, Mass.: Harvard University Press, 1996), 227–31; Schragger, "The Anti–Chain Store Movement"; Ernst and Hartl, "Chains versus Independents: The Fighting Independents."

27. Edward G. Ernst and Emil M. Hartl, "Chains versus Independents: Chain Stores and the Community," *Nation*, Nov. 19, 1930, 545–46; Edward G. Ernst and Emil M. Hartl, "Chains versus Independents: Chain Management and Labor," *Nation*, Nov. 26, 1930, 574–76; Brandeis was quoted in Richard C. Schragger, "The Anti–Chain Store Movement."

28. Robert E. Cushman, "Constitutional Law in 1930–31," *American Political Science Review* 26, no. 2 (1931): 161.

29. Lebhar, *Chain Stores in America*; Joseph Cornwall Palamountain Jr., *The Politics of Distribution* (Cambridge, Mass.: Harvard University Press, 1955).

30. Schragger, "The Anti–Chain Store Movement." For more on the extension of rights to corporations, see pamphlets and resources available through Reclaim Democracy.org and Poclad.org. A good history is Thom Hartmann's *Unequal Pro-*

tection: The Rise of Corporate Dominance and the Theft of Human Rights (Emmaus, Penn.: Rodale, 2002).

31. Lebhar, *Chain Stores in America*.

32. Helen Woodward, "How to Swing an Election," *Nation*, Dec. 11, 1937.

33. Paul Ingram and Hayagreeva Rao, "Store Wars: The Enactment and Repeal of Anti-Chain-Store Legislation in America," *American Journal of Sociology* 110, no. 2 (Sept. 2004): 446–87; Carl George Ryant, "The Unbroken Chain: Opposition to Chain Stores during the Great Depression" (masters thesis, University of Wisconsin, 1965); "Chain Labor Deal," *Business Week*, Dec. 24, 1938, 30.

34. In the past, comprehensive plans were treated merely as advisory documents. But the trend in many states has been to give these plans greater legal weight and to require that local officials use them as a basis for evaluating development proposals. In some states, comprehensive plans have attained a status akin to a local constitution: city officials may not adopt laws or decisions that violate them. See Edward J. Sullivan & Matthew J. Michel, "Ramapo plus Thirty: The Changing Role of the Plan in Land Use Regulations," *Urban Lawyer* 35, no. 1 (2003).

35. See the Institute for Local Self-Reliance's Web site at www.newrules.org/retail for more details and the text of ordinances detailed in this section. Brent Thompson, interview, Jan. 23, 2006; Kathy Grotto, interview, Jan. 5, 2005.

36. Lisa Rother, interview, Jan. 19, 2006; "Taos, New Mexico, Votes to Keep Store Size Limit," *Hometown Advantage Bulletin*, Apr. 1, 2003; "Taos, New Mexico, Battles Big Boxes Again," *Hometown Advantage Bulletin*, Feb. 1, 2003.

37. For more on European superstore regulation, see Ken Baar, *Legislative Tools for Preserving Town Centres and Halting the Spread of Hypermarkets and Malls Outside of Cities* (New York: Institute for Transport and Development Policy, Mar. 2002).

38. Jane Jacobs, *The Death and Life of Great American Cities* (New York: Random House, 1961).

39. Town of North Elba Planning Board, "Statement of Findings and Decision: Proposed Wal-Mart Store," Jan. 9, 1996.

40. Again, see the Institute for Local Self-Reliance's Web site at www.newrules .org/retail for more details and the text of these ordinances.

41. Unidentified speaker at a meeting in Portland, Oregon, Sept. 28, 2005.

42. Mike Mullen, Arcata city planner, interview, Jan. 24, 2006; Tom Conlon, interview, Jan. 31, 2006; Marsha Tauber, owner of Simply Macintosh, interview, Jan. 24, 2006; Paul Cienfuegos, member of the Committee on Democracy and Corporations, interview, Jan. 24, 2006; Ryan Emenaker, chair of the Committee on Democracy and Corporations, interview, Jan. 25, 2006.

43. Mullen interview; Conlon interview; Tauber interview; Cienfuegos interview; Emenaker interview.

44. See "Formula Business Restrictions," at www.newrules.org/retail for details on these communities; "Washington Town Limits 'Formula' Businesses," *Home-*

town Advantage Bulletin, Oct. 19, 2005; *Coronadans Organized for Retail Enhancement v. City of Coronado*, Fourth Appellate District, Court of Appeal of California, June 13, 2003.

45. Ed Bedard, interview, Jan. 25, 2006.

46. Aaron Peskin, interview, Jan. 24, 2006.

47. For examples of purchasing policies that give preference to local businesses, see www.newrules.org/retail; *A Local Official's Guide to Developing Better Community Post Offices* (Burlington: Preservation Trust of Vermont, June 2001); Philip Langdon, "Public Buildings Keep Town Centers Alive," *Planning Commissioners Journal* (winter 2003).

48. See Democracy Unlimited, www.duhc.org, and the Community Environmental Legal Defense Fund, www.celdf.org, for more.

49. John Lipman, chief planner, Cape Cod Commission, interview, Jan. 18, 2006; "An Act Creating the Cape Cod Commission," available at www.capecod commission.org; Jeff McLaughlin, "Debate Pits Regulation vs. Economy," *Boston Globe*, Mar. 27, 1994, 42; Robert W. Smith, "Regional Land Use Planning and Regulation on Cape Cod: Reconciling Local and Regional Control" (Department of City and Regional Planning, University of California, Berkeley, Feb. 2002).

50. Lipman interview; "Regional Policy Plan," available at www.capecod commission.org.

51. Sylvia Lewis, "When Wal-Mart Says 'Uncle,'" *Planning*, Aug. 1994, 15; Elizabeth Ross, "Cape Cod Resists Next Wave: Superstores," *Christian Science Monitor*, Aug. 1, 1994; Constance Beaumont, *Better Models for Superstores* (Washington, D.C.: National Trust for Historic Preservation, 1997).

52. Lipman interview; Felicia Penn, interview, Jan. 30, 2003.

53. Lipman interview; Smith, "Regional Land Use Planning and Regulation on Cape Cod."

54. Act 250 is available at www.state.vt.us/envboard; Elizabeth Humstone, former director of the Vermont Forum on Sprawl, interview, Jan. 24, 2006; William E. Roper and Elizabeth Humstone, "Wal-Mart in Vermont: The Case against Sprawl," *Vermont Law Review* 22 (summer 1998): 755–91.

55. Paul Bruhn, personal communication, Sept. 2005; Shay Totten, "Supersize Me! Wal-Mart Says Bigger Is Better, Rebuffs Efforts to Get Small," *Vermont Guardian*, Oct. 28, 2005.

56. See the Regional Policies section of www.newrules.org/retail; Patricia E. Salkin, "Supersizing Small Town America: Using Regionalism to Right-Size Big Box Retail," *Vermont Journal of Environmental Law* 6 (2004–2005).

57. See "Mandatory Impact Review" at www.newrules.org/retail for more on these bills.

58. See "Big Box Tax" at www.newrules.org/retail for more on these bills.

NINE: DECLARATION OF INDEPENDENTS

1. Julie Simpson, interview, Feb. 7, 2006.

2. Simpson interview; Diane Logan, interview, Feb. 6, 2006.

3. Gina Schaefer, interview, Feb. 8, 2006.

4. Elizabeth Houghton Barden, interview, Feb. 7, 2006.

5. Chad Moles, interview, Feb. 6, 2006.

6. Stacey Swartz, interview, Feb. 10, 2006; Carol Cooke, NCPA external communications director, interview, Feb. 10, 2006; figures on independent drugstores supplied by the National Community Pharmacists Association.

7. Doug Loescher, interview, Jan. 25, 2006.

8. Kennedy Smith, interview, Jan. 9, 2006.

9. Smith interview; Logan interview.

10. Nancy Carmichael, interview, Feb. 3, 2006; *Main Street Success Stories: Corning, Iowa* (Washington, D.C.: National Trust for Historic Preservation, 1997).

11. For market-analysis tools, see the University of Wisconsin's Center for Community Economic Development, www.uwex.edu/ces/cced/dma. Smith interview; Timothy Bishop, director of the Walla Walla Downtown Foundation, interview, Feb. 6, 2006.

12. Smith interview.

13. Gerry Kempen, interview, Dec. 2000; Ali Aghamoosa, interview, Dec. 2000

14. David Fogerty, City of Berkeley community development project coordinator, interview, Feb. 6, 2006; Jay Fowler, interview, Feb. 6, 2006; "Development Grant Leads to Opening of Grand Rapids Bookstore," *Bookselling This Week*, Jan. 11, 2006.

15. Steve Raguski, interview, Feb. 15, 2006.

16. Greg Walker-Wilson, interview, Feb. 6, 2006; Jim King, director of the New York State Small Business Development Center, interview, Feb. 6, 2006.

17. Jan Baxter, interview, Feb. 9, 2006; Kathy Puryear, interview, Feb. 9, 2006; Ellen Shepard, executive director of the Andersonville Chamber of Commerce, interview, Feb. 2, 2006.

18. Baxter interview; Puryear interview; Shepard interview.

19. Carmen Herrera-Mansir, interview, Jan. 20, 2006; Donna Jones, "El Pajaro Helps Latino Residents Start Businesses," *Santa Cruz Sentinel*, Jan. 24, 2004; Carol Jaines, "Assisting Retail Businesses," *NBIA Review*, Oct. 2003.

20. Alex Padro, interview, Feb. 7, 2006. Washington, D.C., has a Commercial Property Acquisition Program to help local business owners buy their buildings, but it has not been funded. The Mission Economic Development Association (MEDA) in the Mission District of San Francisco also has a Commercial Ownership Program that provides technical assistance and gap financing, but MEDA business consultant Oscar Dominguez said property values rose so fast during the dot-com boom that, even with the extra help, ownership is out of reach for most of the business owners he works with. Oscar Dominguez, interview, Feb. 6, 2006.

21. Sabrina Butler, "Potential Uses of the Community Land Trust Model for Commercial Development in Low-Income Communities," unpublished paper, Dec. 10, 2004; Donovan D. Rypkema, "Commercial Gentrification: Beyond the Rhetoric," speech delivered to the Urban Main Street Forum, Boston, June 25, 2002.

22. Steven G. Craig and Pauline Hardee, *The Impact of Bank Consolidation on Small Business Credit Availability* (Washington, D.C.: Small Business Administration, Feb. 2004).

23. Rupert Ayton, Center for the Development of Social Finance, interview, Dec. 16, 2005; Michael Shumam, personal communication, Dec. 20, 2006; Michael H. Shuman, *The Small-Mart Revolution: How Local Businesses Are Beating the Global Competition* (San Francisco: Berrett-Koehler, 2006).

24. Ryan Coonerty, interview, Oct. 3, 2006; "Cal. City Uses Reserve Funds to Spur Local Business Development," *Hometown Advantage*, Oct. 4, 2006; David P. Culver, Santa Cruz finance director, "Investment in Local Financial Institutions," memo to Santa Cruz city manager, Sept. 21, 2005.

25. Ken Witzeling, interview, Feb. 10, 2006.

26. Paul Ramos, interview, Mar. 2004.

27. Witzeling interview; Dave Bonner, "Community-Owned Store in Powell Succeeding, Looking to Expand," Associated Press, Feb. 1, 2006.

28. Tom Bath, interview, Feb. 10, 2006.

29. Jack Smith, interview, Feb. 10, 2006.

30. Dan Leoni, interview, Feb. 10, 2006.

31. Witzeling interview.

32. Steve Alves, interview, Feb. 7, 2006; John Waite, executive director of the Franklin County Community Development Corporation, personal communication, Feb. 8, 2006; Greenfield Mercantile prospectus, Jan. 3, 2006.

33. Richard Dines, program manager of the Food Co-op 500, interview, Feb. 14, 2006; National Cooperative Month Planning Committee, *Cooperative Businesses in the United States: A 2005 Snapshot* (Washington, D.C.: National Cooperative Business Association, Oct. 2005).

34. Stacy Mitchell, "Home Shopping Networks," AlterNet, Mar. 17, 2004, available at www.alternet.org.

35. Christopher B. Leinberger, "Building for the Long-Term," *Urban Land* (Nov./Dec. 2003): 95–104; Christopher B. Leinberger, interview, Aug. 2005; Smith interview; Neil Takemoto, interview, Jan. 13, 2006; Peter Rubin, interview, Jan. 23, 2006; Bruno Bottarelli, managing director of the Marquette Companies, interview, Jan. 23, 2006.

36. Leinberger, "Building for the Long-Term."

37. Ibid.

38. Frank Seely, interview, Jan. 23, 2006; Fred Evins, City of Austin Redevelopment Project manager, interview, Jan. 23, 2006; Shonda Novak, "Second Street Shopping Open for Business," *Austin American Statesman*, Dec. 1, 2005; Dan Hous-

ton, principal with the Austin-based Civic Economics, e-mail communication, Jan. 24, 2006.

39. Melissa Miller, interview, Jan. 19, 2006.

40. Ibid.

41. Ibid.

42. Neil Takemoto, interview, Jan. 13, 2006.

43. Rubin interview; Tasha Flournoy, "Supermarket Brings Vitality Back to Shaker Square," *Cleveland Plain Dealer*, Oct. 11, 2005.

44. Doyle Davis, interview, Feb. 14, 2006.

45. Eric Levin, interview, Feb. 14, 2006.

46. Levin interview; Matt Vaughan, owner of Easy Street Records in Seattle, interview, Feb. 14, 2006; Ed Christman, senior editor at *Billboard*, interview, Dec. 3, 2006; Don VanCleave, president of CIMS, interview, Aug. 13, 2004; John Kunz, interview, Nov. 15, 2005.

47. Paul Hazen, interview, Feb. 16. 2006.

48. Jim Stevens, interview, Feb. 15, 2006.

49. Ken Nichols, Ace vice president of retail operations, interview, Feb. 6, 2006; Scott Olson, "Ace Sees Growth Potential in Central Indiana," *Indianapolis Business Journal*, June 20, 2005; Madhusmita Bora, "A Thriving Hardware Co-op: Indiana-Based Do It Best Grows in Face of Big-Box Rivals," *Indianapolis Star*, Oct. 20, 2004.

50. Stevens interview; Tom Cyr, National Cooperative Bank, interview, Feb. 14, 2006; John Ketzenberger, "Nuts-n-Bolts of Thriving in Big-Box Era? Try Adapting," *Indianapolis Star*, Dec. 13, 2005.

51. Nichols interview.

52. Ibid.

53. More information on purchasing co-ops can be found at the National Cooperative Business Association (www.ncba.coop) and the National Cooperative Bank (www.ncb.coop).

54. Marilyn Shulman, interview, Feb. 16, 2006.

55. *Internet Retailer, Top 300 Guide: Profiles and Statistics of America's 300 Largest Retail Web Sites Ranked by Annual Sales*, 2004 edition, available at www.internet retailer.com; Gary Rivlin, "A Retail Revolution Turns Ten," *New York Times*, July 10, 2005.

56. Nichols interview.

57. Chuck Robinson, interview, Nov. 24, 2004; Luanne Kreutzer, owner of St. Helen's, interview, Nov. 24, 2004.

58. Miller interview; Rebecca Melancon, interview, Feb. 15, 2006; Steve Bercu, interview, Feb. 15, 2006.

59. Bercu interview; Melancon interview.

60. Jeff Milchen, interview, Feb. 2, 2006; David Bolduc, interview, Feb. 11, 2006; Stacy Mitchell, "Homegrown Economics: How Boulder Businesses Are Staying Ahead of the Chains," *Orion Afield*, autumn 2001.

61. For links to each alliance, see www.amiba.net; Jennifer Rockne, interview, Feb. 2, 2006; Nancy Olson, owner of Raleigh's Quail Ridge Books, interview, Feb. 15, 2006; Linda Watson, interview, Feb. 15, 2006.

62. David Kaseman, interview, Feb. 2, 2006.

63. Kaseman interview; "Maui Retailers Join Forces to Reward Customers, Counter Chains," *Hometown Advantage Bulletin*, Aug. 1, 2000.

64. David C. Korten, *When Corporations Rule the World* (West Hartford, Conn.: Kumarian Press; San Francisco: Berrett-Koehler, 1995).

65. Michelle Long, interview, Feb. 3, 2006; Raguski interview.

66. Sustainable Connections, www.sustainableconnections.org; Long interview, Feb. 3, 2006.

67. Rebecca Wiswell, interview, Feb. 20, 2006; Ken Bothman, interview, Feb. 15, 2006; Robinson interview.

68. Long interview; Robinson interview.

69. Merrian Fuller, BALLE's managing coordinator, interview, Feb. 20, 2006; Betsy Burton, interview, Nov. 15, 2006.

70. Robinson interview; Milchen interview.

INDEX